Shifting the Ground of Canadian Literary Studies

TransCanada Series

The study of Canadian literature can no longer take place in isolation from larger external forces. Pressures of multiculturalism put emphasis upon discourses of citizenship and security, while market-driven factors increasingly shape the publication, dissemination, and reception of Canadian writing. The persistent questioning of the Humanities has invited a rethinking of the disciplinary and curricular structures within which the literature is taught, while the development of area and diaspora studies has raised important questions about the tradition. The goal of the TransCanada series is to publish forward-thinking critical interventions that investigate these paradigm shifts in interdisciplinary ways.

Series editor:

Smaro Kamboureli, Canada Research Chair in Critical Studies in Canadian Literature, School of English and Theatre Studies and Director, TransCanada Institute, University of Guelph

For more information, please contact:

Smaro Kamboureli
Professor, Canada Research Chair in Critical Studies in Canadian Literature
School of English and Theatre Studies
Director, TransCanada Institute
University of Guelph
50 Stone Road East
Guelph, ON N1G 2W1
Canada
Phone: 519-824-4120 ext. 53251
Email: smaro@uoguelph.ca

Lisa Quinn
Acquisitions Editor
Wilfrid Laurier University Press
75 University Avenue West
Waterloo, ON N2L 3C5
Canada
Phone: 519-884-0710 ext. 2843
Fax: 519-725-1399
Email: quinn@press.wlu.ca

Shifting the Ground of Canadian Literary Studies

Smaro Kamboureli and Robert Zacharias, editors

WILFRID LAURIER
UNIVERSITY PRESS

Wilfrid Laurier University Press acknowledges the support of the Canada Council for the Arts for our publishing program. We also acknowledge the financial support of the Government of Canada through the Book Publishing Industry Development Program for our publishing activities.

 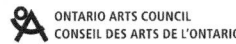

Library and Archives Canada Cataloguing in Publication

Shifting the ground of Canadian literary studies / Smaro Kamboureli and Robert Zacharias, editors.

(TransCanada series)

Includes bibliographical references and index.
Issued also in electronic formats.
ISBN 978-1-55458-365-2

1. Canadian literature—History and criticism—Theory, etc.
2. Criticism—Canada. 3. Literature and state—Canada. I. Kamboureli, Smaro
II. Zacharias, Robert, 1977– III. Title. IV. Series: TransCanada series

PS8041.T73 2012   801'.950971   C2012-900196-1

Electronic monograph.
Issued also in print format.
ISBN 978-1-55458-397-3 (EPUB).—ISBN 978-1-55458-396-6 (PDF)

1. Canadian literature—History and criticism—Theory, etc.
2. Criticism—Canada. 3. Literature and state—Canada. I. Kamboureli, Smaro
II. Zacharias, Robert, 1977– III. Title. IV. Series: TransCanada series (Online)

PS8041.T73 2012   801'.950971   C2012-900197-X

© 2012 Wilfrid Laurier University Press
Waterloo, Ontario, Canada
www.wlupress.wlu.ca

Cover design by Blakeley Words+Pictures. Front-cover collage by Roy Miki, from "A Walk on Granville Island," in *Mannequin Rising* (New Star Books, 2011). Collage © Roy Miki.
Text design by Janette Thompson (Jansom).

This book is printed on FSC recycled paper and is certified Ecologo. It is made from 100% post-consumer fibre, processed chlorine free, and manufactured using biogas energy.

Printed in Canada

Every reasonable effort has been made to acquire permission for copyright material used in this text, and to acknowledge all such indebtedness accurately. Any errors and omissions called to the publisher's attention will be corrected in future printings.

No part of this publication may be reproduced, stored in a retrieval system, or transmitted, in any form or by any means, without the prior written consent of the publisher or a licence from the Canadian Copyright Licensing Agency (Access Copyright). For an Access Copyright licence, visit http://www.accesscopyright.ca or call toll free to 1-800-893-5777.

For Yoko Fujimoto
1955–2011

CONTENTS

Acknowledgements ix

Preface xi
Smaro Kamboureli and Robert Zacharias

Introduction
Shifting the Ground of a Discipline: Emergence and Canadian Literary Studies in English 1
Smaro Kamboureli

National Literatures in the Shadow of Neoliberalism 37
Jeff Derksen

"Beyond CanLit(e)": Reading. Interdisciplinarity. Transatlantically. 65
Danielle Fuller

White Settlers and the Biopolitics of State Building in Canada 87
Janine Brodie

"Some Great Crisis": Vimy as Originary Violence 109
Robert Zacharias

Amplifying Threat: Reasonable Accommodations and Quebec's Bouchard-Taylor Commission Hearings (2007) 129
Monika Kin Gagnon and Yasmin Jiwani

The Time Has Come: Self and Community Articulations in *Colour. An Issue* and *Awakening Thunder* 151
Larissa Lai

Archivable Concepts: Talonbooks and Literary Translation 173
Kathy Mezei

Is CanLit Lost in Japanese Translation? 187
Yoko Fujimoto

The Cunning of Reconciliation: Reinventing White Civility in the "Age of Apology" 209
Pauline Wakeham

The Long March to "Recognition": Sákéj Henderson, First Nations Jurisprudence, and *Sui Generis* Solidarity 235
Len Findlay

bush/writing: embodied deconstruction, traces of community, and writing against the state in indigenous acts of inscription 249
peter kulchyski

Notes 269

Works Cited 303

Contributors 331

Index 335

ACKNOWLEDGEMENTS

Most of the essays in this collection were originally presented at TransCanada Two: Literature, Institutions, Citizenship (Guelph 2007). We would like to thank the members of this event's organizing committee—Lily Cho, Paul Danyluk, Kit Dobson, Sophie McCall, Roy Miki, Donna Palmateer Pennee, and Christl Verduyn—for their hard work and vision, as well as the large number of delegates who attended the conference and engaged in vigorous dialogue. As co-editors, Smaro and Robert would like to acknowledge the work of Hannah McGregor, a doctoral fellow at TransCanada Institute (TCI) and research assistant for Smaro, for her valuable work standardizing the manuscript and tracking down bibliographic materials. Smaro's research assistants Derek Murray, Marcelle Kosman, and Mishi Prokop also worked with great expediency on various editorial issues at different stages of the manuscript's preparation, while Mollie McDuffe, the former Administrative Assistant at TCI, also pitched in to facilitate the production of this work. For the generous funding that has made the conference and this book possible, we wish to acknowledge the Social Sciences and Humanities Research Council of Canada, the Canada Research Chairs office, the Canada Council of the Arts, various offices at the University of Guelph, and the Office of the Vice-President Academic at Simon Fraser University. Our deepest thanks, however, are to the contributors to this volume; the journey from conference to collection has been a long one for reasons not always under our control, and we are grateful for their patience. We are also grateful to Lisa Quinn, acquisitions editor at Wilfrid Laurier University Press, for her patience and ongoing support.

Robert would like to gratefully acknowledge that his work on this project was facilitated by a Social Sciences and Humanities Research Council of Canada Doctoral Fellowship. He would also like to thank Arvelle for her ongoing support; he thanks as well their three children,

Adiah, Samuel, and Talia, each of whom was born in the gap between the original conference and the publication of this collection. Finally, thanks to Dr. Smaro Kamboureli and the wonderful TransCanada Institute, for enabling his work in so many ways during his doctoral studies.

Smaro owes special thanks to Roy Miki and Donna Palmateer Pennee for their feedback on her essay. Needless to say, she is responsible for any blind spots left over after she tried to engage with their queries, especially Donna's detailed response.

The book is dedicated to Yoko Fujimoto, one of the contributors to this book, who succumbed to cancer in the middle of this volume's editorial process. Yoko played an instrumental role in promoting the study of Canadian literature in Japan, especially at Waseda University in Tokyo, where she taught. To the best of our ability, we have attempted to resolve any inconsistencies in her essay regarding references to Japanese titles; for her assistance in this process, we are grateful to Yuko Yamade, from the School of Political Science and Economics, Meiji University in Tokyo, and former student of Yoko at Waseda University.

Guelph – Toronto

PREFACE

Smaro Kamboureli and Robert Zacharias

Shifting the Ground of Canadian Literary Studies examines Canadian literature not simply as a body of texts but as a field and institution that is subject to a host of complex but identifiable cultural, economic, and political pressures. Approaching the field and its contexts from different points of entry, the contributors reflect a shared commitment to the methodological attention that is necessary to trace and intervene into the network dynamics that have recalibrated Canadian literature as a discipline in recent years. This was the chief focus of TransCanada Two: Literatures, Institutions, Citizenship, the 2007 conference for which most of these essays were first written. Because the contexts and concerns of the nation-state and its various institutional structures have shifted under the pressures of globalization and neoliberalism, the foundations and assumptions of Canada's national(ized) literature have been exposed to critique, a development that this TransCanada conference saw as a summons for reconsidering, among other things, what constitutes the proper object(s) of literary studies. Our strategy, as editors, not to standardize how the field of Canadian literary studies is referred to throughout the collection—Canadian literature, Canadian Literature, CanLit—signals, in a small way, our sense that the institutional signature of the field has begun to shift directions. The discrepancies that arise when these signs coexist play a functional role in this collection, gesturing toward the instability of CanLit as an institution while reflecting the various contexts in which it is read today. Following the logic of Raymond Williams's insistence that "culture is ordinary," and that it must be understood as both "arts and learning" as well as "a way of life" (11), the essays gathered here, as the Introduction of this volume makes evident, do not set aside the literary so much as they work to broaden the definition of the literary itself.

In a similar vein, while the preoccupation with the nation-state that has so decidedly marked the formation of Canadian literature as an institution continues in this volume, the contributors turn this cultural habit inside out. Not only does this collection invite us to rethink the assumed homologous relationship between Canadian literature and the Canadian nation-state, but its concern with the latter raises challenging questions as much about its strategies of self-invention as a tolerant and liberal society as about its persistent, and vexing, relationship with the former. Arguably, it would be difficult for a field of study that names Canada as part of its disciplinary signature to avoid the category of the nation-state; yet in this instance concern with the nation-state, as it has become increasingly apparent in critical discourses today, goes hand in hand with its radical questioning in the age of globalization. The widespread reassertion of "national interests" in relation to issues of "security" that followed the attacks on the World Trade Center on 11 September 2001, along with the collapse of the world's financial markets in 2008, has shown that pronouncements of the triumph of global capital and the corresponding death of the nation-state were hopelessly rash. Notwithstanding the changes it has undergone as a result of the economic, socio-political, and cultural processes of globalization; the neoliberal policies of supranational organizations; and the increasingly rapid flow of culture-as-commodity across national boundaries, the nation-state persists, for better or worse, both as a state of mind and as a structuring principle.

Thus, despite the premature announcement of the nation-state's irrelevancy, Canadian literature as an institution remains entangled with the nation-state. Jeff Derksen's essay, "National Literatures in the Shadow of Neoliberalism," which opens the collection, invites us to beware of the critical instruments and methodologies we employ so that we are able to attend to the national as a category without inadvertently replicating its limits. As he persuasively argues, Canadian critics have not paid heed to the ways in which the postcolonial discourses prevalent in the field as of late are aligned with the neoliberal project of disbanding the national space. He is equally critical of the "nonvigilant" poststructuralist mode that relies on tropes such as "migrancy," "nomadism," "hybridity," and "de-territorialization" without recognizing how strikingly close they are to the rhetoric and logic of neoliberal globalization (47). To negotiate the materiality of global relations, he posits scale theory as the conceptual framework that allows for the "embed[ding of] the nation-state into sociospatial relations ranging from the body to the globe" (46). The questions he poses—"Can a national literature adapt to new formations and opportunities and still remain recognizable as a national literature? Is the national a category that can be utilized beyond a distinction within a global commodity culture and beyond its own political borders?... Can the nation ... be turned outward, as a platform of engagement, rather than be reflected back onto the nation-state in the continual reimagining of the cohesive community?" (51)—set the stage for the essays that follow.

Similarly, Danielle Fuller's essay, "'Beyond CanLit(e)': Reading. Interdisciplinarity. Transatlantically.," engages with certain aspects of commodity culture while practising, as its title suggests, a productive reflexivity. Fuller is concerned as much with the methodological and disciplinary turns of her own argument as with how Canadian literature is being read today at new or different levels. The transnational and interdisciplinary scope of Beyond the Book, the project she has pursued collaboratively, offers a large-scale comparative analysis of book clubs in Canada, the UK, and the US that situates Canadian literature not only in regard to other cultures and disciplines but also in the context of its mediatization. Her concern that literary critics "rarely dwell upon our conception of 'evidence,'" let alone "question the validity (appropriateness) of using our textual methods to generate evidence," reiterates Derksen's call for a reconsideration of the methodological assumptions that underpin the study of Canadian literature. Fuller's focus on both the unsettling function of "collaborative interdisciplinarity" (66) and the practical complications born out of intrapersonal, disciplinary, and institutional differences serves as a warning of the challenges that emerge as we navigate the shifting ground of the field.

Echoing Derksen, Janine Brodie draws attention to the ascendance of neoliberal discourses in the late twentieth century. But while his argument is intent on "grasp[ing] the present" (39), Brodie's essay, "White Settlers and the Biopolitics of State Building in Canada," centres primarily on the past to offer a critical genealogy of white settler society and the concept of indigenization in order to "destabilize contemporary national narratives" that celebrate the project of integrating cultural diversity into "the national social fabric" (108). Critical of the tendency to present Canadian citizenship as the evolution of a rights-based collective or the steady progression of ethnocultural accommodation, Brodie employs, in a highly effective way, a "biopolitical perspective" that "does not deny the cold realities of colonialist racism; instead, it suggests that state racism is not reducible to historicized representations of settler culture alone" (98). Just as Fuller's call for a reconsideration of the parameters within which we situate the object of our study includes a direct engagement with readers that are members of book clubs, Brodie's work as a political scientist focuses on a different type of text: the Speeches from the Throne from Confederation to 1946, the year of Canada's first citizenship act. Her close reading of their tropes and contexts exposes the complex "processes of aboriginalization" in relation to white settler culture, while also bringing into relief the extent to which "the biopolitical imperatives of categorization, racialization, and selective exclusion" continue to shape "Canadian citizenship politics" (108).

Operating at a different register but likewise concerned with both the violence that informs the building of the nation and the making of Canadian literature as an institution, Robert Zacharias's essay, "'Some Great Crisis': Vimy as Originary Violence," turns its critical gaze on the Battle of Vimy Ridge. Identifying two related national myths that remain operative in Canadian criticism—that Canada lacks a violent moment at its origin, and that the nation systematically effaces the violence of its construction—he traces their shared concern with "crisis" back to early Canadian literary criticism. He shows that the trope of crisis, employed both by proponents of the nation-state and by early Canadian critics, is key to understanding how and why Vimy Ridge has emerged as a master narrative in "the birth of the Canadian nation" (111). Mythologized as the "founding violence" that had been missing in the Canadian nation-state, the Battle of Vimy Ridge functions as an act of "preserving violence" (119) whenever it is invoked. Thus the violence that accompanies the invention of origins is never too far off when we consider the nation as an ordering principle.

If, as Zacharias's argument demonstrates, violence as crisis is a trope that informs the invention of origins, and if narratives of origins insist on their singularity, Monika Kin Gagnon and Yasmin Jiwani focus on the implications of a more recent cultural and political crisis, that of L'Affaire Hérouxville in Quebec. Their essay, "Amplifying Threat: Reasonable Accommodations and Quebec's Bouchard-Taylor Commission Hearings (2007)," troubles the inherited notion of a single Canadian narrative through an examination of Quebec's complex "race/culture equation." Just as Brodie's essay finds that the biopolitics at the foundation of the

Canadian state remains encoded in the contemporary moment, Gagnon and Jiwani offer a trenchant critique of the political and media furor surrounding L'Affaire Hérouxville and expose how it "pierced the delicate veneer of tolerance that characterizes everyday life and social practices in Quebec" (129). Through a close reading of newspaper reportage employing a *vox populi* approach in order to capitalize on the racialized, religious, and gendered anxieties of its readership, Gagnon and Jiwani question both the instrumentalizing response of the provincial government and the media's coverage of the event. As they demonstrate, the Quebec government and the media worked in tandem to "amplify" the negative impact of the event on Quebec's Muslim community.

Larissa Lai's essay, "The Time Has Come: Self and Community Articulations in *Colour. An Issue* and *Awakening Thunder*," addresses different strategies of articulation and representation that take on questions of racialization and the nation-state. She examines the fraught politics of the genre of special issues as a forum for the voices of minoritized subjects in the anti-racist activism of the early 1990s. More specifically, she considers both the divergent editorial strategies that introduce and shape two special issues dedicated to Asian Canadian literature as well as the poetry included in them. Her close readings offer a highly nuanced understanding of the ways in which "literary conventions tend to reproduce existing power structures in language" (164). Wrestling with the doubled status of special issues as simultaneously privileged sites of collective articulation that are always also supplementary to a reaffirmed norm, Lai suggests that special issues have played a key role in the development of Canadian literature as an institution. Their politics, then, must be understood within the particular moment(s) of their publication, for they offer the power of a collective voice at one moment, while drawing attention to the homogenizing power of racialized discourses the next.

Kathy Mezei's essay, "Archivable Concepts: Talonbooks and Literary Translation," shifts our focus to translation as another major aspect of the formation of Canadian literature as an institution. Intent on showing that Canadian literature is "produced or inflected by a transaction with another language, culture, or medium" (174), she examines the role small presses have played in facilitating the "interactions" of different bodies of literature through translation. She insists, productively so, on "the vitality of these interactions" and their "wide range of cultural artifacts," which are often the result of translation. Because different acts of translation "involve strategies of appropriation or distancing," it is important, she argues, "to develop and interpret" archives of "Canadian translation activities" (174), as a means of understanding the infrastructure of Canadian literature. Employing Talonbooks (the Vancouver small press that pioneered the translation of Québécois texts into English) as her case study, Mezei unpacks the "institutional dynamics, socio-political circumstances, and personal histories" that have fashioned the practice of cross-cultural translation in Canada (176).

Continuing Mezei's interest in the translation of Canadian literature but expanding it into a larger context that resonates with Fuller's transnational and Derksen's global perspectives, Yoko Fujimoto's contribution "Is CanLit Lost in Japanese Translation?" investigates the circulation of Canadian literature in translation and its study in Japan. Just as Fuller's approach involves interviews with members of book clubs, Fujimoto relies, in part, on interviews with editors of prominent Japanese publishing and translation houses. Along with her close reading of the genre of postscripts that accompany Japanese translations, these interviews reveal how the national character of Canadian literature has become nearly irrelevant to its circulation in Japan. Fujimoto, then, makes a strong case for what she calls the "slighting, or the loss of significance, of the national category that occurs in the process of reproducing and distributing Canadian literature in translation" (189). In today's globalized cultural economy, then, it is not the particularities of an individual author or the distinctive character of a national literature that determines which authors and titles are selected for translation. Rather, the "standardized" packaging of best-selling authors, international prizes and their consequent "culture of celebrity," and the "exchange system of knowledge and values" among "multinational publishing companies" (193) are the deciding factors. Thus Fujimoto demonstrates not only "the extent to which the market value system of literary publications in the West is transplanted in Japan" (193), but also how translations of Canadian literature participate in the construction of Japanese modernity and the latter's ambivalent relationship with Western, especially Enlightenment, values.

From the ideologies and value systems that shape the global scene and the various economies within which Canadian literature circulates, the collection moves back to Canada by way of rethinking the colonial legacies, ethical and practical limitations, and political possibilities of the study of Canadian literature today, specifically in the context of indigenous values and concerns. Pauline Wakeham's essay, "The Cunning of Reconciliation: Reinventing White Civility in the 'Age of Apology,'" revisits some of the mythologizing strategies employed in the construction of the Canadian nation-state as they persist in the emergence of the culture of apologies today. Suggesting that the "phenomenon of reconciliation has become naturalized as a product of the 'core' of Canadian beneficence and integrated into a national mythology of magnanimous governance" (209), she extends, and ultimately moves beyond, Daniel Coleman's concept of "white civility" to examine the function of state apologies. In a meticulous fashion, she takes note of the pressures of the global gaze on Canada as a model of civility and positions the "cunning of reconciliation" in Canada as "the strategic co-optation of the ethical project of offering recompense for injustices." As she posits, such practices of apology and reconciliation operate as a political plan "of silencing resistance and manufacturing premature closure upon questions of power imbalances that continue to structure Canadian society" (215–16). She thus resists the hope for a rehabilitation of civility and the liberal promises of reconciliation, seeking instead, through the work of Sákéj Henderson and the field of indigenous legal studies, a more radical form of social change.

Len Findlay's contribution, "The Long March to 'Recognition': Sákéj Henderson, First Nations Jurisprudence, and *Sui Generis* Solidarity," offers an amplification of Wakeham's essay by engaging at length with Henderson's work. His call for "*sui generis* solidarity," solidarity based upon the "history and current realities of indigenous struggles for both recognition and redistribution," reveals "a social and intellectual treasury on which we might all respectfully seek to draw" (245). Arguing that the current "knowledge economy" continues to rely on an Enlightenment tradition that has long since met its ethical limit, Findlay positions Henderson's work (which is featured in the third, and forthcoming, volume based on the TransCanada conferences) as a model "capable of nourishing new (and much needed) pedagogies, [and] new research agendas" (235). Insisting, powerfully so, that there is no neutral political ground for literary and cultural scholars concerned with colonial traditions and institutions, Findlay's argument offers a self-consciously utopian call for critics to participate in the active decolonization of both the nation-state and the academy.

Concluding the volume, peter kulchyski's essay, "bush/writing: embodied deconstruction, traces of community, and writing against the state in indigenous acts of inscription," echoes many of the collection's larger concerns, including the critique of the neoliberal state in the age of global capital taken on initially by Derksen and elaborated in Findlay; the attentiveness to the power of language and signification as examined by Lai; the politics of representation and ethnicity explored by Gagnon and Jiwani, and Lai; and the violence of the nation-state, as examined by Brodie and Zacharias. Most obviously, however, kulchyski's essay resonates with Wakeham and Findlay's turn to indigenous values and perspectives as he criticizes the various ways in which the state functions through what he calls "a certain kind of writing." Challenging scholarly norms at both the affective and linguistic levels, kulchyski intersperses his unflinching critique of neoliberal capitalism with narratives of his own experiences by performing what he calls "bush/writings," that is, "resistant, embodied, creative texts out of the bush" (259). Since writing, as he argues, "is one of the key mechanisms that the state deploys" in its "field of activity," he sets out to contest the state's claims to monopoly over the form and function of communal narratives. Thus he suggests that understanding sites like the "teaching rocks" near the Curve Lake Reserve in southern Ontario or the "footprints" and "the chair" in northern Manitoba as forms of writing—indeed, literature—grants them a destabilizing power in that they "challenge not only the grammatical structure that underlies our literature—the form by which an inscription contains and expresses its meaning ... —but the very mode of inscription that founds the being of euro-western writing" (264).

If, as kulchyski suggests, the nation-state itself is "no more nor less than a certain kind of writing" (254), *Shifting the Ground* can be read as offering a manifold and composite reading of this "certain kind of writing." This collection, then, neither offers a singular vision or critique of the complexities of the study of Canadian literature as of late, nor attempts to be exhaustive. Instead, it offers what we believe to be a representative view of some of the more charged developments in the field today.

Introduction
Shifting the Ground of a Discipline: Emergence and Canadian Literary Studies in English

Smaro Kamboureli

> Canadian criticism is only its fields or contexts.
> Eli Mandel, "Introduction" (1)

Something has happened to English Canadian literary studies. It has a cast of "new" characters. No longer exclusively concerned with Canadian literature's themes and imagery, its forms and genres, or its linguistic nature and structure, it has begun to demonstrate a steady shift toward a foregrounding of the situational and material conditions that influence the production of Canadian literary texts. Richard Cavell's *Love, Hate, and Fear in Canada's Cold War* (2004), Pauline Wakeham's *Taxidermic Signs: Reconstructing Aboriginality* (2008), Julia Emberley's *Defamiliarizing the Aboriginal: Cultural Practices and Decolonization in Canada* (2009), and Lily Cho's *Eating Chinese: Culture on the Menu in Small Town Canada* (2010) are examples that reflect the most recent stages of this shift. As the titles of these studies suggest—Cold War, taxidermy, cultural practices, menus—a growing number of Canadian literary scholars writing today appear to circumvent the literary or, more precisely, to approach it as a sign that is generated by the triangulation of culture, literature, and the nation-state. Now seen as belonging to the larger category of culture—culture in the general sense of "meaning-making activities" (Coleman, Szeman, and Rethmann 1)—now as belonging to particular networks of power relations and economies that make the nation-state, or a combination of both streams, Canadian literature is no longer seen solely as a discrete textual construct, nor is it read exclusively in the context of Canada.

Far from being a current phenomenon, as the opening sentence of this Introduction would suggest, this shift has been taking place for a while now, hence "new" in scare quotes. As Diane Bessai and David Jackel, the editors of *Figures in a Ground*, wrote in 1978: "Twentieth-century literature and literary criticism both reflect and react against the dynamics of change: cultural, political, technological. Changing modes of perception and consequent shifts in values lead in turn to new forms of expression and adaptations of old ones. The critic of twentieth-century literature is continually confronted by the need to understand and evaluate the complexities and idiosyncracies of new creative sensibilities" (n. p.). Here, then, "new" is not meant to suggest that such changes in focus as those noted above usher in an entirely novel stage of critical developments. Rather, it is intended to highlight the noticeable, because progressively more concentrated, emphasis among Canadian literary scholars on the contexts and various conditions, often not readily identifiable as literary, that produce literature and their attendant critical discourses. There have always been critics who study literary texts as a "reliable source of information about anything but [their] own language," the result often being "confus[ing] the materiality of the signifier with the materiality of what it signifies" (de Man 11). Nevertheless, the growing engagement of Canadian literary scholars with the contingencies that influence the making and teaching of Canadian literature demands to be examined in its own right. Such shifts of the critical gaze do not follow a single direction or method. They may veer away from conventional notions of formalism, but they do not entirely disavow all aspects of literariness.[1] If anything, they broaden our understanding of what the literary entails and invite a reassessment of the disciplinary contexts within which we customarily read literature. Signalling what we might call a "contextual approach" (Klarer 74), they reflect above all an intensifying concern with the larger discourses within which the literary is embedded. To put this in both Frygian and non-Frygian terms, we might see these shifts as registering Canadian literature's loss of its autonomy as literature (assuming it was autonomous in the first place).

The TransCanada project,[2] which this book comes from, is designed to provide a forum for exploring precisely the conditions that have generated these critical turns in the study of Canadian literature in recent years.[3] Though I cannot possibly offer here a survey, let alone an exhaustive analysis, of the circumstances that have brought about these changes, I have a double goal in mind: to situate the essays gathered in this collection and to do so in a fashion that provides a critical delineation of what animates the TransCanada project at large, at least from my perspective.[4] In some ways, then, what follows is also an analeptic introduction to *Trans.Can.Lit: Resituating the Study of Canadian Literature* (Kamboureli and Miki, eds.), the volume that focused on the first TransCanada conference. Thus while I pay attention to the larger frames from which I see these essays arising, my guiding principle is shaped by methodological concerns. More specifically, I attempt to examine how the field of Canadian literary studies has been reconfigured as a discipline through what I call "emergent" events or discourses and how such events advance a thematics that is acutely different from thematic criticism. In taking a look at why the latter, though certainly not the single most important approach in the field, has historically been granted a dominant—albeit frequently repudiated—role, I also consider how the study of Canadian literature as a field may remain, predictably so, entangled with the nation, but this entanglement is not methodologically or ideologically stagnant; it displays, as Winfried Siemerling says, "new grounds for re-cognition and revision" (183). A fuller examination of these admittedly complex issues would be beyond the scope of my argument here. My objective, then, is not to offer definitive answers to the issues I identify as deserving close attention but rather to render in bolder relief the contours of the argument here, namely, that the shuttling of the critical gaze from the "inside" to the "outside" of the discipline—along with the characteristic interdisciplinarity it involves—signals yet another important shifting of the ground of CanLit.

Transfiguring the Ground of Literary Studies

These days, *Canada* and *Canadian* do not circulate in critical discourses merely as signs of native circumstance, nor do they signify as transparent descriptors; rather, they demand to be read synchronically and diachronically, locally, transnationally, and globally, that is, as cyphers of a plurisignification process that has recalibrated as much the institutional formation of Canadian literature as the critical discourses about it. So, if scale theories of the nation and globalization (Jeff Derksen); Throne

Speeches and the biopolitics of settler nationalism (Janine Brodie); indigenous knowledge ecologies and bush/writing (peter kulchyski); memorializing Vimy Ridge and the role of crisis in the formation of a national literature (Robert Zacharias); the politics of reasonable accommodation and its media representations (Monika Kin Gagnon and Yasmine Jiwani); transcultural modes of social justice and redress (Pauline Wakeham); book clubs, interdisciplinarity, and collaboration (Danielle Fuller); translation as cultural transfer between minority and dominant cultures (Kathy Mezei) and between nation states (Fujimoto); publishing strategies that combat racialization (Larissa Lai); and indigenous jurisprudence that produces *sui generis* solidarity (Len Findlay)—ostensibly disparate topics—appear together in this volume, it is because they trouble the complexity of the cyphers *Canada* and *Canadian* that have dominated the study of Canadian literature to date.

Read collectively and in relation to each other, the essays in *Shifting the Ground of Canadian Literary Studies* are intricately and staunchly tied together. They are tied as instances of critical practices that reveal the relations and exchanges that take place between the categories of the literary and the national, as well as between the disciplinary sites of critical discourses and the porous boundaries of their methods. Thus, along with the essays that appeared in *Trans.Can.Lit: Resituating the Study of Canadian Literature,* these essays shift our understanding of what constitutes the putative object of literary study: showing literary and critical work to be caught up inextricably in the larger realm of human practices, they expand and by implication interrogate the ground of literary study. If this ground has been shaped by, to adapt Wole Soyinka's words, the Western "habit" of "compartmentalizing ... thought" that turns aspects of human practices "into separatist myths (or 'truths') sustained by a proliferating superstructure of ... idioms, analogies and analytical modes" (37), then by transfiguring the ground of literary study, these essays show the degree to which they are constituting and constituted by complex mutualities both holding together and exposing the rifts within and between the nation-state and culture. While a range of forces that have contributed to the formation of literary and critical discourses fall under these authors' critical scrutiny, their concern with the material effects of the imperial and colonial logics that have fashioned Canada—as well as with the paradoxes, ironies, and contortions that abound in the general perception that Canada has progressed beyond its colonial construction—looms large. To echo Diana Brydon's essay that appeared in *Trans.Can.Lit*, they register the transformation of a discipline.

If the nation and Canadian nationalism[5] have served as the impetus and organizing frames that institutionalized Canadian literature and its study in Canadian universities, as a collection, then, these essays operate as *ex*tensive readings that displace the inherited imperative to practise literary study either as a nationalization project or as a project that defers to the traditional compartmentalization of knowledge. Far from consigning concern with the nation to the dusty drawers of history (after all, it has become a national pastime for Canadianists to "worry the nation"),[6] as a collection these essays show that the substantial transvaluation the nation has already undergone—the nation as concept and Canada as a nation-state—is co-extensive with the changes that have been occurring in the production and study of Canadian literature. These fluctuations, of course, are in tandem with developments in the field of literary studies at large, as well as with how we situate ourselves as critics in humanities departments in Canadian universities.

Read individually, the contributions to this volume offer *in*tensive readings that derive from their attention to specific situations, texts, or contexts.[7] Without assuming a linear chain of events, some of the trajectories they follow are situated in the present, while others take the reader through different historical moments the effects of which remain inscribed in the literary, political, and social discursive sites we engage with today. Similarly, through their different approaches to their objects of study, these essays cumulatively disclose and examine the web of forces with which Canadian literature and the Canadian polity are laced.

Shifting the Ground, then, offers a situational mode of reading whereby the contributors' critical idioms and foci are brought together not by eliding their differences but with the intention of creating a site of "emergence" that is responsive to the thresholds Canadian literary studies have crossed in the first decade of the new millennium. Thus, while the volume is in effect a cluster of singularities—the contributors' individual arguments and approaches that demand to be read in their own terms—it also operates as an assemblage of discourses that pivots both on the *relations* developed among them and on the *questions* raised *by and about* these relations. Reading situationally in this instance means paying attention to the contingencies and locations that have produced these essays, that is, being attentive as much to the particularities in which each essay is grounded as to the larger contours of the collection, along with the specific conditions that have generated it, as a whole.[8]

Nation-state, culture, and indigeneity, understood in broad strokes, are the primary topics the volume addresses, but these topics are redeveloped in concert with the methodological questions they raise. That not all of the contributors in this collection are literary scholars—Brodie is a political scientist and kulchyski a Native Studies scholar—and that some of the literary scholars take on issues that are not, at least not at first sight, directly related to the literary—Wakeham writes about the culture of apologies and Findlay about Sákéj Youngblood Henderson's legal concept of *sui generis*—reflect the design of the TransCanada project: to bring together people from different cultural and academic constituencies in order to explore the interconnectedness of distinct disciplinary and cultural spaces, as well as the transactions that take place among the diverse cultural and political sites scholars and creative writers inhabit. The collapse of the division between the inside and outside of literature *and* its study that this transactional alignment implies is, I think, where the study of Canadian literature has been concentrated since the first decade of this millennium.

Making Strange the Field-Imaginary

It is this unravelling of Canadian literature as an object of study across different thresholds that I had in mind earlier when I said that the new critical directions I am considering do not necessarily do away with literariness. It is worth remembering that literariness, according to Roman Jakobson, who first introduced the concept, is not exclusively a feature of what we commonly refer to as literature. In fact, as he wrote, "The object of literary science is not literature but literariness, i.e., what makes a given work literary" (qtd. in Steiner 201).[9] What makes a work literary for the formalists in particular, or what constitutes literature in general, continues to be discussed with unabated interest;[10] literariness, as Terry Eagleton writes, is "not a thing in itself, eternally fixed and objectively isolable, but a relation between different kinds of discourse" (49). Often misunderstood and misapplied, literariness has proven to be a highly unstable term. But it is this volatility of the term that has enabling possibilities: that literariness does not simply refer to the linguistic or structural properties of literary texts, that it raises questions about the contexts within which literature is produced and those within which it is read, in effect that it is marked by mobility and, thus, "migrates through different levels and functions of linguistic usage" (Bradford 127). Literariness, then, here refers to those elements in literary discourses that exemplify the way another Russian formalist, Viktor Shklovsky, recast literariness, as the concept of *ostranenie*, variously translated as a process of estrangement, defamiliarization, and making strange.

Releasing literariness from pure aesthetic and rhetorical elements, as de Man writes, "one frees the discourse on literature from naïve oppositions between fiction and reality," thus avoiding the trap of mere phenomenalism; by not taking the referential function of literature as an *a priori* principle, that is, by suspending the assumption that the reality constructed by literature and the world outside it share a transparent correspondence, literariness operates as "a powerful and indispensable tool in the unmasking of ideological aberrations" (11). The ability of literariness to make strange produces, de Man says, "negative knowledge about the reliability of linguistic utterance" (10). In this context, knowledge is negative because it does not unfold by way of affirming positivist truths: unstable, and therefore shifting and transforming, this kind of knowledge remains aware that its limits are conditioned by relations of power. Thus it both critiques existing regimes of truth and produces new ways of knowing. In other words, it signals epistemological shifts that challenge master narratives that transmute the shape and boundaries of disciplines. It is these ways of knowing, along with the various materialities they are produced by and embody, that have shifted recently the ground of Canadian literary studies.

Though other critics, including myself, have engaged with the possibilities of defamiliarization, Fred Wah's *Faking It: Poetics and Hybridity. Critical Writing 1984–1999* has given the term greater currency, especially with regard to the politics and poetics of reading Canadian literature against the grain. In the context of Wah's oeuvre, making strange is a crucial aspect to understanding why and how he writes as poet and critic by pulling different methods and devices out of his critical tool box: the act and art of faking it, strang(l)ed poetics, half-bred poetics, *krinopoeia*, trans=geo=ethno=poetics, and poetics of the potent. Yet because literariness is not exclusively a property of literature but of other discourses as well, making strange also operates in certain critical discourses as a tool that unsettles the homologous relationship that is often assumed to exist between the making of literature and the textuality of history, as well as between literature and the public sphere. Dealing with what makes literature strange shows how it is interpellated by various contingencies but also that it has the capacity to turn these forces inside out and upside down. Understanding literariness in this sense materializes the "transing" process of the writing and critical acts. In Wah's own terms, "'[t]ransing'... [is] an important compound in ... writing actions that have to do with translation, transcreation, transposition, i.e., senses of crossing, and shifting" (*Faking* 2).

This transing registers the opening up of the study of Canadian literature: unfolding through emergent events, it identifies moments of crisis that demand retooling, that is, developing new, while simultaneously engaging critically with existing, technologies of knowing, a process that instigates changes in the field-imaginary. I borrow the term field-imaginary from Donald E. Pease's introduction to his guest-edited special issue of *boundary 2* of the same title, "New Americanists: Revisionist Interventions into the Canon," an issue designed to address anew the history and contexts of American studies. He employs the term "to designate a location for the disciplinary unconscious," that is, a given field's "fundamental syntax—its tacit assumptions, convictions, primal words, and the charged relations binding them together" (11).[11] Because a specialist's "primal identity" is formed out of this syntax, it is not possible to "subject [the field's terms] to critical scrutiny ... [They] subsist instead as self-evident principles" (12). Nevertheless, the emergence of certain events—events that cannot be easily accommodated within the field-imaginary, that disturb its terms of self-reference, that are entangled with it in agonistic relations—have the capacity to intercept its normative affairs.[12]

Emergent Discourses/Undisciplining the Discipline

"Emergence" as concept and event encapsulates the process and effects of making strange. I have in mind here Foucault's notion of *Entstehungt* that echoes, in turn, Nietzsche's use of it. As a "moment ... arising" from a conflict of forces, emergence may hold the promise for new configurations but does not embody the "final term of a historical development." Precisely because emergence is just one moment in a "series" of "episod[ic]" occurrences (*Language* 148), it "designates a place of confrontation but not as a closed field"; not necessarily constituting a "common space" but rather a scene of differentiation where competing forces are exposed and perhaps even clash, "no one is responsible for" emergence: "no one can glory in it, since it always occurs in the interstice" (150). In its Foucauldian sense, emergence reflects my perception of the process whereby the Canadian field-imaginary begins gradually but steadily to change its syntax, for example, by stopping the romancing of the nation and of CanLit as a statist institution as the field-imaginary uncovers and examines those relationships between literature and the body politic that have been rendered invisible or contained, and thus suppressed—notably, but not exclusively, indigeneity, racialization, gender, and queerness.

The episodic nature of emergence does not lend itself either to linear chronology or to progressivist development of a discursive formation. Rather, it draws attention to the thresholds crossed at different points and to the effects of such crossings that can be coincident or cross-pollinating, effects that might have a lasting impact but do not necessarily lead to what we might consider a point of maturation or what Foucault calls "culmination" (148). The result of specific circumstances, emergence causes a rupture at a particular moment in the discipline instigated by material conditions that constitute crisis points.[13]

Crisis, which Jörn Rüsen defines as "a certain experience of temporal change: that of contingency," is indeed essential to most cases of transformation that involve resistance; as he writes, "crisis constitutes historical consciousness, so one can say that there is no historical consciousness without crisis" (253). What he calls "catastrophic crises," ones that suspend "historical consciousness's ability to digest contingency," in due course become part of the "meaningful narrative" of historical consciousness that normalizes a departure from regulatory patterns (254).[14] However, this phenomenon of "routinization" (Mbembe and Roitman 326) does not necessarily "reduce crisis to an event whose meaning is exhausted once it has been analyzed and deciphered" (325) or, I would add, incorporated into normative socio-cultural moulds. Though it does not by default change a field's foundations, a crisis event exercises pressure on them by introducing new questions *and* new ways of posing questions about, to loosely echo another Foucauldian schema, the power/knowledge dynamic as well as the various modalities and practices that manage the production of knowledge and the institutional apparatuses within which critics operate.

Emergent discourses are interlinked with knowledge sites—for example, the conception of Canada as a *terra nullius*, the head tax imposed on the Chinese labourers in the nineteenth century, or presuppositions about the discipline—that for a long time have been beyond the conventional domain of the study of Canadian literature. Thus they disturb the political unconscious of the discipline and produce knowledge that is working at the limit: at the limit in the sense that that kind of knowledge has been repressed in the Canadian national imaginary and, as a result, pushed to the edges of the field; in the sense that the emergence of such knowledge upsets inherited orthodoxies; and in the sense that its emergence does not attempt to replace by default the doxa of received assumptions with new positivisms. At once conditioned by and resistant to hegemonic formations, knowledge at the limit denaturalizes what have been constructed as the natural borders of a discipline.

The Women and Words conference in Vancouver (1983), the Third International Women's Book Fair in Montreal (1988), and the Writing Thru Race conference (also in Vancouver in 1994) are events that exemplify the emergence of different ways of knowing. For example, it was in the Montreal event that Lee Maracle voiced the powerful imperative addressed to non-Aboriginal writers and academics to "move over,"[15] an incitement that is directly linked with, among other things, what has been called the cultural appropriation debate.[16] The ripple effect and impact this has had on a number of fronts, ranging from the realm of anti-racist activism to publishing and cultural production, from pedagogy and curricular development to diasporic and postcolonial critical discourses, reflect the impetus such emergent moments create to cross different thresholds.

Emergent events, then, initiate a disruption that triggers what Len Findlay calls, in *Trans.Can.Lit*, "the multilateral sublime." Cunningly deployed as a trope because of its "*un*Canadianness outside the realm of nature or wilderness" (184), the multilateral sublime "must be subverted, discredited, and prohibited because it intimates an alternative sublime that ... represents a loss of power by the dominant as well as the redefinition of power itself by the dominated" (184). Moreover, as an instance of Findlay's strategy of "revisionary citation" (179, 180), resonating as it does with Edmund Burke, the multilateral sublime instantiates a process that renders the familiar strange. Seen in this light, emergent events reconfigure the political unconscious of the field-imaginary by unravelling its sedimentary structure. To appropriate Findlay's words, they operate as a "necessary mechanism of transformation" that discloses "the cunning of production" (178). At once internal and external to the field, emergent events serve in part to remind us of the relationship of the field-imaginary and of literature to the public sphere. Because their multilateral function unmasks the alleged disinterestedness of institutional formations; because they mess up the value systems of cultural, political, and economic capital; because they upset normative paradigms, they constitute at once moments of crisis and of re-vision.

Junctures that constitute turning points in the re-scripting of the field-imaginary do not have to be event-bound, nor time-bound, nor occurring exclusively within the same disciplinary or cultural spaces.[17] Often the result of a converging or incremental process,[18] emergent events take different forms, thus displaying different productive capacities and different amplitudes. For example, Maracle's autobiographical and oratory writings, *Bobby Lee: Indian Rebel* (1975; rev. 1990); *I Am Woman* (1988); and *Oratory: Coming to Theory* (1990); Beatrice Culleton's *In Search of April Raintree* (1983); and Jeannette Armstrong's *Slash* (1985);[19] the volumes of feminist criticism *A Mazing Space: Writing Canadian Women Writing* (1986), which I co-edited with Shirley Neuman, and *Gynocritics/Gynocritiques: Feminist Approaches to Canadian and Quebec Women Writers* (1987), edited by Barbara Godard; the launching of the feminist journal *Tessera* in 1984, edited by the collective of Godard, Daphne Marlatt, Kathy Mezei, and Gail Scott; the avant-garde but short-lived feminist magazine *(f)lip*, founded and edited by Betsy Warland et al. in 1986; and the Telling It Book Collective (SKY Lee, Lee Maracle, Daphne Marlatt, and Betsy Warland) conference in 1988 in Vancouver and the book of the same title that resulted from it (1990)—all these comprise cases of particular *nodes* within the emergence of diverse discourses that seek to question the self-legitimization of the dominant master narratives about Canadian society and culture.

I call such emergent events nodes because they operate within and across different communities as (sometimes loose, sometimes organized) network formations that gradually pick up momentum; the nodal function of emergent events is crucial in that it establishes allegiances through interrelationships that mobilize action across different constituencies. This does not mean that the flows from one node to another are always smooth or that the impact of a node is immediately recognized. Nodes are marked by their own attributes, and they have itineraries of their own that, when they intersect with those of other nodes, can generate shifts that cross boundaries. The intervention a node makes is contingent on the particular spaces and circumstances from within which it emerges, and its importance can flow or ebb. Furthermore, nodes may not fall within the scope of a field's technologies of recognition precisely because the latter render them illegible and illegitimate, but the micro dynamics within the particular community from which these events emerge, while perhaps unnoticed at first, may accrue archival significance in the temporality of their material effects. Thus which events are seen as emergent, coupled with the importance assigned to them, depends in part on circumstances of witnessing and participation; while they may be quiet (or non-) events for some, they constitute an unquiet force for others. They are, then, at once synchronous with the tradition that excludes or is oblivious to them and occurring within a discrepant temporality. Trying to understand the unfolding of a discipline by being attentive to the work produced by individual nodes as well as to how they interconnect creates the possibility of getting a glimpse beyond the restricted economy of the field, a glimpse of the general economy of cultural and critical production that is in the horizon. The nodal function of emergent events, together with the fact that they take place on the periphery of the field-imaginary, allows those involved in them to develop scales of trust in their own terms.

The ambivalent and gradual material effects of the policy of multiculturalism; the Japanese Canadian redress movement (early 1980s–88) and the role Joy Kogawa's *Obasan* (1981) played in animating the Canadian public about it; Linda Hutcheon's *The Canadian Postmodern: A Study of Contemporary English-Canadian Fiction* (1988); M. NourbeSe Philip's *Frontiers: Selected Essays and Writing on Racism and Culture 1984–1992* (1992); Himani Bannerji's *The Writing on the Wall* (1993); and the canon debate that included major critical arguments chiefly between Robert Lecker and Frank Davey (circa 1991–95)—all these are examples of the *process* of emergence. I stress process for, as I have already suggested, it is not always the singularity of an event or a text that marks an emergence; rather, such events or texts serve as conduits through which turning points occur, shifts that are to be gauged by how they upset the restricted economy of the field-imaginary. And since emergence as I am defining it here is not synonymous with completion, nor is it linear, the uncertainty embedded in its episodic structure contains the ability to undiscipline the discipline. In other words, emergent events bare the scaffolding on which the field has relied as a discipline and expose the vested interests that constructed its foundations.

Emergent events, then, also help uncover the collusion that exists between the discursive formation of the nation-state and that of the field-imaginary, thus not only bringing forth changes about the kinds of things we study but also bringing into relief the ways and milieus within which we do so. This entails, on the one hand, devising methodological approaches that alter the scene and environment of the field-imaginary and, on the other hand, developing a sharper awareness of the fact that what we study and how we study it is mediated by the governmentality of knowledge. Thus while many scholars continue to produce criticism by reading literature as a verbal construct alone, a growing number of them have become alert to how what Arjun Appadurai calls the research imagination is interpellated by forces outside, or at the limits, of our disciplines and the profession. Writing in 2001, Appadurai noted that universities, like other sectors ranging from law and medicine to fiction, from marketing to the armed forces, "must demonstrate their foundation in research in order to command serious public attention or funds" (10). But today, as Canadian studies have begun to cross the new millennium, it appears that Appadurai's rationale for research has been upended. It would be foolhardy to ignore the fact that research in the neoliberal lexicon of government policies about universities has undergone a fundamental reduction to economic benefits and quantifiable impacts. While this conception of education and pure research is advocated nominally for the sake of the public's wellness and fiscal responsibility, pure research—and the study of Canadian literature falls largely under this category—is gradually rendered inconsequential. Since this has been in the offing for a while now in the various "transformations" the research landscape in Canada has been going through,[20] the TransCanada project also engages with this larger domain of *critical* affairs within which the study of Canadian literature takes place, one reason for the range of issues addressed in *Trans.Can.Lit* as well as in this volume and the third one that follows.[21]

My point here is not to opine an imperative, namely, that the field-imaginary of Canadian literary studies must at all costs engage with the plight of the humanities today, but rather to suggest that what shapes the research imagination, the field's political unconscious, is inextricably enmeshed with what is happening "out there." Emergent moments can restructure the research landscape by redrawing the boundaries that separate critical discourses from the material conditions that lie outside them; moreover, they bring to our attention the need to rework the terms of what is interior or exterior to critical discourses, in other words, to question what constitutes the proper subject of the Canadian field-imaginary or what constitutes disciplinary propriety. For example, much of the fervor in the debates in the 1960s, '70s, and '80s about Canadian literature revolved around who was a Canadian writer, with reviewers displaying the tendency to first identify an author's origins before talking about her or his writing, while critics obsessed about the Canadianness of a story or a poem.[22] Similarly, there are still critics today who assume that the proper object of the field of Canadian literary studies is literary commentary, and that literary critics should write exclusively about literary texts. Were such proprieties the rule by which disciplines are to conduct themselves, then there would be no Asian Canadian or Caribbean Canadian literatures, or gender or race studies of Canadian literature today. Disciplines, Foucault writes, are "made up of errors as well as truths ... errors which are not residues or foreign bodies but which have positive functions, a historical efficacity, and a role that is often indissociable from that of the truths" ("Order of Discourse" 60). In this context, emergent events can destabilize disciplinary boundaries by showing the pliability of their coordinates.

Inside and Outside the Field-Imaginary

In many respects, there is nothing "new" about such disciplinary shifts. Nevertheless, what is relatively recent in the larger schema of things is precisely the increased awareness of the forces that have shaped the Canadian field-imaginary as a discursive formation.

What is "new," then, is disciplinary consciousness. Were I pressed to identify only one thing that has given rise to this consciousness in the recent course of Canadian literary studies that would be what we might call its outward mobility: what lay outside the discipline's purview as proper subject because it didn't match, and thus disfigured, the field-imaginary's self-image, what was rendered improper by virtue of its absence, has moved in. But it is crucial to understand that what has entered the primary scene of the field through this movement has not automatically been co-opted or assimilated; instead, while initially seen as a sign of disfiguration, it has revealed its capacity to create impetus for transformation.

The institutionalization of the study of Canadian literature and how it has begun to shift its parameters must be examined, naturally, in terms that are particular to the Canadian milieu, but as a disciplinary discourse Canadian literary studies must also be seen in the larger setting of disciplinary formations. In this context, I find the topic Foucault chose for his inaugural lecture at the Collège de France in December 1970, "The Order of Discourse," to be à propos of the emergence process I am discussing here. Foucault spoke of the "profound logophobia, a sort of mute terror against ... the *surging-up* of" events, things that could be "discontinuous, pugnacious, disorderly" ("Order" 66; my emphasis). "[T]here are monsters on the prowl," he said, "whose form changes with the history of knowledge" (60). These "monsters" that haunt the disciplinary unconscious, whose stalwart irascibility puts to test the "principle of control" that a discipline is, throw into upheaval a discipline's proper subject. Foucault's trope of the monstrous speaks to the logophobia that "polic[es]'" ("Order" 61) what constitutes the inside and outside of a discipline or, to put this in Michel de Certeau's terms, it "manifests a *heterogeneity* relative to the *homogenous* wholes established by ... [a] discipline" (81).[23]

If the iteration of gender, race, and ethnicity has long reached the point of operating virtually as a cliché, a strategy (in part) of scholarly accountability, it was not too long ago when these categories of subjugated subjectivities were relegated entirely outside university culture and critical discourses, and in the margins of the social realm. But mere incorporation within a discipline's domain of those other subjects or of different ways of knowing does not necessarily disrupt its political unconscious; inclusion can become an instance of policing and fetishization, a means of containment, a strategy designed to pre-empt any radical restructuring of the discipline. Granting a place inside the discipline to those unruly others[24] is not inevitably synonymous with their exercising their own agency; as long as their entry into the field-imaginary casts them into subjects-as-objects, as long as their representational role is guided by the discipline's sense of propriety, these others remain guests of the discipline's putative beneficence as host, speaking through critical acts that are nothing more than acts of ventriloquism.[25]

Hence my stressing that emergent events are not marked by the teleology that usually characterizes a discipline, especially a discipline that, like its subject, CanLit, has played an instrumental/ized role in discourses of the Canadian nation-state. Foucault's critique of disciplinary discourse as "a violence which we do to things" draws attention to the need to reconceptualize the outside and inside of disciplinary formations, one of the "rules" he proposed by way of curtailing or avoiding this violence. "We must not go from discourse toward its interior," he admonished his audience, "but … go towards its external conditions of possibility, towards what gives rise to the aleatory series of these events, and fixes its limits" ("Order" 67).[26] Far from reifying the outside and inside of field-imaginaries as a binary, Foucault's incitement suggests that what lies outside of disciplinary discourses is not constituted by them. That emergent events may appear to be aleatory when seen from a discipline's vantage point does not diminish their possibilities; rather, such a disciplinary perspective reinforces the disjunction of temporality between itself and emergent events and helps make visible the constitutive force of exclusion. For example, an event may be perceived as emergent and thus disruptive within the temporal and spatial dimensions of a discipline's status quo, but it might very well be continuous with the spatio-temporal scope of the constituency that produces it. The exclusion of the outside, then, delimits what lies inside; it develops a kind of topography of distance and difference, a map of conflictual relations. Significantly, the outside as a space of intervals, writes Gilles Deleuze in *Foucault*, is configured as "'non-place': … the place … of mutation," mutation in that "things are no longer perceived or propositions articulated in the same way" (71).[27] If "[e]mergence, change and mutation affect composing forces, not composed forms" (73), then the force embodied in emergent events does not only agitate a discipline's mastery over its proper subjects; it also articulates its process of becoming—becoming its own inside as it were—not by aspiring to be the same as the inside of the field-imaginary but, instead, by asserting its own propriation, that which is proper to itself, that which belongs to it.[28]

Emergent Events and Paradigm Shifts

It must have become apparent by now that I was not referring to a distinct paradigm shift when I earlier said that, at least in my reading of things, the object of Canadian literary studies has expanded substantially beyond the world of literary texts and toward a wide range of directions that enlist discourses that are other than distinctly literary. As I have argued, emergent events bring about fluctuations that gradually pick up speed, but the result of this process does not constitute without fail a change of paradigms. Some of the shifts that the emergent events I referred to above have generated may have become part of the habitus of Canadian literary studies[29]—mainly, the preoccupation with otherness and the movement outwards—but deployment of the major turning points this emergence process has initiated does not automatically alter the political unconscious of the discipline. A field's political unconscious can rescript its primal scene only via epistemic and methodological shifts. The political efficacy of emergent events as I have attempted to theorize them here does not lend itself to the kind of mastery that disciplinary formations conventionally strive for, a mastery often achieved by enforcing the primacy of certain critical parameters that can result in closure. Because emergent events each launch their own concerns, they do not necessarily produce a shared narrative that can reroute the trajectory of the discipline in the coherent fashion that paradigm shifts require. Moreover, because of their episodic structure, because of the different temporal and spatial zones within which they occur, because of the situated knowledge they produce, and because they gain leverage only gradually and often in sites that are different from those of the discursive formation of the discipline, the agitation emergent events cause in the field-imaginary may initiate a reshuffling of priorities in the discipline, but this does not as a matter of course translate into a paradigm shift. The forces they unleash may well prove to be incommensurable.

In considering the developments of Canadian literary studies in recent years, I lie somewhere in between the Kuhnian doctrine that argues for sudden transitions—non-linear periodic shifts (not always identical with emergent events)—and its critics who argue for gradual change, that is, between "revolution" and reformation by degrees, or my preferred term, retooling.[30] Rather than indicating a relativist position, this reflects my sense that, despite the many fundamental changes that have occurred in Canadian criticism since the early 1980s, it would be hard, if not downright impossible, to identify a single methodological shift, let alone a particular study, that has ushered in a rapid transition in a singular way "from one dominant paradigm to another" (Patrick Colm Hogan's definition of a paradigm shift, 323). The high drama of sudden paradigm shifts does not appear to be a model in Canadian literary studies; indeed, even Kuhn's theory concedes that abrupt paradigm changes are not the norm in the humanities. When we consider what has been happening on the stage of the Canadian critical scene, the position of Kuhn's critics who argue that paradigm shifts take time to develop better reflects some of the changes we have been witnessing in Canadian critical discourses since the mid-1980s.

Interestingly, Kuhn also draws attention to the processual way in which such changes may occur:

> Led by a new paradigm, scientists adopt *new instruments* and look in *new places*. Even more important, during revolutions scientists see new and different things when looking with familiar instruments *in places they have looked before*. It is rather *as if* the professional community had been suddenly transported to another planet where familiar objects are seen in a different light and are joined by unfamiliar ones as well. Of course, nothing of quite that sort does occur: there is no geographical transplantation; outside the laboratory *everyday affairs usually continue as before*. Nevertheless, paradigm changes do cause scientists to see the world of their research-engagement differently. (111; my emphasis)

The fact that everyday affairs may go on as usual diminishes a paradigm shift's immediate impact. Underscoring the importance that a paradigm shift can be applied as much to familiar as to new places, Kuhn suggests that to "see" the light of a new method is not enough; one has to develop new research instruments and "look" as much inside as outside the discipline. This necessary retooling of the discipline should ideally involve the various technologies that determine a field-imaginary, both from within and without; otherwise, any changes would simply amount to a dress-up game. As a method of "re-equipping and redesigning" (Coleman and Kamboureli 263), retooling entails both a reorganization and a reconceptualization of disciplinary formations, a process that requires an acute sense of disciplinary consciousness encompassing as much pragmatic change as a renewal of the terms and methods that normally define a discipline's canonical values. Thus, the point of a paradigm shift is making a discipline strange to itself. Simply changing one set of tools with another does not make the familiar strange; disciplinary consciousness in this instance implies that the familiar is not a natural category, that the self-sufficiency defining it is, more often than not, based on exclusion and suspect or exhausted beliefs.

The question of whether a sudden shift has occurred in critical discourses about Canadian literature is based on the assumption that there was a single, or easily identifiable, dominant paradigm in the first place to be replaced suddenly by another one. I don't think this has been the case. What is more, it is important to understand that naming a given approach to Canadian literature dominant is not just a matter of identifying a method widely used by a community of scholars. While the dominance of a paradigm is perforce communal, such a naming act also involves antagonism among different optics and ideological positions; it recognizes a normative state of affairs, but it also points to the institutional and political forces that have interiorized the paradigm's dominance in the discipline. The methodological and ideological prisms from which a body of critical work is read in a given period are determined by the master narratives at work at that time, indeed by the field-imaginary's political unconscious. To pursue further the complexity of this issue would take me into the realm of literary history, which is not my purpose here. Still, I would like to linger a while longer on this point in the hope of showing that the permutations I am talking about here, and which this collection reflects (upon) as a whole, do not constitute a paradigm shift as such but rather nodal points in the development of Canadian literary studies: crisis as what destabilizes submission to conformity; making strange as what disturbs the legitimate frames of the discipline.[31]

Forging the Discipline: The Paradigm of Canadian Thematic Criticism

If there is a single dominant paradigm that recurs in discussions of the formation of Canadian literature as an institution, this is indisputably that of thematic criticism in the 1970s. But what constitutes the dominance of this mode of reading? We may have "survived the paraphrase" (Davey, *Surviving*) of what we have come to dub thematic criticism, but that thematicism persists as the foremost paradigm that critics refer to, mobilized as it was by the double intent to institutionalize Canadian literature and to establish a close rapport between it and what was assumed to be the character of the Canadian nation-state. As Barry Cameron wrote in 1990, "Canadian criticism since the late 1960s may be characterized as one *governed* by a (modified) poetics concerned with establishing a general grammar of Canadian literature as a whole and discovering certain kinds of patterns in Canadian literary texts" (125; my emphasis).[32] But the irony here is that it has not been so much thematicism that has governed Canadian criticism but the critics' obsession with the idea of it. How could this approach have achieved such prominence when, as Russell Brown rightly states, "within ten years of the publication of *The Bush Garden*, thematic criticism had gone so completely out of fashion that even John Moss, one of the critics most identified with this critical mode ... had renounced thematics" (657)?[33] Granting thematic criticism credit as a paradigm that a large number of Canadianists began critiquing soon after it was produced,[34] one that, as Heather Murray puts it bluntly, "is of course now universally despised" (221), is tantamount to composing literary history that privileges a single narrative order, an order that presents a neat, and therefore reductive, account of what transpired in that period.

The emphasis on the thematic paradigm says as much about the prominence of certain critics at the time when Canadian literary studies had begun to come of age as it says about their later counterparts composing a history of critical approaches. As E.D. Blodgett reminds us, "The narrative of literary history ... does not simply tell a story; it is designed, no matter how obliquely, to argue a kind of supremacy." The supremacy, as it were, at stake here reflects the desire, in Blodgett's words, "to find a means of unifying what may appear to be disparate parts and to suggest that in the process of finding unity meaning will emerge" (*Five Part* 6). The plot that emerges, predictably, centres on the nation. Yet even in the heydays of thematic criticism, a period usually identified with the publication of Margaret Atwood's *Survival: A Thematic Guide to Canadian Literature* (1972), D.G. Jones' *Butterfly on Rock: A Study of Themes and Images in Canadian Literature* (1970), and John Moss's *Patterns of Isolation in English Canadian Fiction* (1974) and *Sex and Violence in the Canadian Novel: The Ancestral Present* (1977), there were other kinds of thematic and non-thematic discourses that disturbed the idea of a singular critical model, that did not obsess with the nation, and that did not posit the national character of Canadian literature as the determining feature.

For example, Imre Szeman may be right to identify Warren Tallman's 1960 essay "Wolf in the Snow" (published in two parts) as an "influential ... precursor" (*Zones* n. 11, 229) to these critical studies—studies that as recently as 1998 Linda Warley, John Clement Ball, and Robert Viau referred to as "foundational" (1)—but Tallman was practising a different kind of thematics. Though, in ways that anticipated Atwood's survival theory and Moss's theme of isolation, he identified "[t]he desire to prevail" (Part Two, 42; 43) as a central theme in the fiction he examined, and he focused on landscape and the particularities of place,[35] unlike them, he was not interested in producing a Canadian national narrative. The "fictional house" he examined might have been located in province-specific sites, but his use of this trope operated in a centrifugal manner; "it is best to enter the fictional house at once," he wrote, "and move across rooms to where the windows *open out*" (Part One, 7; my emphasis). This *opening out* did not gesture toward Canada, nor did it aim to address what constituted Canadian identity; contrary to the thematic critics who adopted a nationalist/culturalist approach, Tallman wrote from a continental perspective.[36] As he put it, "[t]he continent itself—the gray wolf whose shadow is underneath the snow—has resisted the culture, the cultivation, the civilization which is indigenous to Europe but alien to North America even though it is dominant in North America" (Part Two, 43). Thus what has become an article of faith in discussions of Canadian thematic criticism in the 1960s and early '70s, what Szeman calls "the persistence of the nation," is loudly absent in Tallman's work. And if, as Donna Bennett claims, the thematic criticism of the 1960s and '70s was an early exercise in rendering Canada and its culture postcolonial ("English Canada's" 125), the lack of any declared interest in the nation in Tallman's twin essays—essays that were rendered "classic" soon after they appeared—points to the development of a continental critical discourse that anticipates (structurally) Robert Kroetsch's aphoristic statement that "Canadian literature evolved directly from Victorian to the Postmodern" ("A Canadian" 1). Besides, this development is more akin to transnational issues than to postcolonial discourses' concern with disturbing the colonial roots of settler nations.

Tallman was not the only critic who wrote around the same time but did so in ways that, if not decidedly anti-thematic, shifted the gravitational pull of the thematicists away from the nationalism and positivism that characterized their work. Employing comparative literature's reading methods that, implicitly as well as explicitly, challenged the principles of transparency and overdetermination inscribed in that criticism, Blodgett, for example, situated Canadian literature in a comparative and world literature context, and worked, unambiguously so, against the drive toward national unity and cultural homogeneity that the emphasis on (mythic and other) patterns of thematic criticism displayed ("Preface" 8). Writing in 1981, to introduce his collection of essays—*Configurations: Essays on Canadian Literatures*—that had originally appeared in the second half of the 1970s, he talked about Canada "not [as] a unified country in either a political or a cultural sense" ("Preface" 8). Rather, he saw it as "a nation-state ... whose model is that of a commonwealth, a *multinational* society where one is *always at home and abroad*" ("Canadian Literatures" 34; my emphasis), thus contesting the dream of homogeneity that held sway in thematic criticism. "The survival of Canada—if such a phrase is appropriate ... ," he stated, "depends upon a genuine *Aufhebung*, a genuine negation and transmutation of the major, if not the unique, impasse in the emergence of a genuine Canadian culture" ("Preface" 9). Equivalent, for my purposes here, though by no means the same, to Tallman's *opening out*, Blodgett's *Aufhebung* pointed to the need to abolish the prevailing ideologies in Canadian criticism at the time by practising a method "guide[d]" by a "re-spective glance"; this method required that the critic "be ... on a threshold ... contingent, fragile, unwilling to accept ... the illusion of the universal solution, self-absorbed, unguided by the enigmas of the other presence" ("Canadian Literatures" 35). Posing Canadian literatures as a "problem," he was not interested in forging a discipline in the name of a homogeneous nation. Indeed, his comparativisit approach in the late 1970s anticipated in substantial ways some of the debates that have revitalized the field of comparative studies, debates that addressed the universal values ascribed to the subject of that discipline at the time of its inception.[37]

A similar turn away from nationalist criticism is also displayed in most of Eli Mandel's work in that same period. For example, in his "Preface" to his edited collection of essays, *Contexts of Canadian Criticism* (1971), Mandel lamented the "paranoiac self-consciousness" of criticism at the time and called for an "expan[sion of] the notion of literary criticism in Canada to include the work of historians and philosophers." As he wrote, "[w]hatever the explanation for this obsession with self-consciousness and theoretical configurations, this much is obvious: any collection of critical essays that aspires to represent Canadian critical writing fairly and accurately will obviously present selections concerned not only with traditional comments on patterns of literary development but with the history and form of Canadian society and with problems in poetic theory as well" ("Preface" vii). As his collection's title and contents make apparent (it includes essays, for example, by George Grant, Marshall McLuhan, H.A. Innis, Northrop Frye, and Dorothy Livesay), the interdisciplinarity this collection strove toward was not of the kind we usually encounter today whereby methodologies from different disciplinary areas converge and/or cross-fertilize each other in a single reading. Nevertheless, this was clearly what Mandel's editorial project "aspire[d] to": his emphasis on contexts,[38] his situating literary and critical discourses within, and juxtaposing them to, the various conditions, elements, and relations that participated in their production, posited a model for criticism that worked at cross-purposes with that of the thematic critics by "tr[ying] to find its boundaries *outside itself*" (Introduction 3; my emphasis).

Emphasizing the importance of contingencies that Blodgett talked about, especially with regard to his concern with modernity, while also displaying his abiding interest in language, Freudianism, and phenomenology,[39] Mandel called, in his Massey Lectures (1966), for a "savage" criticism (*Criticism* 71). He thus exposed the conceit of civility underlying nationalist thematic criticism—a term that has returned in our days, albeit with a critical difference, thanks to Coleman's study, *White Civility: The Literary Project of English Canada*. Contrary to the thematic critics' obsession with compact tropes—survival, garrison mentality, wilderness—intended to identify (read construct) a cardinal narrative for the Canadian nation as a family of the same, Mandel willfully imagined a family that "*was not*" his own (*The Family Romance* ix).[40] Via Freud and Harold Bloom, the trope of the "family romance" allowed Mandel "to seek ... scenes of nomination, identification, origins" (x) and thus interrupt the standpoint of homogeneity that configured the cultural space of Canada at the time in terms of what Jean-Luc Nancy would call "being-together" or "being-in-common" (90). That he acknowledged the "unequivocally male ... bias" of the theories he worked with in *The Family Romance* (xi), as well as the fact that the essays gathered in that collection were "only incidentally about the margin" (xii), also caused a fracturing (at least in my view) in thematic criticism and expressed a concern with marginality that was far from being common at the time.[41]

Why then does Bennett insist, in what is surely one of the institutional/izing contexts of literary and critical discourses, *The Oxford Companion to Canadian Literature*, on seeing Mandel as belonging to the group of thematic critics, albeit as "the most literary and wide-ranging" figure of them (252)? Her entry on criticism reiterates her earlier comment that "the thematic approach ... dominated Canadian criticism from the late sixties to the mid-seventies" (194), in effect producing the kind of monologic perspective that Donna Palmateer Pennee, rightly so, argues is impossible to discern (see "'Après Frye, rien'?"). Such perspectives of the history and development of critical discourses about Canadian literature reflect the disposition to read with the grain. I am inclined to think, then, that thematic criticism has been constructed as the single dominant mode of reading because of the perceived need that a unified critical paradigm was crucial to granting validity to a discipline in the process of formation. A paradigm may establish the parameters of scholarly pursuits, but it also institutes the boundaries of the research imagination, thus introducing degrees of legitimacy and relevance of methods. In this light, considering thematic criticism to be the dominant paradigm operates as an integrationist approach that speaks to and compensates for the anxiety that has accompanied the belatedness of Canadian literature and its study.[42] I borrow the term "integrationist" from Houston Baker, who sees it as "institut[ing] an optimism that reads documentary statements of ideals as positive signs of a promised land to come." His remark that "integrationism validates ... an epistemology with sharply exclusive horizons" (69) thus echoes my understanding that the identity/identification goals of thematic criticism were intent on devising parameters that would establish the distinctiveness, and thus the exclusionist character, of the representational value of CanLit.

Cross- and Intra-Generational Shifts and Emergent Events

A way of understanding the concurrence of different critical discourses in the 1970s would be as epistemological or ideological turns to ways of thinking and issues that the so-called normative paradigm at the time failed to respond to. Such shifts, as I have already argued, come both from within and from without the field: Davey's *From There to Here* (1974) is an example of a critical approach that, although it remains in some respects akin to the thematic model, sets out to displace it, and thus signals change from within the field while also taking into account the technological advancements at that time; and the gradual turn to literary theory and feminist discourses that began appearing around the same period was also a major shift mobilized, in large part, by influences external to the field (i.e., continental European and American theories). These departures from what is taken to be the norm operate in a manner that is similar to what Houston Baker calls a "generational shift." Here, however, I do not take "generational" to designate a group of critics that belong to a distinct chronological period. Instead, I employ the term as demarcating critical voices and approaches, across generations but also within the same generation, that flag a departure from established norms in the same time frame, hence my qualifying the term as cross- and intra-generational. For instance, while feminist criticism in Canada was certainly influenced by different kinds of feminist theory, Women and Words, one of the examples I mentioned earlier as an emergent event, shows that it would be highly reductive to attribute the turn toward feminist, gender, and queer discourses exclusively to imported feminist theories in the 1980s. The galvanizing impact that event had on those of us who were there and its productive consequences across diverse constituencies had a whole lot to do with the particular kinds of knowledge and experiences participants of different generations and communities brought to it.

Baker employs the term "generational shift" to articulate a "vernacular theory" of Afro-American literature and criticism that refers to "an ideologically motivated movement overseen by young or newly emergent intellectuals dedicated to refuting the work of their intellectual predecessors and to establishing a new framework for intellectual inquiry" (67). He reinforces his definition by citing Lewis Feuer, who argues that "'in its experience, each such new intellectual generation feels everything is being born anew, that the past is meaningless, or irrelevant, or non-existent'" (qtd. in Baker 67).[43] Nevertheless, his own critical practice does not privilege Feuer's binary logic, which evokes the agon in which the Bloomian ephebe poet engages in order to withstand the influence of his predecessors, an agon that involves misprision and power politics cast largely in psychoanalytic terms.[44] Such a generational shift would entail skipping over history to reinvent the wheel, a battle between the "old" and the "young," the past and the present. Instead, Baker transfers the generational aspect of this combative encounter away from individual authors and critics and onto the conceptual and ideological swerving points in the development of Afro-American literary studies. A generational shift, he says, "begins with the assumption that changes in the 'categorical structure' of thought are coextensive with social change" (108), a view that aligns Baker's theory with Kuhn's paradigm as a "tropological vehicle" (76). Thus, rather than singling out the instantaneity, as it were, of paradigm shifts that could stop the clock of knowledge production in order to have it ticking again through new mechanisms that so many of Kuhn's supporters and detractors focus on, Baker draws attention to the *process* that accompanies epistemological changes.

This broader perception of the term "generational" is relevant to understanding the different critical models and emergent discourses that have shaped Canadian literary studies. Coming as they do from within discrete socio-cultural and intellectual communities, emergent discourses bring about ideological and methodological reorientations that operate in the name of difference rather than in the name of identification. As the figure of "outward" suggests—Tallman's *opening out*, Blodgett's *Aufhebung*, and Mandel's *outside itself*—critical discourses that trope not inwards, toward the legitimized and legitimizing centre of the discipline, but rather centrifugally do not fit easily the integrationist model that normally determines the construction of disciplinary fields; rather, operating as nodal points, they demand to be read not in the kind of consensual manner that would have their differences subsumed but in ways that would allow their multi-accentual discursive re-articulations to signify in terms of their disjunctive temporalities. The cross- and intra-generational forces that have contributed to the field's development, then, are the direct result of the fact that, as I have already suggested, emergent discourses coincide temporally with the critical models that institute, and are instituted by, the discipline.

This is what I think Barbara Godard has in mind when she refers to "the characteristic features of contemporary Canadian criticism [since 1974], notably an idiosyncratic use of terminology and the class of critical ideologies, frequently self-contradictory" ("Structuralism" 57). Godard does not question the existence of a Canadian critical tradition; it is its "specificity" that she finds "elusive" (54). Her summation of how and why such contradictory modes of thinking coexist with each other anticipates the argument I have advanced here:

> While the debate surrounding the death of the subject is being waged in English Canada, as elsewhere, between phenomenology and structuralism, its evolution in timing and configuration is unique. For the

appearance of these two critical theories on the Canadian scene has been nearly simultaneous with the arrival of semiotics, deconstruction, and feminism. Forty years of European critical theory have been absorbed in ten brief years, resulting in hybrids which the respective grandparents, French and German philosophy and Saussurian linguistics, would have difficulty recognizing. For this reason, any study of contemporary Canadian literary theory is an exercise in comparative literature. When read for the silences and gaps, for the unexpected swerves and twists which occur when divergent cultures come into contact, this "new new criticism" testifies to an ongoing dialectic between tradition and imported innovation. (54–55)

It is both ironic and affirmative of the dialectic she is talking about that the occasion on which she originally presented this paper is the 1986 Future Indicative: Literary Theory and Canadian Literature conference in Ottawa. This was surely an instance of the field nodding toward those it had considered up to that point to be dissenters from its proper object;[45] as Linda Hutcheon put it in the critical dialogue that concluded the event, "for the first time in Canada, I have felt that I have not had to stand up and apologize for giving a theory paper" ("Present Tense" 243).

Still, in his introductory remarks to the book of the same title that gathered together the conference presentations, John Moss, the conference's organizer and editor of its proceedings, having already taken a tentative step beyond thematic criticism (see this Introduction note 33), makes a concerted, albeit awkward, effort to acknowledge a degree of urgency in swerving, to use Godard's word, away from "its exhausted tradition" (1). He sees the gathering of participants representing different generations[46] as "splendid proof that a cacophony of critics is at least as loud as a commune" (2). Cacophony here not only gestures, however reluctantly, to the coexistence of different critical approaches but also concedes to the fact that, at least at that time, any departure from a cohesive reading of CanLit was seen as discordant action that threatened it as an institution. In a belletristic and highly metaphorical fashion that reveals, while also trying to conceal, his discomfort with theory, and that employs vintage thematic tropes, he calls the contributors "demanding," "obscure," and "esoteric." Nevertheless, in what is surely a coming-out event from the perspective of the discipline—"that is the point of such a book as this—to open up or expose to the light what might otherwise remain the arcane pleasure of a few genuine and brilliant eccentrics"—"the maverics" are let in: as he writes, "*they* have been deconstructing the box in which *we* have tried to contain our culture; not peering over the garrison walls but walking right through them" (3; my emphasis). At the same time as this generation of "new" critics is imaged as dissenters and malcontents, they are also granted the uncanny ability to walk through walls, too—a metaphor, apparently, for Moss's understanding of deconstruction. The Us/Them paradigm, along with the other tropes in this statement, clearly performs the garrison tactics of the Canadian literary field.

I see this textual and temporal moment as an instantiation of the field-imaginary's political unconscious experiencing a rupture and reaching a truce with those critics that questioned its formation, methods, and interests. It is not a coincidence that, in the penultimate paragraph of his short introduction, Moss uses the adverb "suddenly" three times in quick succession:

> Suddenly, people working from a literary base ... are bringing critical theory from Paris and Oxford and New Haven to bear ... in Vancouver or Fredericton or, yes, even Ottawa, on literary experience of their own country.... Suddenly, it seems reasonable to think about critical theory in a Canadian context. Suddenly, it seems appropriate, even essential, to think of Derrida and Bowering, Bakhtin and Kroetsch, as interpenetrating figures in a common ground. (Introduction 3)

Besides contributing to the high rhetorical flare that marks Moss's introduction, the emphasis on the swiftness of the phenomenon he comments upon exhibits the field's recalcitrance and blindness in that it can envisage change only as materializing abruptly, emerging virtually out of nowhere, and thus lacking a sense of causality. If the ground of the field can shift that suddenly, it is because Moss constructs it around the traditional notion of paradigm shifts.

Things, as Godard notes above, did happen in a rather condensed fashion, but theory certainly didn't appear in Canada as suddenly as Moss would have it. Speaking through the voice of the field's political unconscious, he makes an (intentionally) comical effort to naturalize the continental theorists whose ideas punctuate the book: "As Bakhtin leaps from the sidelines to centre stage, as Derrida clambers out of the orchestra pit and into the prompter's box, and Lacan swings from the flies, as Foucault,

Lévi-Strauss, Saussure, Barthes, and a throng of others rhubarb their way through the text, one recognizes just how connected all the disparate elements of this critical extravaganza really are" (2). No longer bushed, these theorists, and what they represent, are allowed to enter the field in a manner that reiterates both its garrison mentality and the nation's self-declared magnanimity; while Moss welcomes the "trends" they usher in, he also manages to maintain intact the presumed naturalness of CanLit, its rhubarb folksiness. Thus, they may be in, but they are still configured as suspect or squabbling immigrants.

From her own vantage point, Godard, certainly holding the lead in that group of mavericks, sees the influx of these theorists as enabling Canadian critics "to 'configure difference,' to wrestle with the Canadian 'plus'" ("Structuralism" 55). As she writes in the penultimate paragraph of her own essay in the same volume, this

> Canadian "plus" is all meaningful in the present conjuncture [the mid 1980s] preoccupied with figures of difference. To be a Canadian, as to be a woman, is to inhabit a colonial space from which one perceives discourse as a form of power and desire.... That all these theories [structuralism, semiotics, phenomenology, reception theory, poststructuralism, feminist theory] are themselves imported with their carpet bags stuffed with ideological positions is yet another paradox: a new colonization to free oneself from colonial status.... there is nonetheless a perverse logic at work in the pattern of borrowing, one that foregrounds the Canadian "plus." Through its recombinant genetics, this new new critical theory seeks to unmask power and to focus on the study of "Canadian forms of language and language alone." And it borrows freely from or subverts to its own end the dominant critical theories of the North Atlantic triangle. (82)

It is interesting, of course, that Godard sees the advent of these theories as a form of colonization. She anticipates, I believe, the array of critiques Fredric Jameson's at once influential and maligned essay about "Third-World" literature and allegory (1986), engendered.[47] While her statement certainly reverberates with the outward mobility characterizing certain kinds of Canadian criticism that I have noted above, it also lets slip a certain anxiety. But what is most important for my purposes here is that what she calls the "recombinant genetics" that has given rise to these Canadian critical discourses point to a veering toward "metacritical reflection," namely "the discovery that methodology does more than reveal: it actually creates the object of study" (55).

A Thematics of Critical Difference

It is as a response to this shift toward metacritical reflection, more specifically pondering not only on the methods but also on the institutional and material conditions that have shaped CanLit and its study as an institution since the early 1990s, that the TransCanada project has been conceived. Not isolating a particular method as an object of critical consideration but rather acknowledging that the broad assemblage of approaches in the Canadian critical scene is itself a sign of the times, a sign that itself merits attention, the TransCanada project has invited scholars and cultural practitioners to take note of, largely, precisely what our times entail: the various and often contradictory economies—restricted and general—that have formed of late as much the literature we study as the sites, contexts, and conditions within which we study it. The essays included in *Trans.Can.Lit*, in this volume, and in the third one forthcoming, along with other papers that it was not possible to include in these books, engage, at least in my view, with these issues in ways that open up new and important possibilities.

Shifting the Ground of Canadian Literary Studies in English, then, posits itself simultaneously as a critical recognition of and response to the conceptual challenges that have altered the study of Canadian literature as an institution. Situated both within but also beyond the narrowly circumscribed disciplinary site of Canadian literary studies, the essays collected here enact a variety of critical approaches that engage and/or are informed by findings in other disciplines. By studying the different economies that shape Canadian literature as an institution; by investigating literary productions that operate in the interstices of CanLit as a disciplinary construct; by exercising a self-reflexivity with regard to their critical tools; by engaging with textual constructs that are not exclusively literary; and by dialoguing with other disciplines, they track the relation of literature as well as culture at large to wider discursive formations.

A critically different thematics, then, emerges from them, a thematics that, at the risk of oversimplifying things here, is intent on revisiting and examining, on the one hand, what in Roy Miki's words constitutes "[m]uch of the thrust of nationalist Canadian literature," namely, the "narrative of conquest and settlement that appropriates the nativization process to acculturate the lands taken" (*In Flux* 124) and, on the other, the global and neoliberal policies and ideologies that inflect, and are embraced and/or resisted by, both the production and study of Canadian literature and the unfolding of the Canadian nation-state. While some of the essays lean more toward the former concern (those by Brodie, Gagnon and Jiwani, Wakeham, Findlay, kulchyski, and Zacharias) and some veer toward the latter (those by Derksen, Fuller, Lai, Mezei, Fujimoto), all of them engage with three main areas of interest: methodological reflection that is usually exercised via different kinds of interdisciplinarity; a resolute desire to address issues regarding the nation and/or citizenship, racialization, and aboriginality; and the urge to practise criticism responsibly and ethically. While these concerns can be traced in distinct ways, at a certain suprastructural level they all converge: ethically responsible criticism predicates a metacritical stance and methodological self-reflexiveness, while the ethical issues at the core of these arguments revolve, almost invariably, around what the nation's neo-/post-/colonialism has bequeathed to its citizens. With the tightening of citizenship, as a result of both neoliberalism's consumerism—including its attendant impact on the commodification of knowledge production—and the nation-state's in/security vis à vis certain demonized others, how scholars perform citizenship has become a paramount concern, indeed an issue that matters ethically and otherwise.[48]

These areas of concern reflect not merely that the field has already shifted its ground in response to what I call emergent events but, above all, that they exhibit a vested interest in a thematics that exceeds the so-called paradigm of thematic criticism. Neither exclusively interested in the intragenetic relationship between Canadian literature and the Canadian nation-state, nor exactly bent on identifying structural and narrative patterns, the thematics that looms large in this collection is diametrically opposed to the thematic criticism of the 1970s. Whereas the latter was decidedly marked by positivism[49]—trying to answer, while misreading (I believe), Frye's seminal question "Where is here?" by in effect positing a rejoinder to its own question "What is Canadian identity?"—the former is cast as a multifarious riposte to, and moves beyond, the perceived need to define CanLit and Canada within the parameters of inherited paradigms. This is, then, not the kind of thematics that, as

Werner Sollors says in *The Return to Thematic Criticism*, "dares not speak its name today" (xiv); rather, it registers an "antithematic affect [that] seems so deeply ingrained that one might think of it as an episteme of contemporary criticism" (xiii).

This epistemic shift in thematics takes theme to be not a subject perceived as a stable or transparent construct that can be interpreted exhaustively and thus mastered but as a continuously unfolding constellation of interrelated (though perhaps on the surface disparate) issues that resist an exegetic approach. Such themes demand a renegotiation of their parameters. They operate at the limit of the meanings that have been assigned to them, thus behaving as Derridean supplements or as Barthean texts of bliss. If bliss sounds a discordant note here, given that such themes, as is the case in this book, involve displacement—and its consequent affects and material knowledge of a subject's loss, trauma, and disempowerment—then in this instance it should be understood ironically, but also as the gratification—a compensatory pleasure—that comes when the cultural, political, and economic codes that produce and demarcate these anti-thematic themes are exploded. (Think of Kroetsch's trope of the exploding porcupine.)[50] The turn to this thematics is mobilized by the ethical and political concerns mentioned above and materializes as the byproduct of methodological transportability.

Transing Disciplinarity: A Certain Kind of Interdisciplinary Practice

Among the changes that the Canadian literary studies' field-imaginary has undergone since the early 1990s, interdisciplinarity features as a recurring trope. From being commonly understood as a methodology that crosses the boundaries of two or more disciplines, it has become a trope in that it is employed as a value-added element in humanities scholarship. This tropological shift has been gradual and has been taking place in concert with another shift, the privileging of knowledge-as-commodity in university culture. Thus interdisciplinarity and its ancillary development, collaboration, have "emerged as instruments of strategic importance" (Coleman and Kamboureli 28). This does not mean that all manifestations of interdisciplinarity in the field of CanLit studies serve exclusively the strategic interests of the institutional structures to which scholars are accountable. Rather, interdisciplinarity, as I see it, is now operating both horizontally, as a "dialogue across different fields of knowledge" (Schagerl 106), and vertically, as a strategy that reflects the management of knowledge production in academia. Accordingly, while the move toward interdisciplinarity in Canadian literary studies reflects the various scholars' own methodological and subject pursuits, many of which could be seen as the effects of emergent events, we must also acknowledge that the widespread use of the term in the field—from Social Sciences and Humanities Research Council grant applications to conference abstracts, from published scholarship to course descriptions—also chronicles the economic instrumentality attributed to interdisciplinarity, as well as the trend it has become.[51]

This double function of interdisciplinarity—how it works epistemologically and tropologically—has been one of the TransCanada project's major concerns. Essays in both the first volume and this one, as well as the one forthcoming, whether they take on interdisciplinarity directly or indirectly, raise fundamental questions about how to understand (their) methodology, as well as about the relationship of the discipline to their subject material and vice versa. That interdisciplinarity does not operate in a singular way in this context indicates that it is a hard notion to define, as well as a complex and diverse practice to perform. One of the things that has become apparent to me is that interdisciplinarity as manifested in the Canadian field-imaginary is not always strictly speaking interdisciplinarity. If, as Jürgen Mittelstrass states, "interdisciplinarity properly understood ... removes disciplinary impasses where these block the development of problems and the corresponding responses of research," then most scholarship in Canadian literary studies today practices what would be best described as a "commut[ing] between fields" (Mittelstrass 497). Though this may be anathema in purist approaches to interdisciplinarity, it nonetheless invites us to confront the limits, as well as the possibilities, of different kinds of interdisciplinary practice.

Alan Liu's distinction between "*thin*" and "*thick*" interdisciplinary models alerts us to the complex permutations of different kinds of interdisciplinary work. As he writes,

> On the one hand, the representation of knowledge embodied in the other discipline is simply compensatory: it confers extra validity on home knowledge because it seems to represent an infusion of intuitive or natural truths.... The thinner the interdisciplinary project, ... the more home knowledge is content to see in the other discipline

only such a deictic, "there-it-is" representation of truth—only, that is, a romance of the other.

On the other hand, the thicker or deeper the project, the more it will discover that romance is a dark interpreter.... The representation of knowledge glimpsed in other disciplines, that is, can have the uncanny or unhomely effect of utterly *hollowing out* the home field's sense of valid knowledge. The moment when a discipline is entranced by the knowledge of other disciplines, after all, is also the moment when its own knowledge dissolves into a centerless relativism of paradigms, methodologies, theories.... Put in academic ... terms, few of us today have any knowledge anymore; we all have approaches instead. (181–82)

Because it does not do away with the notions of individual disciplines and specialization, Liu's argument offers a more candid reading than most of the other accounts I have read of how interdisciplinarity works in literary scholarship. Echoing his position, Ria Cheyne posits that whereas "true interdisciplinarity" should involve "*a synthesis of disciplines*," most interdisciplinarity is "a kind of sequential movement back and forth from one discipline to another" (104). However, this shuttling back and forth, an instance of thin interdisciplinarity, doesn't inevitably result in real dialogue between disciplines. It may produce a discursive site where discourses from different disciplines coexist, but there is no guarantee that these disciplines move in the same direction or that there is a shared intention between or among the disciplines in question to dialogue with each other. The latter point also implies that the discipline one borrows from to practise interdisciplinarity would not necessarily approve of how its methods are employed in the results produced. In effect, to employ Liu's rhetorical terms, in thin interdisciplinarity the scholar operates methodologically as a tourist, following the "allure" of the other discipline and using it to enrich "the validity of home knowledge to itself" (181). This is obvious in the fact that most Canadian literary scholars who posit their work as interdisciplinary continue to publish virtually exclusively within their field.[52] Furthermore, it would be safe to argue that while a lot of criticism about Canadian literature practises and promotes a certain kind of interdisciplinarity, the same cannot be said about most of our peers in the social sciences and legal studies.[53] Far from suggesting failure at the individual level, such instances point to the larger disciplinary and institutional structures and protocols that determine the parameters of fields and assess scholarly work.

But the apparent limits and problems in this kind of interdisciplinary work do not cancel out the benefits that come from thick interdisciplinarity. This kind of interdisciplinary project, as Liu suggests, has the capacity to produce a kind of self-reflexivity that directly impacts on the scholar's work as well as on the field's political unconscious. In this instance, the traffic from one discipline to another speaks not only to the themes addressed that demand for their investigation a broadening of disciplinary boundaries but also to the need to challenge and recalibrate one's field-imaginary; furthermore, it is accompanied by recognition of the limits of knowledge and methods, so that "the romance of the other" (Liu 182) becomes one of the things troubled and examined. And this is precisely where the potential of interdisciplinarity lies, namely, in its capacity to create "not only an alluring rhetoric for knowledge, but also a rhetoric that senses, without being epistemologically clear about it, that it has yet further limitations to reconfigure, further forms of closure to try out" (183).

Thus, if the thematicists of the 1970s constructed CanLit and CanCrit by writing about and on behalf of the nation-state without considering how the latter and its attendant concepts of citizen/ship, multiculturalism, immigration, race, or aboriginality were treated by, say, political scientists and theorists, philosophers, or legal scholars, then the scholars in this collection move, when necessary, precisely toward that direction. The outcome of this criss-crossing of boundaries both at the writerly and readerly levels[54] does not necessarily produce a "new discipline altogether" (Davis, Lennard B9), the kind of "new, single, intellectually coherent entity" Julie Thompson Klein argues defines interdisciplinarity (57); nor does it "integrate" by default "the methodological and conceptual view of the other disciplines in their shared efforts," as Terry Weech and Marina Pluzhenskaia would expect an interdisciplinary project to do (157). It is chiefly for this reason that I think transdisciplinarity would be a more accurate designation for the metacritical and methodological turns that mark the contributions to this volume on the whole.

As "a critical evaluation of terms, concepts, and methods that transgresses disciplinary boundaries" (Dölling and Hark 1195),[55] transdisciplinarity performs in *Shifting the Ground* both thematically and methodologically. If transdisciplinarity reflects at once an awareness of the territoriality of disciplines and an intention to transgress their boundaries as an act of practising criticism responsibly, then the disciplinary territorialism troubled here is consonant with territoriality as it concerns aboriginality and land claims; white settler society, sovereignty, and the nation-state; cultural and publishing spaces claimed for by racialized and diasporic subjectivities; the travel of literature across languages and their cultural domains through translation; and market places where CanLit as a national or globalized formation circulates. The articulation and treatment of these themes demand that they be addressed contextually across and through the different discursive sites where we encounter them. The territoriality inscribed in these contexts, then, operates "as the crisis in the relationship between the nation and the state" (Manning xix) but also as the crises brought about by various emergent events that have reconfigured CanLit's field-imaginary. In *Shifting the Ground*, then, territoriality—like transdisciplinarity—emerges as a theme that is inscribed large as much in this collection as in the one to follow.

National Literatures in the Shadow of Neoliberalism

Jeff Derksen

At the same time as national literatures are deeply temporal and spatial, and are produced by contested histories and spaces, they themselves produce national narratives and the spatial imagination of a nation. Yet both of these big categories—space and time—have been reconfigured by the concept of globalization as a surging movement of ideas, people, capital, and images and by neoliberalism's contested "end of history." While this may appear to fulfill Marx's outcome that the creative destruction of capitalism annihilates space with time, globalization theory and the temporal aspects of neoliberalism work to blur the antagonistic edges of counter-narratives and oppositional spaces within globalization. Investigations of the nexus of the spatial and the temporal are therefore crucial today to grasp national literatures within the long moment of neoliberalism and the geography of globalization. A "strategic interdisciplinarity"[1] troubles the strain of the cultural language of globalization that is quick in proposing that nation-states and national literatures would dissolve upwards into a global culture. To agitate this language is not to recuperate nation space and nation narratives after globalization, but to turn to an interdisciplinary method to locate the role culture plays within this spatiotemporal knot. Shifts within the definition and possibility of culture as well as historical changes in the role of nations in this post-euphoric moment of globalization—a moment distinguished by the ideological software of neoliberalism—play dialectically off of theories of the cohesive and unitary nation that can be, simultaneously, the anchor and site of critique in critical theory.

Culture, and the analysis of culture, builds and circulates the "spaces of representation" (Lefebvre, *Production* 42–43) that give an image to globalization. Cultural theory is tugged through a narrative of globalization that carries the tensions of process, policy, and development. As Timothy Brennan poses the question: "Is globalization theory about describing a 'process': that is an amalgam of material shifts, spatial reorderings, anonymous developments and movements, the inexorable concatenation of changes in communication, transportation, demographics and the environment? Or does it describe a 'policy' whose purpose is to project a world order that a small group of national and/or financial interests ardently desires for the rest of us?" (129) Between the openness of process and the closure of policy (paralleling Antonio Negri's categories of "constituent" and "constituted" power),[2] a developmental strain of cultural thought regarding globalization accepts the model of globalization as determined by capitalist trade and a world market. As Imre Szeman points out, "[t]he critical agenda is thus set by the operations of globalization *qua* global capital: the need for criticism to concentrate its own energies on movements and border-crossings, while not entirely misplaced, comes across as a rearguard manoeuvre to catch up with phenomena that have already taken place at some other more meaningful or important level" ("Poetics" 155). The economic determinates on cultural theory may place it in a belated position, but tracing the role of culture in globalization and neoliberalism, through the reorderings of time and space, can bring us to the unstable present.

Michael Denning has identified a "nation turn" in cultural theory that focused on "the concepts that produce a people" (89), a turn that signifies a "break between the theme of the national-popular and those of hybridity, flexibility, and the diasporan" (10). This narrative of solidity and fragmentation, or of unity and de-territorialization that Denning points to, does not encompass existing cultural practices within and above the nation, yet it has become a touchstone within cultural theories of globalization. And, as Denning asserts, it can lead to a pairing of a global "culture of transnational corporations" and an "alternative global culture" that are then both read through a "relatively ahistorical logic of global cultural flow, produced, commodified, consumed, hybridized, co-opted, and resisted" (32–33). This view of global flows, springing from Manuel Castells's critique of Henri Lefebvre and understood as a "spaces of flows" model, can splice with a view of globality shaped by a market model that speeds up global processes at the expense of the nation. Despite having the advantage of engaging with the reach of capital and the intensification of globality as a form of knowledge (as well as a form of trade), this position gives up the strategic space of the nation and ignores tactical uses of the state by social movements in the shadow of neoliberalism. In fact, in order to set up the poles of this schema, "theory conjures an abstract state as its enemy—outside space and time" (Brennan 20) and configures the nation as the hardening of space and time.

In order to propose a spatiality other than the global-flows model, and to propose "structure and struggle" (Gordon 9) rather than process and policy as the poles of a dialectical globalization theory, I will turn to concepts of the production of space and scale theory. While Len Findlay's powerful imperative to "Always Indigenize!" is a call to take apart the "legal, religious, political, and cultural armatures of colonization [that] constantly circulated the notion that Canada was an *empty land*" (310) in order to arrive at social justice in the present, the method I am proposing is to "always spatialize" as a means to grasp the present, but also as a means to locate and understand potential politics and nonconformist knowledges. Spatializing breaks the colonial myth of an "empty land" and brings in a concept of spatial justice in which "space—like justice—is never simply handed out or given, but ... both are socially produced, experienced and contested on constantly shifting social, political, economic and geographical terrains" (Bromberg, Morrow, and Pfeiffer 2). Scale theory has the advantage of making space more material in globalization and in neoliberalism's restructuring, but it also provides the possibility of highlighting discursive and cultural practices. Eric Swyngedouw argues that "Scale becomes the arena and moment, both discursively and materially, where sociospatial power relations are contested and compromises are negotiated and regulated" (140). Sallie Marston proposes scale matters because "scale making is not only a discursive practice; it is also the tangible outcome of practices of everyday life as they articulate with and transform macro-level social structures" (173).

But, scale has the disadvantage of implying a nested set of spaces stable in their relationships, or the reflection of a given hierarchy, and that "local to global conceptual architecture intrinsic to hierarchical scale carries with it presuppositions than can delimit entry points into politics—and the openness of politics—by preassigning to it a cordoned register for resistance" (Marston, Jones, and Woodward 427). I use scale in a broader way, I hope, in which "scale is the spatial repository of structured social assumptions about what constitutes normal and abnormal forms of social difference" (N. Smith, "Scale" 197) and as a way to recognize "spatial difference." Following Neil Smith, I'm proposing that, in the spatial restructuring of neoliberalism, the nation-state has not been overcome, but has been transformed and extends throughout globalization both as engine and as platform. As a result, our expectations of what occurs at what scales has also been bent rather than broken. This restructuring is not isolated to the de-territorializing of globalization, but is linked with the re-territorialization of neoliberalism.

Spatially, neoliberalism is drawn out through two tensions familiar to discussions of national cultures and globalization—the macro-political, which sees neoliberalism as an "economic tsunami" (Ong, "Mobile" 3) or as a "totalizing economic master narrative" (Roberts, Secor, and Sparke 887) and the "path-dependent" (Brenner and Theodore 349) emphasizing how neoliberalism from above adapts to local conditions and practices as it migrates and is picked up by governmental structures (for instance, the manner in which a neoliberal urbanism is becoming policy in Canadian cities).

Temporally, neoliberalism gets stretched out from an economic seed in neo-classical economics (Lebowitz; Tabb); springs from a kernel in liberal philosophy of the seventeeth and eighteenth centuries (N. Smith, *Endgame*); and breaks ground in a brutal legitimization by the "Chicago Boys," the gangsters of free market economics lead by the unlikely Al Capone of the market, Milton "Hidden Hand" Freedman. David Harvey, in his *A Brief History of Neoliberalism*, chooses Tuesday, 11 September 1973—the day of the coup overthrowing Salvador Allende that levered Pinochet into power—as the date, and Chile as the place, of the first "neoliberal state experiment" (7). Following this forced introduction, Jamie Peck and Adam Tickell describe two strong stages or mutations of neoliberalism: "roll-back neoliberalism" and "roll-out neoliberalism." Rollback neoliberalism of the 1980s sought to retract social programs, social entitlements, and nation-scale regulations to liberate the global market and to unfetter the individual, the nation, and the city for vigorous activity in the market. Rollout neoliberalism, from the early 1990s, is characterized by government intervention that projects neoliberalism beyond freeing the market to a broader engagement with "new modes of 'social' and penal policymaking, concerned specifically with the aggressive reregulation, disciplining, and containment of those marginalized or dispossessed by the neoliberalism of the 1980s" (389). Peck and Tickell associate these changes with neoliberalism's engagement with both an "external" crisis (blamed on the institutions of welfare state) and with the "internal" contradictions and conditions created by neoliberalism itself.

Yet both of these phases point to a contradiction in the neoliberal relationship to the state. As Harvey points out, this shift from "government" to "governance" creates "the paradox of intense state interventions and government by elites and 'experts' in a world where the state is supposed to not be interventionalist" (*Brief* 69). If we take this timeline, we see neoliberalism forcefully restructuring a state and entering the world system at a strong moment of the Canadian cultural project and just as official multiculturalism is expanding in the public discourse. This neoliberal unravelling of the discourses of the nation was, however, a strong period of state intervention.

In order to solidify some aspects of this uneven present that theories of culture strive to grasp, I use the nation-state as a fulcrum space within the territorial structure of neoliberal globalization rather than as an absolute space or as a container that holds and isolates bodies, literatures, and economies. The question that emanates from this position is not how national spaces have been eroded and unraveled but rather where national spaces have reformed and what the possible politics of these spaces and literatures are. This has the advantage of not disarticulating the nation-state from the production of global neoliberal space, nor positioning the nation as a passive target of the processes of globalization. What is more, this move also has the advantage of tracking how new cultural spaces are opened, new publics imagined, and how critical cultural practices address the present moment.

Creative practices that jump into and off the altered or transformed space of the nation in order to engage with neoliberalism can be characterized, on the one hand, as forceful examples of "nationalisms against the neoliberal state," to paraphrase David Lloyd, and, on the other hand, as the cultural use of nation-scale politics that address neoliberalism as it is embedded in state actions, urban territories, and across spatial scales. In order to catch some of the possibilities of this type of work, I will look at several tendencies visible within contemporary Canadian critical and cultural texts and the manner in which they reflect or deflect neoliberalism's project. On the one hand, I look to a poetics that provides a "global" critique of the cultural and economic logic of neoliberalism from an embedded position in the national scale. Roger Farr (*Surplus*) and Dionne Brand (*Inventory*) have produced big projects, taking different tones that grasp at these scales as well as at the processes and policies, structures and struggles of globalization. Stephen Cain's *American Standard/Canada Dry* reinvigorates a poetics that is both critical of, yet informed by, the twists of Canadian cultural nationalism to return to the refigured discourse of the nation within neoliberalism. From a different political economy, I read the highly lauded novel by Timothy Taylor, *Stanley Park*, as the narrative construction of the city in a neoliberal distortion of cosmopolitanism as consumption, and difference as taste (literally figured through food). Consumption is both a theme and a formal determinate in this novel, and to understand its influence I turn to its reception within the structure of literary awards. The limited spatiality of the novel foregrounds the global-local in order to reify the local as out of time and naturalize gentrification. Yet, approached spatially and temporally, all of these texts circulate around the present.

Nation Time, Nation Space

Following a shift in postcolonial theory from "engaging in the process of 'imagining' the nation," and then "embarking on what is seen as a much more sophisticated examination of identity and hybridity" (Szeman, *Zones* 26); to early statements such as Stephen Owen's that "[i]n the contemporary literary world the very possibility of 'national literature' is dissolving rapidly" (122) and Homi Bhabha's casual statement asserting "the breakdown, in a more international field, of the national experience as a stabilizing force that establishes a consensual commonality amidst subjects of difference" ("Anxious" 202); to Arjun Appadurai's influential command that "[w]e need to think ourselves beyond the nation" (*Modernity* 158); to Hardt and Negri's space- and nation-annihilating *Empire*; to the cosmopolitics of a global civil society, the time and space of the nation has been imagined as both productive and oppressive space, as both a homogenous time and a contested temporality. It has moved from a given frame for cultural meaning to a fading political force.

Yet, the shift away from the nation in globalization theory is strikingly at odds with political theories of the nation-state that see it maintaining a refigured, yet key role within global processes and policies. From Linda Weis's argument against a "new era of 'state denial'" (2) (epitomized by Kenichi Ohmae's *The End of the Nation State*), to Ellen Meiksin Wood's long view that "'globalization' is characterized less by the decline of the nation state than by the growing contradiction between the global scope of capital and its persistent need for more local and national forms of 'extra-economic' support" (177), to Jamie Peck and Adam Tickell's phase theory of neoliberalism, to Aihwa Ong's view that neoliberalism both "fragment[s] and extend[s] the space of the nation-state" (*Exception* 7), we have a differentiated discourse available to situate the role of nation-states and cultural practices in the present moment.

Culturally and politically, the possible positions toward the nation in Canadian state theory and cultural criticism are more tangled, complicated by our relationship with the USA and the relative clarity of the previous national project of culture building. For instance, in contrast to Hardt and Negri, Leo Panitch does not see the nation-state giving way to a stateless globalization or centreless Empire. For Panitch, even a narrative of the shifts in the state function in global capital that takes it "from buffer, to mediator, to transmission belt … is perhaps too brittle" (21). Instead, he is definitive in posing that "capitalist globalization is a process which also takes place in, through, and under the aegis of states; it is encoded by them and in important respects even authored by them; and it involves a shift in power relations within states that often means the centralization and concentration of state powers as the necessary condition of and accompaniment to global market discipline" (13).

Canadian literary critics, even as they cast Canadian literature in a perpetual crisis, do not unanimously predict the demise of the nation-state and the folding up of the tent of Canadian literature, or the flipping of the CanLit downtown condo to an offshore owner. Rather, there is a strong current in Canadian criticism toward a critique of the state and toward a questioning of the cultural construct of the nation. For instance, nation-scale politics can be hailed to resist erosion from the outside, as in Frank Davey's call for a politics against "multinational capitalism" through "participating in the arguments of a nation that is being continuously discursively produced and re-produced from political contestation" (*Post-National* 24). Or, in a conservative political register, the idea of the nation separate from the state can be evoked to stabilize internal restructuring, as in Stephen Henighan's crisis of representation within the nation caused by postcolonialism and globalization. Or, closer to trends of "cultural transnationalism" (Hitchcock) or "critical transnationalism" (Lee), Roy Miki calls for a national pedagogy within globalization that "would not only reveal that globalization is not a movement 'beyond' the problems of the nation-state, but a mode of translation in which previous hierarchies undergo reconstruction in their 'interaction with transnational cultural referents'" ("Globalization" 95). Paul Hjartarson joins this urgency by proposing, "Now, more than ever, cultural critics and theorists need to understand not only culture's relation to the nation-state or how nation-states are transforming themselves in the global era, but the changing place of national cultures and literatures in those developments" (110). In an alternative politics of nation formation, Daniel Heath Justice argues that "[t]o dismiss nationhood from analysis, especially when it is the concern of Indigenous peoples themselves, once more silences Native voices and perspectives and reinforces the dominative power of Canadian colonialism" (149).

Perhaps because of the persistent troubling of the fictive unity of Canadian identity and of the reflective cohesion of Canadian literature that marks a strain of CanLit criticism and denies Canadian literature an "immutability" (Kamboureli, *Scandalous* 35), the anxiety of the global throughout Canadian literary criticism does not obscure the nation. The nation is understood as constructed and affective, and the state is seen as an apparatus cut by both antagonism and responsibility. As Donna Palmateer Pennee argues, to work through "the space and moment of the nation" and "the *category* of a national literature" is also to work at a historical limit, and "it might be necessary to invest a little longer in the ongoing power of the nation as a referent and a concept in the literary domain, even if we may disagree with the term's uses, or may have become wary of practices in its name" ("Literary" 78). Pennee proposes, in the negative, that "the category of the national is *not negligible* for literary analysis," in order to move positively to define the national as not "content but as method, as a set of relations, as potential" (79).

Nonetheless, there is an anxious critical language of the diminishing of the role of the nation in globalization and a waning of state influence within global capital: this language hints at a relative separation of the national project and the state from global processes. Yet, this hesitation reflects a stage, I believe, in the cultural negotiating of the nation-state in relation to globalization—a hesitation theoretically propelled from a number of positions. However, this hesitation requires a strong reexamination due to its relation to the imagination of the nation and the state in the neoliberal project. In criticism, such as I cite above, there has been a vigilance toward national narratives that cut off spaces of difference, and toward narratives that conjure a blank history to insert a colonialism armed with a developmental humanism, yet neoliberalism's discourse of a weakened nation (often obscuring the state for the nation) at times aligns with critiques of the nation aimed at unravelling both its false unities and its false pluralities. The gradual appropriation of critical positions against the nation and the state by discourses of neoliberalism (with the state being the space where neoliberals and Leninists meet) has confused not only the language of critique but also the reconfiguration of state functions and national invocations in neoliberalism itself.

The Imagination of the Nation and State in Cultural Theories of Globalization

Given the historical relationship of the nation-state with globalization, the nation is not the most obvious formation to be threatened by global processes. Yet, why have the nation and the nation-state emerged as the weak points within globalization? From a cultural angle, three interlocked positions have downplayed the importance of the nation-state within globalization. Curiously, a time-released Leninism that obliquely agrees on the withering away of the nation (rather than his view of the state being eradicated) within global processes that are seen as dramatically new or intensified, drifts through both cultural views of the nation and free-market utopianism. This perspective, which has reached its end, emerged from an accumulation of theoretical shifts including tendencies to make space metaphorical, a theory of the weak state rather than its adaptive or transformative qualities (Weis), and a radical openness grafted from poststructuralism onto the political terrain of the nation.[3] Alongside these shifts was a tendency to see the work of the nation as *merely* cultural and temporal, constructing and repressing identities; this tendency does not structurally have to loosen the state and identities from the determinants of capital, but the cultural emphasis (and a theoretical tendency to see the economical as necessarily reductive) tends to obscure the relationship of capitalism and the state in the function of the nation and nationalism.

In this theoretical nexus, the nation is imaged spatially in two manners that separate it from the production of space globally and from the geography of capitalism. Built metaphorically as an *absolute* space that is a pre-existing field or container that holds the national economy and contains national identities, the nation-state is rendered static in its spatiality, vulnerable to spaces above and below it rather than tied into and productive of these other scales via spatial practices that cross scales. When Appadurai asserts "[t]he nation-state relies on its legitimacy on the intensity of its meaningful presence in a continuous body of bounded territory" (*Modernity* 189), he invokes an absolute space, a space ready to be breached.[4] Simultaneously, the nation is also figured as an *abstract* space independent of the social processes that produce it: social processes are understood to be "happening 'in' or 'across' an equally given spatial field" (Smith and Katz 74) in absolute space rather than space and the relationships between spaces being the outcome of social production. This "deadening of space," as Neil Smith and Cindi Katz argue, lends power to metaphors that escape the problem of space: this is played out through metaphors of flows, erosion, dispersal, and a de-territorialization uncoupled from re-territorialization. Once the problems of space can be avoided, and once the problems of the nation have been frozen, there is also a spatial escape from the processes that produce the nation.

Second, in a serial shift, the nation-state is exempted as an actor within globalization and is generally viewed as the vulnerable point with a false unity that is beginning to unravel rather than as an enduring adaptive structure with a political, economic, and affective function. This radical disarticulation (or de-territorialization) pits globalization *against* the nation-state rather than grasping the historical role of the nation-state within capital accumulation at a global scale. This is first set in motion by imagining the nation as an absolute space: like a modernist architectural module, it can be plugged into or lifted out of the structure of globalization. In contrast, viewed from scale theory, which embeds the nation-state into socio-spatial relations ranging from the body to the globe, "[t]he national scale ... represented a platform for globalization that already preceded and produced it" (N. Smith, "Scale" 203). Once national economies and state functions are falsely believed to be dissolved (rather than extended and altered) by global processes, then the nation-state as a scale necessary to capital is jumped over or replaced by the articulation of new scales rather than a re-territorialization of nation-scale politics. The nation is unplugged rather than refigured.

Third, as an arrested space, the nation had a set of textual biases derived from poststructuralism projected onto it. These biases solidified the nation as an apparatus that closed meaning at a national scale as well as arrested the emergence of contestatory and resistant possibilities from the sub-national, the local, the urban, the neighbourhood, and the body. The problem of the fixed nation could then be overcome by pluralization, hybridity, and excess that breaches its ability to lock the chain of signification at the national. Part of a progressive "desire to transgress the codes of Nation" (Hitchcock 14), this tendency is, Brennan forcefully argues, "part of a set of ethical postulates popularized by poststructuralist theory: the striving for ambivalence as a matter of principle; the ardent belief that answering a question forecloses it; the elision of meaning in pursuit of epistemological doubt as a desired goal; and, most of all, the deployment of a variety of tropes such as 'migrancy,' 'nomadism,' 'hybridity,' and 'decentring,' which are marshaled in order to make the case that mobility and mixedness—not as contingent historical experience but as modes of being—are states of virtue" (139–40). This set of postulates certainly circulates easily in globalization theory, so it is also important to question, as Rey Chow subtly warns, that, "[i]f textually vigilant postructuralism specializes in foregrounding the alterity that is inherent to, that is an inalienable part of, any act of signification, has it not, by the same token of its insistence on linguistic self-referentiality (or inward-turning), essentialized such alterity (or its process of reinscription) in the form of a final determinant—a lurking reference, no less?" (*Age* 63).

Spatially, alterity as a final determinant can lead to a privileging of "de-territorialization" as a process disarticulated from "re-territorialization," and without really taking into account the contestations in the production of space. Absolute space is broken apart to release a contained mobility (of meaning, of culture, of identities) into the potential of global flows and hybrid spaces. Yet these global spaces can only be figured as spaces of alterity by foreclosing other spaces and failing to examine the determinants of globality. That this language of flows so closely parallels the language of trade and of finance, as many commentators point out, creates a troubling nexus of the language of neoliberalism and the qualities that cultural theories of globalization (figured through a non-vigilant poststructuralism) take as a virtue. "Waking up to the limits of their own reliance on the nation as a key organizing principle," Szeman writes, "literary studies and poetics have thus come to insist on the need to take into account the global character of literary production, influence, and dissemination" ("Poetics" 154). Yet, he continues, "[m]uch of contemporary literary studies have focused correspondingly on the transfer and movement of culture" (154) and have thus mirrored capital's dominant frames of globalization. To jump out of the container of the nation—its lid held down by the oppression of the state or state policies (with the state imagined in a singular way, which cuts so deeply against the ways that we see states mobilized against neoliberalism today)—into the liberatory flows of global potential cannot be the only imagined state of a cultural politics and it can be, as Szeman suggests, playing on a field already limited in its possibilities.

These shifts I have outlined align with the state "as a monolithic ghost rather than a variable political form" (Brennan xiii) and with a general understanding of the state as a "special repressive force" (Engels qtd. in Lenin, *State* 18) not predominantly of labouring people, but through the management and repression of identities, the administration of culture, and maintenance of narrowly national interests in the face of global forces of heterogeneity. Caught in absolute space, the nation-state then became a container to jump out of, or the apparatus to be eroded away by global flows. In another view, "the life of the state," as Gramsci puts it, can be "conceived of as a continuous process of formation and superseding of unstable equilibria ... between the interests of the fundamental group and those of the subordinate groups—equilibria in which the interests of the dominant group prevail, but only to a certain point" (qtd. in Harvey, *Spaces* 277). The "unstable" aspects of hegemony, which prevail "only to a certain point," get lost when the state and the nation are made static in space and in time, and we forget other histories of the state and of the nation. This is not to suggest that the state does not oscillate between coercion and force, mediated by corruption, in order to maintain hegemony, nor that a progressive history of the nation would escape the brutal history of nationalism, but rather to insist that we must examine the state and the nation in their complexities within neoliberalism. Otherwise we are swatting at images of the state that cohere from perfect theoretical storms rather than from the very flexible powers that tie the state to new capital strategies, such as accumulation by dispossession, and to the hardened forms of nationalism we see at every border crossing.

Through this position-taking, I'm not proposing a potentially benevolent state that should be heralded as localized force field against globalization, nor a hidden history of the state we can call on to refigure the present. Nor is a state-led model necessarily a progressive alternative to globalization (Panitch 30–35). But I am rejecting the abstraction of the problem of the state, an abstraction that tends not to account for contestation of the state by social actors and misses what Lefebvre identifies as "[t]he dialectical movement at the heat of the State: social forces acting from 'the bottom up' and political forces exerting their action from 'the top down'" (*State* 119). In this model, states function, internally and externally, in a much more contradictory and varied manner, both in terms of their articulation to emergent publics and transnational social actors and of new forms of surveillance, interpellation, and capital accumulation that states create. Yet, what cannot be forgotten is that "[t]he state does not exist independently of struggle or human agency; and nor is struggle, in turn, autonomous from the state" (Gordon 8). This dialectic of structure and struggle, framed spatially, provides a model of locating state function and allows for clarity on the possible instrumentalization of discourses of the nation (and nationalism).

Viewed as a process with adaptive capacities, the state works through the relations of economic and political power, juggling the conditions of capitalist accumulation and strengthening property rights (key today for the neoliberal state), while also providing a structure for social reproduction. Yet, it can also be a platform from which political claims are made and bent. What is at stake, aside from the necessary and important position-taking within cultural theory (which is perhaps even more vital at the nation-scale in Canadian literary debates), is the way that the political is figured in relation to the cultural, and the possible spaces where a public sphere or civil society can materialize. Pennee argues for a space for "[l]iterary studies organized under the rubric of the national [to] create a space to ask civic questions of state policies and inherited notions of nationalism" ("Literary" 81). And Nancy Fraser has defined the shift in which "it has ceased to be axiomatic that the modern territorial state is the appropriate unit for thinking about issues of justice, and that citizens of such states are the pertinent subjects of reference. The effect is to destabilize the previous power structure of political claims-making—and therefore to change the way we argue about social justice" ("Reframing" 71). This shift that Fraser describes is also common to a tension within neoliberalism that discursively pushes the diminished role of the nation in the political realm, while relying on the state to implement drastic economic and social reforms that erode rights.

Yet rescaled notions of rights and citizenship that jump up to the global, or cohere around cosmopolitanism, are not so clearly libratory. As part of a spatial imagination, such a jump overlooks a powerful strain of social and spatial justice movements at the urban scale. Chantal Mouffe argues against David Held's model of cosmopolitics and against Hardt and Negri's view that "[t]he demise of the sovereignty of the nation-states is perceived as a new stage in the emancipation from the constraints of the state" (108). For Mouffe this "post-political" position does not grasp hegemonic neoliberalism and rejects the modern concept of sovereignty in order to augur in a democratic model not attached to national or regional politics. A politics that tries to annihilate space by pluralism is difficult to imagine and is at odds with actually existing place-based politics—from the politics of water in Bolivia and India, to the struggle for land rights by First Nations in Canada (a struggle that contests neoliberal forms of ownership), to neighbourhood formations countering gentrification.

In a proposition that opens political possibilities, Neil Smith suggests that today we are in a "period of scale reorganization in which an inherited territorial structure no longer fulfills the functions for which it was built, [and] develops new functions, or is able to adapt to new requirements and opportunities" ("Scale" 201). This series of shifts does not dissolve the nation as one of the possible scales of a public sphere or a civil society; rather, it opens the question to how nation-states function within neoliberalism and what the stakes for the nation-state are.

Scaling Literatures and Neoliberalism

If, in the restructuring of the geography of globalization and the spaces of the nation, "[e]ntrenched assumptions about what kinds of social activities fit properly at which scales are being systematically challenged and upset" (Smith, "Scale" 193), as we see in the discussion of rights and citizenship, it is time to ask how the scales of a national literature are actually challenged and upset. To ask such a question presumes neither the disappearance of national literatures nor the recuperation of earlier national cultural projects. Likewise, to return to the question of the nation in the shadow of neoliberalism is not a turn to regressive nationalism (so often posed as the default option for the nation within globalization and a force we see in the USA today), but a question of scale bending in which a politics is bent from its usual scale in order to form a new politics within neoliberalism. Can a national literature adapt to new formations and opportunities and still remain recognizable as a national literature? Is the national a category that can be utilized beyond a distinction within a global commodity culture and beyond its own political borders? Can the critical terrains of transnationalism be imagined as simultaneously national, linking cultural projects into new or adequate cultural formations without uploading into the ether of cosmopolitanism (and this is a question to be asked of new avant-gardist formations as well)? Can the nation also be turned outward, as a platform of engagement, rather than being reflected back onto the nation-state in the continual reimagining of the cohesive community (pressured from the inside by the restructuring of the state and from the outside by the processes of globalization)? As I've suggested above, in radical formations of democracy that are not "beyond hegemony" (Mouffe) or imagined in a smooth space of globalization, the national is not a scale that can be pulled out of the project of democracy (and it is key to note that democracy, rather than transformation, is the organizing call of anti-globalization politics at the moment).

The Cultural Project of Neoliberalism

Given that neoliberalism is generally described as a force of individuation, privatization, and atomization, it can also be seen as a force that scrapes against the cohesive aspects of the project of the nation sprung free from the hyphen of the nation-state. The state seems to hold a knife to the throat of the national project that it (not so long ago) was active in building (and which was vigilantly critiqued by those swept into the culture industry). The necessary critique of the state by Canadian cultural interventions was taking shape just as the state was outsourcing its power to other arenas, doubling back to accommodate the critiques in a neoliberal space of super-individualization that promised both new forms of freedom (for the many) and new forms of repression and violence (for the few, both in the name of the many and in the name of the nation). In the context of anti-racist cultural formations in Canada, Larissa Lai articulates this conundrum as follows: "Just at that moment when it looked possible that the voices repressed by the old (not-quite) democratic state might be admitted into that old (not-quite) democratic state, the old (not-quite) democratic state began to morph into the neoliberal state we have today" ("Community" 121). The neoliberal cornerstones of free trade, competition, flexible labour, "active individualism," and self-responsibility (Peck and Tickell) are the social imaginary of the terrain of rollback neoliberalism, and rollout neoliberalism has added an aggressive dispossession of public goods and common spaces to refigure the (not-quite) democratic state and to answer the fiscal crisis brought on by the storm of neoliberalism. In Canada, we are at a temporally complicated intersection of these two phases: rolling out belated neoliberal policies after they have proven to fail through the shattering of social stability and the acceleration of internal inequities (Stephen Harper!), yet having cleared space and hollowed out functions in a succession of rollbacks (Mulroney! Chretien! Martin!). It's from this intersection that we hear the zombie voices call for tax cuts, cultural cutbacks, the unravelling of labour agreements, and the loosening of environmental laws. While I have argued that there are disturbing parallels between poststructuralism and neoliberalism, the one aspect that neoliberalism lacks is any degree of self-reflexivity (hence its singular narratives and dogged insistence).

Harvey argues that a curious relationship of the nation and state exists in neoliberalism: "In principle, neoliberal theory does not look with favour on the *nation* even as it supports the idea of a strong state" (*Brief* 84). In fact, he argues, this relationship is necessary to the development of neoliberalism: "The umbilical cord that tied together state and nation under embedded liberalism had to be cut if neoliberalism was to flourish" (84). Neoliberalism does not so much erode the nation and state as seek to transform the relationship of citizens to the nation and the state, and through this, alter the relationship of citizen to citizen (now, individual to individual). Here is where a dramatic contradiction arises— taking place in a complex national temporality—between the state in neoliberalism and the former project of nation building. The neoliberal state, and its actions, is at odds with the type of community formation (imagined or otherwise) that would bring a nation into modernity or solidify its position in the world system. Yet a key ethos of neoliberalism is to disrupt forms of social collectivity not based on finance (unions withered away, anonymous mutual funds increasing rapidly). Harvey duly notes that "[a] contradiction arises between a seductive but alienating possessive individualism on the one hand and the desire for a meaningful collective life on the other" (*Brief* 69).

This reveals a cultural project (as massive, perhaps, as the previous national cultural program) where national subjects are asked to reimagine themselves along the matrix of neoliberal values and common sense: property rights trump human rights; state programs interfere with daily life rather than ameliorate conditions; forms of collectivity are repressive; competition between spaces and places characterizes the world; and in general one must live one's life through negotiating the market rather than negotiating or contesting the state. Althusser's policeman, who hails a subject in the name of the state, is replaced by the stock market or a hedge fund, calling sweetly with a state-subsidized whistle. Yet this reimagining does not do away with national difference (or nationalism), as we know, which is figured, on the one hand, as a value-added aspect in the global market (Žižek) and, on the other hand, mobilized in hardened national identities played out in the race and class politics of borders and migrant labour. New flows hit new forms of hardened borders, surveillance technology, and the liminal spaces of the exception of law. A very small percentage of free-floating neoliberal global subjects above the nation are actually sprung free—even after the market crash of 2008, Lear Jet still could not make private planes fast enough for the demand.

By proposing that there is a neoliberal cultural politics that is both an extension of earlier nation-based cultural projects and a radical refiguring of it, a number of speculative questions arise. At what scale is this project located—is it the reshaping of the earlier homogenizing threat of a global culture? What role does the state play in this project, particularly given that the state organizations that were the infrastructure for national culture have been weakened during the rollback period? Are national literatures drawn up into the neoliberal project, or are they platforms of resistance to it? Does a national literature sway to the state or the nation? And does the narrative of Canadian literature alter when it is read alongside neoliberalism?

Stanley Park, Timothy Taylor's popular novel set in Vancouver, illustrates the complex tension of the national and neoliberalism as it migrates to other scales. But this novel unplugs the nation as a scale in order to foreground the global and the urban to develop a rich neoliberal urban landscape of consumption, taste cultures, and competing forms of gentrification. One part of my reaction to *Stanley Park* is affective, as I have lived and worked in the areas of the city that are represented, yet within that exists the challenge to read this novel as an effective example of the tendencies of neoliberalism as they hit urban territories and transform them. But the novel is intricate in the way that it folds localism into the global-urban nexus—this is made even more complex by the way that its reception has strengthened its representational power of the city of Vancouver and of Canadian urban space. This reception, through the One Book, One Vancouver contest, which *Stanley Park* won in 2003, is at such odds with the narrow view of the city that the book actually builds, that it (both in its image of the city and in its reception) is constructive of the city, aligning with the generalization of gentrification and "urban regeneration" as a neoliberal project (Smith and Derksen). One Book, One Community contests emanate from the USA and have been picked up by Vancouver, Cambridge/Kitchener/Waterloo, and Ontario First Nations; the Vancouver version, through the Vancouver Public Library, defines itself as "a book club for the entire city, cultivating a culture of reading and discussion in Vancouver by bringing people together around one great book" ("One Book"). Yet, *Stanley Park* itself is remarkable in the manner in which it flattens the antagonisms and contradictions of global-urban space, as well as the narrow range of racial, ethnic, class, and cultural positions it throws into the urban mix. In Mouffe's terms, this is a "post-political" urban territory. Specifically, the novel builds a narrative of a chef devoted to local cuisine and his struggle to open and maintain his own restaurant without being bankrolled by a soulless global coffee-shop entrepreneur who has designs to blandly globalize the bistro and to use it as an anchor in his restaurant empire and in the gentrification of the Cambie and Hastings area, the border between the city centre and the most contested neighbourhood in Vancouver, the Downtown East Side. The struggle in the novel plays out as a struggle over soft local gentrification (chef Jeremy and his local restaurant plans) and hard global gentrification (Dante's homogenous and inauthentic global empire). The landscape of gentrification that the novel builds is based on strong representations of urban frontiers (N. Smith, *Urban*) that are settled by taste-wielding urban pioneers—devotees of the Hundred Mile Diet, secret restaurant club members, and "foodies"—and shaped into new consumptive landscapes.

What is remarkable for a novel that has such strong claims on representing Vancouver within the global-urban nexus is that there is no opposition to gentrification itself in the novel, even though the fictive bistro is situated just a few blocks from the former Woodward's building, a flashpoint for gentrification in the city, and the site of a major squatting action. My point is not that the novel fails the test of realist representation but rather that it presents gentrification as a naturalized and inevitable process at the moment when gentrification is both being hotly contested and as it moves into a critical public discourse.

Far from being a process of urban regeneration, gentrification is central to the neoliberal program for cities globally: it ties together the role of the state in opening national-city spaces and asserts property rights over collective or community claims of ownership. In this light, *Stanley Park* is a complex smoothing out of the politics of urban processes in neoliberal globalization: it reflects an idealized neoliberal urban landscape back onto a city that is still in transition, and a city where political claims against neoliberalism take shape in the public debates about social housing and homelessness.[5] Importantly these claims are made to various levels of government as all three—the city, the province, and the federal government—are involved in shaping urban policies. In the post-political cosmopolitan landscape of *Stanley Park* these are absent, lifted out of the imagined community. On the one hand, I'm hesitant to reduce the novel down to a mere symptom (borrowing this term from Jameson) of neoliberalism, but on the other hand the striking parallels of a generalized neoliberal policy of gentrification that migrates globally and is picked up and adapted to local conditions is uncritically reflective of the intensely political ways in which the local is figured in neoliberalism, as well as the ways in which a class makeover of the city characteristic of gentrification draw on a generalized culture embedded into the local.

In *Stanley Park,* the capability of the local to resist, deflect, and alter the global (key for early formations of culture in globalization) is intimately absorbed. Through an affective relation (for we have to be vigilant not to elevate affect to a default form of resistance to globalization or neoliberalism) with the local, developed through an extended metaphor of the local as "bounty" and food, the local has its more resistant aspects buffed off—it returns as connoisseurship and taste cultures, as a value-added aspect of the global-urban experience. This subtle grasping of the local as a powerful particular used within a global project is also a defining aspect of how culture has moved to a central position within the remaking of cities and also marks a shift in the uses of culture, as others have noted, from a reflective and constructive national project to a commodity-based relationship (Fuller and Sedo). Yet, viewed in the spatial relations that I have suggested above, this shift from national to commodity does not bypass other scales or eclipse the national entirely: there is a complex oscillation that moves a commodity culture across the spatial scales (rather than the local and the national being the particular that resists global commodity culture). Crucially, in a counter move, other critical uses of culture and creative practices spring up. Culture as a process is not boiled down to these abstractions of gleaming commodity or clear reflection of existing social and economic relations: even more so now culture is a flash point in the long neoliberal moment, a moment that arrives and develops with varied temporalities. *Stanley Park* is therefore an important book, not a mere symptom, for it makes a compelling and affective argument for a neoliberal city, a global dream city.

In contrast, several long poem sequences also jump into the contestations of the global-urban nexus and engage with neoliberalism as both an ideological software that provides the interface between spaces and places and as a growing common sense to be derailed from its logic by counter-arguments and other articulations of the global, national, local, and urban. Roger Farr's sonnet sequence from *Surplus* ranges from a philosophical investigation of the roots and logics of neoliberalism to the emergent and historical forms of resistance. It is a sequence that has a very active spatial politics, addressing positions, histories, and moments across the spatial scales. This spatiality, I think, is able to engage with the extension and fragmentation of the nation-state that I've suggested is characteristic of the neoliberal restructuring of spatial difference. Like Dionne Brand's *Inventory*, a poetics of witness processes an array of neoliberal causes and global effects—materializing the varied temporalities of rollout neoliberalism. While Farr's work is less an affective forging of cause and effect that the global (and localized media) will not make, this sequence works off of formal disjuncture and semantic conjunction. There is no ironic distancing in the disjuncture: the "flows" that Farr tracks are more links across the uneven geography of globalization and the place-specific resistances of neoliberalism. This place is both material and localized, as well as rooted in the counter-philosophies to market logic and neoliberalism (taking in the Italian autonomists, Marxist economic analysis, and new social movements). For instance, Sonnet III acts as a sort of phatic agit-prop address, a hailing of citizens across this uneven terrain:

> Hello Citizens, here is your room.
>   Here is an SGE 400 and
>   Here are your demands.
>   Here are some traditional actors.
>   Here is a transitional stage.
>   Here is a letter from West Papua it says "just leave us alone."
>   Here is a donation to the Free Jeff Luers Fund.
>   Hello, are you still there?
>   Here is the widening gap.
>   Here is an expert to explain how it widens.
>   Here is a camera, do you see how it is pointed?
>   Here is a sentence in lieu of a slogan.
>   Here is the story making the headlines tonight.
>   Hello Citizens! Hello? Hello? (11)

I say phatic agit-prop because the closing line tests the phatic function of the poem, checking to see if the connection is made, if the various conjunctures can cohere into an address made to a citizen vigilant enough to hear them: the historical avant-gardist tendency of "awakening" the political here, I think, is drawn across the terrain of the anti-globalization movement and across a number of other struggles—environmental, anti-colonial, and anti-capitalist. It is a large claim for fourteen lines, but the specific nature of the references and the semantic density of the poem leads to this. The two specific references to political action—"Here is a letter from West Papua it says 'just leave us alone.' / Here is a donation to the Free Jeff Luers Fund"—are drawn from such actions. The quoted assertion "just leave us alone" is the final demand from the Free Papua Movement (OPM), their statement beginning with: "We are not terrorists! / We do not want modern life! / We refuse any kinds of development: religious groups, aid agencies, and governmental organization." On the website "Solidarity South Pacific," the OPM provides the historical and political reasons for the OPM's fight for self-determination and their refusal of development from above—currently West Papua is invaded by Indonesian troops with UN and USA supervision.

From that anti-colonial or anti-imperialist context, Farr's next line brings a more "local" political engagement in relation: Jeff Luers is an environmental activist who was sentenced to twenty-two years in prison for torching three SUVs in a Chevrolet dealership in Oregon. The complex linking that Farr sets up—joining very different contestations of dispossession and forms of resistance in the poem—is also tied to the virtual communities that are made through the websites devoted to these eruptions of political moments.[6] This potentially global linking of struggles—the accumulation or inventory of a politics of resistance—complicates that address to the citizen. At what scale does that citizen reside? Is it the citizen of a global movement who is nonetheless place-specific—which would articulate an imagined community based not on identity but on a shared political position in relation to imperialism, capitalism, and neoliberalism? The spatial politics, along with the enjambment of politics across a global terrain, is sharpened by several other semantic levels in the poem. The combination of "Here are some traditional actors. / Here is a transitional stage" pushes toward a questioning of how historical formations of resistance and social transformation might take shape. Similarly, the combination of "traditional actors" with "transitional stage" points toward the debate of emergent social actors and sites of resistance in relation to the "traditional" actors, in this case setting up a relationship of class as the engine of transformation to environmental and indigenous resistance. Here, I think Farr's sonnet reflects the shift in a politics of transformation from a temporal one to a spatial one. In response to the restructuring of politics globally, the spatial question is: at what scales can action and transformation take place? In terms of Smith's "scale reorganization," Farr's sonnet raises a question of how new social actors and political movements produce new spatial arrangements and bend the scales of place-based politics. This discursively counters the inevitability of a neoliberal restructuring of the social and political economy. The Citizen addressed in the poem has already been issued an SGE 400 (a lightweight Techno-Pro gas mask), a set of demands, a camera, and a "sentence in lieu of a slogan." "The widening gap" (presumably of rich and poor, as the "expert" will explain) has been designated and the connection checked: "Hello Citizen! Hello? Hello?"

I have isolated one poem from the book and the sonnet series to examine, but Farr's project itself is not isolated; rather, it is tied into a growing body of poetry in North America that is critically and intensively engaged with the politics and restructuring brought by neoliberalism. As I've suggested, this engagement is spatially complex, neither eroding nor unplugging the nation from a hierarchical spatial scale but also articulating the effects and discourse of neoliberalism from its global heights to its impact on bodies, identities, and possible social formations on the ground. A short list of these works would include Rita Wong, Louis Cabri, Rachel Zolf, Roy Miki, Bud Osborn, Dorothy Lusk, Clint Burnham, Nancy Shaw and Catriona Strang, Dan Farrell, Larissa Lai, George Stanley, Mark Nakada, Stephen Collis, Stephen Cain, Adeena Karasick, Reg Johanssen, and in particular Kevin Davies's highly influential book *Comp*.[7]

I've limited this cursory list to Canadian writers, but they cannot be isolated from other North American writers nor from the translation projects that are bringing this work into Italian, French, and German. From my position as a writer and editor, the "post-national" moment of poetry and poetics in North America is a dynamic regeneration of a political project that encompasses aspects of a poetics of witness (exemplified in Canada by Pat Lowther), media critique, vigilant poststructuralism and the politics of poetic form, transnational (rather than cosmopolitan) avant-gardism, and the transnationalism of what Barbara Harlow called "new geographies of struggle." Because this formation of writers, or of this critical tendency within poetics, is itself spread across the spatial scales—being urban, local, national, and global in many senses—it has a friction with critical tendencies that would define a national literature as a literature within the absolute space of the nation.

Yet, as I've been leading to, the Canadian writers that I have listed are engaged with a national project, working with a spatially dynamic sense of the national within neoliberalism, working through the fragmentations and extensions of the nation and the state sprung by neoliberalism and globalization. The national is not by any means the dominant scale in many of these works, but neither is it a "lost geography" made vaporous by de-territorialization. In particular, Stephen Cain's *American Standard/Canada Dry* re-engages with the left cultural nationalist project within Canadian literature but through the intensification of the commodification of culture and history, and through the torqueing of nationalist history by the time line of neoliberalism—its progressions, coherences, and moments. Likewise, a tracking of Dionne Brand's *Inventory* illustrates a highly varied geography, dense with information not easily excavated from the mass media but more available through alternative networks. As an affective anchor, the body figures centrally in Brand's geopolitical landscape, but I would also argue that the nation is integral to the position-takings in this long poem. As Diana Brydon notes, Brand's work "has never been simply nation based" ("Brand's" 3), and it does not turn away from the place and function of the nation in neoliberalism, particularly the place of USA in the return to the dispossession or smashing of national common goods (Iraq's oil, and Iraqi archives and museums being the most egregious examples). In this manner, it is far from the centreless empire of Hardt and Negri where imperialism is a stage relegated to bad history and far from antagonism-free global space. As I'm pointing out, these poetic texts take the nation in both its particularities (the focus on Canada by Cain and others) as well as its generalities (the nation as a scale within the processes of globalization and as a site neoliberalism migrates to).

In this way, the texts I have touched on can be thought of perhaps as nation-scale literatures—with an acknowledgement that scales "operate by way of networks that are 'deeply localized' as well as being extensive in their reach" (Marston, Jones, and Woodward 418). Embedding the nation-state, and the nation as scale, as a necessary and productive agent of the neoliberal restructuring of the geography of globalization allows a deeper historical grasp on the present: it counters the presentism of neoliberalism's claims of the end of history, of the end of geography. The post-euphoric terrain of globalization, the market utopia of the very few versus the rising dystopia, the "widening gap" that we don't need an expert to explain, marks neoliberalism. Neoliberalism promises modernization without modernity for the developing world, and a "level playing field" for those trying to hold onto or gain position: in this landscape of competition, nations and nationalism are neither lost nor merely regressive—they are central. It is therefore hard to speculate on the simple erosion of national literatures.

The dynamic question is: How have national literatures been restructured and what roles can they be mobilized for or pulled into? This sounds drastically instrumentalist, but the tendency to agree on the demise of the nation-state and of national literatures is also densely instrumental. At a moment when the expectations of where social activities, forms of governance, civil societies, cultural formations, and new social actors cohere and take place are open for scrutiny, no scale or place can be excluded. National literatures of course are never wholly or merely national, and they can play both a negative and positive role in the geography of neoliberalism. On the positive side, national literatures can be cultural markers of the way the nation functions culturally and how the nation-state grounds a set of expectations—ranging from personal rights, to citizenship, to economic stability. Here I am thinking of how literary representations of cities could tie into the movement to re-establish a national housing policy in Canada to alleviate homelessness at the urban scale, or the manner in which the nation was invoked by cultural producers to protest against the recent round of cultural funding cuts by the federal Conservatives (and the shift here was that the argument was made toward the necessity of a nation's relationship to culture rather than the economic argument that insists on culture's rank in national industries).

Alternatively, a national literature can function as a negative dialectic in the shifts of the role of the state and the nation. For instance, in Canadian literature, Jane Rule's novel, *The Young in One Another's Arms* draws a set of past positions of the state so forcefully that it is a cultural marker of a particular politics that has been eroded by neoliberalism. In *The Young in One Another's Arms*, Vancouver is transformed by its shift to a "life style" city and the wave of gentrification that began in the late 1970s in the city's west side, as well as politically transformed by an influx of Americans fleeing the draft and the impact of the Viet Nam war. Alongside *Stanley Park*, *The Young in One Another's Arms* holds a strikingly different history of the city and of the state, and also a radically different social imagination.

This complex temporality that marks neoliberalism (rather than merely periodizing it) is used critically by Larissa Lai to refigure the 1994 Writing Thru Race conference within its context of late 1980s and early '90s "anti-racist cultural gatherings" at the national scale, alluded to above, but also within the frame of the neoliberal reformation of the nation. Lai points to the tension in temporality between the state and activists: "While anti-racist artists, writers, and activists were pushing to get their voices heard within a liberal democratic federal system, the conservative right was pushing for the weakening of that system in favour of 'common-sense' populism; that is, the power of global capital masquerading as the power of the people" ("Community" 121). Lai's retroactive assessment of that moment opens Writing Thru Race beyond the nation scale (and beyond the cultural) and uses the conference as an effective gauge to reread the assumptions of cultural strategies and the tactics of the state. In the language I have been using, the push Lai locates was directed at the nation-state (and the institution of Canadian literature and the Canadian museum system) just at the moment of a scale-bending that tried to evacuate the national as the platform for such claims; hence these claims were deflected out of the "national" public, as Lai writes, and down to the individual (122–23).

Here I could propose an inversion of the function of a national literature within neoliberalism, an inversion that does not do away with the category, nor jump up into global flows as a means to refigure a crisis, but an inversion that would read literature not to find out who we "were"—the popularized trope that classic Canadian literature was built around in the cultural nationalism project, the national literature that I stepped into as a writer and a reader—but to read through literature the place and role of the nation and the state. This recalls Roy Miki's assertion for cultural work that is "a mode of translation in which previous hierarchies undergo reconstruction" ("Globalization" 95).

This inversion I am identifying is also an inversion of scale: to read national literatures as simultaneously literatures productive of and produced by globalization (inverting the residual dominance of the national scale and troubling the global as the new dominant) but also to read the making of new limits of national literatures. These limits have often been figured as stasis, as borders of an absolute space, but they are also philosophical and ideological limits—that is, limits to thinking and knowing. Here the production of a nonconformist knowledge that reads the historical process of globalization and the powerful shaping of neoliberalism as a common sense—a common sense, as I have argued above, that is not only a forceful "making economic" of the cultural but a refiguring of value as economic—could break this mirror of the production of globalization and the scale-crossing common sense of neoliberalism. The neoliberal theory of value is the opposite of Marx's labour theory of value, which has its basis in the expenditure of labour, a fact driven home by the ratio of the remuneration of financial or immaterial speculation to the real wages of material labour. This revaluing of value along economic lines, from pins to people, from neo-classical economics to how we make personal decisions under the determinants of a neoliberal philosophy, is where the crisis lies, and cultural criticism and literary criticism can turn to an unravelling of this logic.

The cultural program of neoliberalism, and its revaluing, which has slid into dominance, has had a distorting effect on both the production and consumption of culture (just as it has distorted the relationship of consumption and production across the uneven geography of globalization—an unevenness so desperate that the current economic crisis is born out of this divide). My reading of *Stanley Park* aligns with a broader statement from Miki regarding consumption and production (a statement that is entirely central to his reading of the circulation of power in Canadian literature): "The pressure to provide more transparency of form and subject positionings that ride the crest of consumer-based dominants has undermined the critical power of cultural work, particularly its power to resist and oppose normative assumptions, offering in their place alternative approaches to the real" ("Globalization" 93). In this moment, the pressure that Miki identified has become the object of criticism by creative production, as I have tried to show above, through both formal and thematic alternative approaches to the real.

To borrow a term mobilized by Len Findlay, both cultural production and critical practices now have the "*bad instrumentality*" ("Always" 324) of neoliberalism's effect on the cultural and the social, as well as on the function of the nation, as a clearly visible limit. These are hard limits to knowledge, and also real limits to social, economic, and spatial justice. A part of the project of criticism and literature is to open Canada's *bad history* to other sensibilities, as Jacques Rancière has asked of history as a discipline, and to open as well a refigured global present that is not stubbornly predictive, in order to, as Peter Hitchcock advocates, "keep alive capacities for change that don't simply mirror the imaginary relations of globalization [and neoliberalism!] as currently construed" (200). Szeman too has proposed that "[t]he focus should ... be on the production of new concept-metaphors that might open up politically efficacious re-narrativizations of the present with the aim of creating new visions of the future" ("Poetics" 157). To come back to the spatial and temporal aspects of national literatures, I have pushed here for a spatial critique of the present. Along with this critique, research that finds already existing collective or insurgent concept-metaphors and already existing modes of organizing and living should also be our focus. The tools of criticism and the forms of creative knowledge that were forged in the critiques of the nation can be scaled up and brought into the present both for and against the nation and the state in neoliberalism.

"Beyond CanLit(e)":
Reading. Interdisciplinarity.
Transatlantically.

Danielle Fuller

"Beyond CanLit(e)" is an exploration of the methodological challenges of investigating reading as a social practice. My aim in this essay is to articulate problematics, to formulate some questions, and to share some critical reflections about the process of working on a collaborative, transatlantic project that involves non-professional readers and cultural workers.[1] I believe in interdisciplinary scholarship involving the humanities and social sciences and view its various and potential formations, including collaboration with practitioners outside the academy, as essential pathways for future research about Canadian Literatures.[2] However, I wish to complicate the apparent taken-for-granted ease with which the terms "interdisciplinary" and "collaborative" are often employed by academics, funding agencies, and university managers (at least in the UK, where I am employed). My analysis is grounded in my experiences of collaborative interdisciplinary teamwork and in the insights offered by some of the readers and organizers who have contributed to the study during its main primary research phase (2005–8). Beyond the Book is a research project that aims to produce a transnational analysis of mass reading events and the contemporary meanings of reading in the UK, USA, and Canada.[3] This essay offers a snapshot taken at a moment (Autumn 2007) when the researchers were moving into the beginnings of data analysis and the complex intellectual work of figuring out how to make sense of the knowledge that their research participants had articulated. In my experience, such a process takes time, and given the large amount of material generated by our multi-site project, there are still many conversations ahead of us.

The purpose of this essay, then, is not to offer a polished final account of a research project, or indeed, a full treatise on the topic of "interdisciplinarity." Rather, my purpose is to be an advocate for process, not a predictor of its possible end points or outcomes. I make an argument about the benefits of interdisciplinary work when it is undertaken in collaboration with others, because despite the challenges involved, such work can be generative of new paradigms and methods. Interdisciplinary approaches suit problems and projects that are too vast or complex for a single discipline, and the TransCanada project challenges scholars of Canadian Literature to tackle complex political and social issues. Through various activities, including symposia, book series, and the three TransCanada conferences, TransCanada Institute's work has signposted several such large-scale issues, including "institutions," "citizenship," "ecology and mobility," "First Nations: treaty rights and justice." These topics all invite critical responses that engage with contemporary and/or historical material conditions, power relations, and the competing ideologies that impact on them. In terms of methodology, such issues implicitly invite the respondent to shift her ground and to move well beyond the interpretation of literary texts, even while the method of textual criticism and the concepts of critical theory might usefully inform her response. Another significant aspect of these TransCanada topics is the way that they gesture beyond the nation-state of Canada by referring to economic structures, legal statutes, or world views that exist as trans- or supranational formations, thereby posing further theoretical and methodological challenges to researchers.

The TransCanada project, as I understand it then, is not only about practising interdisciplinarity, but also about undertaking that work collaboratively and, perhaps, even transnationally. My essay offers a critical reflection upon my own experiences of attempting such work as a "foreign" Canadianist engaged in an investigation of the relationships between reading and popular culture in three nation-states. Through a series of narratives and commentaries about work process, I move toward a conceptualization of the terms in my title, before concluding with a broader consideration of what collaborative interdisciplinarity might offer the field of Canadian Literature.

"Beyond CanLit(e)"

A decade ago, my Canadian-born, British-based colleague Susan Billingham and I published a brief examination of the commercial, critical, and institutional success of Canadian writing within the UK (Fuller and Billingham). Our analysis included examples of the Canadian government's role in the export of CanLit through the delivery of boxed sets of Canadian books to university libraries in the early 1970s. We jokingly labelled this sample set "CanLit(e)," not only as a reference to the export of Canada's less palatable beer brands to overseas markets but because the boxed set offered a resonant symbol of how cultural goods had been employed for purposes of cultural and political diplomacy. While we had ideological misgivings about the "Canada" represented by the box and its contents, we were convinced about the significance of the provision, via Department of Foreign Affairs and International Trade (DFAIT), of funding for research and teaching about Canadian Literature across three decades. Such support, we argued, made an important contribution to the institutionalization of Canadian writing and even to its commercial success in the UK. Since we had both benefited directly from programs sponsored by DFAIT, and we also occupied (and continue to occupy) posts that were originally created with seed funding from the Canadian government, we were keenly aware of our position as part of the systems, economies, and policies that we were critiquing. We had the unsettling sense that we were also cultural goods made by or in Canada, and thus a part of a state-funded nationalist CanLit project.

As a form of "soft diplomacy" DFAIT's Academic Relations programs were successful in the UK, particularly during the last two decades of the twentieth century, before funding cuts began to impact upon the training of future Canadianists. As teachers of British students, we drew upon knowledge gained in Canadian (as well as British) institutions and through subsequent funded visits to Canada for research purposes and also to assist in the design of new courses. Without the finance for these activities, it is likely that we, as well as other Canadianists working outside Canada, would have devoted far fewer classroom hours (if any) to teaching students about Canadian culture. Of course, we did not simply reproduce normative or pronationalist ideas about Canada and its literatures as a result of our pedagogical trips. We were (and remain) committed to teaching students to interrogate the politics of textual representation, to critique different discourses of multiculturalism and "race," to attend to the ways that Canadian Literature may seduce them as "outsider" readers of a familiar-looking, yet often enticingly different, culture.

Yet sometimes, in spite of all our careful professional and critical strategies, as we confessed to each other, we literally forgot where we were and, standing in a classroom, would say "here" instead of "there" to denote Canada and our location. It was easy to understand why Susan, a dual citizen who had lived the majority of her life in Canada, would make this slip, less obvious why I, as a British citizen whose passport registered me as either a "visitor" to or a "student" in Canada, would do so. Our sense of being outsiders within two cultures was not identical, but we both experienced moments when we were made aware of the privilege of such a position and its literal and intellectual mobility made possible by money, education, and the historical relationship between our natal nation-states. Unlike many people who are forced to seek asylum, or members of diaspora produced through histories of enslavement, we had the privilege of forgetting where, and sometimes even who, we were.

While we were working together on our article, we reminded each other about our positionality, and this helped us to think critically and more explicitly about what and how we practised our trade as Canadian Literature specialists. The process of collaboration helped to defamiliarize our professional work because we had to discuss, nominate, and negotiate the differences that disguised our apparent sameness. We also had to confront our complicity with, and indeed our emotional investment in, some institutional structures (educational and governmental) that we found ideologically and intellectually problematic. For me, this collaborative experience, which was focused around the interrogation of one of Canadian Literature's transatlantic journeys, brought home the critical responsibility involved in being a "foreign" CanLit scholar: to remain open to the experiences of estrangement; to resist romanticization; to critique the structures, institutions, and ideologies that supported my attempts at knowledge production. It was also a process that made me think "transatlantically" about the material production and transnational distribution of Canadian books, about my own literal to-and-fro travels across the ocean, and in a more conceptual sense of the term, about "transatlantic" as a discursive space in which subjectivities, including my own sense of self, were produced. I was hooked on the institutional history of Canadian

Literature whether I liked it or not. I was also high on the intellectual stimulation and emotional affect provided by a process of collaboration that traded upon the trust and knowledge of a collegial friendship.

The movement between estrangement and connection that this relationship and our shared training enabled was not something that I had expected, even though it was not my first experience of collaboration. As I thought more about how and why some Canadian books travelled overseas, and in particular began to wonder about their reception by nonacademic readers in different geographical locations, I also felt a longing for that combination of intellectual energy and affective engagement. I became intrigued by the proliferation of popular formations of shared reading that, inspired by the success of Oprah's Book Club, took up the model of a reading group but on a bigger, more public scale. These models existed on both sides of the Atlantic, some as mass-mediated broadcast events on radio and television, and increasingly as the new century progressed, in the form of One Book, One Community programs (OBOC). These are usually city-wide and involve a series of events focused around the themes and issues of a selected book. Over five hundred such community-wide reading events are now held each year in a number of countries, including Australia, Singapore, and the Netherlands, and they are capable of bringing featured authors and books not only new readers and media attention but also significant commercial success. The broadcast events (e.g., the UK television's *Richard and Judy's Book Club* and *Canada Reads*) can increase sales of featured books by as much as one thousand percent.

Since I was a CanLit and Canadian Studies scholar first and foremost, I decided to begin with an investigation of the CBC's radio show *Canada Reads*, which at that point (2002) had just been broadcast for the first time. I also decided to find a research partner who could help me make sense of the ideological work that these events were performing for their organizers, for the institutions that sponsored them, and for readers. Once I began to talk with DeNel Rehberg Sedo, a communications scholar born in the United States but working in Canada, the questions multiplied. What, we wondered, about the political economy of these mass-reading events? How did the globalized structures of English-language publishing impact on events, and what was at stake in the various combinations of public funding, private sponsorship, and voluntary labour that delivered them? What about differences and commonalities across the USA, Canada, and the UK in terms of the meanings of reading that events produced or reproduced? Could such community-building initiatives attract new readers, promote intercultural understanding, achieve any kind of social change? As these questions indicate, I was moving "beyond CanLit(e)" in scope (three nation-states), in scale (the investigation of multiple events in different locations), in media (although books were the central object, broadcast media and online communications were involved in promoting and facilitating the sharing of reading), and in method ("why do people come together to share reading?" was not a research question I could answer only through the analysis of printed materials).

Since we had both previously worked on aspects of Canadian literary culture, Canadian books, readers, and events were central, rather than marginal, to the conceptualization and design of our study. Our understanding of reading, writing, and publishing communities was shaped by our knowledge of how these operate in anglophone Canada and the critical and commercial success of Canadian Literature abroad. We began our investigations with *Canada Reads* and our pilot study was One Book, One Community in Kitchener-Waterloo-Cambridge, one of the earliest Canadian iterations of a One Book, One Community program. Those studies changed our research tools, altered the logistics of our larger project, and foregrounded intellectual themes for further investigation, themes such as notions of literary value and readers' pleasures, for example. Canada is thus neither marginal nor a bit player within our conceptualization of the "transatlantic," which denotes a geographic area, a northern industrialized subregion, but also a culturally constructed space criss-crossed by literary traffic, including ideas about why reading books matters.

Reading Matters

We designed Beyond the Book as a study that examines reading as a social practice, rather than privileging the investigation of reading as a hermeneutic or interpretive practice (while recognizing that these practices are imbricated: shared reading is also, in part, an interpretive process of rereading). Our fieldwork focused on ten sites across three nation-states.[4] Recognizing the cultural specificities that inflect class, race, and gender formations and attitudes to literary culture, we decided to undertake context-specific case studies of reading events. We chose sites either because we were familiar with the local print cultures in the selected locations (Vancouver, Birmingham, and the Maritimes); or because of their significance to the OBOC "movement" (Seattle was the very first program, while Chicago was the model encountered and adapted by the first Canadian organizers in Kitchener-Waterloo-Cambridge and the first British organizers in Bristol); or to establish a range in the scale of events and communities studied (large cities located at a distance from metropolitan centres such as Liverpool, alongside smaller cities such as Huntsville, Alabama). Guiding our project design was our commitment to feminist-standpoint epistemology, which in terms of research process, advocates a continual "back and forth" movement between theory and practice (Stanley and Wise). Feminist-standpoint theory also emphasizes the importance of beginning analysis from your research subjects' own accounts of their everyday lives (e.g., D. Smith, *Everyday*; Code). Within Beyond the Book, this means that we use the readers' and cultural workers' own articulations and analyses of their shared reading practices and event experiences as a starting point from which to analyze the cultural work that mass reading events perform and enable. In doing so, we are also seeking to understand and to analyze dominant and subordinate kinds of knowledge; that is, knowledge created, informed by, and sometimes resistant to the ruling relations of power (D. Smith, *Everyday*; *Texts*). This epistemological approach to the study of shared reading enables us to identify and theorize the ways that readers negotiate the meanings of reading within the contemporary "matrix of communication" (Long 216). Within this matrix, the mass media possess tremendous symbolic power, while the more traditional ruling relations of power, represented by educational and governmental institutions, for example, lend particular social meanings to shared reading that do not always coincide with reader experience. A particularly striking example of the latter is the desire, expressed in a press release from the National Endowment for the Arts in the USA about their large-scale sponsorship of One Book, One Community programs, to get Americans talking about literary books with their neighbours, or as they gather around the water cooler at work, rather than chatting about episodes of *Desperate Housewives* (NEA). The hierarchy of cultural value around different media inferred here is not necessarily shared by all readers, nor is the practice of casual book talk the most likely outcome of a city-wide reading event.

Many—although not all—of the experiences described by the readers quoted in this section are more or less invisible to professional literary academic readers if they employ exclusively text-based methods.[5] Moreover, empirical methods, including a quantitative survey and a range of ways of working with human subjects, were essential tools for our investigation since without them and the data they generated we would have been restricted to an analysis of printed and online texts produced by event organizers and the media. Such an approach would have omitted readers' own understanding of their experiences entirely or, where reader's views were cited, represented them within the ideological frames of reference of an organizing agency eager to report the success of their program.

Attending to the voices of non-professional readers is fascinating and provocative for an academic literary critic since they suggest a series of reasons why reading books still matters in the digital age, as well as indicating some of the ways that readers outside the academy encounter, re-encounter, and share books. Two readers from our pilot study in southern Ontario offered insights into their enjoyment of One Book, One Kitchener-Waterloo-Cambridge (KWC) that suggest different experiences of reading print books as part of mass-reading events. Their comments indicate potential pathways for further research and analysis in order to generate new critical vocabularies of pleasure, for example. One questionnaire respondent articulated a desire to learn about the author's creative process and biography—a desire we were to hear many times over from readers in other fieldwork sites. She wrote, "The event puts me in touch with the real person behind the book. I like to know more about the author and the 'why' behind the book" (Questionnaire respondent, Kitchener-Waterloo-Cambridge, September 2004). As this reader's words indicate, author events bring writers literally face-to-face with readers' various desires, including a desire for intimacy with the person behind the text. Such a desire may be coupled with a reader's urge to authenticate the text via knowledge of the writer's life, or to authorize and recontextualize the text as a culturally valuable object either for themselves, for a particular cultural group, or as occurred in the events featuring Nino Ricci (whose novel *Lives of the Saints* was the 2004 KWC One Book selection), for their local community. Meanwhile, Trudy, a middle-aged woman who took part in one of our focus groups, expressed the fun of affective identification made possible by the literary bus tour that has formed part of the annual activities for the KWC program for several years. In the summer of 2003, a group of about

50 readers toured some of the sites depicted in Jane Urquhart's novel *The Stone Carvers*. Trudy recalled her experience with great enthusiasm:

> I really enjoyed [*The Stone Carvers*] and the bus tour really bought that book alive.... because you went to places that were described that were part of the book and somehow it seems real, you know—I know it was a novel, but just, you know you could see the characters, you see the places ... you felt that what was described could have happened and you were where it, you were where these places were. (Trudy, focus group participant, Kitchener-Waterloo-Cambridge, September 2004)

For Trudy, the tour offered a pleasurable opportunity to construct a mimetic identification between textual representation and the physical environment. Her sense of having stepped into the world of the book in both an imaginative and physical way moves her from an abstract textual world (a bookish space familiar to literary critics but not comfortable for all readers) to a more material relationship with the text. Trudy's embodied and sensory experience prompts a form of identity work in which she "feels" (and by implication comes to know) the events of the novel both emotionally and physiologically. Her experience also indicates the legitimacy that One Book, One Community events can lend to vernacular forms of reading.

A more imagined or cognitive kind of identity work is desired by the following respondents to our *Canada Reads* questionnaire, respondents who are both reflecting upon the question, "What type of book is the best choice for *Canada Reads*? Why?"

> A book that says something about Canada and Canadians, who we are, what is important to us, what we want others to know. It must be well written, but not necessarily a best seller.

> Ones about Canadian life. It is so varied across the country and books can give the readers more insight into Canadians. (*Canada Reads* questionnaire respondents, April 2006)

The ideological work that Canadian Literature may perform for the reader through hermeneutic encounters with representations of difference is referenced by these readers and will not surprise Canadian literature scholars. But it might be instructive for us to examine further the relationship between the "materializing" of the book experienced by particular groups of readers such as the Kitchener-Waterloo-Cambridge participants, and the cognitive-imaginative text-reader encounter described by these *Canada Reads* readers.

Significant for Beyond the Book, a project that is focused on the contours, purpose, and meanings of shared reading, are readers' desires for the connection and a sense of community that can be built via public and broadcast reading events, even if the community is ephemeral, or as in the case of the *Canada Reads* respondents, imagined. Stuart Dybek, a Chicago writer whose short-story collection *The Coast of Chicago* was featured as that city's One Book Spring 2004 selection, recognized these desires when he remarked that, One Book, One Chicago makes "reading social without destroying the relationship between the book and the individual reader" (Interview, Chicago, Oct. 2004). Dybek infers that solitary and shared reading are not mutually exclusive to a reader's enjoyment or understanding of a text. His comment prompts critical reflection about the respective value conferred upon these different types of textual-social encounter by readers located both within and outside the academy.

Adding a further dimension (and complication) to our potential understanding of reading as a social practice, Emma, a teenaged group member of Get Into Reading in the Wirral (UK), movingly articulates the therapeutic possibilities activated by a model of shared reading that does not depend on print literacy but rather on reanimating the text through orality: "[Being read to] calms us down, cos, like, we're normally dead loud. We're normally dead loud outside. And it does calm us down.... So when we go home we're dead chilled (February 2007)." Initiated by Jane Davis in 2001, Get Into Reading (GIR), the scheme in which Emma was a participant, is a not-for-profit organization and a registered charity running reading programs. Under Davis's direction, the GIR team has developed a model of small-group shared reading that involves people reading stories, poems, and novels aloud in the company and under the guidance of a trained facilitator. GIR deliberately selects socially and economically marginalized groups living in and around the Wirral, an area situated on a peninsula between the rivers Mersey and Dee due east and in sight of the city of Liverpool in North West England. The reader-text encounter that Emma describes above involves her physical body as well as her emotions and enables her to achieve relaxation and, by implication, better mental health.[6]

Experiences like Emma's suggest that, for some people, sharing reading with others promotes well-being that can be individually transformative in psychosocial ways. How and why this occurs is the subject of collaborative interdisciplinary research involving medical doctors, neuroscientists, literary scholars and psychologists.[7]

While these readers' commentaries represent a very small selection of voices from our study, they illustrate the range and complexity of contemporary readers' engagement with shared reading and book cultures. They also speak to the apparent power of reading and books to bring people together, to offer various kinds of pleasure, to change world views or mental states. Such scenarios are especially seductive for those of us who are professionally invested in the promotion of reading. As members of what sociologist Wendy Griswold conceptualizes as "the reading class," we have benefited from the social prestige accorded to book reading and indeed, as teachers of literature, we help to maintain the notion that being an adept book reader creates cultural capital (Griswold 37). At the conference that formed part of our project, Jonathan Davidson, Artistic Director of the Birmingham Book Festival, offered the assembled audience of academics, public librarians, and community activists a salutary caveat: "Let's not sanctify books" (Sept. 2007). We might usefully borrow Davidson's caveat to apply more particularly to our role as Canadian Literature specialists. We might ask ourselves, for instance: in what ways do our various activities as teachers, researchers, readers, and students of Canadian Literature "sanctify books"—to what ends, and at whose expense? How can we defamiliarise what we do with, and in the name of, Canadian Literature?

Certainly, I view collaborative interdisciplinary work that crosses the humanities and social sciences in terms of its methods as one strategy that is capable of denaturalizing what "I do" as a person trained in (Canadian) literary studies in ways that, I hope, will be generative of methodologies for investigating reading as a social practice in the contemporary moment. In the second half of this essay, I offer a (necessarily partial) account of Beyond the Book's research process. My commentary is inflected by a key methodological question: how can a researcher hear the voices and attend to the analyses that nonacademic readers and cultural workers, such as those quoted in this section, are making? My belief, as I have begun to indicate in my discussion of the various reading experiences articulated by actual readers, is that the humanities cannot provide all the tools for this purpose, and my aim here is to suggest how mixed-method research conducted as a collaborative interdisciplinary investigation may help us to "retool."[8]

Interdisciplinarity

Our interdisciplinary approach draws upon our combined research expertise in textual and empirical methodologies: the result of our training in the humanities (Fuller) and social sciences (Rehberg Sedo). For this project, we developed a multilayered investigation involving: qualitative interviews with event producers, focus groups with event participating and nonparticipating readers, participant observation of activities, and the collection of quantitative data through a trilingual online questionnaire that we have adjusted for use in each site. To use the vocabulary of mixed-methods research analyst John Creswell, DeNel and I chose to adopt a methodology somewhere between a concurrent triangulation strategy and a concurrent nested strategy (Creswell 217). Simply put, we decided to collect qualitative data "in the field" within each research site, while running our quantitative questionnaire at the same time; hence, our research practice was "concurrent." Findings generated through one method were used to "attempt to confirm, cross-validate, or corroborate findings" arrived at through another method (217), hence, "triangulation." However, we put much more effort into our qualitative research and, in fact, employed multiple qualitative methods (participant observation, focus group interviews, interviews with cultural workers, collection and analysis of event artifacts). In this sense, our mixed methods have looked more like a "nested" strategy in which the quantitative data (gathered from our questionnaires) is given less priority than our qualitative methods during collection and analysis. As Creswell notes, very little analysis of concurrent nested strategies exists (218), and so we hope that one of the ultimate outcomes of our interdisciplinary collaboration will be a critical account of our methodology's strengths and limits.[9]

In practice, undertaking this type of research methodology is difficult, because it is time consuming, labour intensive, and energy draining, although it is also occasionally exhilarating. It requires more money than traditional humanities methods that are text-based, and demands that its research subjects assume and enact ethical and social responsibility that can not only be proven to institutional authorities but also demonstrated toward research participants in ways that make sense to them. Success of such multilayered mixed-methods research, which involves so much face-to-face interaction with human beings, also depends on the development of trust among team members and the facility and ability to take risks—intellectual, social, and emotional. The researcher must step beyond her comfort zone, whether that involves the challenge of talking to people from a wide variety of backgrounds, grappling with new software programs, or "groping" toward knowledge while learning new methods (Bal 20).

Yet methodological "groping," intellectual grappling, and emotional risk taking are also fundamental to the process of collaborative interdisciplinarity as I understand it. While I believe that it is possible to undertake interdisciplinary work as an individual scholar, and in the arena of reading studies Janice Radway's research is exemplary in this regard (e.g., *Reading the Romance*), becoming fully conversant with the paradigms and practices of more than one discipline is incredibly difficult to achieve. The overt and ongoing negotiations required for effective collaborative work, however, also produce the benefit of one being confronted by another's viewpoint. Although the moments of intellectual surprise can lessen across the time of a collaborative relationship, the different epistemological frames that differently trained scholars bring to bear on both the gathering and the analysis of data is a valuable aspect of collaborative interdisciplinarity. As my account of philosophical "clashes" will illustrate, these moments of intellectual surprise can generate awareness of disciplinary assumptions, which in terms of defamiliarization are not unlike the earlier same-discipline collaborative experience I described in the opening pages of this essay. However, the process of intellectual negotiation, exchange, and to-and-fro movement across critical paradigms, methods, and theoretical concepts required by interdisciplinarity coincides with the dialogic and social demands of collaboration to produce "interactional expertise," or new knowledge (Collins and Evans). Sometimes such knowledge is capable of transforming existing disciplines or even creating new ones. Collaborative interdisciplinarity is thus both an ontological process of enacting social relations as you study them, and an epistemological goal toward which its subjects are always moving, admittedly sometimes in faltering steps, as the following work narratives demonstrate.

Problematizing the Interdisciplinary Methodology of Beyond the Book

In this section, rather than dwelling on the pragmatic difficulties arising from our choice of research methods, I would like to focus on the issue of paradigm clashes and philosophical tensions. These inevitably occur when humanities and social sciences methods are merged in order to study shared reading in event-based cultures, and I have chosen just two problematics among many possible examples to support my contention that collaborative interdisciplinarity that is also transformative is tricky but important work.[10]

Problematic 1: What is evidence?

As Linda Hutcheon and Michael Hutcheon have noted, "disciplines have different notions of evidence" (1366) and "different standards of evaluation" (1365). Social science demands high standards of evidence, so methodology has to be designed to achieve those standards (e.g., via triangulation and by achieving saturation). In literary studies (as in the humanities in general) "evidence" is usually provided through textual interpretation and sometimes supported by the analysis of contextual material (historical, cultural, social, political). If, as teachers of Canadian Literature, we say to a student, "Where is your evidence for this comment?" or (one of my own default essay comments), "Don't just state: demonstrate!" we are usually seeking proof via the close textual analysis and interpretation of a text. We may, depending on pedagogical context, require a demonstration that the writer can draw upon concepts from specific literary and/or cultural theory in order to make their analysis more nuanced and convincing. However, we rarely dwell upon our conception of "evidence" or, indeed, question the validity (appropriateness) of using our textual methods to generate evidence.

Within most social science disciplines, students are explicitly taught to address issues of validity and evidence by learning about different research methods. Using an appropriate type or types of method to investigate your research question (validity) has to be a consideration; otherwise your fellow social scientists will not consider your eventual findings or your analysis of them to be reliable evidence. In turn, reliability depends upon hearing and identifying consistencies across research subjects, case studies, and the like and confirming or complicating these consistencies through at least one other form of investigation. Further, whereas in literary studies we are always already in interpretive mode, social science students are encouraged to think self-reflexively about whether they wish to take an interpretative or realist world view to their research practice (roughly equating to and translating into qualitative and quantitative methods) and to understand the philosophical and practical consequences of doing so. Although we do consider these world views within literary studies, it is usually as philosophical standpoints.[11] We may, in fact, use our philosophical reflections upon these standpoints as a means to identify dominant and resistant ideologies and their articulation within a literary work (maybe also within other cultural forms such as visual art or performance). This is a useful and important method used extensively within cultural studies, as well as by many literary scholars, but it is one that depends heavily on the authority of the academic critic and their deconstructive (interpretative) skill. To social scientists, wherever they would locate themselves along the quantitative-qualitative/positivist-relativist continuum, this textual approach, used in isolation from other forms of investigation, cannot generate reliable evidence.

Given that Beyond the Book's research questions include "Why do people come together to share reading?" and "Do mass-reading events attract marginalized communities, foster new reading practices, and enable social change?" we could not rely (in all senses of that word) upon the analysis of text (even upon the analysis of interview transcripts) as our only way of producing evidence. Investigating social practice demands methods that can engage with that set of social practices as lived, embodied experience rather than only rely on narrative or textual accounts of it. Hence, the employment in our investigations of participant observation techniques and face-to-face interviews with groups of people (sometimes known to each other, but often strangers) actively making sense through dialogue of why they share reading, do or do not participate in events, and so on. Even though we selected a series of methods, including the design of a quantitative questionnaire (which includes open-ended questions and thus is in itself a "mixed method"), we have to continually recognize the limitations of each method and the relationships among them as we work toward an understanding of the data that we have gathered. Recruiting to our focus-group interviews was a recurring problem, for instance, and the membership of groups was neither as full nor as cross-cultural as we would have liked. Added to this, is the complication of the frames (institutional, contextual, and even moral) of our project, which involves both a practice (reading) and an object (print books) that are inscribed with various cultural meanings and value (sometimes moral value) within the nation-states in our study. Given that all interviews are a type of performance by all parties (researcher and subject) (Fuller), what status does the data gathered through this method have in evidential terms?

In Chicago, our second research site, my response to DeNel's concern about the size and demographics of our early focus groups was, "Hey, it's all qualitative to me!" At the time, I meant that I could take the narratives offered by the participants and analyze them, no matter how few of them there were. For DeNel, my textual-analytic skills were not good enough in and of themselves, and she was not about to let me run wild with a clutch of interview transcripts. Her communications training demanded that we work with several groups of people in each research site so that we would begin to hear certain phrases, desires, ideologies, and pleasures articulated, and analyses or attempts at analyses (e.g., of the role reading plays in people's everyday lives) repeated, albeit with context-dependent variations. About two research sites later, I recall her saying with relief, "We're getting saturation!" (My immediate thought was: but it's not raining!) However, even this is not the end but the very beginning of being able to say that we have some evidence of, for example, why people come together to share reading. Any consistencies, hints, and analytic clues generated from focus-group or individual interviews must be cross-validated with data from the questionnaires and insights drawn from our participant-observation work at event activities, complicated by our analysis of event artifacts. And all of these efforts at triangulation must include a critical account of frames and the practical problems that have produced a very particular data set about groups with specific demographics, despite various efforts to alter how we recruit participants in later sites. Only then, may we say that we have "evidence" to support our findings and analyses.[12]

Problematic 2: Interpretation

"Interpretation" haunts the preceding discussion of standards of evidence and the differences in research methods across the humanities and social sciences as an additional (yet related) problematic. Once again, working with a social scientist has encouraged me to think about it in terms of research process and methods. DeNel's professional training as a market researcher and professional communications researcher leaned toward the positivist model of social science, so that interpretation involved making sense of statistics gathered via quantitative methods: this is what the respondents said; this is what the stats show us; ergo, this is the finding. I am going to highlight, but put aside, the problem of objectivity, which has been helpfully interrogated, debated, and reconceptualised by (among others) feminist epistemologists working within social science and the natural sciences as "strong objectivity."[13] My point here is that the positivist model demonstrates much less faith in the researcher's knowledge and analytic ability than modes of interpretation that are bound up in qualitative and text-based methods. Our employment of a multi-site online questionnaire and the Statistical Package for the Social Sciences (SPSS) software, through which the datasets can be managed, manipulated, and interrogated, has foregrounded the different paradigms of interpretation operative within our particular humanities and social science trainings.

SPSS is a statistical software program that enables you to process data quantitatively, so the questionnaire responses, which include answers to both tick-box-type responses and open-ended questions (data that could be described as a mixture of quantitative and qualitative in both its method of collection and in its expression), had to be grouped and boxed up into "crunchable" units so that the program could assign values and locate consistencies. In order to prepare the data so that you can run queries, any open-ended responses need to be labeled (or coded), that is, put into some type of category. The coding categories that we have used are partly derived from earlier data collected during a pilot study, but they are also functionally descriptive in a way that felt very strange and restrictive to Anouk Lang and to me (both of us literary studies scholars by training). One day we sat down with a list of categories prepared by DeNel, and reworked them by applying our close reading skills to a particular set of open-ended responses. Our impulse was to add more and more categories, in order to account for the various interpretations we produced as we attended to the variations in language use and narrative strategies across the range of respondents.

A very brief (and relatively simple) illustration of our "humanist interpretive impulse" will have to suffice here. One of the open-ended questions asked respondents to comment on what they thought the best book choice would be for the reading event in question (e.g., *Canada Reads* or *Liverpool Reads*) and to explain why.

Even isolating one out of nearly nine hundred responses to this question within the *Canada Reads* data set foregrounds our dilemma: "That is difficult to answer because I wouldn't want just one type. My preference would be a book that combines history/suspense/good character development—and that one can thoroughly enjoy without having to feel virtuous for having read it."

While this response can be coded under the category label "variety of genres," none of the initial categories captured the resistance of this reader's response to the implied moral imperative of the show ("[a book] one can thoroughly enjoy without having to feel virtuous for having read it"). It was easy to suggest that we might add a category "book with good character development" (or similar), and there were certainly other responses that merited that addition. However, adding a category "resistant response" opened up a whole other can of (book?) worms around definitions of resistance. Anouk and I tended to examine the open-ended responses for not only implicit meanings but also ambivalence, but in our doing so, DeNel felt that we were sometimes overinterpreting or using our own critical frameworks rather than those of the respondents.

In practice, in order to capture all the nuances that our textually trained minds desired to preserve and deemed to be valuable, Anouk and I altered the entire list of categories for "Book Choice"—giggling together as meanings proliferated and the list of categories (labels) grew in length. Some of those alterations included complicating the descriptor "Challenging" by creating two categories: "Formally or Stylistically Complex" and "Content/Ideas Complex." Our discussion about the categories "Prize Winner," "Classic," and "Middle Brow" was intellectually stimulating, but our ever more nuanced list of labels arising from it proved to be impractical. DeNel accepted only a handful of our alterations and rejected many of them because, from a quantitative standpoint, we were in danger of rendering the data unusable and thus meaningless, not least because some of the categories would only contain one response. The saving grace for the literary-trained mind is that you can recover the string (open-ended) responses and treat them as qualitative material should you wish to do so at a later date.

Why use this method within our research design if, from the standpoint of my own original training, it seemed to be constructed upon a reductive notion—even a dismissal—of textual interpretation? First, mixed-methods research demands that researchers should not rely on their statistics alone, especially if convenience sampling is used (as we have done), and even when the total data set reaches a statistically valid number of responses (as ours, at over three thousand, does). I believe that the employment of mixed methods promotes a practice of interpretation capable of complicating and problematizing data, whether it takes the form of words or numbers. The practice may proceed in ways that are somewhat unfamiliar to me, but the attention to complication satisfies my desire to decode and critique signs. I recognize and trust that these methods, used extensively within different branches of social science, can produce a nuanced analysis of how specific groups of people value books, or how they define and practise shared reading.

Second, being able to produce some statistics offers us a language that can assist the practitioners (librarians, community activists, reading event organizers) whom we have met during our research. Statistics about what people read and why help them to make a case to funders and policy-makers for whom qualitative data is useful but not easily translatable into dollars and pounds. While, strictly speaking, ours is not a "solution-focused" piece of research, we have always envisaged our work as being useful not only for academics (in various fields: cultural studies, book history, sociology of culture, literary studies) but also for cultural workers. To that end, we have continually tried to communicate our preliminary analyses via short reports (an example is posted on our website); consultation meetings with organizing agencies (e.g., OBOC organizing committees or members thereof in Chicago, Liverpool, and Huntsville) and related organizations (e.g., the UK's The Reading Agency); and via presentations to practitioners (e.g., the public librarian's professional conference at North York, 2005; the 2007 Canadian Library Association conference; and Reader Development Day, Napier University, 2008). We also invited a range of practitioners to participate in our conference, both as part of the plenary panels "Reading and/as Social Change" and "Creating Communities of Readers" and as presenters within parallel sessions. I claim no originality in our research practice or politics by offering these examples: many feminist scholars within humanities and social science would also understand these communications as integral to their work as feminists.

Third, interpreting numbers alongside language is one of the most intellectually exciting and potentially generative aspects of our mixed-methods work. Since Beyond the Book is also employing textual-analytic methods, for example, to deconstruct the rhetorics of promotional materials and the branding of mass reading events, we are not ignoring the value of textual methods but resituating them within our toolbox of qualitative and quantitative approaches. As researchers whose work is shaped by feminist-standpoint theory, we are continually trying to generate explanatory categories from the field and from our research participants so that our theories will be induced from our empirical data rather than deduced from pre-existing hypotheses. As Klaus Jensen suggests, feminist standpoint and grounded theories have "attract[ed] renewed attention to the practical, lived categories of understanding with which people engage media and other social interaction" (261). The process of becoming an attentive listener within this type of investigation requires a range of skills, and a critical-sceptical understanding of how meanings are made and the discursive work that language is made to perform can be a very useful part of that skill set.

Concluding Thoughts: Bringing It Back Home to CanLit

I began this essay by stating my belief in interdisciplinary scholarship involving the humanities and social sciences. I view its various and potential formations, including collaboration with practitioners outside the academy, as essential pathways for future research about Canadian Literatures. I have outlined one project that attempts to combine methods from different disciplinary traditions and have identified some of the practical challenges and philosophical tensions that have arisen. I set out to complicate the terms "interdisciplinary" and "collaborative" through a discussion of research process and a reflection on methodological problems, for several reasons. First, not only funding agencies but also Canadian Literature specialists invoke these terms repeatedly. However, I do not think we have yet given enough time or credence to discussions of method within our own field or to collaborative discussion with scholars and practitioners with different trainings to be able to understand or to identify all of the different modes of "interdisciplinary" investigation available to us.

Second, as anyone who has undertaken any type of collaborative and/or interdisciplinary work will know, it is intellectually, physically, and emotionally demanding. Frequently it requires a great deal of human and economic resources. We have to become more practical scholars and benefit from the management experience of colleagues such as Marjorie Stone, Diana Brydon, and other senior academics involved in the TransCanada projects, people who have acquired knowledge about planning, team building, and large-scale strategic thinking. Third, if as Canadian Literature specialists, we want to move further into interdisciplinary work (and I fully accept that not every literary-trained scholar does), we have to become more "sociable" human beings. If we want to move beyond our textual methods, our books, and computer screens, we can begin by drawing upon our best-practice classroom skills. But we also need to retool in ways indicated in my essay and in others that I have not been able to discuss—or indeed to imagine—here. We need to do so in order to investigate the proliferating social and cultural formations of Canadian literatures: their readers and listeners, the institutions that play roles in producing and evaluating them, the political economies of the global publishing structures that have made "Can Lit" not only "fit for export" but a prestige brand (at least, in some parts of the world) (Fuller and Billingham). Lastly, whatever type of collaborative interdisciplinary project we choose or are able to practise, we must continually ask ourselves: "Whose knowledge is this? Who is this knowledge for?" The stakes can seem high: we love books, but they are being reconfigured by nonprint media and new technologies; we are paid with public money and need to consider how we can be "accountable" to various audiences without compromising intellectual endeavour or simply aping the utilitarian discourse beloved by conservative politicians on both sides of the Atlantic; many of us desire a more equitable world and want our paid work to contribute to that project, however modestly. At the same time, we have to be mindful of—and humble about—our relatively privileged role as knowledge producers. We can only begin from our recognition of our situation within the discipline, and the Canada, that made us.

White Settlers and the Biopolitics of State Building in Canada

Janine Brodie

Introduction

In recent years, there has been an explosion of studies investigating the meaning and status of national citizenship in an era of economic globalization and unprecedented international population mobility (Isin). In the early twenty-first century, citizenship continues to designate a legal status that identifies someone as a full and equal member of an internationally recognized nation-state. Once popular representations of liberal-democratic citizenship as an ever more inclusive unfolding of individual and social rights, however, have been progressively undermined by contemporary public policies that have significantly eroded many hard-won civil liberties and social security programs. Feminist and critical race theorists also rightly argue that advanced liberal democracies never fulfilled their promise of universal citizenship rights and equality for all.[1] These critics demonstrate that the declaration of citizenship equality, the "we-ness" that purportedly holds national polities together, is premised on the fabricated "other-ness" of identifiable groups located both inside and outside of the territorial boundaries of the state (Sharma). Contemporary citizenship studies thus have interrogated the contradictions and tensions embedded within the very idea and practice of modern citizenship and national identity, both of which take the national state as a primary conceptual and historical point of reference (Sassen 281–86). This essay follows in the latter tradition by examining the ways in which the iconic national citizen, as well as racial and ethnic hierarchies and exclusions, were embedded in the formative biopolitics of Canadian state building. We begin with a brief survey of popular approaches to the study of Canadian citizenship practices.

Citizenship Quandaries

The right to have rights

Although the story of Canadian citizenship has been told and retold in many different ways, this essay recounts only three motifs—the universal rights-based story, the more broadly cast ethnocultural account of the accommodation of Canadian diversity, and an alternative approach that emphasizes the triangular underpinnings of the national narratives of white settler societies such as Canada. The rights-based story, which is commonly found in introductory political science texts, borrows from T.H. Marshall's influential account of the development of citizenship rights in liberal democracies. Writing in Britain at the end of WWII, Marshall provided a progressive and universal reading of the evolution of citizenship rights across three centuries of liberal governance. The crux of Marshall's argument is that liberal-democratic citizenship developed in three distinct stages, becoming an ever more inclusive and substantial rights-based institution of modern governance in the process. Reflecting on the European experience, he traced the growth of citizenship rights from state recognition and protection of *civil rights*, relating to individual freedoms, property rights, and equal protection under the law, to *political rights*, such as the right to vote, participate in politics, and hold governments accountable, to *social rights*, which ensured all citizens a right to claim from the state a minimal level economic security and social welfare. According to Marshall's template, the undifferentiated citizen of liberal democracies secured fundamental civil rights in the eighteenth century, political rights in the nineteenth century, and social rights in the twentieth century.

Marshall's rights-based model of the evolution of citizenship was widely influential in the heyday of the welfare state, not least because it resonated with the socially progressive policy paradigms that animated western democracies in the immediate postwar period (Brodie, "Social"). A proliferation of universal and ameliorative social programs following WWII seemed to affirm both the promise and irrevocability of social citizenship rights. However, Marshall's formulation of the evolution of citizenship rights also drew criticism from a variety of quarters. Feminist and critical race scholars, for example, pointed out that, far from being a universal story, Marshall's account largely reflected the privileged experience of securely employed white men, and veiled systemic social exclusions in the mirage of universalism. Precarious workers and gendered and racialized groups did not experience a similar sequenced expansion of citizenship rights; nor did they have the same access to citizenship rights enjoyed by Marshall's iconic postwar citizen. To name a few examples in the Canadian case: women were granted political rights before they achieved essential civil rights relating to legal autonomy or bodily integrity; First Nations did not gain basic political rights until the 1960s; and the promise of universal social rights for citizens needing social welfare programs for their very survival, disproportionate among them single mothers, the disabled, and the chronically unemployed, proved elusive. Access to many social welfare programs was not a right of citizenship but conditional upon state surveillance and myriad disciplinary practices. As important, the ascendance of neoliberalism in the late twentieth century triggered the elimination of many universal social programs and the destabilization of the very idea of collective social provision. All of these factors have diminished the popularity of universal accounts of evolution of citizenship rights.

The challenge of diversity

A second perspective on Canadian citizenship takes as its point of departure the idea that citizenship involves much more than formal membership in a national state and the right of citizens to claim rights. Citizenship, as Bryan Turner explained, is best understood as a "*set of practices* (juridical, political, economic and cultural) which define a person as a competent member of a society and which, as a consequence, shape the flow of resources to persons and social groups" (2; emphasis added). Elaborating on this more expansive understanding of modern citizenship, Jane Jenson developed the idea of a citizenship regime. According to Jenson, a citizenship regime consists of a broad range of institutional arrangements, laws, and state discourses that: first, establish the boundaries of state responsibilities and those of markets, individuals, and communities; second, enunciate and enforce the terms of national membership, identifying those who are entitled to citizenship rights and protections and those who are not; third, legitimize specific forms of political engagement and modes of claims making on the state; and fourth, contribute to prevailing definitions of nation, nation building, national identity, and exemplary citizenship ("Social"). Citizenship regimes embroider formal citizenship status with multiple and shifting narratives about a shared national history, national interests, and national identity. More specifically, these national narratives promote a particular image of national space, an image of the master of this national space in the form of the iconic citizen, and an image of the "ethnic/racial other" within this space (G. Hage 28; Sharma 13).

The recognition and accommodation of ethnic and cultural diversity is a dominant theme that weaves through popular iterations of Canada's national citizenship narrative. Vintage representations of Canadian diversity, such as "two nations (English and French) warring within the blossom of a single state" or as "two solitudes," however, have been supplanted in recent years by more complex diversity imaginaries. Popular social commentator John Ralston Saul, for example, weaves a diversity narrative from what he terms as the "triangular foundations of Canada"—native, francophone, and anglophone. "No matter how much each may deny the others at various times," Saul insists, "each of their existences is dependent on the other two" (*Reflections* 30). Jane Jenson refines this genre of national narrative by arguing that Canada's distinctiveness rests in the fact that it has always been diverse. "Living in an immigrant society, implanted in the territories of indigenous peoples, with a national minority whose presence predates the political hegemony of the English-speaking majority, Canadians have had to struggle to find a political expression of respect for diversity" ("Building" 15).

William Kymlicka, a prominent student of Canadian multiculturalism, similarly argues that "the accommodation of ethnocultural differences has been a constant challenge for Canadian politics and a constant factor underlying the Canadian approach to citizenship" ("Multiculturalism" 47). He dissects the Canadian political community into two internally diverse but sociologically generic categories: first, national minorities, consisting of Indians, Inuit, and French, which meet the sociological definition of "nation" as being complete societies before being involuntarily incorporated into Canada; and, second, the variegated stream of immigrants that settled on the northern half of the continent under both British and Canadian law. For Kymlicka, Canada's story is one of developing strategies, through deliberate state policies, to construct an artificial but, nonetheless, shared sense of national identity among sociologically, ethnically, and culturally diverse populations, which history has "thrown together" in a radical way ("Multiculturalism" 47–51). The "we-ness" in this Canadian project, in other words, emerges out of the ongoing challenge of reconciling competing, contradictory, and sometimes antagonistic national or cultural differences and forging one grand Canadian narrative premised on respect for individual rights and cultural diversity ("Ethnocultural Diversity").

Kymlicka and others working within this ethnocultural accommodation motif have carefully woven a story of Canadian nationhood and identity that, although grounded in historical practice, is very recent in origin. This new variation on the "colony to nation" tale characterizes Canada's earliest citizenship regime as an ill-fated and exclusionary Anglo-conformity model. Having written limited accommodation mechanisms for francophone/Roman Catholic citizens in the British North America Act, the core Anglo-Celtic diaspora both embraced their privileged colonial status as members of a global imperial network and celebrated the ideal citizen as a loyal subject of the British crown.[2] This dominant ethnic group controlled the fledgling settler state and deployed its power to build a new country that reflected its norms, values, and interests (Sharma 53). Aggressive territorial expansion and ambitious infrastructure development were accompanied by an unfolding sequence of legislation designed to contain and control those named and categorized as Aboriginal peoples and exclude others who were deemed incapable of assimilating into the dominant cultural, ethnic, and racial formation. Francophone Canadians were increasingly isolated in the province of Quebec, where for many decades Anglo elites maintained a firm grip on the levers of economic power; immigration policies aggressively sought to increase migration from the United Kingdom and, failing that, Northern (white) Europe; other forms of federal legislation targeted racialized groups for special entry taxes (so-called "head taxes" that were imposed on the Chinese in 1885 and South Asians in 1907), while immigration laws were constantly fine-tuned to effectively bar non-whites from settling in the country; and the 1876 Indian Act reduced once self-governing peoples to the status of wards of the federal state. Most were isolated on reservations and denied basic citizenship rights in the new settler regime unless and until they renounced their indigenous identities and religious, political, and cultural practices (Galabuzi 29, 79–80; M. Smith).

The Anglo-conformity model, according to this recent ethnocultural citizenship narrative, failed to accommodate Canada's foundational national/cultural diversity and was replaced in the second half of the twentieth century with a still unfolding pluralistic and multicultural citizenship project (Kymlicka, "Multiculturalism" 54; "Ethnocultural Diversity"). This new regime was prompted in part by the wave of concern for human rights and national self-determination that washed over the international system in the aftermath of the atrocities of WWII. Exposed as a laggard, if not as an archaic, bastion of "icy white nationalism" (J. [S] Henderson, *Treaty Rights* 415), Canada's new citizenship regime promoted a pan-Canadianism that affirmed the equality of all citizens, regardless of racial or ethnic background or country of origin, as the foundational principle of Canadian citizenship and identity (Brodie, "Elusive Search"; Jenson and Papillon). Canada's first citizenship act was implemented in 1947 and, during the next few decades, the remnants of the Anglo-conformity model were systematically chipped away: an ostensibly colour-blind point system would guide immigration practices; Canada's bicultural and then multicultural essence would be celebrated; the inherent rights of indigenous peoples would be gradually but progressively affirmed; public apologies would be offered for a tarnished history of internal colonialism and state racism directed at, among others, indigenous peoples, South Asian, Chinese, and Japanese Canadians; and new vectors of religious and racial prejudice would be acknowledged as important new challenges to overcome.[3] Canada's national story was thus rewritten as an ongoing and incomplete project of recognition and accommodation of cultural diversity and represented as a model for other diverse national polities.

Admittedly, this ethnocultural perspective on Canadian citizenship generates a more nuanced scholarship than the abridged story that I have outlined above. All too often, however, this version of Canada's national story betrays an unacknowledged monologue about Canadian citizenship and national identity that can only be told from the standpoint of the dominant group's iconic citizen. To put a more provocative point on it, it is a "whitewashed" narrative that veils and contorts as much as it reveals and celebrates. For example, the naming and categorization of indigenous peoples as an Aboriginal sociological nation reproduces a colonialist gaze, obscuring both the violence and dislocations of European colonialism in North America and the ongoing deep disparities between indigenous peoples and post-settler populations. Additionally, the prioritization of, if not singular focus on, cultural diversity to the exclusion of other vectors of social, economic, and political difference both conceals systemic inequalities grounded in historically shifting constructions of race and isolates voices that challenge dominant narratives about the primacy of cultural difference. Remembering to forget the genesis and history of white settler societies; a singular focus on cultural difference to the exclusion of systemic inequalities in power and position; the recent confessional voice and collective apology for past practices of state racism; the celebration of the Canadian project as an ongoing project in the recognition and accommodation of diversity—these are stories that only the dominant group can tell. Each of these "race fictions," as Malinda Smith explains, reinforces a "stubborn complacency" to recognize the imprint and experience of racism in our national narratives, citizenship practices, and public policies (124). The tensions, contradictions, and complexities of Canadian citizenship, in other words, exceed a singular and celebratory ethnocultural monologue about learning to live together.

Triangulating settler narratives

In contrast to the above two perspectives, David Pearson argues that the citizenship narratives of former white settler societies such as Canada, Australia, and New Zealand have been shaped through the interplay of three distinct processes of identity construction: first, the indigenization of settler populations; second, the creation and recreation of ethnicized hierarchies; and third, the invention and reproduction of Aboriginal minorities (991; 1000). The process of indigenization generally takes the form of a colony-to-nation tale told first from the standpoint of Anglo-Celtic settler and then later from the standpoint of differently configured post-settler majorities. A distinctive national narrative and national identity were slow to develop in white-settler states, in large part because, for many decades, Anglo-Celtic settlers identified as part of "a transnational British kin group, sharing the family status of monarchical subjects," and "bound together by ties of race and national origin" (994).

This core group identified itself as "the majority" and as the normative (superior) culture from which all others were measured as deviations. Indigenization occurred, according to Pearson, when native-born post-settler generations gradually distanced themselves from the imperial centre by cultivating a distinctive civic national identity. Grounded in New World sensibilities, these new national narratives gradually replaced the colonial idea of "home there" with the nationalist idea of "home here" (1004–5; 1007).

Settler-state citizenship regimes were interlaced with discourses and public policies that positioned "other" ethnic (non-Anglo) and racial (non-white) groups as being less desirable citizens or, indeed, ineligible for citizenship. Ethnification processes, the naming and ranking of ethnic groups for differential treatment, informed restrictive immigration policies, which served as official filtering devices. For many decades, these and other public policies used "degrees of cultural and/or physical distance from majority group norms as a yardstick for rules of admittance and conditions for membership in settler societies" (Pearson 994). Ethnification creates and reproduces "ethnic others" by combining diverse cultural and often racial backgrounds, which differ from those of the core majority, into supposedly transparent (from the vantage of the dominant group) identities and objects of public policy. This fabrication is then treated as the most meaningful signifier of the person or group. Ethnic categories such as "Asian," for example, were and are produced and reproduced in immigration laws, census data, and political discourses, even though this and other such ethnic categories veil a "wealth of internal economic, cultural and political diversity" (Pearson 1002). Ethnification also weaves through post-settler national narratives, which are based on differently configured majorities and multicultural constructions of nation. Multicultural narratives invariably privilege some members of the new post-settler majority, by virtue of their ethnic origins, as being more "at home" in socio-cultural terms than other segments of the multicultural matrix (Pearson 1007; Bannerji). Indigenization and ethnification processes thus work in tandem: nationalist narratives about being at "home here" also provide a platform for some to tell others to "go home" (Sharma 13).

Pearson's use of the term "indigenization" is unconventional given that, in both Canadian and international settings, indigeneity typically refers to populations and societies that predate European colonization.

Pearson's theoretical framework isolates the moment in the history of white-settler societies when the dominant group names itself as a new nationality and as the sovereign master over the territory that it occupies. I prefer, however, to use the term settler nationalism to describe this moment because the term "indigenization" conjures images of taking root rather than uprooting, and inadvertently authorizes settler narratives about founding peoples. Settler nationalism advanced narratives about "our home and native land" rather than "our home on native land," thereby rendering indigenous peoples invisible, if not homeless (Sharma 9). Pearson argues that indigenous peoples were incorporated into settler states through various processes of aboriginalization, that is, discourses and governing practices that excluded these diverse populations from full political membership (1001). Unlike prospective immigrants, indigenous peoples could not be turned away at the gates of settler and post-settler states: they existed as members of many different non-state political orders long before British colonization (1003). Thus, echoing anti-colonial theorist Franz Fanon, Pearson reminds us that it was the act of colonization itself that brought such categories as "Indian" or "Aboriginal" into existence, and that this political identity has been variously reproduced ever since through different models of governance. Aboriginal minorities were and are constructed through the discursive and legislative contours of coexistence: formed through their colonial relationship with settler majorities who established prevailing conceptions of membership, sovereignty, and authority; and, then, reformed as post-settler states eventually grappling with the challenges of reconciling different social and political orders within the territorial and conceptual boundaries of a single modern state (1001; 1006). A seemingly intractable challenge revolves around the reconciliation of competing indigenous and settler conceptions of citizenship, especially when the latter claims jurisdiction over the former (P. Wood 374). Indigenous ontologies with respect to collective identity and environmental coexistence, for example, do not mesh with dominant liberal constructions of individual rights, self-determination, and private property. As Isabel Altamirano-Jimenez further explains, the capacities of those variously named and governed as Aboriginal to negotiate an inclusive citizenship regime have been limited by the white experience and the "whiteness" of prevailing forms of knowledge, values, privileges, and dominance (126).

Pearson's triangulated framework complicates settler and post-settler citizenship narratives by insisting that the "others" in such societies are not so much recognized and accommodated as produced and reproduced through concrete discursive and governing practices. His work, nonetheless, privileges the cultural rather than racial underpinnings of these practices, attributing a large part of the state's apparent compulsion to name, rank, and exclude various others (non-Anglo immigrants and indigenous peoples) to cultural dissonance and colonialist discourses. These discourses, however, were often cast in explicitly racial, if not racist, terms. Pearson does point out that contemporary multicultural citizen narratives often include racial categories, but they are interpreted as representing ethnocultural difference. For example, the term "visible minority," which groups together into a single racialized (non-white) category both citizens and non-citizens of highly diverse ethnic, cultural, and geographic origins, now stands in for "the 'true ethnics' on a scale of migrantness" (1002; see also Bannerji; Razack, *Race*). An alternative perspective is that the use of ethnicity and culture, both in national narratives and in citizenship studies, although often unacknowledged, stands in for race and racism.

Biopolitics and State Racism

A growing body of literature examines racism, not as the unfortunate consequence of individual prejudice or cultural misunderstanding, but instead as a form of governance that is deeply rooted in the logics, strategies, and institutions of the modern state.[4] Critical race scholars depict the modern state as a racial state that deploys its power to "exclude (and include) in racially ordered terms" through the law, policy-making, and a variety of governing practices such as "categorizations, inverted histories and traditions, and ceremonies and cultural imaginings" (Lentin). David Goldberg, for example, argues that the modern state has functioned as a racial state through naturalism, which defines indigenous peoples as premodern, and historicism, which represents Europeans as the singular bearers of modernity/progress and all others as variously backward or deficient (see also Lentin; McWhorter). Many others pursuing this theme have been attracted to Michel Foucault's 1976–77 Collège de France lectures because of his insights into the integral link between state racism and the rationalities of modern governance (published in English in 2003 under the title *Society Must Be Defended*).

Although not focused specifically on the experience of settler states, Foucault argued that "a biological and centralized racism" emerged in the nineteenth century as an expression of a new form of political power—what he terms as "biopower" (244). He contended that biopower differs from the sovereign and disciplinary powers of the state with respect both to its object of governance and the knowledge and strategies it deploys. Disciplinary power takes aim at man-as-living-being, relying on, among other things, surveillance, training, and punishment to render diverse populations into "useful and docile individual bodies" (242; 249). In contrast, biopower focuses on an entirely different kind of body, the population or man-as-species, "as a political problem, as a problem that is at once scientific and political, as a biological problem and as power's problem" (245). The operation of power through the individual body and on the population is linked and rendered coherent by norms embedded in governmental rationalities and popular discourses.

With the birth of biopower in the nineteenth century, the challenges of government expanded from the exercise of sovereignty and the disciplining of individuals to include the production and reproduction of populations, whether through the monitoring and promotion of fertility or the prevention of illness, epidemics, and other factors that were identified as threats to population health, productivity, and growth (Foucault, *Society* 244). It is at this point, Foucault argued, that state racism was engraved onto the practices of government. States sorted subpopulations into biological continuums of good and bad, ascribing hierarchies of superior and inferior, and sorted groups and behaviours that needed protection and promotion, things that "must live," in contrast to things to "let die," things identified as threats to a vibrant population, as degenerate and abnormal, including those deemed as inferior races (Tanke 695).

As Foucault explained, racism was not invented by the state but, through biopolitics, it took on a particular murderous logic: "If you want to live—the other must die." He continued: "The more inferior species die out, the more abnormal individuals are eliminated, the fewer degenerates there will be in the species as a whole ... the more I—as species rather than individual—can live, the stronger I will be, the more vigorous I will be" (255). Foucault further clarified that the state's role in letting others die does not simply involve "murder as such, but also every form of indirect murder: the fact of exposing someone to death, increasing the risk of death for some people, or, quite simply, political death, expulsion, rejection" (256).

Although Foucault's ideas about the biopolitics of state racism are admittedly provocative, they do provide a different perspective on formative policies of settler societies, a perspective grounded in the practices of state building, that is, in what states do rather than in what people think (Valverde). A biopolitical perspective does not deny the cold realities of colonialist racism but instead suggests that state racism is not reducible to historicized representations of settler culture alone. The next part of this essay explores the ways in which early settler state discourses and practices in Canada inscribed settlers, other immigrants, and indigenous peoples with different biopolitical logics. We will track state citizenship discourses through eighty-two Speeches from the Throne (hereafter Speeches) from Confederation until 1946, when Canada's first citizenship act was introduced, marking the official transition from a settler to a post-settler citizenship regime.[5] These official transcripts, written by the sitting federal government of the day for the opening of a new session of parliament and read by the governor general, are valuable longitudinal records of prevailing discursive constructions of nation, nation building, and citizenship, and are now easily accessed online (see Canada, *Speeches* 1867–2009).

White Settlers and the Biopolitics of Nation Building

Reading these Speeches, one is immediately struck by the absence of inspiring appeals to national purpose and national identity that now embroider these transcripts. At the opening of Canada's first parliament, Governor General Viscount Monck did note that Confederation "laid the foundation of a new Nationality" and was "a fresh starting point for the moral, political and material advancement of the people of Canada" (*Speeches* "1867" 58). With few exceptions, however, these early Speeches are workmanlike documents, intensely focused on the project of nation building through territorial expansion, institutional and infrastructural development, and economic and population growth. The early Speeches also project the imperial voice, not the least because they were read by a succession of governors general recruited from the British aristocracy (Canada's first native-born governor general, Vincent Massey, was not appointed until 1952). The Speeches take the form of imperialist stock-taking, providing a running inventory of successes and failures with respect to harvests, levels of immigration, the loyalty and mood of the people, and the appropriation of indigenous territories. In fact, immigration and relations with what were then termed as "Indian Tribes," especially those located in present-day Western Canada, were overriding preoccupations of Canada's settler state. For Canada's first half-century, almost every Speech assessed the government's progress in attracting larger numbers of the right kind of settler to Canada, while relations with indigenous peoples consumed successive federal governments. Notably absent in this reservoir of official state narratives is any mention of French Canadians or Canada's so-called bicultural foundations: these themes only began to appear in the early 1960s. Although social and economic practices assigned French Canadians a lower status in early ethnicized hierarchies, the Speeches were completely silent on relations between what later would be commonly referred to as Canada's "two founding peoples."

Very much in keeping with Pearson's template, three iconic characters consistently walk across these official transcripts—the inhabitant, the immigrant, and the "Indian." The term "citizen" rarely appears in these transcripts,[6] which is not surprising, considering that Canada did not have a citizenship act until 1946. By law, Canadian nationals were simply British subjects born or residing in Canada. The Speeches thus variously identify iconic subjects as the "the people of Canada," "the Canadian people," or, most often, "the inhabitants," who, unlike "Indians" or "immigrants," were politically empowered by their place and role in the British imperial network. As the 1870 Speech explains, "the inhabitants of the Dominion are well contented with their position and prospects, and that the wish nearest their hearts is to avail themselves of the franchises and full powers of legislation, which they possess, in order to build up as a portion of the British Empire, institutions of their own choice, by laws of their own making" (13). The inhabitant is assigned only a minor role in these official settler-state transcripts when compared to the immigrant and the "Indian." This is perhaps because the Speeches already "speak" for the British subject position and their colonialist imaginary of nation building. But these early Speeches consistently convey a biopolitical construction of ideal inhabitants, casting them as the occupants of public space who are loyal, contented, and hopeful. Inhabitants are described with such terms as "enterprise, contentment and loyalty"

("1875" 13); "well being, contentment and hopefulness" ("1885" 19); "loyalty, cordiality [and] public spirit" ("1894" 15); "abounding loyalty and public spirit" ("1895" 12); "toil and enterprise" ("1891" 9); "loyalty and affection" ("1897" 16); and "full of hope and confidence in the future" ("1906" 10). From a biopolitical perspective, these were precisely the qualities that needed promotion and protection to accomplish state building, territorial expansion, and economic growth. In Foucault's terminology, inhabitants were represented as embodying the behaviours and attitudes that the state had to cultivate or "make live."

The proof of the inhabitants' worthiness, however, resided in their willingness to fight for the British Empire in international arenas. The small contingent of Canadian soldiers who fought for Britain in the Second Boer War (1899–1902), which resulted in the conversion of the South African Boer republics into British colonies, was celebrated in the 1900 Speech as a demonstration of "loyalty and patriotism" and as "a matter of pride and gratifying to the people of the dominion" (17). Similarly, the inclusion of Canadian troops within the ranks of British forces during the First World War was represented in the 1915 Speech as "most abundant and convincing evidence of their firm loyalty to our sovereign and of their profound devotion to the institutions of the British empire" (2). In 1916, the Speech again praised "the self-sacrificing and loyal spirit shown by all the Canadian people who have freely dedicated their manhood and substance to the common defence of the Empire" (12). Canada's war effort demonstrated "the fine spirit of loyalty displayed by the people of this Dominion who have freely dedicated their energies and their material resources to the common defense of our Empire" ("1917" 6). Yet, less-than-ideal subjects also lurked between these celebratory lines, subjects who would be immediately recognized by the audiences of the time. Francophone Canadians strongly resisted Canada's participation in these international episodes in defence of empire. Moreover, during the First World War, immigrants and many naturalized Canadians of Austro-Hungarian descent were prohibited from joining the Canadian forces, categorized through federal legislation as "enemy aliens," and denied basic civil liberties and political rights.

Turning to ethnification processes, immigration concerns, especially in the early years of confederation, were almost entirely focused on the biopolitical project of increasing the population and settling the vast western territories. From Confederation until the late 1920s, the

Speeches consistently monitor this population-building exercise, for example: "I look forward with confidence to the addition of a large and valuable class of settlers to our population during the coming season" ("1870" 13); it is the government's "duty of promoting ... early settlement by the encouragement of immigration" ("1871" 14) and "to make ample provisions for the steadily increasing stream of settlers that may hereafter be annually expected to add to the population, wealth and strength of the Dominion" ("1873" 22); "the prosperity of the Dominion depends on the rapid settlement of the fertile lands" ("1878" 20); "the steady flow of settlers [into Manitoba and the North-West Territories] ... promise well for the early development of those fertile and salubrious regions" ("1883" 27); and "the number of immigrants ... is a proof that the better Canada is known the more it is valued by those seeking a home in the new world" ("1884" 9). In 1905, the Speech noted: "This favoured land ... is attracting people on an ever ascending scale ... As the opportunities for settlement under the advantageous conditions which exist are better known, this Dominion will become the home of an increasing number of happy and contented people, whose character and prosperity will add strength to the great Empire of which you are so important a part" (20). The settler state's vision of the ideal immigrant is consistently expressed in terms of place of origin: most notably, the British Isles, followed by the USA, and to a lesser degree Europe. The Speeches "congratulate ourselves on the number of settlers [coming from] Great Britain and the United States as well as the old provinces of the Dominion" ("1880" 14); and are gratified to "note the increasing proportion from the British Isles" and the "many coming from the British Isles" ("1906" 5; "1907" 16), as well as "the larger measure than usual ... drawn from the British Islands" ("1912" 21). At other times, the Speeches refer to the "character of these new inhabitants of Canada [which] seems to be of the highest and promises no small addition to the wealth of the country" ("January 1901" 18) and to "a copious and well ordered stream [of immigrants] drawn from the best elements of the British Isles, the United States, and Continental Europe" ("November 1909" 13). These examples point to the biopolitics of immigration as a necessary component of nation building and to an ethnic and racial hierarchy that valorizes the "imperial kin" of the British Isles.

This hierarchy among immigrants was more clearly and forcefully articulated after the implementation of the 1910 Immigration Act, which established a series of measures that defined desirable and undesirable classes of immigrants based on, among other things, skills and perceived ability to integrate into Canadian settler life and adapt to the Canadian climate. Thereafter, the Speeches are less concerned with country of origin, although they continue to celebrate the recruitment of British immigrants until the late 1920s, than with official classifications and rankings of desirability. The 1914 Speech, for example, notes the "large stream of desirable immigration … from other countries" ("1914" 5). Later Speeches underline the need to: "attract to our country the most desirable class" ("1922" 23); increase the "flow of desirable settlers" ("1923" 6); attract "the right class of immigrants to Canada" ("1925" 3); welcome "settlers of the classes which can be absorbed into our population"; and maintain "a flow of immigrants commensurate with Canadian requirements and selected strictly for their ability to promote the general prosperity of the country" ("1929" 3).

Immigration legislation effectively ensured that desirable immigrants would be racially and culturally similar to Anglo-Celtic settlers, thus fulfilling the biopolitical imperative of protecting the populations from those things deemed dangerous or abnormal. The 1910 Immigration Act, the 1914 Naturalization Act, the 1921 Canadian Nationals Act, and a variety of legislative amendments and orders-in-council all contained provisions that effectively excluded non-whites as a desirable class of immigrants to Canada (Knowles 31–40). However, these transcripts also provide examples of less passive forms of ethnification and racialization, especially with respect to those divided off from the population and categorized as Chinese, Oriental, or the Asiatic race, a term used in the 1923 Chinese Exclusionary Act. Chinese workers had been explicitly recruited to perform the most dangerous and backbreaking work in the construction of the transcontinental railroad, but immediately after the railroad was completed, these workers, so critical to the nation-building project, were cast as undesirables (Galabuzi 79). The completed railroad was celebrated because it promised "a steady increase of valuable settlers" ("1884" 9) but also raised concerns about "Chinese immigration" and "those social and moral objections which have been taken to the influx of the Chinese people into Canada" ("1885" 19). The ethnification and racism that permeated state discourses in these years is evident in Prime Minister J. A. Macdonald's 1885 comments in the House of Commons regarding the enfranchisement of Chinese Canadians: "The Chinese are not like the Indians, sons of the soil. They come from a foreign country; they have no intent, as a people of making a domicile of any portion of Canada; they come and work or trade, and when they are tired of it they go away, taking with them their profits. They are, besides, natives of a country where representative institutions are unknown, and I think we cannot safely give them the elective franchise" (qtd. in Strong-Boag 88). Such sentiments led to a special head tax placed on Chinese immigrants in 1885 and South Asian immigrants in 1907, in response to "the unexpected influx from Oriental countries into British Columbia [which] aroused a strong feeling of opposition" ("1907" 17). Signalling the slightly higher status of South Asians, resulting from their membership in the British Empire, this group's head tax was set at $200, compared to a levy of $500 on Chinese immigrants. An outright prohibition of Chinese immigration was implemented in 1923 and remained in effect until 1947 (Galabuzi 79; Knowles 31–40).

The treatment of indigenous peoples in the Speeches also clearly reveals the subtle and not so subtle ways in which state racism was written into the settlers' biopolitical project of nation building. As discussed above, Pearson and others have argued that the process of becoming an "Aboriginal" or "Indian" is an outcome of European imperialism and an identity that has been periodically renegotiated through various governmental models of coexistence. And, indeed, across Canadian history, this diverse population has been variously named in the Speeches as "Indian Tribes" (1860s and '70s), "Indians" (1880s to 1950s), "Indians and Eskimos" (1960s), "Natives" (1970s), and "First Nations," "Aboriginal peoples," "Aboriginal communities," and "Aboriginal Canadians" (1980s to present). The following focuses on the shift in indigenous-settler relations that accompanied the interpolative shift in the Speeches from "Indian tribes" to "Indians."

In Canada's first decades, the federal government was preoccupied with territorial expansion to the "North-West Territories" (present-day Saskatchewan, Alberta, and parts of Manitoba) and with placing this vast expanse of land under the sovereign control of the Crown. The 1869 Speech announced that a deal had been struck with the Hudson's Bay Company to relinquish its control over parts of this territory, while federal officials launched with western "Indian" tribes a protracted process of treaty making that resulted in the appropriation of much of their land, and their capacities for self-governance. In these early years, indigenous peoples were referenced in the Speeches either by their specific identity or as "Indian Tribes," terms which convey a sense of their autonomy as self-governing peoples. For example, in 1875, a year before the implementation of the Indian Act, the Speech described "the negotiation of a friendly treaty with the Crees and Sauteux *of the North-West* for the cession of territory," a treaty that, it added, may be regarded "as a further guarantee for the continuation of amicable relations with the Indian tribes of that vast region" (13). Two years later, the federal government announced "further Treaty arrangements with certain of the Indian tribes of the North-West Territories, by which their title is extinguished to a very large portion of the territories west of Treaty No. 4" ("1877" 18). Again, in 1878, the Speech announced another "Treaty with the Blackfeet, Blood and Piegan Indians, by which *the Indian is extinguished* over a territory of 51,000 square miles," adding in a satisfied way that "the entire territory west of Lake Superior to the Rocky Mountains ... has now been acquired by peaceful negotiation with the native tribes, who place implicit faith in the honour and justice of the British Crown" (20; emphasis added).

It is clear from these transcripts that the goal of the early settler state was to extinguish Indians on the land, depriving them of their traditional livelihood, culture, and autonomy. At the same time, the Speeches reflected a certain satisfaction with the manner in which the Canadian settler state had executed these acts of displacement. The 1877 Speech, for example, noted "the deplorable war waged between the Indian Tribes in the United State territories, and the Government of that country," and then reasoned that "the expenditure incurred by the Indian Treaties is undoubtedly large, but the Canadian policy is, nevertheless, the cheapest, ultimately, if we compare the results of those with other countries; and it is above all a humane, just, and Christian policy" (18). Later, the 1882 Speech expressed "confidence in the continuance of the kindness and justice which has hitherto governed the relations between the Government and the Aborigines" ("1882" 18). But the Speeches also betray the coercion and force that underwrote these representations of colonial appropriation through Christian gentility: the role of the Royal Northwest Mounted Police, which was founded in 1873 to police the territories, was praised in several Speeches. One noted that "the influx of a white population has greatly increased the danger of collision between the settler and the Red man ... [and] renders an augmentation of the

Mounted Police a matter of urgency" ("1882" 19).[7] At another point, a Speech indicated that the topic of Indian affairs "would be incomplete without an allusion to the valuable services of the North-west Mounted Police" ("1896" 10).

Beyond the treaty-making process, it was the implementation of the Indian Act in 1876 that grounded the indigenous-settler relationship, progressively redefining Aboriginal subjects from members of autonomous communities with the capacities of inter-governmental (inter-national) negotiation to infantilized wards of the state. This infamous colonialist legislation was introduced in the House of Commons as "Acts relating to the enfranchisement of Indians and the management of Indian affairs" ("1876" 16). This reference to enfranchisement related to section C-18 of the act, which enabled "Indians" to acquire full legal status as British subjects by "relinquishing their ties to Aboriginal culture, traditions, and any Aboriginal or treaty rights" (J. Henderson, "Treaty Citizenship" 434, note 18; Canada, *Aboriginal Peoples* 255–332). Only 249 Aboriginal people took up this overtly assimilationist provision between 1876 and 1920; only one indigenous person responded to a similar citizenship-swap deal between 1857 and 1876 (Kymlicka, "Multiculturalism" 52). According to the provisions of the Indian Act, those declining the invitation to become British subjects were defined by law as non-persons and thereby ineligible to make claims to the status and rights of legal personhood. Section 12 of the Indian Act read: "The term 'person' means an individual other than an Indian, unless the context clearly requires another construction." This indirect murder through political exclusion was revised in 1886 and again in 1927 to say: "The expression 'person' means any individual other than an Indian." Exemplars of the biopolitics of state racism, these various legal constructions of Aboriginal peoples as non-persons, as less than and inferior to settlers and immigrants, remained as provisions of the Indian Act until 1951 (Henderson, "Treaty Citizenship" 435, note 16).

The extinguishment of Aboriginal title and of personhood are two biopolitical mechanisms of letting some groups die (indigenous peoples) in order to make others live (settlers and selected immigrants). This process of letting the indigenous way of life die can be quite clearly traced through the Speeches describing the condition of western indigenous peoples after they were sequestered on federal reserves and cut off from traditional sources of subsistence. The February 1880 Speech lamented "the entire failure of the usual food supply of the Indians of the

North-West" and "a large expenditure … necessarily incurred to save them from starvation. It is hoped that the efforts now being made … to induce them to betake themselves to the cultivation of the soil, may prevent the necessity of similar calls for relief in the future" (15). Later in the same year, the Speech repeats that "no effort will be spared to induce the whole of the aboriginal population to betake themselves to agricultural pursuits" ("December 1880" 14). After again noting the ongoing problem of food supply (starvation) for the Indians and the likelihood that their food supply would need to be supplemented for some years, the 1882 Speech further explained that

> Every exertion has been made to settle the Indian Bands on Reserves, and to induce them to betake themselves to the raising of cattle and cultivating the soil. These efforts have met with a fair success, but we can only expect by a long continuance of patient firmness to induce *these children of the Prairie and the Forest* to abandon their nomadic habits, become self-supporting, and ultimately add to the industrial wealth of the country. (19; emphasis added)

Later, residential schools were commended as a promising mechanism for integrating indigenous children into the dominant norms and expectations of settler citizenship. Touring some "Indian Industrial Schools" at the end of the nineteenth century, the governor general noted that he "received hearty demonstrations of loyalty and good-will" and "proofs of proficiency and intelligence on the part of the children" ("1896" 10).

The processes of aboriginalization, as these passages demonstrate, involve the configuration and reconfiguration of indigenous peoples in the early years of the Canadian settler state as a single population that was qualitatively different from the immigrant and incompatible with, if not a threat to, the settler project. At first inscribed with the self-governing capacities to make treaties with the colonist state, indigenous peoples were removed from their land and livelihood, rendered non-persons in law, infantilized through public policy as wards of the state, and impounded on reservations (a governing technology that was later imported by apartheid South Africa). These governing practices may have been situated in or justified by imperial culture or Anglo-conformist values, but they also exceed cultural explanations for these practices of settler states. These practices were emblematic of a state racism that subdivided populations and marked some off as threats to the biopolitical project of nation building and thus as populations that the state could let die directly or indirectly through "political death, expulsion, rejection" (Foucault 256). Indigenous peoples possessed the land upon which the very project of a settler society was premised; they refused the settler state's invitation to citizenship that had been extended to immigrants from other countries, albeit with varying degrees of enthusiasm and inclusion; and they failed to embrace the industry, loyalty, and contentment of the iconic settler. These were biopolitical threats. The settler state astutely pursued policies to optimize or "make live" loyal and contented settler populations but also established a regime to "let die" indigenous communities through appropriation, isolation, and control.

Conclusion

This preliminary investigation of the interplay between settler nationalism, ethnification, and aboriginalization begs a more extensive treatment of the ways in which these three vectors of differentiated citizenship have been written into Canada's post-settler narratives about nationhood and citizenship. Such an analysis would reveal how processes of ethnification continue to name new minorities such as "visible" minorities, new majorities who are tolerant of their internal diversity, and new formulations of aboriginality. We need only turn to the most recent Speeches to understand that these vectors of differential citizenship have survived the settler era as an integral part of Canada's national story. For example, in the 2006 Speech, newly appointed Governor General Michaëlle Jean celebrated our iconic threesome as "the new generation of Aboriginal entrepreneurs who are creating new opportunities"; our "two great linguistic communities"; and "families newly arrived in Canada who seek to contribute to our society and our country's collective wellbeing" (1). In 2007, the Speech outlined the latest contours of who we are: "And although Canada is a young country, its history is marked by our unwavering willingness ... to be and to continue to be a generous society. A society that is concerned about the well being of others. A society that is protective of the spirit of this bountiful land, a deep respect learned from Aboriginal peoples. A society that is committed to finding solutions to today's challenges. A society that is open to creation and quick to innovate" (2). Of course, all countries engage in a continuing process of imaging and reimagining themselves. As Benedict Anderson is often quoted, national "communities are to be distinguished, not by their falsity/genuineness, but by the style in which they are imagined" (6). Some imaginaries, however, are more of a chimera than others. One of my goals in writing this essay was to demonstrate the ways in which racialized hierarchies were embedded in the formative narratives and practices of Canada's settler state. My second motive has been to destabilize contemporary national narratives (often advanced by the ethnocultural perspective discussed above) that represent the Canadian experience as a celebratory and ongoing tale of learning to live with cultural diversity. This national narrative, I have argued, is a relatively recent construction that veils past as well as current state discourses and practices that differently configure, rank, and racialize three recurring characters in the citizenship regimes of settler and post-settler societies: the iconic national citizen, the Aboriginal, and the immigrant.

Drawing on Foucault's work, moreover, this essay demonstrates the links between the biopolitical project of nation building and racialized constructions of good and bad citizens, the healthy and productive in contrast to the suspicious and threatening. Over the course of Canadian history, these initial formulations have been contested by Québécois and indigenous nationalism, and new waves of global migration. Older state-configured racial categorizations and hierarchies also have receded in the face of different biopolitical conceptions of population vitality and productivity, and the identification of new threats to the biopolitical life of national populations. In the contemporary era, biopolitical logics are bound up with citizenship discourses and public policies that have slowed refugee claimants to a trickle; erected new barriers to economic immigrants, especially those from the South; placed new restrictions on alleged citizens-of-convenience; named Aboriginals as populations "at risk"; and questioned the capacity of selected religious and racial groups to integrate into the national social fabric. These practices remind us that, in contrast to dominant narratives about the recognition and accommodation of diversity, Canadian citizenship politics continues to be shaped by the biopolitical imperatives of categorization, racialization, and selective exclusion.

"Some Great Crisis":
Vimy as Originary Violence

Robert Zacharias

Immediately following Confederation in 1867, members of a nationalist movement named "Canada First" pronounced that the Canadian nation was yet to be founded. The British North America Act, they suggested, was nothing but a legal construct that had created an empty shell of a state, while a true nation required a crisis to be born. David P. Gagan notes that the Canada First movement has been "criticized for its pre-occupation with the visionary, rather than the practical aspects of Canada's 'new nationality'" (36), but it is precisely their concern with the vision of violence as being necessary to forge a national Canadian ideal—albeit through what Gagan calls "relatively hollow rumblings of aggressive intent" (38)—that the Canada Firsters established what would become a common concern for Canadian nationalists. In 1869, for example, Canada Firster Robert Halliburton complained that Canada had "crawl[ed] into existence in … a humdrum, common place, matter of fact way," and suggested that in order to become a great nation, it would have to be "purified" by "fiery ordeals" (qtd. in Gagan 37). In "The Duty of Canadians to Canada" (1871), George Denison similarly insisted that nationalist sentiments would arrive in Canada only with a "violent struggle for political existence" (qtd. in Gagan 39). The Canada First movement would dissolve rather quickly, but their anticipation of a crisis sufficient to found the nation would not.

By 1881 the call for crisis was ubiquitous enough that the Canadian poet K. Seymour MacLean could wrestle with it as an open question. In an essay entitled "Education and National Sentiment," MacLean acknowledges that patriotism is to be found "lying dormant and unsuspected until called forth by some great national peril or emergency." In questioning what I call the "crisis thesis," MacLean provides a colourful account of its rhetoric: "Is it true that patriotism is a plant which will flourish only on the soil of battlegrounds, whose root must be nourished by the blood and tears of the brave, and whose fair white flower unfolds only in the lurid air of cannon smoke, fanned by the breath of dying heroes?" (191). By 1892 Wilfred Campbell could declare in his widely read "At the Mermaid Inn" column in *The Globe and Mail* that, due to the many disparate regions and cliques of Canada, it *"goes without saying* that we will never have a true national spirit until ... at a grave national crisis the patriotic spirit will conquer them all" (emphasis added).

Given the investment in nationalism that accompanies the establisment of national literatures, it is of little surprise to find early Canadian literary critics awaiting a crisis as well. In 1890, for example, L. O'Loane looked longingly at the difficulties of Russia, suggesting writers like Tolstoy could not be found in Canada because "they could not learn war here, they could not be fired by the daily, hourly, human agonies ... that a Russian sees" (84–85), concluding that, in order to produce a national literature, "Canada must be born again" (85). Archibald Lampman's well-known 1891 essay, "Two Canadian Poets," argued that the formation of a distinctly national literature demanded "the passion and enthusiasm of an entire people [to be] carried away by the excitement of some great crisis"; he, too, noted sadly that "we have yet to reach such an hour" (38). Four years before the outbreak of the First World War, L.M. Montgomery wrote in a similar vein: the nation "has not yet fused her varying elements into a harmonious whole," she claimed, adding that it is unlikely to do so "until they are welded together by some great crisis of storm and stress." Only then, she continued, might a "real national literature ... be born" (qtd. in Vance 226). Finally, in 1944, E.K. Brown expressed the crisis thesis in terms that resonated with both political and literary nationalists, writing that it would require "a national crisis of supreme intensity [to] call forth emotions of such a strength and purity as to issue in a significant expression in the arts" (17). Blithely ignoring the country's involvement in the First World War as well as its mounting losses in the Second, Brown referenced Lampman's much earlier essay on Canada's lack of a founding moment and complained that "we are probably as far, or almost as far from such a crisis in 1944 as in 1891" (17).

My point here is not to offer anything approximating a survey, nor to reroute all of Canadian criticism through this particular preoccupation, but to demonstrate the prevalence of the crisis thesis in early Canadian critical writing. The concern with a lack of a violent crisis at the birth of the Canadian nation has remained such a central thread in the debates over the nature of Canadian identity that it has become something of a critical cliché. In his 1998 study *Worrying the Nation,* for example, Jonathan Kertzer names it the "familiar puzzle about the elusive Canadian character," sarcastically reciting it as follows: "Unlike the United States, Canada casts no heroic shadows because our bland, practical citizens lack the historical traumas and the responsive imagination to expose the dreams on which the nation was built" (37). To consider what is at stake in the crisis thesis as an enduring trope in Canadian literary criticism, I turn to the battle of Vimy Ridge, long and loudly celebrated as the "birthplace" of the Canadian nation.

The Search for an Originary Crisis

There are at least two related stories about the relationship between the nation and violence operative in recent Canadian literary criticism, each of which implicitly hinges on an acceptance of the crisis thesis. The first, which we might call the "myth of the empty origin," imagines the history of Canada as a blank slate. Some critics have celebrated the nation's lack of a violent historical origin as enabling an openness to plurality and multiplicity. Others, as we have seen, have responded to the country's apparent lack of history by anticipating a crisis on which it would be possible to found a distinct nation. The second, which we might call the "myth of national amnesia," offers something of an explanation for the empty-origin myth. Insisting that Canada's history is, in fact, littered by violent events, it holds these events have been systematically ignored, forgotten, or intentionally effaced. If Canadians believe they have no history, according to this second story, the reason is that the nation's move toward unity has demanded a forgetting of the divisive violence of its past. By understanding the blank state of Canadian history as constituting a fundamental lack, the first story assumes that an originary moment of violent crisis is natural or necessary to nations— an assumption the second story implicitly affirms by insisting that such moments can be found in Canadian history if only we know how and where to look.

The myth of the empty origin, as I noted above, was commonplace in early discussions regarding Canadian nationalism. It was enshrined in Canadian literary criticism, however, through Northrop Frye's massively influential "Conclusion" to *Literary History of Canada*. The paragraph that ends with the oft-quoted claim that "Canadian sensibility ... is less perplexed by the question 'Who am I?' than by some such riddle as 'Where is here?'" (222) begins with an equally remarkable (if much less discussed) passage. Frye argues that the "organic rhythm" of a nation demands a foundational period upon which it can build its cultural history, and announces that Canada has "never had it":

> Cultural history, we said, has its own rhythms. It is possible that one of these rhythms is very like an organic rhythm: that there must be a period, of a certain magnitude, as Aristotle would say, in which a social imagination can take root and establish a tradition. American literature had this period ... between the Revolution and the Civil War. Canada has never had it. English Canada was first a part of the wilderness, then a part of North America and the British Empire, then a part of the world. But it has gone through these revolutions too quickly for a tradition of writing to be founded on any one of them. (221)

If we should wonder what it is that the nation is lacking, or what it takes to "found" a national tradition, we should note that, for Frye, this vital period seems violent by definition: not only does he offer two bloody American wars as examples of what bookended the period but, when looking for a turn of phrase to describe the "organic rhythms" of a nation, he turns to a famous definition not of nations but of Greek tragedy. The phrase "of a certain magnitude" comes out of the sixth section of the *Poetics*, in which Aristotle defines tragedy as "an imitation of an action that is complete, and whole, and of a certain magnitude," all of which is aligned to inspire "pity and fear" (38). A definition of the "tradition" or "cultural history" of the Canadian nation that comes via Greek tragedy may seem surprising, but it is, in fact, fully in keeping with the crisis thesis. At the very least, Frye's turn to tragedy demonstrates the gravity he associates with this period in the rhythm of the nation's past, and ought to give us reason to pause and consider its implications.

It is also interesting to note the particular version of Canada Frye constructs in this passage. Not only does his slippage between "Canada" and "English Canada" implicitly naturalize their conflation—that is, there may be other, competing nations within Canada, and this period of "magnitude" might help cement "Canada" as coequal to "English Canada"—but his self-confessed "foreshortening of Canadian history" (221–22) goes further, skipping the status of nation altogether. If "English Canada" lacks the type of traumatic historical moments necessary to found a nation, it only makes sense that he should read its history as leaping from "wilderness" to "North America and the British Empire" to "a part of the world." This, then, is the immediate context for Frye's famous question for Canada: an argument that the "cultural history" of the country lacks a period of sufficient "magnitude" that the "organic rhythms" of all nations require in order to found a singular "tradition of writing." "Where is here?" suddenly looks less like an expression of a garrison mentality than as a lament for Canada's lack of history.

Although his "Conclusion" is likely the most prominent of locations for the myth of the empty origin, Frye, as we have seen, was working in a well-established tradition, one that continues to operate in more recent criticism.[1] For all its pervasiveness and longevity, however, the myth seems to beg a number of questions. In what sense can a crisis be said to "found" a nation, and how does that originary crisis function in later national discourse? And if such a foundation is actually necessary, what about all the rather obvious crises that can be found in Canada's past? The most common answer of contemporary Canadian critics (especially those informed by postcolonial theory) has been to bypass the first two questions in order to answer the last one by countering that the myth of the empty origin is the result of a whitewashing of history. Canada's colonial history, it is argued, has a host of violent events—including several major events that could presumably serve as originary crises—but these have been effaced over time by the dominant, homogenizing national narrative that would have us imagine its history as a peaceful, teleological development that has naturalized and justified its present condition. The question of *how* a crisis founds the nation is set aside, and the idea that Canada lacks such a history is attacked.

The argument that the nation insists we forget the past, which I am calling the basis of the myth of national amnesia, is often traced back to Ernest Renan's 1882 lecture "What is a Nation?"[2] Renan points to the Germanic invasions of the Roman Empire between the fifth and tenth centuries as the emergence of the modern nation-state, suggesting that the defining feature of those emergent nations was "the fusing of component populations" that followed these invasions, a fusing in which language, religious, and cultural (but not class) differences were collapsed in the name of a single community bounded by territorial boundaries. The most remarkable feature of these attacks, he felt, was how quickly the defeated populations forgot the brutality of the invasions that precipitated their new political formations and how willingly they adopted the new nation as their primary, or even sole, structure of identification. Notwithstanding his earlier claim that these Germanic invasions became the "mold of the nation ... *in spite* of the extreme violence" (144; emphasis added), a key element to Renan's argument is his insistence that nations solidify their claims over a population by means of a systematic effacement of their inherently violent origins—a process that is itself a kind of violence. "To forget and ... to get one's history wrong ... are essential factors in the making of a nation," he writes, from which he concludes that "the advance of historical studies is often a danger to nationality" because "historical research ... casts fresh light upon those deeds of violence which have marked the origin of all political formations, even those of which have been followed by the most beneficial results. Unity is always realized by brute force" (145). Renan's passage is remarkable because if the idea of the inherent violence of the *state* is not unusual,[3] the nation has more often been considered violent in its effects than its origins. Scholars like Benedict Anderson have since defined the nation as an imaginary construct, and those building on Homi Bhabha have recognized this imagination can be violently homogenizing, but Renan's much earlier formulation is significant for its suggestion that nations are *necessarily* violent not only in their consequences but also in their inception.

The ethical turn in contemporary Canadian criticism[4] has largely followed Renan's suggestion that "progress in historical studies often constitutes a danger for [the principle of] nationality" (145), systematically uncovering acts of violence that lie beneath the nation's rhetoric of its own benevolence. Daniel Coleman's recent study, *White Civility*, is exemplary of such an approach. Coleman argues that English Canada has been "obsessed" with constructing, and maintaining, an image of itself as a "civil" nation, congratulating itself on its enlightened policies while systematically effacing histories that would contradict this self-portrait. Citing Renan in a consideration of another of the country's most cherished myths, Coleman argues that "a whole range of injustices ... must be repeatedly forgotten if White Canadians wish to sit comfortably with their claim to multicultural civility," and suggests that "a major antidote to nationalism's determined disavowal, therefore, comes in a refusal to forget the history of genocide and cultural decimation of Indigenous peoples in Canada" (8). Cataloguing a series of historical brutalities that have been repressed by the nation, Coleman points out that "many Canadian anti-racist scholars have recently worked to re-educate themselves and broader Canadian society" (8–9). Although certainly not exhaustive, it is a list worth recounting here in full:

> Mainstream Canadians have been reminded about the extermination of the Aboriginal Beothuks in Newfoundland, the deportation of the French-speaking Acadians of Nova Scotia, the discrimination practiced against Black Loyalists and their descendants from 1784 onwards, the head tax upon and eventual exclusion of Chinese immigrants after 1923, the internments of eastern Europeans during the First World War and of Japanese Canadians during the Second World War, the refusal of entry of Jews fleeing Nazi Europe, and the ongoing criminalization of Indigenous and Black Canadians. (9)

I quote Coleman at length because his gesture here is paradigmatic of recent cultural criticism inflected by the ethical turn. Critics informed by postcolonial, queer, feminist, and Marxist approaches have undertaken the task of returning to the forgotten annals of the nation's past to bring to light the injustices that underpin the historical rise of Canada, much of which has been effaced by the celebratory rhetoric of the national narrative.

As necessary as this critical work continues to be, however, it has rarely sought to address the function of past violence as an originary moment. In fact, the historical acts of violence that are being uncovered in such criticism are more commonly positioned as acts that *challenge*, rather than *found*, the nation. It is important to uncover the national acts of violence that we have been asked to forget, but my focus here is on an opposing demand of the nation: if the national narrative operates by effacing the violence of its past, how are we to understand the Battle of Vimy Ridge, unabashedly celebrated as Canada's triumphant founding moment?

Vimy as "Opportunity"

Well before Vimy would become the focal point of Canada's growing sense of national consciousness, it was recognized that the country's entry into the First World War might serve as the long-sought crisis upon which the nation could be founded. As early as 1915, Prime Minister Robert Borden spoke publicly of "an awakened national spirit" occasioned by the war, and author Lintern Sibley christened the war "a new birth-song for Canada" (Vance 227; 228). In a widely published 1916 open letter to Henri Bourassa, Talbot Papineau argued that Canada's losses in the war were necessary to "acquire that Soul or create that Pride without which a nation is a dead thing and doomed to speedy decay and disappearance." Referring to the war in terms that resonate with the anticipation of an originary crisis—he calls it Canada's "moment of travail and tribulation" and "the birth pains of her national life" (18)—Papineau argued that the Canadians' sacrifice would "cement a foundation for a true Canadian nation" (23). As the war continued in 1918, W.D. Lighthall called Canada's military successes the country's "new starting point" (xlvi), writing that "the war is a greater, wider, nobler event for us than Confederation" (lxi), and feverishly announcing "this is our Homeric Age ... the story is too grand to be forgotten" (lxii). The unabashedly pro-Canadian war reports of Sir Max Aitken, published around the globe, struck a similar tone, declaring that the gas at Ypres had "baptized the Dominion into nationhood" (qtd. in Buitenhuis 98). When L.M Montgomery wrote in her journal that the war had answered her earlier search for "some great crisis of storm and stress" to fuse the nation (qtd. in Vance 226), she was apparently expressing the views of many.

As the war came to an end, the effort to commemorate Canada's involvement began. Memorials, newspaper articles, and poetry poured forth celebrating the Canadian accomplishments and, occasionally, lamenting the country's losses. In the notable absence of immediate academic or official publications on Canada's wartime involvement, the largely sentimental and patriotic interpretation of the war portrayed in the "cult of remembrance" that emerged in the postwar years quickly became the standard public version of the war (Williams, *Media* 24).[5] The belief that the First World War effort marked a coming-of-age for Canada began during the war itself, then, and it continues to be "the standard method of judging the impact of 1914–18" (Vance 10).

No single battle holds more weight in this "cult of remembrance" than the Battle of Vimy Ridge. Indeed, the belief that Canada came of age at Vimy began in the immediate aftermath of the battle itself and continued unchallenged until only recently.[6] As Ted Barris recounts in his study *Victory at Vimy: Canada Comes of Age*, newspapers both inside and outside of Canada immediately presented the victory as a distinctly Canadian achievement. *The New York Times* wrote (prophetically, as it turns out) that the day would "be in Canada's history one of the great days, a day of glory to furnish inspiration to her sons for generations," for example, while the *New York Tribune* declared that in the victory the soldiers had won "the opportunity to write the name of Canada on the war map of Europe" (qtd. in Barris 214). The French press, meanwhile, referred to the victory as "Canada's Easter gift" to their nation (qtd. in Barris 212). Although the international praise died quickly—Pierre Berton notes that "after the first burst of publicity, the impact of the battle was blunted everywhere but in Canada" (244)—in Canada the legend of Vimy was just beginning. Desmond Morton and J.L. Granatstein are the most clear in positioning Vimy as the answer to the empty-origin myth, writing that the war itself "forced Canadians to look into the abyss in their own confederation," and declaring that "for Canada … the Great War was a war of independence" (1). Other prominent authors writing in the same vein include D.J. Goodspeed, who insists that "[n]o matter what the constitutional historians may say, it was on Easter Monday, April 9, 1917, and not on any other date, that Canada became a nation" (93). It is a message that has become firmly a part of the national narrative through repetition. In a passage that supports Anderson's argument that printed texts enable a people to "think the nation" (25), Berton catalogues a collection of sources that have posited and affirmed Vimy as Canada's originary moment: "For seventy years it has been said so often—in Parliament, at hundreds of Vimy dinners and in thousands of Remembrance Day addresses, in newspaper editorials, school texts, magazines articles, and more than a score of books about Vimy and Canada's role in the Great War—that it is almost an article of faith" (244). Indeed, Canadians have been told, time and again that, while Confederation created the state, Vimy created the nation. But what does this mean?

Crisis as Foundation

While it is true that wherever a nation corresponds to a political state it derives much of its authority from the state structure, I want to propose that Vimy's much discussed status as the origin of the nation suggests that the nation receives at least some measure of its authority from its own violent inception. If Anderson's reading of Renan has become the standard means of understanding the function of nationalism for Canadian literary critics, it is no surprise that the focus has been on what is being forgotten rather than remembered. Given the prevalence of the myth of Vimy as a source of the violent birth of Canadian nationalism, however, it is clear the horrors of history do not always need to be downplayed or sanitized to legitimize a nation. To the contrary, one could argue war serves as the origin of a nation precisely *because* of its extreme violence. In this context, to call for a violent period of "a certain magnitude," or a "grave national crisis" of "supreme intensity," is not merely to call for a break from the past or to bind a community in shared sacrifice but also to look for a moment of violence sufficient to ground and legitimize the subsequent authority wielded by the nation in order to maintain the unity that Renan recognized is "always realized by brute force" (145). That is, a violent origin is necessary because its invocation is what grants the nation the authority and cultural force to inspire devotion, to demand loyalty, and, yes, to efface the acts of violence that have followed its inception.

What I am proposing here is essentially an adaptation of the argument presented by Walter Benjamin's 1921 essay "Critique of Violence," which suggests that a state receives its enormous power and influence over its citizens not by effacing the brutality of its past, nor by any shared agreement to a social contract, but rather by repeatedly appealing to the act of founding violence that established its sovereignty. Just as Renan drew attention to "those deeds of violence which have marked the origin of all political formations" (145), Benjamin argues that at the origin of every state there is a moment of great instability, prior to the establishment of the law, that is paradoxically both created and managed by a singular act of violence—what he calls the state's "founding violence."

Benjamin sees this moment of uncertainty, when the authority of the state's law-to-come is suspended to allow for its own constitution, as a deep internal contradiction that the state must continually govern or manage by resorting, time and again, to acts of "preserving violence"; all subsequent appeals to the authority of the state, he suggests, are nothing but appeals to, or invocations of, this originary act of violence. Renan suggests that the nation encourages us to forget this moment of violence, and Anderson extends Renan's argument to suggest that we are called to "remember/forget" this violence as disputes within a single community and think of it as "reassuring fratricide" that bonds the community through a history of shared sacrifice (201). Benjamin, however, suggests the state's originary violence is remembered for another reason altogether: to serve as a threat that can silence those who might consider opposing the national narrative, and to re-enforce state control. The violence at the origin must be remembered, he suggests, because it comes to constitute the spectre of force by which the state draws its remarkable authority.

Although Benajmin's essay is concerned primarily with the formation of the state and its control of the physical apparatus of force—the military, police force, and so on—we know that the nation, too, has its form of force.[7] I take Jacques Derrida's reading (in "Force of Law" 1989) of Benjamin's essay as an opportunity to extend its logic to the construction and function of authority within a nation. Derrida suggests the violence Benjamin locates at the origin of the state is "always" there, "even when there have not been those spectacular genocides, expulsions or deportations that so often accompany the foundation of states" (269)—helping to explain the half-century between the relatively bloodless moment of Confederation in 1867 and the violence of Vimy Ridge as the start of the nation, in 1917. What is more, Derrida insists that this violence is "present, sometimes invisible but always effective, wherever there is preservation of the social order" (278)—and the nation, at least as it is commonly understood by critics drawing on Anderson, is nothing if not a primary means of "preserv[ing] the social order."

Derrida's extension of Benjamin's argument helps to explain how those calling for crisis expect that an act of violence might help to establish a nation in a way that Confederation could not.[8] In 1875, for example, Charles Mair—another of the "Canada Firsters"—wrote that every nation requires "a national idea, or sentiment, which has for its internal condition *unity*, and for its external aspect *force*," adding that "wise nations instinctively utilize this force" to ensure their unity (153). Although Mair goes on to suggest that "nature" might serve as Canada's idea, Benjamin's essay suggests that the "force" behind the national idea may well be a "force" in a quite literal sense of the word. As Derrida writes elsewhere, the "originary violence" of the nation is both "constitutive and still vaguely active" in other forms ("Interpretations" 185); as acts of "preserving violence" that are not necessarily literally or physically violent, they nonetheless rely upon, and so repeat, the authorizing violence of the originary, nation-building act. In the logic that proposes the common refrains that Vimy constitutes a "nation-building event," every invocation of the national as a naturalized form of structuring society—from the national anthem to a tank with a maple leaf emblazoned on its side to the institution of Canadian literature—can be understood to be drawing on the authority gained by the violence of Vimy.

Monument and Memory: Vimy "in Story and in Sacrifice"

There are, of course, a host of much more obvious reasons why the Battle of Vimy Ridge has been connected to the birth of Canada. The battle was a significant and tangible Ally victory that offered much-needed positive news in an otherwise bleak period (Christie 1), and it represented a uniquely Canadian victory: the Canadian Corps that managed to take the ridge was fighting together for the first time, both literally and symbolically uniting men from across the country. The French and British armies' repeated attempts to take the ridge had ended in costly failure; in accomplishing a feat that its two "founding nations" could not, the Canadian victory at Vimy represented as much a victory over its colonial past as it did over the Germans. What is more, Prime Minister Borden was able to use Canada's military record in the war to demand a position for the country in the League of Nations, beginning a political movement that culminated in the 1932 Statute of Westminster granting Canada control of its own foreign policy. As the most prominent battle in the country's Great War efforts, it is, at least in this sense, fair to trace something of Canada's sovereignty as a nation-state to Vimy Ridge.

Recently, however, the understanding of Vimy as a nation-building event for Canada has been under substantial academic reconsideration. As Jeff Keshen points out, the fact that Canada entered the war as a colony that was "intent upon demonstrating [its] worthiness within the Empire predetermined that monumental significance would be placed upon [its] battlefield encounters" (220). While it is true that the Canadian Corps were fighting together for the first time at Vimy, it is less commonly remembered that not only were they fighting under the British command of Lord Byng, the key staff officers were also British regulars—as were the vast majority of soldiers in the "Canadian" Corps. And yet, as Gary Sheffield writes, "the British elements of the force that fought in the battle have been airbrushed out of popular memory" (27). Moreover, while the battle was clearly a military success, the victory was short lived, as the day's successes were largely mitigated by the failures of the larger battles of the subsequent days. Michael Valpy points out that "Canadians, and only Canadians, call it the Battle of Vimy Ridge ... In everyone else's historical lexicon, it was a limited tactical victory in the First World War's horrendous Battle of Arras, which the British and their allies lost" ("Making" F4). In fact, as the editors of *Vimy Ridge: A Canadian Reassessment* point out, not only did the Germans enjoy some success in the larger Battle of Arras, it "should not be surprising" to find that "many post-war German unit histories also proclaimed a victory, or at least a draw, at Vimy" (Hayes, Iarocci, and Bechthold, 3). Finally, inasmuch as the losses at Vimy helped convince Prime Minister Borden to renege on his election promises and institute conscription—a decision that sparked massive protests in Quebec and the beginning of what some have called "the most divisive political debate in Canadian history" (316)—at least one critic contends that the Great War ought to be considered as "the unmaking of Canada as much as the making" (Fulford qtd. in Keshen 3).

The relationship between myth and military history is always tight, of course, but it is worth noting how the use of Vimy as a national origin story has enabled its complete reimagining. Although it was made in the midst of the war—and a full year before the battle of Vimy Ridge—Papineau's call for public support of the war effort best demonstrates the logic that dismisses historical detail in the name of burgeoning nationalism. Calling Canada's involvement in the war "the great opportunity for the true Nationalist" (18), he insists: "Canada was at war! Canada was attacked! What mattered then internal dissentions and questions of home importance? What mattered the way and wherefore of the war?" (19). The dismissal of the "way and wherefore of the war" in the name of nationalism would become vitally necessary in Canada, because without it the country's sacrifices in the war lacked compelling ethical justification. The idea that the assassination of an Austrian archduke in Sarajevo results in the death or wounding of well over 200,000 Canadians seems to demand an alternate explanation, lest Vimy become, as it has for a few, nothing but "a bloody mess in a pointless war" (Korski 13). To this end, it is rare to come across a celebration of Vimy that even attempts to point to a moral cause for the battle or to locate it in the war's larger political or military contexts. The focus is always on the abstract result—*the birth of the nation!*—because both the cause behind the larger war and the tactical victory of Vimy are so unpersuasive. The detachment of Vimy from its ethical, political, and historical contexts reveals its reification in the national narrative as an act of founding violence.

Nothing demonstrates the process by which the Battle of Vimy Ridge took on such symbolic importance in Canada's national memory as clearly as the government's official commemoration of the war effort. In 1920, a competition sponsored by the newly formed Canadian Battlefield Memorials Commission (CBMC) proposed that there be eight separate monuments to mark the most significant battlefields in which the Canadians participated, with one identified as a national monument. The proposals poured in, with Walter Allward's design completely dwarfing all other entries in both ambition and scale. Allward envisioned two soaring stone pillars, representing Canada and France, atop a massive stone base adorned with symbolic figures. In a decision that at once reflected and established Vimy as the centrepiece of Canada's war efforts, the CBMC selected Allward's monument as the country's national memorial and decided to locate the monument on the ridge at Vimy, where it would be visible from kilometres around.[9] As opposition leader Arthur Meighen explained as he gave his consent to the monument's construction, Vimy is "beyond comparison" for Canadians because of "all that the war involved in story and in sacrifice" (qtd. in Hucker 285). Its final cost of $1.5 million was a staggering amount during the lean years of the 1930s, but the sacrifice had been made, and no expense would be spared in the construction of the story. Unveiled sixteen years after the competition was announced, the monument consists of well over six thousand tonnes of stone quarried and transported from present-day Croatia, rising well over eighty metres above the field. "To mark this briefest of all battles," as Berton writes, "the Canadian government commissioned the most massive of all monuments" (302). The enormity of Allward's monument, so disproportionate to the military significance of the battle it commemorates, indicates both the mythological importance the battle held for the war generation and the government's determination that it would retain its mythic power for generations to come.

Allward's remarkable monument is notable not only for its size but also for the unique way in which it presents the country's war effort less as a glorious victory than as a national tragedy. For if Allward's monument represents the foundation of the Canadian nation—or if it is, as Valpy suggests, "the manifestation of our national psyche" ("Setting")—it is not the celebration of victory one might expect. Instead, it is a foundation of violence and sorrow, both in terms of the "sacrifice and story" of the war. Not only is its entire base a symbolic tomb on which stand the names of the 11,285 Canadian soldiers who died in France but whose bodies were never found, its allegorical figures also stress the pain and loss of the war. The largest figure on the monument, entitled "the Spirit of Canada," portrays Canada neither in symbolic birth nor in triumph but as a young woman weeping over the loss of her sons (Fig. 1). "Vimy is

FIGURE 1. "Spirit of Canada," the Vimy Monument. Photograph by Michiel Hendryckx, Wikimedia Commons.

not a victory monument," states Jacqueline Hucker. "There are no signs of victory there at all" (qtd. in "Vimy, 90"). According to Hucker, there were few precedents, nationally or internationally, for a war monument that focused less on the glories of military victory than its cost (280). In being crowned "the very essence of the emerging Canadian nation" (Durflinger 291), the Vimy monument locates the birth of the country in an act of devastating violence and heartbreaking loss. With large sections of the land surrounding the National Monument still off limits due to unexploded artillery from the two wars, the violence is more than simply remembered by the monument.

A short paragraph in a 1990 pamphlet entitled "The Canadian National Vimy Memorial," published by Canada's Department of Veterans Affairs, demonstrates both the country's questionable historical understanding of Vimy and how it is used to position it as a mythical origin. The pamphlet provides a brief history of the battle that implies the Allied victory was somehow assured by the Canadian victory at Vimy, and then offers the standard version of Vimy as origin myth, presented as historical fact: "The victory at Vimy Ridge was a turning point for the Allied forces in the First World War. One and a half years later, the Germans were defeated and the war was over. Back home in Canada, the victory at Vimy Ridge united Canadians and established their country as a proud young nation."[10] Reading official publications in light of the recent reappraisal of the standard interpretation of the Battle of Vimy Ridge, and alongside the battle's manifestly disproportionate commemoration, it is difficult to avoid Christie's conclusion that "the capture of Vimy Ridge in 1917 was as much a propaganda victory as a military one" (1).

Vimy as "Magic Elixir"

Through a combination of military success, patriotic news reports, poetic melodrama, and outright embellishments, then, Vimy became the focal point of Canada's contributions to the Allied victory in the First World War. Hailed as the birth of the nation, it bound Canadians together in their sense of pride and shared sacrifice—and, when those failed to unite people, Vimy quickly became the force that silenced dissenting voices. Using the force of the war abroad as a threat to ensure a particular politics at home began almost as soon as the soldiers left for Europe. In 1916, for example, the soldier Papineau threatened Bourassa over the latter's refusal to encourage Québécois participation in the war: "Beware lest we return with revengeful feelings, for I say to you that for those who, while we fought and suffered here, remained in safety and comfort in Canada and failed to give us encouragement and support," he wrote, "we shall demand a heavy day of reckoning" (22).[11] Once the war was over, this threat, manifested as the "memory of the war," was used to stifle dissent in the service of constructing the homogeneous nation. "Those people who believed that the war had almost single-handedly fashioned a national consciousness saw in the war tremendous potential as a constructive force in the life of the country," writes Vance. "It was at once an object lesson, a source of inspiration, and a focus for unity; it was the magic elixir that could cure the country of any ill … [including] the subversive elements that menaced postwar society" (229). Recalling Renan's prescription that "unity is always realized by brute force" (145) and Mair's call for "wise nations" to "utilize th[e] force" of the national idea to secure its unity (153), Vance's study shows how the memory of the war was often "mobilized for the national good"—that is, used as a threat to anyone who dared stand up against the dominant understanding of the nation.[12] Like the threat implicit in the currently popular "support stickers" that read "If you don't stand behind our troops … feel free to stand in front of them," the memory of the war was simultaneously used to garner support for the soldiers and to mobilize their spectre as a threat.

It was during the Second World War, however, that the propaganda surrounding Vimy was at its height. When the Germans recaptured Northern France in the early stages of World War Two, the fate of the monument became a means to garner support for the Canadian war effort. Serge Durflinger's essay, "Safeguarding Sanctity: Canada and the Vimy Memorial during the Second World War," recounts how the Canadian media's reporting of a German bombardment of the monument "stimulated war consciousness and instilled visceral anger towards the enemy" (291). The monument was never damaged at any point during the war, yet on 1 June 1940—only six years after Allward's memorial was unveiled—the Montreal *Daily Star* ran stories under the headlines "Famous Memorial Blasted by Huns" and "Vimy Memorial Smashed by Nazi Bombers." The paper went on to announce that "New heights in [the Germans'] deliberate fiendishness have been reached in Flanders Fields," reporting that "German fliers smashed [the] beautiful remembrance to bits," and that the "obviously deliberate" bombing "tore dead Canadians from their graves" (293–94). Two days later, *The Globe and Mail* quoted Allward himself as saying "the Huns have gone quite mad. This is a sad commentary on civilization" (294), and the *Daily Star* hyperbolically announced that "one of the greatest memorial works of art ever produced by man, a thing of such majestic beauty and significance that it belonged to no single nation but to the whole world, has been senselessly destroyed." Declaring that Germany's actions revealed their complete lack of "human dignity and decency," and had proven "with sickening certainty that the Hun is always the Hun," the editorial concluded, unsurprisingly, that "[s]uch fiends are surely unfit to live" (294). According to Alex Walker, Dominion president of the Legion during the war, "[n]othing since the outbreak of the war ha[d] so helped to crystallize Canada's determination to fight to the finish" (qtd. in Durflinger 295). Indeed, the destruction of the Vimy memorial became such a story that Adolf Hitler himself had his portrait taken with the undamaged monument to disprove the published accounts. A photo of Hitler inspecting the monument on 2 June 1940 was released with the accompanying caption that read, in part: "This picture is documentary proof that shows the impertinent lying of English propaganda" (295). Canada's monument to the First World War had become an ideological weapon in the Second.

In April 2007, the celebrations occasioned by the ninetieth anniversary of the Battle of Vimy Ridge served as a reminder that the memory of Vimy as a moment of authorizing violence continues to be operative in Canada's national narrative. The anniversary was marked by the rededication of the restored Vimy Memorial, attended by some ten thousand participants, including the French prime minister, the British queen, and Canadian Prime Minister Stephen Harper. The celebrations, which garnered front-page status in Canada's national newspapers and were carried live on Canadian television and radio, seemed choreographed to reinscribe the position of Vimy as the birthplace of Canada. "Every nation has a creation story to tell," Prime Minister Harper declared, and "the First World War and the Battle of Vimy Ridge are central to the story of our country" ("Prime"). "The Canadians here today are a long way from home," he continued. "But there may be no place on Earth that makes us feel more Canadian, because we sense all around us the presence of our ancestors." Although obviously rhetorical, the gesture affirms a mythological understanding of Vimy—which is, after all, how the prime minister framed his comment. Tellingly, *The Globe and Mail* emphasized Harper's gesture by dropping his caveat that Canadians at Vimy were actually far from home, quoting him simply as presenting Vimy as being more Canadian than Canada (Saunders). In fact, the suggestion that Vimy is the site of an essential Canadianness was echoed throughout *The Globe*'s coverage, including by Michael Valpy, who described the monument as "a proclamation to the world of Canada's unhyphenated identity" ("Setting"). Julian Smith, the former Chief Architect for the National Historic Sites at Parks Canada, who led the recent Vimy Memorial restoration, agrees. "I love the layering of identities in Canada. I think that's what makes us Canadian," he said. "But Vimy exists outside that. It exists in a kind of pure form as being a Canadian monument" (qtd. in "Setting"). Postcolonial critics would recognize what is at stake in such claims: here, the myth of national amnesia shifts the aim of nationalism from unity to purity, naturalizing an idealized, abstract Canada that is packed with assumptions about the oppressive "hyphens" or "layering of identities," all the more powerful for its passing as "pure."

Vimy has long been a trope for politicians. Mackenzie King, for example, appealed to Vimy in the debate over "Maritime Rights" in 1926 (Vance 233), and Lester Pearson invoked the unity of Vimy in his call for Canada to become a peacekeeping nation (Stewart). Showing how thoroughly Vimy has shed its connection with sparking the divisive conscription crisis, Brian Mulroney invoked it in his efforts to promote national unity in the wake of the failed Meech Lake Accord (Stewart). It was to be expected, then, that the ninetieth-anniversary celebrations would be used to garner support for the nation's most recent military adventure, with speakers repeatedly tying Vimy to Canada's controversial war in Afghanistan. The day before the anniversary, for example, Harper compared Kandahar to Flanders Fields (Freeman and Saunders A1), while Mr. de Villepin used his speech at the monument's rededication to "pay solemn tribute to all Canadians that fell on French soil. I also have in my thoughts, the six soldiers that fell in the line of duty yesterday in Afghanistan" (qtd. in Freeman and Saunders A5). The Queen, meanwhile, literally rededicated the Vimy memorial to the Afghan mission in her speech, declaring: "To [the soldiers at Vimy Ridge's] eternal remembrance, to those who have so recently lost their lives in Afghanistan, to Canada, and to all who would serve the cause of freedom, I rededicate this magnificently restored memorial" (qtd. in Freeman and Saunders

A5). Connecting Kandahar to Vimy effaces a world of significant differences, and it shows how the cultural force of Vimy-as-origin continues to be wielded in an effort to garner support for, and silence dissent over, the military's present engagements.

Conclusion: Oh, *That* Origin

Vimy Ridge ought to give Canadian critics reason to pause, for it clearly contradicts two of the most common myths of the nation that continue to cycle through Canadian critical discourse. An act of violence widely hailed as the birth of the nation, the narrative of Vimy runs counter to the myth of the empty origin; the unending demand that we remember it nearly a century later runs counter to the myth of national amnesia. What this means is that even as we uncover acts of violence effaced as part of the nation's celebratory self-image, we should remain conscious that the nation as a category—within which Canadian literature as an institution continues to function—is enabled through an "originary violence" that is, as Derrida writes, both "constitutive and still vaguely active" ("Interpretations" 185).

Critics have long recognized Canada's Great War literature as wrestling with the question of the birth of the nation—Lighthall started this tradition in his 1918 "Canadian Poets of the Great War"—but understanding the way that the crisis thesis continues to underpin much of Canadian literary critical discourse demands a wider engagement with Vimy as origin. When Joseph Boyden's *Three Day Road* places Cree sharpshooters as fighters at Vimy Ridge, or Jane Urquhart's *The Stone Carvers* inserts a same-sex love story into the construction of the Vimy Ridge Monument, we ought to recognize that, in returning to Vimy, these authors are returning to the mythological birthplace of Canada to insert difference—Aboriginal, queer—into the very heart of the national narrative. Even when Canada is invoked in passing as a signifier of the Edenic, as in Rohinton Mistry's *Family Matters*, or when that Edenic signifier is ironically played upon, as in Rawi Hage's *De Niro's Game*, we should recognize that the originary crisis continues to animate the national signifier. More than this, however, we should recognize that inasmuch as a given novel circulates as part of Canadian literature, it is *of* the nation even when it is not *about* it. And there is no invocation of the nation that is not at the same time an invocation of its originary violence.

Amplifying Threat: Reasonable Accommodations and Quebec's Bouchard-Taylor Commission Hearings (2007)

Monika Kin Gagnon and Yasmin Jiwani

In January 2007, the small town of Hérouxville, near Quebec City, gained international attention and, from some quarters, acclaim, for issuing resolutions concerning prospective immigrants. These resolutions specifically banned the stoning of women, the covering of women's faces through veiling, and a host of other such prohibitions, all in the name of maintaining the province's "civilized" culture. Quebec Premier Jean Charest's response to the resulting brouhaha was to strike a blue-ribbon Study Commission to criss-cross the province and address the question of "reasonable accommodation" through a series of town hall events and a consultative process that took place in the fall of 2007. Headed by philosopher Charles Taylor and historian and sociologist Gérard Bouchard, the Bouchard-Taylor Commission itself unleashed an unforeseen maelstrom of racist opinion, repressed anxieties, and resentments, as well as a deep-seated malaise that pierced the delicate veneer of tolerance that characterizes everyday life and social practices in Quebec. L'Affaire Hérouxville, as it has come to be called, and the ensuing Bouchard-Taylor Commission, offered yet more baffling examples of the complexity of the Quebec race/culture equation, with its particular versioning of colonial histories, its linguistic divides, and oppressive religious legacies. Much attention has been brought to the legal concept of "reasonable accommodation" and how it has become the central structuring notion in the Bouchard-Taylor Commission and their final report.[1] On 27 October 2009, eighteen months after the Bouchard-Taylor Commission Report was deposited, Montreal's *La Presse* published their survey results on "accommodements raisonnables," with headlines that affirmed, "Les Québécois disent non: 18 mois après le dépôt du rapport Bouchard-Taylor, la question demeure sensible. Et les balises restent floues" (Quebecers say no: 18 months after the deposit of the Bouchard-Taylor report, the question remains sensitive. And the markers remain unclear), citing of 76–90 percent of Quebecers who were saying no to various questions relating to reasonable accommodations. The significance of the central concept of reasonable accommodation to the commission, these debates, and their related analyses have also precipitated an abstracting function that overlooks the broader effect of the commission on people of colour and for Quebec's Native communities, and disavows its contribution to normalizing racist attitudes in the public at large, implicit, for example, in former Bloc Québécois candidate, May Chiu's observation that the commission was "faites par des Blancs pour des Blancs" (made by Whites, for Whites) (Lévesque). This essay begins with an account of l'Affaire Hérouxville, which is the backdrop to the Bouchard-Taylor Commission, then proceeds to examine the texture of the ambient environment during the Bouchard-Taylor Commission province-wide consultations from 10 September to 13 December 2007, highlighting this ambiance and general public atmosphere through some newspaper representations from this consultation period. We are therefore less concerned here with the commission's outcomes and conclusions, outlined in detail in their final report, than with understanding the dynamics of racialization and racism that occurred during this specific time frame. Our analysis suggests that, during the period of the commission hearings, the media initially amplified the discord and disgruntlement that were apparently extant in the population at large. As Bouchard and Taylor were themselves quoted as stating: "Nous avons perdus nos repères: Gérard Bouchard et Charles Taylor sentent clairement qu'il y a un malaise au Québec à l'égard des immigrants" (We have lost our bearings: Gérard Bouchard and Charles Taylor clearly sense a malaise with regards to immigrants in Quebec) (Péloquin). The media amplified this perception in three ways: by not immediately challenging and critiquing the debate's frames of reference that informed the appointment of the commission; by conflating democracy with populism; and, finally, by confusing cultural and religious symbols and affiliations. We conclude with a more substantial examination of the role of racialized gender in the formation of these debates and, more particularly, the representations of women wearing the *hijab* and *niqab* and their congealing of anxieties about difference and the perceived Other in Quebec culture. In this, we hope to dismantle and challenge, in a preliminary way, some of the discursive logics of racialization that have come to the forefront of contemporary Quebec society in the last few years.

L'Affaire Hérouxville

On 25 January 2007, the small municipality of Hérouxville, located 160 kilometres northeast of Montreal and with a population of 1338 residents, adopted a resolution regarding "les normes de vie" (living norms) at its municipal meeting. The document designed for the "immigrants éventuels" (eventual immigrants) was sent to six Quebec ministries, amongst them Relations Internationales, Immigration, and Famille, Ainés et Condition Féminine, as well as federal Foreign Affairs Minister Peter MacKay and Secretary of State Helena Guergis. The resolution outlined modes of behaviour that were deemed "acceptable" for new immigrants by the municipal council, and seemed to express the councillors' strange fantasies and outdated stereotypes of Muslim culture. By early February, this "Code of Conduct" for prospective immigrants had attracted wide international and local media attention. This attention was initially dismissed within Quebec as a media fabrication that exaggerated and sensationalized the issue, even by journalists, as *Gazette* columnist Jeffrey Heinrich characterized in his article "Media stir up storm over 'accommodation'" (February 2007), as if the declaration did not speak for itself. "No Stoning: Don't stone women to death, burn them or circumcise them, immigrants wishing to live in the town of Hérouxville in Quebec, Canada, have been told," announced the headlines for *BBC News* on 29 January, while the *New Zealand Herald* declared, "You can stay in Canada as long as you don't stone your women" (1 February 2007). In contrast, the French newspaper *Libération* brought some critical perspective and referred to a "croisade xenophobe" (xenophobic crusade) (Dolbec). At the same time in Canada, national and local papers tended toward reporting decontextualized testimonies without offering any critique and without addressing the particularities of location. Town councillor André Drouin announced that the declaration was not racist: "Bien sûr, nous avons voulu choquer en parlant de lapidation ou d'excision, mais il était temps que quelqu'un mette ses culottes et regard plus loin que le bout de son nez. Si on s'adapte à tous les nouveaux immigrants, qu'adviendra-t-il de notre culture québécoise dans 10 ou 20 ans?" (Certainly, we wanted to shock people in speaking of stoning and female circumcision, but it was time we "put on our pants" and saw beyond the end of our noses. If we adapt to all new immigrants, what will become of our Quebec culture in ten or twenty years?) (Dolbec).

Based in part on a peculiar survey undertaken in the region of Mékinac in mid-December 2006, in which 196 residents responded to nineteen questions (ranging from "Would you define yourself as a racist person?" and "Can a woman walk alone in a public place?" to "Do you think we should reserve a space for prayer in schools?"), the declarative resolutions of the Hérouxville resolution, when combined with the gendered expression uttered by Drouin—"mettre ses culottes," or "putting on one's pants"—in order to take a strong (read manly) stance, reveal the interlocking discourses of racism, paternalism, and sexism that were deeply embedded in these events. The city of Hérouxville's website offered downloads of most of the documents pertaining to the resolution, as well as its coat of arms; a recent issue of the magazine *Les immigrants de la capitale* (the voice of immigrants in Quebec); a letter from Grandmère Chayer entitled *Je me souviens,* reflecting on the tyranny of the Roman Catholic Church, particularly regarding gender equality; and a letter to Premier Jean Charest requesting amendments to the Quebec Charter of Human Rights and Freedoms regarding "reasonable accommodations" (see Municipalité Hérouxville).

In the post-9/11 era, the Islamophobia that is at work in the Hérouxville document is unmistakable in its condemnation of particular cultural practices (such as stoning of women or the covering of the face with a veil) that were not being practised by any citizens of this small town. (Islamaphobia is understood here in its most basic definition to be an unreasonable fear and prejudice against Islam and Muslims.) As Jasmin Zine argues in her analysis of the various flashpoints concerning Muslim minorities in Canada, the Herouxville "Citizen's Code"

> is an invisible line that maps the terrain between the familiar and the strange, insiders and outsiders, belonging and otherness. Not only are

the boundaries invisible, but the objects of the Code's negative attention are never explicitly named. Dangerous foreigners remain encrypted in the subtext—a haunting otherness lurking in the shadows of the town's imaginary and taking the form of a veiled Muslim woman. (147)

Six surrounding municipalities in the Mékinac region responded to the controversy by declaring their solidarity with Hérouxville, as other regions scrambled to distinguish themselves (in often equally racist, if slightly different, terms). Premier Jean Charest continued to tout racist expressions as "isolated" and aberrant positions. In these particular characterizations, a polarization and distancing takes place between *les regions*, or the rural municipalities, and the cosmopolitan, multicultural urban centres of Montreal, Quebec City, and Gatineau. In doing so, the official stance was to downplay and dismiss such racist behaviour and expressions as marks of an uneducated, homogenous, and rural population, a racism therefore rooted in ignorance. This marginalized the need to responsibly address and analyze the violence of such gestures and the hostile social climate that was created as a consequence. Premier Charest continued to reiterate that Quebec was a tolerant province, that it in fact needed its immigrant citizens to thrive economically, and followed suit with the formation of the Bouchard-Taylor Study Commission to investigate "reasonable accommodation," with a mandate to deliver recommendations by March 2008.

In responding to the term "reasonable accommodation" as the organizing principle of the Commission, we argue that Hérouxville's Islamophobia was sanctioned and reified as an actual problem facing Quebec's national identity. That the figure of the "veiled Muslim woman" signifies the site of contestation raised by this declaration is a point we will address as key to this series of events. (This has most recently culminated in the introduction of Bill 94 in March 2010, a bill that would restrict women wearing the *niqab* from accessing government services in Quebec, and which followed the introduction of legislation in spring 2010 to ban the *niqab* in other European countries.)

Montreal-based human rights and immigration lawyer Pearl Eliadis summarized the peculiarity of "reasonable accommodation" as a term for debate on CBC Radio's 25 February 2007 *Cross Country Checkup* on the subject of "How do you avoid cultural conflicts in a multicultural society?" Referring to section 15.1 of the Canadian Charter of Human

Rights, wherein "Every individual is equal before and under the law and has the right to the equal protection and equal benefit of the law without discrimination and, in particular, without discrimination based on race, national or ethnic origin, colour, religion, sex, age or mental or physical disability," she stated that Canadian human rights law had morphed from pure legal rule to a social discourse in Quebec.

> I think the debate in Quebec has become a strange social phenomenon of what is actually a very well-known legal concept in Canada. The concept of "reasonable accommodation" has existed in every single province, including Quebec, for decades. What it means is that if there is someone who runs up against an established rule, and they are trying to exercise their religion or get into a building because they have a disability, that the person on the other side of that request is obliged, under Canadian human rights laws, to respond to that reasonably. What has happened in Quebec is that has appeared, [sic] like a social virus, and jumped from a pure legal rule to a social discourse about expressing preferences. The general comment I want to make is that we live in a liberal society where we need to start with, "You get to do what you want to do, you get to live the way you want to live, you get to express the preferences that you want to express, without needing permission first." That is what our culture and society is built on. The strange thing that has happened in Quebec—and I'm thinking of the Hérouxville example, which is a small municipality which has done a code of conduct in rural Quebec—is that this has now become a debate about how you are going to live, and almost needing permission if you are going to engage in a kind of conduct that is different from the majority.

Speaking in early 2007, as the Hérouxville controversy was at its zenith, Eliadis highlighted the peculiar use of "reasonable accommodation" within the Quebec context and how its usually legal function had taken on an aggressive, socially prescriptive dimension. With the ensuing unconventional usage of this term over the last few years, there has been a normalization of this prescriptive dimension that has stretched the boundaries of permissible behaviour on issues of racialization and racism.

As the first wave of l'Affaire Hérouxville persisted into 2007, independent groups undertook damage control on behalf of their own communities. The Muslim Council of Montreal issued conciliatory press releases

(2007)[2] while, in February 2007, nine women from the Canadian Islamic Congress bravely visited Hérouxville for a two-hour meeting with town residents to dispel myths of the Islamic faith and to confirm and affirm their equal status as Quebecers. Within this social climate, racialized religious minorities were put in the position of educating particular publics about their cultures and religious practices and, further, compelled to prove their allegiance to the Quebec nation. As Gada Mahrouse observed once the Bouchard-Taylor Commission commenced:

> Once the hearings began, it became evident that participants from minority communities were expected to play a very particular role. Against the backdrop of Quebecers lamenting the loss of the mythical days when Quebec identity was untainted by the threat of "cultural differences," members of immigrant communities were expected to soothe such fears by defensively justifying their presence, and asserting their civility. This was made clear in an editorial in *The* (Montreal) *Gazette* (8 September 2007) that called the commission "a good-faith effort" and called upon minority groups to "defuse the angst" of the majority. (20)

Mahrouse's point highlights a notion of a "golden past" uncontaminated by cultural differences, and reaffirms the perception of a culturally homogenous nation state. This framing is a boundary marker that, as Zine underlines, defines those who belong to this nation and those who must legitimate and earn their presence within it.

Mediations: Framing, Vox Populi, Legitimizing Hate

We will examine early coverage of l'Affaire Hérouxville in Quebec's five major newspapers, Montreal's *La Presse*, *Le Devoir*, *The Gazette*, *Le Journal de Montréal*, and *Le Soleil*, in order to understand the discursive strategies that the media utilized in identifying, framing, and constructing racialized "Others." Our analysis below draws from Stuart Hall's seminal work on the media, as well as Teun van Dijk's research on press coverage of racism (*Racism*; *Elite*). In his analysis of the media's treatment of moral panics, Hall describes what he calls the "amplification spiral," whereby exaggerated coverage of a problem can have the effect of worsening it, in the following way: "If the official culture or society at large comes to believe that a phenomenon is threatening, and growing, it can be led to panic about it. This often precipitates the call for tough measures of control. This increased control creates a situation of confrontation, where more people than were originally involved in the deviant behaviour are drawn into it" ("Treatment" 26). Thus, when racialized "Others" are regarded as threats and given sustained media coverage that consistently links them to social problems, such representations of them can generate moral panics that call forth, within the public, support for a law and order agenda. Since the dominant media constitute a public sphere (Habermas), the constructions that are nurtured and circulated in media discourses, as well as the privileged frameworks of interpretation, provide a lens through which we can apprehend the national imaginary at work, as well as the racial dynamics that are involved.

In l'Affaire Hérouxville, as we elaborate below, this media amplification rested on a number of key issues: the mechanisms and rituals of press reporting, the conflation of democracy with populism, and the ensuing flattening of the field upon which the commission took place, so that both racist and antiracist statements were construed as being "equal" in a rhetorical sense. The legitimation of hate speech occurred in ways that permitted it to come across as a credible and authentic response on the part of a population besieged by the (presumed) onslaught of difference. Throughout these events, the figure of the veiled Muslim woman remained a dominant motif threading the mediated discourses concerning racialized "Others." The continued prevalence of the veiled Muslim woman in contemporary coverage is suggestive of its semiotic weight as a sign coalescing national anxieties, as we demonstrate in the remainder of this essay.

The Quebec media's representation of immigrants as a threat to the nation of Quebec has been no less intense and pejorative than representations of people of colour in the English language media in the rest of the country, as has been more extensively researched by Canadian scholars.[3] That being said, there was an intensity with which the Quebec media focused on the commission's hearings. In part, this was due to the provincial nature of the event being covered, combined as it was with the fact that the dominant media tend to report on the actions of government and other elites. As well, the concentrated ownership of the media within Quebec also influenced the heavy coverage of the events leading up to the commission and the hearings that followed.

The mainstream print media in Quebec is largely monopolistic for, despite a number of newspapers that reach a wide population in terms of circulation figures, the press is controlled by a small number of owners. Quebec's two big media chains are Quebecor Media (which publishes, among others, the *Journal de Montréal*, Canoe.com, and the television station TVA), and Gesca (which publishes, among others, *La Presse* and Quebec City's *Le Soleil*). Each of the five papers examined in our analysis aims to address a specific target population. While three of these French papers tend to be populist, the fourth—*Le Devoir*—is the only independently published paper within this landscape and caters to a more affluent and educated class of readers. As the mainstream English language paper in Quebec owned by Canwest Corporation, our fifth newspaper, *The Gazette*, serves a distinctive audience and thus occupies a similarly distinctive ideological position.[4] *The Gazette* also reflects the anglophone position, continually striving to show how tolerant the English are as compared to the francophone community.[5]

In the early coverage of the commission's hearings examined in these papers, the media broadly conflated democracy with populism and strictly remained within the frames defined by the commission itself. It is clear that throughout the commission's hearings the newspaper coverage we examined (from 10 September 2007 to 13 December 2007) took on different inflections in response to different political events. Midway through the commission's hearings in the autumn, the controversy became embroiled in a provincial election; thus the coverage became notably more heightened and contradictory when the Parti Québécois introduced Identity Bill 195 on 18 October and later, when Premier Charest responded with an "Open Letter to Quebecers" on 30 October. This open letter was an attempt to contain the Parti Québécois strategy to foment a rudimentary nationalism centred on its separatist platform. These two events can be seen as further exacerbating the high-pitched racism that set the ambient tone in the province's press coverage during the entirety of the commission's hearings.

Parti Québécois (PQ) leader Pauline Marois presented the inflammatory Bill 195, which proposed guidelines for Quebec "citizenship" for new immigrants based on fluency in French, galvanizing a particular nationalism at this already volatile moment, and projecting a future in which Quebec "becomes" a nation actually able to legislate citizenship. In response, Premier Charest restated the Bouchard-Taylor Commission's mandate in his "Open Letter" on October 30, in the starkest terms: "Quebec is a nation. By its history, its language, its culture, its territory, its institutions. The Quebec nation has values: the equality of women and men, the primacy of French, the separation of state and religion. These values are fundamental. They come with Quebec. They cannot be subject to reasonable accommodations." In claiming the province as a nation, and primarily French, Charest effectively erases the history of French colonialism, suggesting that the province was *terra nullius*, that is, devoid of Aboriginal inhabitants, and coming into existence only through its inhabitation by the French.[6] Underlying his text, in stating the equality of women and the separation of state and church, is the historical fact that women in Quebec were the last to receive the right to vote in Canada in 1949, and an allusion to the *révolution tranquille* of the 1950s and '60s that saw the controversial secularization of the province. However, more than that, Charest's articulation of the principles mandating the commission makes apparent the binaries underpinning their construction of "Others." Whereas the Quebec nation is considered to be egalitarian, the culture of its minority communities is, by comparison, seen to be unequal and patriarchal. Similarly, while Quebec now enjoys the separation of religion from the state and, hence, secularism, or *laïcité*, the "Others" bring with them cultures that fuse the two. Such binaries introduce a dualistic structure of relations that suggests that only Quebec national culture is civilized. Implicitly, the "Others" remain uncivilized. This "clash of civilizations" is thereby a familiar organizing paradigm within the very term of "reasonable accommodation" and the ensuing rhetoric that was repeated throughout the commission and its aftermath.[7]

The coverage of l'Affaire Hérouxville and the Bouchard-Taylor Commission focused on the participation of citizenry in the consultation process. One news story reported from the commission's stop in Trois-Rivières "Commission Bouchard-Taylor Islamistes et journalistes vertement critiques" (Bouchard-Taylor Commission: Islamists and journalists sharply criticized), suggesting that even from within the commission there was the perception that testimonies were uncritically portrayed in reporting:

> Parmi la trentaine d'interventions, beaucoup prenaient directement à partie les islamistes et leur résistance à s'intégrer dans une société d'accueil. Plusieurs personnes ont raconté des anecdotes relativement à leur travail, à des voyages à l'étranger ou à de simples conversations

avec des femmes voilées, tendant à prouver que l'islam est une religion où le prosélytisme est plus courant que l'intégration. (Plante) (Among the thirty presentations to the commission, many commentaries were about Islamists and their resistance to integrating into a host society. Several people told anecdotes regarding their workplaces, their travels abroad, or their conversations with women wearing the veil, which they considered to be ostensible evidence that Islam is a religion in which proselytism is more likely than integration.)

From the first seven weeks of reporting on the Bouchard-Taylor Commission until late October 2007, the coverage in the five papers was dominated by the perspectives of particular citizen testimonies, mostly expressing negative opinions about immigrants and immigrant cultures, religious affiliations, and practices. In privileging a *vox populi* perspective—the individual voice of the man or woman making *their* two-minute presentation to the commission, which largely characterized the initial style of coverage—the media conflated democratic processes with populist sentiments. This is evident in numerous headlines from this initial period. *The Gazette* reported that there was "Much ado about what people wear; Longueuil residents sound off. 'We shouldn't concede anything to fanatics like that—not one thing,' man says of Sikhs" (Heinrich, "Much"). And again, the testimony that "'Here, it works like this'; ... Newcomers must conform, mayor insists" (Dougherty). Further, *La Presse* summarized other accounts that "Ils craignent les demandes d'accommodements: Des employeurs évitent les musulmans" (They fear the demands of accommodation: Employers avoid Muslims) (Perrault).

Only rarely was there any in-depth coverage of briefs presented by organizations, and when organizations were featured—as for example with the coverage concerning the Quebec Council on the Status of Women's statements in October—the focus was predominantly on negative viewpoints. In the latter instance, the statements of the Quebec Council were used to convey the point that the issue of women's equality was central to any debate concerning cultural diversity and accommodation.[8] The Council advocated a banning of the *niqab*, and the elimination of all religious symbols, except for small crucifixes, in public institutions, similar to what occurred in France.[9] The media's emphasis on *vox populi*—accessing the voice of the common person on the street or at a hearing—is laudable in the ideal sense of giving space to popular sentiments. However, within news discourse, this move serves a two-fold function. On the one hand, it allows the media to appear non-partisan and to show concern about the views of the common people. As well, employing a discourse of *vox populi* provides a human interest angle that has accessibility and thereby increases the potentiality of profits.[10] On the other hand, if the audience itself is steeped in a colonial and colonized history of racism, then should the audience's perspective, especially when it is racist and xenophobic, be valorized?

In apartheid South Africa or the *antebellum* South during its reactionary response to the civil rights movement, the dominant or majority population was racist. Had the world and minorities listened to those voices, had they believed that perspective because it was considered legitimate and legitimized by the media, apartheid would not have been dismantled and the civil rights movement would likely have died. Our point is that the audience of media messages is just as crucial as the messages themselves. In the context where xenophobic and racist sentiments have already been stirred, the media's amplification—through repetition, privileging, and lack of critical framing—simply legitimizes racist viewpoints and makes them seem to be commonsensical knowledge.

On the other hand, the *vox populi* approach effectively levels the field so that, in mediated discourses, the hierarchies of race, class, religion, ability, and sexuality are less apparent (Hall, "Culture"; "Media"). Within this "level" playing field, the racist and antiracist perspectives are treated as equally valid—each reflecting a different viewpoint, although they are different in terms of their moral value and their acknowledgment of power inequalities.[11] The equation of such opposing positions fails to consider the resonance of racism in a particular climate and context, a generalized ambience, and simply offers these two perspectives as evidence of a diversity of opinions. Notwithstanding some rare moments of intervention by commission chairs Bouchard and Taylor into citizen testimonies that were extremely racist or anti-Semitic, the media as a sanctioned space of testimony created a context that supported racist perspectives and legitimized racist behaviour in the public sphere. Van Dijk (*Elite*) has argued that elite racism (as in the racism of those with material and cultural power), propagated by the press, is often organized around the construction of immigrants-as-a-threat—a threat to the nation, its culture, and its socio-political and economic order. Within this context, immigrants were construed as a threat to the cultural and social order, with religious symbolism a potent identifier in the mix serving to define those who were different and non-assimilable to Quebec society.

While the French-language press differed in terms of the coverage afforded by the elite press (*Le Devoir*) as opposed to *Le Journal de Montréal* or *La Presse*, the English-language *Gazette* offered a new angle.[12] Poised as an advocate of minority groups—notably the anglophone minorities—the paper sought consistently to portray the racism of the francophone press and populace. Indeed, Jeffrey Heinrich, the key reporter for *The Gazette* covering the commission's hearings, was the first to disclose in the press the recommendations of the commission's final report—much to the chagrin of the francophone press.

The Gazette was quick to publish Jewish groups' responses to the hearings, especially those reactions concerning anti-Semitism. Nevertheless, it is interesting to note that even though the individual stories consistently recounted the violently racist diatribes against Muslims that were articulated at the hearings, the issue of Islamophobia as a systemic form of racism was never identified. *The Gazette* did, to its credit, emphasize the discrimination that most racialized immigrants encounter in obtaining employment. Yet, this was tempered by the inclusion of immigrant voices at the hearings that also insisted on immigrants having to adapt to Quebec society. The central terms of the debate—reasonable versus unreasonable accommodation—were left untouched. In other words, it was up to the immigrants to adapt, integrate, or assimilate. The nuances between these various terms were left undefined. It was never a question of Quebecers having to adapt to an increasingly multicultural and multi-religious society. Yet, *The Gazette*'s reportage was also discerning in its political analysis. It was quick to highlight how the commission's hearings were being utilized by the political opposition parties to suggest that the only solution to the issue of accommodation was Quebec's separation from Canada. The discourses of nationalism entrained and harnessed the ideological force of the rabid Islamophobia and anti-Semitism (the latter was specifically directed against the Hasidic Jews). The discourse of dominance was also evident in the repeated reporting of polls indicating that Quebecers were less tolerant than their counterparts in the rest of the country, thereby underscoring the view of English Canada's presumed and greater tolerance of difference.

A Nation under Siege

Newspaper coverage pertaining to the first segment of the commission's hearings in September and October focused on the racist diatribes and sense of siege experienced by what some media openly called "pure laine" and "Québécois de souche," or "old-stock Quebecers"—which constructed the "authentic" Québécois in opposition to the implied "inauthentic" newcomers, or even more insidiously, to people of colour and Aboriginal people in general. For instance, Fleury's editorial, "Accommodants, dites-vous?" (Accommodating, you say?) on 21 October in *Le Soleil*, outlines the persistence of the "us" and "them" divides at the commission's hearings and his discomfort with the prevalent terminology that designated the "Québécois de souche" and the "ethnics," terminology that was simply assumed in much of the early coverage (see also Nieguth and Lacassagne). What is interesting is how racist statements articulated by persons presenting to the commission were subsequently psychologized under the rubric of "cultural anxiety" and "insecurity" and "malaise identitaire." These terms became commonplace throughout the commission (see, for instance, Croteau and Cliché) and evacuated the violence of hate in the discourse. Instead, "anxieties and insecurities" became legitimate expressions for a "common sense" response that seemed to imply that anti-immigrant sentiments were merely a natural outcome or response to a perceived threat. Neither the threat nor the anxieties it apparently catalyzed were interrogated. Rather than questioning the broader frame that had created the occasion for these voices to be given a sanctioned space and audience attention, the media's treatment of this issue naturalized and normalized hate.

The second key discursive trope in the media's treatment of the hearings was the conflation and confusion between cultural and religious symbols and affiliations. What began as an attempt to deal with cultural differences quickly shifted into a debate about religious differences, though it was not so much a debate as a condemnation. By and large, the print media's emphasis dwelt on specific religious groups, such as Muslims and Orthodox Hasidic Jews, that were seen as being highly problematic and inassimilable. The assumption was and continues to be that immigrants must assimilate and the religious differences must be either forsaken or privatized to such an extent that they are inoffensive to the general public and require no tolerance or space within public institutions. In Quebec, Muslims and Hasidic Jews have been singled out as prototypically deviant and nonconforming immigrants. The rights to pray, practise dietary requirements, or celebrate particular holy days, as well as the right to wear symbols of religious identification, have been regarded as offensive to secular public sensibilities and exploitative of public goodwill. One instance that led to this overall sentiment involved the notorious "cabane à sucre" episode, wherein a Muslim group was made pork-less baked beans at a sugaring-off cabin, an episode that propelled the media into "reasonable accommodation" debates (Perrault).

By late October 2007, as provincial election campaigning began and the various political parties were exploiting the volatile climate created by the commission, the full extent and damage of such conflations seemed to be apparent enough that the very frames defined by the commission itself were now themselves under interrogation. At this time, a discernible shift in media perspective is evident with an added critical distance. In addition to expressing concerns about Quebec's image on the world stage, *Le Devoir* reviewed national press coverage of Quebec's identity debates, precipitated by PQ leader Pauline Marois' identity bill, with the commission as a backdrop. In an opinion piece in *Le Devoir* on 5 November 2007, Concordia political science professor Guy Lachapelle recommended that the commission abruptly conclude their work, and stated: "Je le dis et je l'écris: la communauté arabo-québécoise ne merite pas d'être traitée de cette facon sur la place publique." (I have said it, and I will write it: the Arab-Québécois community does not deserve to be treated in this way in public.) And columnist André Pratte wrote in *La Presse* on 1 November, noting the broader social events that had led to the moral panic fuelled by the media: "Tout a commencé avec l'histoire d'un jeune sikh qui voulait porter un kirpan à l'école. Quelques mois plus tard, nous voici plongés dans un émotif débat sur l'identité Québécoise, sur la survie de la langue française, sur les cours de religions, sur le sort des Autochtones et sur les habilités linguistiques … du capitaine des Canadiens de Montréal, Saku Koivu." (This all began with the history of a young Sikh who wanted to wear a *kirpan* to school. A few months later, here we are, plunged into an emotional debate on

Québécois identity, on the survival of the French language, on religious curriculum in schools, on Aboriginal culture, and on the linguistic ability of Saku Koivu, the captain of the Montreal Canadiens hockey team.)

Gendering the Nation

A key site of the discourse pertaining to the commission's hearings and the media discourses emanating from it centred on the figurative and material symbolism of the Muslim veil—the *hijab* (the headscarf) and the *niqab* (the full face veil). As noted earlier, the idea of the veiled Muslim woman figured predominantly in the Hérouxville affair and its aftermath. She was predated by the debates over Muslim girls wearing the veil in Quebec schools (see Lenk), as well as in the infamous case of Asmahan Mansour, the eleven-year-old Muslim girl who was banned from playing soccer because her *hijab* contravened the rules of the Quebec Soccer Federation. The veiled Muslim woman was again a point of attention and contestation during the Quebec elections in 2007, when the chief returning officer issued an order stating that women wearing the *niqab* would not be allowed to vote. *Le Devoir's* coverage on 30 October 2007 quoted le Centre culturel islamique de Québec (CCIQ) in Quebec City on the damage that fixations on veiled women had had on their communities in general. Spokeswoman Fatima Zahra Benjulloun stated that Muslim women had not requested to vote while veiled, nor cross borders with the *niqab*: "C'est sur le dos des femmes qui portent le voile qu'on fait tous ces debats-là pour stigmatiser encore davantage la communauté musulmane." (It is on the backs of women who wear the veil that these debates are staged in order to further stigmatize Muslim communities) (Dutrisac). That only a minority of Muslim women wear the *niqab* and, further, that none had requested permission to vote wearing the *niqab*, suggests how volatile the issue of the veil had become. The veiled Muslim woman signifies the inassimilable immigrant susceptible to death by culture (Narayan), and in this case, death by religion, wherein Islam is represented as strangling and impeding her progress, from which she must be rescued.

The fixation on the bodies of Muslim women is a common pattern in provincial, national, and international coverage.[13] As Bullock and Jafri have observed, Muslim women in the Canadian press tend to be represented as non-Canadian "Others" who do not fit the normative image

Amplifying Threat   145

of the citizen. However, what is noteworthy about the use of Muslim women's bodies as markers of national boundaries—locating them outside the nation—is the semiotic significance of gender as a sign denoting the capacity to reproduce the nation.[14] In other words, which bodies are considered suitable for reproducing the nation is the benchmark defining women whose bodies are valued as opposed to those who are considered expendable and disposable. Further, the palpable fear of miscegenation and the threat of being engulfed by a growing foreign population is averted, if not diffused, if the threat posed by Muslim women is neutralized, through either their ejection from the body politic or their assimilation/conversion. However, even here, belonging remains a tenuous and conditional status contingent on the racially marked body.

The veiled woman was featured repeatedly in the Quebec media during the period of l'Affaire Hérouxville and the commission, as evident in an advertisement that appeared in *The Gazette* before the hearings began. (See figure 1.) In it, the Muslim woman in *niqab* is portrayed opposite the white male. His baldness, open face, and direct gaze stand in stark contrast to her veiled appearance and sideways gaze. The title above her "Unreasonable Concessions? Let's talk" appears ambivalent. The question mark indicates that the subject is open to debate, hence the topic of the radio talk show. On the other hand, that her gaze is directed away from the audience suggests an inability to talk, as the *niqab* here symbolizes her muteness.

FIGURE 1.   Radio-station advertisement in *The Gazette* (Montreal), 8 May 2007, p. A17.

The figure of the veiled Muslim woman also serves a strategic purpose. It functions to deflect attention from the oppression of women in general across North America. Sonya Fernandez reasons that:

> The focus on gender issues such as veiling, honour killing and forced marriage acts as the perfect prop for justifying the forceful imposition of western values on the cultural Other, by pointing to the oppression of women in Other cultures while simultaneously ignoring the oppression of women within the dominant culture. The construction of these particular practices as particularly *Islamic* has wrought a blend of mistrust, suspicion and hostility towards Muslims fundamentally rooted in racist thought. The effect is to disguise the imperialist motivations and generalizations that demarcate Other cultures as inherently *more* patriarchal, rather than *differently* so, behind a concern for gender equality. (271)

Thus, with the media's preoccupation on veiled women as a sign of the *ultra*patriarchal nature of Islam, violence against women in Canada is effectively elided and patriarchal structures within the nation are obscured (Jiwani "Mediations").

Veiling, as in the practice of wearing the *hijab* and/or the *niqab*, is also freighted with multiple layers of signification. Meyda Yeğenoğlu has observed that the veil signifies premodernity in the dominant Western imagination, connotating a perception of the backwardness of Islam and the essentialized "ultra" patriarchal force of Muslim men. However, as much as it stands for a fossilized and static past, the veil also connotes sexual allure. Franz Fanon commented on this when he drew attention to the French colonial desire to unveil the Algerian woman and, by corollary, to unveil and possess Algeria. The forced unveiling of Muslim women is then suggestive of their possession by dominant powers. Indeed, critical analyses of representations of veiled Muslim women in the press explicitly link the militarized intervention in Afghanistan to the desire of Western powers to unveil Afghan women, thereby making these women "like us" and as belonging to the West.[15]

Muslim women become acceptable as conditional citizens when they show signs of assimilation—when they in fact become "good Muslims." These acceptable Muslim representations often demonstrate signs of gratefulness for the benevolent safety afforded by the West.[16] "Good"

Muslim women also ventriloquize the dominant sentiments of the West and elite powers (see Razack, *Casting*). As Sunaina Maira observes, "In the post-9/11 period ... notions of the assimilability of Muslim women and men are intertwined with gendered discourses of neoliberal citizenship and imperial nationalism that are couched in rhetorics of Western modernity, democracy, and the 'American way of life'" (632). Having native informants that buttress dominant sentiments serves to affirm the national sense of identity and reinforces the notion of the benevolent national self. Within Canada, that sense of self is rooted in the image of a peaceful kingdom textured by British civility, and, in the case of Quebec, by francophone aspirations and history of the struggle for sovereignty against both the state power of the English and the religious order of the church. Within this context, the veiled Muslim woman becomes a repository of all that is considered oppressive—by the dominant English and French societies as a sign of the unliberated and oppressed woman, and by the French as a sign representing the dangers of fusing religion and governance—a reaction grounded in the rejection of a Christian state and the embrace of *laïcité*, or secularism.

Zine contends that three thematic tropes organize representations of Muslim women: "(1) Disciplining Culture, (2) Death by Culture and (3) Death *of* Culture" (152). We have already discussed the notion of "death by culture" as indicative of the notion that the presumed patriarchal nature of Islam is responsible for the oppression of women (see Fernandez, Narayan). The trope of "disciplining culture" refers to the various strategies used by the state to contain and discipline unruly cultures. The idea of "reasonable accommodation" constitutes one such form of disciplining culture, as it invokes the notion that in order for particular cultures to be accommodated, they have to change. In other words, they have to assimilate and divest themselves of signifiers that are deemed problematic, as, for example, wearing the veil. Zine's last trope—that of "death of culture"—signifies the fear of being engulfed by a foreign Other, and the death of the domestic culture. In this case, the anxiety fuelled by the image of the Muslim woman is a reactionary projection of the fear of the "Other," a fear of white decline. Drawing from Ghassan Hage's work, Zine posits that:

> The [Hérouxville] Code is an attempt to preserve the "homeliness" of the nation from the onslaught of estrangement and unfathomable

cultural difference personified as the body of a veiled Muslim woman. Muslim women become "imperiled Muslim women imperiling the nation." The difference they embody is an imperiled difference; they are threatened by the barbaric misogyny of their culture and religion and at the same time they pose a threat to the sanctity of the nation as a space for dominant liberal, Christian, Eurocentric values to prevail. (158)

We have quoted Zine at length so as to portray the backdrop that accentuated the moral panic fuelled by the perceived intransigence of religious and racialized minority groups in refusing to relinquish their adherence to cultural practices and religious symbols of identification. The notion of the potential and/or imminent death of francophone culture operates as the "equation of concern" as Hall et al. define it, into which the issue of accommodation was inserted. The commission's hearings stoked these pre-existing anxieties and fanned the moral panic against religious and racialized groups.

Conclusion

At a recent international workshop on cultural dialogues, religion, and communication, one of the audience members, a prominent Québécois academic in the field of communication studies, commented on how the "reasonable accommodation" hearings in Quebec had afforded the population within the province a very positive and therapeutic opportunity, a view also echoed in the press (Breton).[17] This "therapeutic" experience was borne at the cost of the further stigmatization of Quebec's racial minority groups that were and continue to be constructed by the media as a moral panic threatening the province's fragile sense of national sovereignty. In positing the experience as "therapeutic," the academic's point was that it had allowed the population at large to vent its frustrations regarding "Others."

While the Bouchard-Taylor Commission has ended and its final recommendations have been made public, little has changed, as *La Presse* highlighted on its front page article, "Les Québécois disent non" in October 2009. The issue of accommodation has become submerged and may reappear at the next opportune moment when ruling powers seek to harness populist sentiments toward political ends. Yet, to date, little has changed with regard to the situation of racialized and religious minorities in Quebec. There is little contestation of the widespread Islamophobia that marks the cultural and economic terrain. As sociologist Rachad Antonius stated during another conference, the damage endured by Quebec's Arab and Muslim communities as a result of l'Affaire Hérouxville and the Bouchard-Taylor Commission has been enormous.[18] Muslims continue to be cast as the problem—the men as potential terrorists and ultrapatriarchs, and the women as oppressed, inassimilable others. In the end, one has to ask: Who benefited from the commission? Certainly, as we have argued, it was not a therapeutic exercise for those who were targeted by the press, by the populace, and by the elites.

The terms of the debate that informed the appointment of the commission were translated by the media into a language that could be readily understood by the intended audience (i.e., other Quebecers): namely, how far do *we as Quebecers* have to go to "accommodate" minorities? Had the terms been reversed—as in, how much do cultural minorities have to change in order to feel accepted and gain a sense of belonging to the nation—the coverage might have been very different. Had the media adopted such a perspective, the audience might have learned of the ongoing struggles that individuals from minority communities face upon immigrating, settling, and acculturating into a new terrain, and in Quebec in particular. The audience might have also learned that many of the so-called "minorities" have been here for a generation or more and are not new immigrants as their stereotypic portrayals suggest. Finally, had the terms of the debate been interrogated and inversed by privileging the voices of racialized Others in Quebec and their histories of exclusion, the outcome would have been different, resulting in a more productive debate from a humane, informed, and critical perspective.

The Time Has Come: Self and Community Articulations in *Colour. An Issue* and *Awakening Thunder*

Larissa Lai

Collective Strategies

In the late 1980s and early '90s, special issues of journals offered an imperfect but productive way of bringing into presence histories, experience, and subjects who had little articulated place in the Canadian cultural landscape until that point. These collective, community-based forms of publishing made space for multiple voices to be heard. What was and is productive about the special issue as a form is that it includes a notion of the collective in its conception. Like autobiographies by minoritized subjects, special issues serve the function of "breaking the silence," creating a forum for marginalized voices to articulate histories and experiences not previously granted legitimacy or space within mainstream Canadian literature. Special issues require host journals whose regular stream of publication is necessarily interrupted by the production of "special" issues. The special issue becomes a disruption in the linear flow of a periodical's history and continues, paradoxically, to marginalize those voices even as it grants them a forum, as Ashok Mathur discusses in his editorial introduction to *Race Poetry, Eh?*, a special issue of *Prairie Fire* (8). Special issues on racialized writers or racialized writing engage the Hegelian "master/slave" dialectic that Monika Kin Gagnon has so clearly articulated in her book *Other Conundrums* on anti-racist cultural production in the 1980s and '90s: "My sense of the contemporary dilemma is that naming racism's operations means naming oneself and others within the very terms and operations that have historically enabled racist discourses to proliferate" (22). In order to free oneself from a history of racism, one must name that history, but in so doing the old colonial binary ("white"/"of colour") and its attendant social relations are necessarily re-engaged and re-enacted. I will not go so far as to suggest that special issues on the subject of "race" are the only kind of special issue that necessarily engages this binary. But there is always something of the supplement, in Jacques Derrida's sense, that is called up in relation to the special issue; in other words, it points to that which, as "other" to the regular stream of periodical publication, is always both greater and lesser than the regular stream. Always already secondary, it bolsters the legitimacy of the "regular stream" even as it asserts its content, as Smaro Kamboureli has noted with regard to the social labour of "ethnic antholog[ies]" in relation to canonical anthologies (*Scandalous* 134). The flipside of the special issue's supplementary function, however, is that even while it is "lesser" and debased in relation to the regular stream, it is at the same time "more than" the regular stream—exalted, "special." The dedication of an entire issue to questions of racialization or marginality points to the importance of the "issue" in the moment of publication, and serves as a fresh reiteration of a subject that has always been with us, albeit valenced differently, and placed in the service of older power structures, but from a non-dialectic logic it may at the same time remain continuous with the regular stream. Significantly, these tensions can co-exist.

My objective here is not to offer a statistical survey of the relative absence or presence of racialized voices in the mainstream of Canadian literary magazine publications, though I do take it as a given that marginalization is a historical fact. What I am interested in examining, instead, is exactly what kinds of subjectivities get reproduced[1] through the deployment of the special issue as an anti-racist political tactic.[2]

In this essay, I closely examine two special issues of the 1990s: *Awakening Thunder: Asian Canadian Women*, a special issue of *Fireweed* produced in 1991, important because it was the first Asian Canadian women's special issue; and *Colour. An Issue*, a special issue of *West Coast Line* that came out in 1994, important because of its focus on the language of race and racialization. I explore the politics of framing, modes of production, editorial content, as well as creative and critical content to ask what kinds of communities, futures, and models of liberation these special issues produce. I ask to what extent the strategies of their production are a question of the historical moment and what other factors might play into their differing strategies. Finally, I take into account the tension between the ideal of accessibility in *Fireweed* and the drive to break down and reinvent white patriarchal language in *Colour. An Issue*.[3]

Subjectivities in Double Time: *Awakening Thunder*

Fireweed's special issue *Awakening Thunder: Asian Canadian Women* was a groundbreaking text in the 1990s' "moment" of anti-racist cultural production and one of the earliest special issues to emerge in a decade that saw the publication of *Asian Pacific Authors on the Prairies*, a special issue of *Prairie Fire* (1997); *Prairie Asians,* a special issue of *absinthe* (1998); *Asian Canadian Writing*, a special issue of *Canadian Literature* (1999); as well as, at the beginning of the following decade, a special issue of *West Coast Line* entitled *In-Equations: can asian pacific*. The same year that *Awakening Thunder* was published, SKY Lee published *Disappearing Moon Cafe*, and Paul Wong launched the exhibition *Yellow Peril: Reconsidered*, which featured the work of twenty-five Asian Canadian artists working in contemporary media. To my mind, *Awakening Thunder* represents a (contingently) pure moment in the movement because it is uncompromising in its ideals. It also emerges at the beginning of a new wave of discussions on race and racialization that were very productive in laying the groundwork for the emergence of communities of racialized writers, artists, and activists engaged in what Cornel West called "the new cultural politics of difference" (19). The kinds of qualifications, provisions, and uncertainties (not necessarily unproductive) that mark the editorials of later special issues are absent in this one. *Awakening Thunder* was edited by five strong, intelligent, and hopeful Asian Canadian feminists—Sharon Fernandez, Amita Handa, Mona Oikawa, Milagros Paredes, and May Yee. The playfulness of the editors' biographical notes gives some hint as to the delight and empowerment experienced in the assembling of the special issue. The visual artist Sharon Fernandez, who would later become the Cultural Equity Coordinator for the Canada Council for the Arts (1996–2003), is described as "a completely sexy and fascinating visual artist with a wild sense of humour and one incredibly fine tuned and youthful body" (136). Amita Handa, described soberly as "currently studying at the Ontario Institute for Studies in Education

(OISE) in the sociology department" (137), subsequently completed her Ph.D. and currently teaches at the University of Toronto's Institute of Communication and Culture. She also hosts a radio show called Masala Mixx and DJs for clubs in Toronto. Mona Oikawa's biography says she "hopes to continue to explore her history, back through Toronto and British Columbia to Japan" (137). Oikawa also went on to complete her Ph.D. and is now a professor at York University, currently working on a project called Racial Formations in Settler Society: Japanese Canadians' Relationship to Colonialism. Milagros Paredes, like Amita Handa, was a graduate student at OISE at the time of *Awakening Thunder*'s publication. Her biography says she is "trying to write on her own terms." At the moment of this essay's writing, I can only assume she has escaped to "hot, sunny, fine sand and deep blue sea beaches," as her biographical note states she wishes to do (137). May Yee taught English in the workplace at the time of *Awakening Thunder*'s publication. Her grandfather was a Head Tax payer. Thoughtfully, her biographical note declares, "[h]er year in China is a journey from which she is still returning" (138). What is important in this context is that the editors for *Awakening Thunder* were not "professionals" at the time of their editorial work. Rather, they were students and cultural workers engaged in the new cultural politics of difference and keenly aware of its possibilities.

The editorial for *Awakening Thunder* articulates a feminist, antiracist politics in clear, certain terms that, I argue, produce Asian Canadian women's identity in a way that is particular to that historical moment, though not necessarily "new." The editors propose a kind of silence breaking that is invested in "resisting racist stereotypes of Asian women" (7). Through reading Himani Bannerji's text "Sound Barrier" (included in *Awakening Thunder*), the editors of this special issue recognize the difficulty of representing experience that occurs across a range of cultures and languages, particularly the difficulty of representing that experience in imperial English. They write: "We often break through that sound barrier as part of our struggle against isolation and the racist portrayal of Asian women as passive, submissive, and silent" (7). There are, then, two breakages instigated here: the breakage of a sound barrier that is shattered through the act of speaking and the breakage of a stereotype of Asian women as silent and passive.

The possibility of both breakages depends on an existing but unarticulated reality brought into the light of day through the power of a strong liberatory politics. This unarticulated reality that the editors voice is a Marxist materialist one: "We have never been silent, only ignored. The creative workers in this anthology have drawn from the courage of their foremothers' and forefathers' voices raised to protest the injustices of their lives. Our strength comes from these histories of resistance. Our work articulates this inheritance of struggle" (7). "Histories of resistance" and "inheritance of struggle," then, are the moral and epistemological foundations upon which this special issue builds validity, community belonging, and political knowledge/power. The editors specifically reference the Japanese Canadian internment and the Chinese Canadian Head Tax and Exclusion Act as founding traumas. They applaud the (at-the-time) recently achieved the Japanese Canadian Redress Agreement and note the connection between the Chinese Head Tax and Exclusion Act and current unjust immigration laws. They emphasize the intertwining character of racist and sexist oppression from immigration process to domestic violence to military occupation to prostitution, particularly as the contributors to this special issue document their experiences of these oppressions. Further, these experiences are connected to racist and sexist events occurring at the moment of the issue's publication, in order to recognize the continuity of the oppressions of the past with the oppressions of *Awakening Thunder*'s present. Specifically, the editors note the 1989 massacre of fourteen women at the Ecole Polytechnique in Montreal that later became known as the Montreal Massacre; the Toronto police shooting of a Black woman called Sophia Cook; the police beating of a Chinese woman called Kay Poon; and the killing of a young Vietnamese man by Toronto skinheads. The editors also note the beginnings of inquiries into residential school abuses of Aboriginal children in Manitoba and Nova Scotia.

Bringing the texts included in this issue together in this manner makes a range of disparate experiences coherent in a way that they formerly were not. Through the logic of the future anterior, a political consciousness of the present makes coherent and legible what was not coherent or legible under earlier historical conditions of silence and invisibilization. *Awakening Thunder* actively builds community in the moments of production and publication by providing a conceptual framework through which Asian Canadian women's experiences can be understood and related to one another.

Awakening Thunder begins with an epigraph, or an invocation, ascribed to one of the editors, Sharon Fernandez:

> According to Hindu tradition we are in the age of Kali … in that tradition she has "historically" been depicted by masculine-biased commentaries as cruel and horrific, a warrior sprung from the brow of Durga to fight demonic male power and restore equilibrium. I have imagined her in my own aspect as a creatress and nurturer: the essence of fiery and substantial love. I feel a transformation of consciousness occurs when we create identity through the energizing force within us. It is this creative engagement with our organic and cultural roots that illuminates the vast memory and connectedness of the human spirit outside of dominant repressions. (2)

Through both this invocation and the title itself, a dual temporality is called into being. "Awakening" suggests both a birth and a rebirth. The invocation of Kali calls up a mythic past beyond the reaches of patriarchal history and, at the same time, through Fernandez's reimagining of Kali as "creatress and nurturer," produces the present as a break from the immediate past, even as it is connected to an imagined older (her)story. An alternate present is called into being through the invocation of a mythic past, which Fernandez describes as "organic and cultural." This invocation also drives toward a hopeful future. Between the mythic past and a hopeful future, Fernandez thus produces a community-based present, an Asian Canadian women's reality that emerges as a kind of Butlerian "repetition with a difference" at the moment of the special issue's publication. What I am arguing, in other words, is that the present of *Awakening Thunder*'s production and publication is both continuous with the histories it references and discontinuous—a breakage—from those histories. There is a difference (from the prior moment) and a possibility produced in the framing and circulation of *Awakening Thunder* that the special issue, like the goddess Kali, creates.[4]

In its Hindu specificity, the invocation of Kali poses both a problem and a possibility. Insofar as such an invocation is culturally specific, it hails only those women identifying as Hindu. However, because Fernandez's Kali is a "creatress," a mother figure from whom new kinds of women are born, she offers the possibility for imagining new kinds of kinship—kinships that emerge from histories of trauma, kinships based both productively and problematically on the term "Asian," historically used in the colonial context to marginalize, silence, and exclude.

As Gagnon has noted in *Other Conundrums*, such a reclamation always contains a dilemma (22). There is empowerment in voicing the terms through which one has been oppressed in order to point out that such oppression has existed and continues to exist, and to demand re-evaluation and restitution. On the other hand, to repeat the name of race—Asian, Black, Native—is to reiterate old colonial relationships, to reinscribe the white/colour binary and deepen its power. If Kali can offer us a transformation of the name, a mother figure in whose arms cultural-activist women can coalesce, then there is a woman-centric empowerment there. I suggest that the problem of Kali's Hindu specificity is also a boon, as she is a figure of specific South Asian cultural experience. Her centres are thus Asian and non-Western. However, insofar as her cultural signification is not pan-Asian, it seems to me that there is room for a politics and poetics of relationality, one that is present in the spirit of *Awakening Thunder*, though perhaps not fully explored or articulated. If "Asia" is a colonial cartographer's category, then the relationship among "Asians" needs another name in order to have another, freer being. For the moment of *Awakening Thunder*, that name could be "Kali." There is a brave, slightly idiosyncratic but intensely hopeful act of creation and coalition building that occurs under the name of the creatress Kali and brings at least a momentary cohesion to a range of voices that might otherwise be regarded as disparate. Under this rubric oppressive silences are broken and Asian women fight back.

By reproducing the mythic past in feminist terms, the *Awakening Thunder* collective produces both a possibility and a reality embodied by the text itself. But what is interesting about this production of history is that it is retrospective. It emerges as much from the "reality" of the present as from the "reality" of the past. And yet, paradoxically, the "reality" of the present is produced only in this invocation of the past—the Japanese Canadian internment; the Chinese Head Tax and Exclusion Act; and all the personal, daily experiences of suffering that have been part of life in Canada for many racialized families since the nation's inception(s).[5]

In *Awakening Thunder*, this mutual production of the past and present emerges through the logic of the future anterior. The past is reconstructed so that it seems to predict and produce the present, but it is precisely the force of the present moment that makes possible such a reconstruction of the past. As Marjorie Garber explains with regard to prophecy in Shakespeare's history plays, to write about the past from the present moment, in such a way as to make the present seem an inevitable consequence of that articulation of the past, gives the text an almost mystical sense of legitimacy (307–8). In Shakespeare's history plays, a national, patriarchal history is validated in this way. I argue that, in the case of *Awakening Thunder*, subaltern histories can also be validated through this way of thinking. In both cases, however, the logic of the future anterior is a logic that leaks: it pokes holes in the seamlessness of national histories and opens potentially liberatory (but also potentially violent) gaps for subaltern ones.

Indeed, as Homi Bhabha has taught us, alternate temporalities can produce moments of liberation. The haunted temporalities lived by subjects of trauma are markedly different from official history's linear temporality. Bhabha writes:

> to dwell "in the beyond" is also ... to be part of a revisionary time, a return to the present to redescribe our cultural contemporaneity; to reinscribe our human, historic commonality; *to touch the future on its hither side*.... The borderline work of culture demands an encounter with "newness" that is not part of the continuum of past and present. It creates a sense of the new as an insurgent act of cultural translation. Such art does not merely recall the past as social cause or aesthetic precedent; it renews the past, refiguring it as a contingent "in-between" space, that innovates and interrupts the performance of the present. The "past-present" becomes part of the necessity, not the nostalgia, of living. (*Location* 7)

Awakening Thunder illustrates the cultural productivity of such an encounter with "newness." Its voices are the voices of Bhabha's "past-present," erupting and diminishing through the non-linear logic of the haunted "beyond."

The politics produced in *Awakening Thunder* are thus both pragmatic and programmatic, and quite historically specific. The editors actively set out criteria for selection and decide that the works they include ought to: "reflect the importance of communicating our common experiences as Asian women. We also looked for accessibility of language and image, and pieces that were written from a critical perspective free of sexism, racism, classism and heterosexism. While in their entirety, these selections show our common bonds, we were ultimately drawn to work that clearly conveyed the writer's or artist's presence, her uniqueness, her history" (6). While emphasis is placed on common experience, the tension between the collective and the individual is highlighted through the notion of the writer's "presence" and "uniqueness." There is a tension in that historical moment between the Enlightenment and Western democratic ideal of individuality on the one hand and, on the other hand, an ideal of social interconnectivity and sisterly solidarity that is rooted in class struggle. Most cannily, there is also a comprehension and a claiming of the multiple possibilities inherent in the term "Asian women." The editors recognize it at once as a naturalized "race" category that continues to have contemporary cultural currency, a racist appellation that has made those marked as "Asian women" the objects of racism, colonialism, and patriarchy, and at the same time as a label that can be reclaimed for the purposes of self-empowerment.

While these different modes of the term's circulation are recognized in the editorial, the temporal zone of this special issue is one in which reclamation is emphasized.[6] "Awakened thunder" signals, then, a breaking of silence in order to recognize a common bond for the purposes of self-empowerment. Tied to a mythic past, this politics emerges specifically, as I have said, from a particular moment in the late 1980s and early '90s in which the possibility and reality of empowerment are simultaneously produced, making room for the articulation of histories and politics for which there were no words and no forum in the contiguously previous moment. Arguably, however, such eruptions have occurred at other historical moments that may or may not be read as causally related to this one. Without official state histories to bestow the appearance of linearity, these moments of eruption belong to fragmented time. In the language of psychoanalysis, they are returns of the repressed. In performance theory terms, they are repetitions with a difference. For a generation of artists, writers, and activists raised under Trudeau's multiculturalism, the possibilities of articulation and thus self-fashioning mark a clear break from the whitewash of the previous era. Thus, whether or not this moment is "new," it has the appearance and feel of newness for those who engage it. With newness goes an attendant risk, for through the articulation of injustice one might gain entry into the public life of the state but, alternately, or additionally, one might be further marginalized. In the 1990s, racialized artists, writers, and critics recognized the timeliness of their work as being "in fashion." Many worried about what would happen to their work and their newfound place in the public eye when they were no longer the "flavour of the month."

The problem of reclaiming the racist name, then, is not solved by *Awakening Thunder*. *Awakening Thunder* embraces the liberatory power produced in the oppositional aspect of naming. It does not concern itself with the problem of reinscription. I suggest, in fact, that part of what makes the moment of *Awakening Thunder* both radical and productive is precisely its refusal to address the reinscribing aspect of the white/of colour dialectic. In the "in-between" time of *Awakening Thunder*, the problem of reinscription does not exist.

The problem is, of course, that in the outside time of right-wing populist discourse, this reinscribing aspect is the only aspect that exists. The charge of racism against whites, or "reverse-racism" that was to emerge with such force during the Writing Thru Race conference, had not yet arrived at the fullness of its rhetorical power in the moment of *Awakening Thunder*, though that rhetoric and the storm clouds that accompanied it were certainly gathering in that same (linear) historical moment.

While the tension between liberatory naming and the reinscription of the racist name, as well as the attendant reinscription of old colonial relationships, is not engaged in *Awakening Thunder*, what is engaged are smaller movements within the liberatory possibilities of naming difference. Gilles Deleuze offers us another, less dialectic, way of thinking about difference. For him, identity is never selfsame, but always differing within itself. If change does not occur in the grand, synthetic steps but rather in smaller, less predictable ones, through the interplay of small differences within a time of repetition, then the conundrum that Gagnon describes in *Other Conundrums* need not be so determining. John Rajchman, in "Diagram and Diagnosis," suggests:

> A "history of the present" is a history of the portion of the past that we don't see is still with us. Thus it involves a concept of historical time that is not linear and is not completely given to consciousness, memory, commemoration. But Deleuze thought it involved something more—a relation to the future. He would put it this way: "Not to predict, but to be attentive to the unknown that is knocking at the door." It was this relation to the future that made the "present," whose history Foucault proposed, something untimely, creative, experimental. (*Becomings* 47)

I read certain special issues, such as *Awakening Thunder,* as "histories of the present" that recuperate, however they can, a marginalized past for the purposes of opening out onto a more hopeful, open-ended future.

Editorial Strategy

As the co-editors of *Colour. An Issue* (1994), a special issue of *West Coast Line*, Roy Miki and Fred Wah constituted a very different kind of editorial team from the team that assembled *Awakening Thunder.* At the time of *Colour. An Issue*'s publication, both were professors—Miki at Simon Fraser University, Wah at the University of Calgary. *Colour. An Issue* was published six years after the Japanese Canadian Redress Agreement, for which Miki and a small group of committed activists had worked incredibly hard. By the time of *Colour. An Issue*'s publication, Miki already had a strong record of publication behind him, including two poetry books (*Random Access File* and *Saving Face*), *Justice in Our Time* (an account of the Japanese Canadian redress movement, co-authored with Cassandra Kobayashi), *Pacific Windows* (an edited collection of the late Roy Kiyooka's poetry), and *Meanwhile: The Critical Writings of bp nichol* (also an edited collection). Similarly, Wah was an impressively accomplished writer at the time of the special issue's publication, with sixteen poetry books to his credit, including the Governor General's Award–winning volume *Waiting for Saskatchewan*, as well as numerous chapbooks, broadsides, and articles. Interestingly, the contributors' notes for *Colour. An Issue* do not provide information about either of them. If *Awakening Thunder* can be characterized as emerging from a youthful, streetwise quickness, *Colour. An Issue* seems to emerge from an attentive sense of responsibility backed by the wisdom of experience. It is probably overdeterministic to suggest that *Colour. An Issue* takes its cue from *Awakening Thunder*, but I think it is important to note that it was graduate students, emerging artists, and unestablished cultural workers who took the early risks in the anti-racist movement of the 1980s and '90s wave.

Rather than declaring a politics, as *Awakening Thunder* did, *Colour. An Issue* lays its parameters a lot more contingently, without driving toward a synthesis, a liberated "end of history" or "revolution." Rather, its (very short) preface foregrounds the utterance of "race" as a moment of breakage, a moment at which the speech of linear history is radically disrupted, and reduced to meaningless noise:

> "Race"—that four letter word, making a headway on visibility: the zone of the body scanned by surveillance monitors. The squawking of ruffled feathers shakes loose the tiles which spill into the public squares. There is nothing more apparent, and nothing more transparent, than the signs of "race" that circulate in the everyday lives of people of colour. Drop it into most public conversations on writing, culture and representation and the whole mainstream hall shudders, as the shutters come down and all the mechanisms of power fill up the stuttering spaces with the discourse of muzak muzak muzak. (Miki and Wah 5)

As in *Awakening Thunder* the racialized body remains in focus, but it is the body under surveillance, the body already drawn into signification as a site of contention that holds the editors' attention here. "Race" is a dirty word, a swear word, that brings on stuttering and empty mall music in the halls of power. What is repeated in the stutter, or in the mechanical blandification of the music of bygone times? The racialized body, the visible body "of colour" remains in the panoptic eye (of the state or the shopping mall), as a disruption in the flow of unmarked, "colourless" bodies. But articulation of this difference is unacceptable, especially when that articulation emerges from the mouths (or pens) of the wrong bodies.

Through the swear word "race," as much a promise as a curse, the language of the colonial moment returns with a difference and a vengeance. Those against whom it was applied, as I have described in relation to *Awakening Thunder*, have produced a new kind of power in its redeployment. Time is out of joint. The empire is haunted by the ghosts of its own violence. But the ghosts (of colour) have to live out the haunting if we are to be empowered by it. And this living out is no easy task.

Colour. An Issue lacks the optimism of *Awakening Thunder*. But it is also less prescriptive. "Colour," unlike "Asian women" (in the contexts of the respective issues), is not an identity, or a politics. While *Awakening Thunder* emphasizes set criteria—"common experience;" accessibility of language; critical perspectives; and absence of racism, classism, and heterosexism (6)—*Colour. An Issue* is consciously contingent. "Colour" is deployed as an open-ended term around which thinking, being, and writing coalesce: "*Colour. An Issue* is not an anthology, a collection of texts that have been selected, arranged and edited into a "whole" that advances the coherence of the collectivity. The methodology adopted proposes an open-ended process that could yield much more provisional patterns of interconnections for the diverse materials included" (5). One could, of course, argue that the refusal to set criteria is a kind of setting of criteria and that the refusal to select is actually a kind of selection. In the historical moment of this text, as poststructural as it is postcolonial,[7] it is impossible to ignore the ways in which the privileges of class, education, access—all those things that *Awakening Thunder* is so conscious of and determined to undo—still shape any text, "edited" or not. However, the drive toward contingency is very different from the drive toward common experience. While *Awakening Thunder* emphasizes commonality, specifically in the experience of race and gender oppression, *Colour. An Issue* emphasizes diversity and "provisional patterns." Its editors recognize profoundly the incompleteness of conversations about race, and indeed the fact that the power of these conversations lies precisely in their incompleteness.

I have been discussing these two texts comparatively not in order to ascertain whether one organizational strategy is "better" than the other but rather to ask how they work, both separately and together, within practices of community separated by (a short) time and (a short) geographical distance, but nonetheless closely related in terms of their political and imaginative projects.

As the historically prior text, *Awakening Thunder* could be said to lay groundwork. The pieces included in this special issue tend to be biographical or autobiographical in nature, and emphasize experiences of oppression based on race, class, gender, and sexuality. Formally, the fiction included in the issue follows realist literary conventions; the poetry tends to be lyric in form; the essay pieces strive for clarity and transparency. The contributions include, for instance, an oral history from the then-in-progress book project *Voices of Chinese Women*; "Safer Sex in Santa Cruz," Mona Oikawa's delightful account of an Asian lesbian retreat in California; Kaushalya Bannerji's poem, "Remembrance Day: for Anthony Griffin age 19 murdered November 11/87 Montreal Canada"; and "English Classes for Immigrant Women: A Feminist Organizing Tool," an extraordinary account by an immigrant academic woman, Pramila Aggarwal, of how she worked with immigrant women at a pizza crust factory to organize for better working conditions. The linguistic transparency of these works is precisely what gives them their impact and their liberatory power.

Indeed, one of the stated criteria for inclusion in the issue is "accessibility." The issue and its editors are not directly critical of formal innovation. However, what is not questioned in the production of this issue are the ways in which literary conventions tend to reproduce existing power structures in language. There is a real tension, then, between the practice of writing and the practice of disrupting white supremacist norms in the world of work and everyday life.

In a poem called "Grief" in *Awakening Thunder*, Kim-Man Chan writes:

> Loneliness
> A sense of not belonging
> A sense of not being at home
> A need to talk to somebody
> Who would understand me
> A need to be appreciated
> For what I am, and where I came from.
>
> Neither here nor there,
> Not working class, not middle class.
> Children of a proprietor
> But lived in a storeroom,
> Slept under table, worked seven days a week,
> Scrambled money for groceries—ten apples, ten oranges ...
> Member of the petty bourgeois?
> A text-book case of the integrated structures
> Of patriarchy and capitalism? (106)

Chan, we are told in the biography section of this special issue, is from Hong Kong. She came as a visa student to Canada and, at the time of publication, worked as an English instructor with immigrant workers. She has not gone on to write books; she is not a known figure in Asian Canadian Literature. (Does this mean she is less commodified or commodifiable?) Whether the writing is "good" or "bad," the "I" asserted here is full of pathos. A silence has been broken. The poem "Grief." fits perfectly the criteria laid out in the editorial—it is accessible, it is free of racism, sexism, classism, and heterosexism. It expresses a unique history and at the same time recognizes common experience. As such, it works in support of the social/political stance taken by the editors. In a sense, its publication, if not its writing, becomes an inscription as much of the editors' agency as of the author's own.

As Kamboureli notes in her discussion of ethnic anthologies, however, writing that foregrounds immigrant experience without full attention to language and form raises the question of how we are to understand such work in literary terms (*Scandalous* 150). Kamboureli suggests such work, in fact, fulfills the expectations and funding criteria of government officials by presenting the voices of racialized subjects in the form they expect—that is, in mimicry of accepted colonial form and with content that confirms what the colonizer already expects of the colonized (151). As such, poems like Chan's serve to reinforce the stereotypes of the mainstream and, in so doing, undermine the liberatory project they appear, at the first pass, to support. Kamboureli suggests that such work raises the question of whose aesthetic values are reproduced in such instances. Her argument echoes the point I make in another article in which I consider this problem in relation to autobiography by racialized writers. There, I conclude that the articulation of experience is an important step in the marginalized subject's entry into subjecthood and citizenship, but that the texts produced invariably function to fold the subject in question rapidly back into the containing norms of the state. Such texts, especially when actively marketed as objects of white atonement, give the state and its mainstream citizenry the appearance of having made up for the violence of the past, even as such violence continues, unremarked upon, in the present.

The remaining eight stanzas of Chan's poem go on to document the tortured emotional state of a young immigrant woman whose family struggles for pride as much as for connection among its members. As much as the poem's speaker is a "textbook case" of immigrant misery, the poem's structure is a "textbook case" of lyric mimicry, complete with capitalized letters to begin each line and a culturally non-specific, mimetically universal "I" who outpours her grief:

A hand on my hair, long long time ago.
Tears streaming wildly down my face as I write this,
At twenty-three supposedly a grown woman. (107)

For me, in cold critical mode, the poignancy of Chan's expression is undermined by the knowledge of the state-preserving service to which this poem and others like it are routinely put, as in fact are the subjects who produce these heart-wrenching confessional texts. But the textual moment, like the critical moment, matters. I recognize here that the cathartic and community building power of such texts can sometimes outweigh the cold critic's concern or even the inevitable return to state containment that regularly occurs with regard to such texts.

While *Awakening Thunder* occurs at a specific moment in history—1990—I would argue that its temporality can erupt unexpectedly at any time and produce important and necessary catharsis and community for individuals deeply in need of it. I am conscious of my politically liberal use of the word "individual" here; confessional lyric poems like Chan's are about the production of Western liberal subjectivity—but always with a supplemental difference that, as I have argued elsewhere in relation to the poetry of Evelyn Lau ("Strategizing"), necessarily produces the need to write more, since the racialized subject writing from a lyric location can never have the originary citizenship bestowed on the nation's founding races.

The "I" of Mark Nakada's "marginalia" in *Colour. An Issue* expresses similar dislocations to Kim Man Chan's, but these are explicitly integrated into the formal structure of the poem.

```
          cant feel how this sand   place  (a beach    is an area where    if not for
greed                                                                          lust
                                                                               land
only                                                                           power
nine                                                                           dominance
i pick                                                                         c. 1609
up a                                                                           a chance
handfull                                                                       movement
of sand                                    e                                   escape
these                                         g                                denial
okinawans                                      a                               forgetting
(relatives to           here eh                 u                              i might
what                                           g                               have
speak to                                       n                               been
me                          l                              a                   margin
```

```
in my            u              l                         the
own lost         f                                   language
tongue           e                                     almost
i slowly         s                                       mine
spill my         u                                        can
grains                                                  never
back into                       e                 really be
the foreign                     r                       but a
beach                                  o             canadian
they                                   m             nonsense
wait
for me to answer    but i cant    perhaps my unintelligible okinawan
words                                                     are a
                                   (29)
```

Nakada's consciousness of the formal rules that conventionally govern a page of poetry allows him to deliberately place his words in the margins. He offers breakages in the seamlessness of the lyric "I." The poem's structure reproduces, for the reader, its speaker's struggle with Okinawan language and the frustration of not being able to communicate with his Okinawan relatives. The text, then, is conscious of the histories of colonialism and displacement that lead to the way English rolls off Nakada's tongue.

It may be that Nakada means to deride texts like Chan's with his empty pointer, "more useful language," running backwards up the centre of the page, unsettling further the reader's capacity to register sense in his text. It takes slow and careful puzzling to work out the fact that the apparently random letters in the centre of the page say "more useful language." In this way, the reader is confounded by Nakada's language in ways that parallel the poet's unsettling experience of being confounded by speakers of his mother tongue.

Like Chan, Nakada recognizes his own marginalization. But the structure of his poem also recognizes a kind of training that Chan may have also encountered, although in all likelihood has not. So she places her lyric language in the centre of the page, following lyric convention. Nakada's poem is more "successful" than Chan's in the sense that it disrupts the linearity of official English and presses its reader into a reading experience that parallels the speaker's experience and deployment of his two fraught tongues—Okinawan and English. The temporality of its social usefulness is thus different. If Chan's text is an early disruptive rumble of thunder (and here I mean "early" not just in the sense of linear time but in the sense of the temporality of engagement with "race" issues in a racist society), Nakada's belongs to a moment of contemplating "colour" as "an issue." It resists the reincorporation into state understanding that Chan's falls easily prey to.

Formally, one might read Nakada and Chan's texts as oppositional to one another. But in the sense of "common bonds" (6) that the editors of *Awakening Thunder* value, these are ally texts. It would be interesting to pursue a politics of coalition building between or among these writing practices in order to understand what their relationship can be to one another. They might speak differently to one another than they do to the centres that they address. It would also be worth asking what might happen to those centres if marginal texts ceased to address them but addressed one another instead.

Formal innovation does not make Nakada's text any less lyric than Chan's. In its desire for an "I," Nakada's poem might be thought of as a lyric/anti-lyric in the sense that Douglas Barbour describes—"lyric straining against itself" (19), blasting out of tradition even as it repeats it. What is interesting about both poems is the production of excess to identify that element that identity cannot name—the "evacuated subject" Miki describes in *Broken Entries*.[8] The "more useful language" of Nakada's poem or the "neither here nor there" of Chan's might just as easily be a language that articulates the inarticulable void Miki describes. "More useful language" and "neither here nor there," in other words, point to an impossible text, a magical text that frees the marginalized subject from the name of her or his oppression, a text that Chow might posit as existing at the moment of the racist name's disappearance. Contemplating the problem and the possibility of reclaiming the racist name, which both frees the racialized subject from silence and reinscribes the dialectic relationship between "colour" and whiteness, Chow concludes in *Ethics After Idealism* that the "void," that is, the site of inarticulation that exists in excess of the possibilities of articulation, is a place of hope and possibility (54). In the present imperfect, in which we are always inheritors of colonial history, we cling to the name of race as our only out—even as it produces and reproduces melancholy subjects like the speaker in Chan's "Grief." The magic time that I envision here is a moment when we escape the bonds of racist history and thus no longer need the name of race. This is, of course, the moment that mainstream Canada imagines we already occupy, not understanding or not wanting to acknowledge how the traumatic past roils beneath the surface. It is thus an impossible time that can never arrive in the linear order of national history, and yet a time that those of us who still cling to some utopic impulse still long for because resignation and cynicism are even less appealing options. If the mimetic humanist feeling in "Grief" is also a Marxist feminist grief, then I claim a moment of strategic individualism in the early time of *Awakening Thunder*.

In *The Cultural Politics of Emotion*, Sara Ahmed makes a useful distinction between the fetishization of the wound that leads so easily to its commoditization, on the one hand, and the need for testimony in order to "break the seal of the past" (33) and mobilize pain into political action, on the other. It seems to me that both "Grief" and "marginalia" do this work. In more complex ways, so do the special issues that they appear in.

What if Nakada's "more useful language" were not the language of oppression at all but a liberatory language belonging to an alternate temporality—language from the future for which one can leave only a blank space, a space that waits? The unknown knocks at the door. The phrase "here, eh" indicates at once a circumscribed national and a much more open-ended site of possibility. As a distinctly "Canadian" interjection, "eh" locates "here" as a tightly delineated (white) national space. But "eh" is also an interjection of uncertainty, a sort of verbal question mark. "Here" is thrown into contest. It is open-ended. It could mean anything and contain anyone, even someone with such a hybrid body and experience as Nakada—or Chan. Nakada does not specify whether "here" is also "now." The phrase "more useful language" ironizes the position of the master tongue, but it does not close that discourse off as the only possible discourse that might fill in the blank. I want to suggest here that the ontology of the future does not include "I": rather, it conceives of "I" as a much more open container than an Enlightenment humanist ideology might allow.

As co-editors, Miki and Wah are more interested in "you" and "we," but these are pronouns that oscillate, that jump from body to body depending on the moment:

> Or "Colour" with a "you." How "we" has to figure it out. How some
> of us can't make a move without thinking it. How some of you never

think it, don't have to, don't even bother because it is no bother to you. How some have to double-think it, hyphenate it, dilute it, disappear into it. Yellow on the inside, white on the outside. Invisible. Except for a name, a history, a dream, a resonance, a trace taste that becomes a hunger, a deep need, to spit it out. (*Colour. An Issue* 5)

Because it includes "u," the Canadian spelling of "colour" can be read as more open to relation than the USA spelling of "color." "U" sounds like "you"—the "Other." But the "u" whom the co-editors refer to is a hostile "u," a "u" with a colonial history and continuing white privilege that prevent it from seeing the marginalized histories and bodies that hold it up. Not that the USA is without its colonial or its neo-imperial masters. But to embed the master into "race" ("colour") is to recognize the deep intertwining of the two concepts. Thus "we" has no natural being; it is a subject position to be occupied rhetorically in order to work out power differences that are nonetheless highly material. "You" is embedded in colour but never thinks of it; it is the normalized white universal. But "you" is other to the speaker. This is a turn from its habitual usage in the (neo-)colonial sense that it is usually the white speaker addressing the brown "Other." Subjectivity and power bounce through the pronouns "I," "you," and "we" in a way that destabilizes all three. In the movement of pronouns through a range of bodies, those that are racialized and those that go unmarked, the social relationships of those bodies are reorganized. The "you" of privilege is drawn out of blindness, is made to recognize its own privilege, is suddenly held responsible. "You" is used to point out the ways in which positions of power are not recognized as such but allowed to pass as normal. Through this usage, power relations are made manifest. By destabilizing the assumed gender, race, and class of the speaker, co-editors Miki and Wah call a different kind of "I" or "i" into being, or rather into becoming, in ways that are hopeful and productively incomplete.

Strategy's Timing

The cultural moment of *Awakening Thunder*'s publication was one that emphasized the historical as a mode of legitimation and empowerment. Indeed, the notion of the historical is something that is repeatedly recognized in the editorial itself: "Many of the stories and articles in this issue of *Fireweed* show how the histories of Asian women and men are also part of the history of colonialism" (8). And later, referring to eruptions of violence against women and people of colour near the time of publication, the editors write: "Although these events are being portrayed as 'isolated incidents' by those in power, we know they are all interconnected as part of the long history of racism in this country" (8). The liberatory model proposed is one that recuperates history for the purposes of empowerment. In naming the violence that has been directed against racialized subjects, the editorial sees that liberatory power lies in testimony. To the extent that testimony can rapidly be fetishized and consumed, *Awakening Thunder* requires, indeed demands, an audience able to inhabit the uncomfortable but potentially liberatory time/space of Fernandez's Kali.

The future of *Colour. An Issue* is not liberation or revolution but rather possibility: "this 'issue' is a transitional zone that functions, in this instance not as a showcase but as a catalytic kindling of marginalized discourse, imagined possibilities in language and thought—the intent of a dialogue, a forum of diversity, finally, shared" (5). By including "issue" in the title itself, *Colour. An Issue* foregrounds its own situation in fleeting time, in the sense of being just one issue in the flow of *West Coast Line*. By locating itself within the genre of special issues, it declares its solidarity with other special issues like *Awakening Thunder* and the concomitant politics of contingency that recognizes the issue's "special status." But further, "issue" implies an orientation toward the future, as in "to issue forth." It also offers "issue" in the sense of "offspring": a kind of child, full of hope, the intellectual and creative issue of communities cross-fertilizing. And of course, "issue" invites controversy. "Colour," unlike "Asian," is not an identity, in spite of that moment's preferred terminology for the racialized—"person of colour." It is a conundrum, a problematic and, as Wah and Miki write, a kind of kindling to fuel the flame of that moment's already burning politics.

These two issues, then, emerge from different moments within the anti-racist movement, which might account for some of the differences in their orientation toward politics and the future. Further, while *Fireweed* is a Toronto-based feminist magazine with Marxist feminist underpinnings, *West Coast Line*, with its roots in the critical journal *West Coast Review* and the experimental-poetics journal *Line*, tends toward embracing open-ended experimentation. If there is tension between the two special issues, it is marked by their classed, gendered, and geographic differences. Here are a few productive questions: To what extent does desire for recognition by the centre emerge from the fact of living at the centre of the nation? To what extent does the rush into a more fragmented, fleeting kind of liberation belong to an already established Western dream of the ever expanding frontier? To what extent is literary experimentation a realm of masculinist/academic discourse? To what extent does the need for the immediacy of accessibility override the long-term uncertainty of time invested in the experimental and the contingent? These are highly ideological questions that I could not possibly begin to answer here, except perhaps by way of saying that a linguistic strategy for speaking into silence depends on the moment in both linear and haunted time, as well as on the intentions of the speaker. That one issue occurs later in the linear historical trajectory than the other, however, is not a coincidence. The contingent and open-ended require a prior certainty and idealism to posit themselves against.

I would like to suggest, in conclusion, that between the time of *Awakening Thunder* and the time of *Colour. An Issue*, the shift in the capacity of the subject to articulate experience parallels a shift on the global stage, in which the power of subaltern discourse to bring about liberatory change becomes incorporated into the power of neoliberal capital to control international markets and the flows of subjectivities and bodies that follow those markets. The steer away from the lyrically mimetic "I" to the shifting "I"-as-container parallels a shift in the capacity for anti-racist work to draw marginalized subjects into the nation as full citizens. To the extent that citizenship in liberal democratic states depends on the coherent ego of the lyric "I" to declare allegiance, mark a ballot, and take on civic duty, the recognition that no real freedom lies there complicates matters, as does the evacuation of the power of citizens by neoliberalism in the same moment. In its "special" status, the special issue both interrupts and continues the regular flow of journal publishing. It hails its audience slightly differently. In so doing, it opens the possibility for journals to take alternate directions. Thunder could (re)awaken at any moment. "Colour" continues to issue possibility in the imperfect present before the disappearance of the name of race.

Archivable Concepts: Talonbooks and Literary Translation

Kathy Mezei

> In an enigmatic sense, which will clarify itself *perhaps* ... the question of the archive is not, I repeat, a question of the past. It is not the question of a concept dealing with the past that might *already* be at our disposal or not at our disposal, *an archivable concept of the archive*. It is a question of the future, the question of the future itself, the question of a response, of a promise and of a responsibility for tomorrow. The archive: if we want to know what that will have meant, we will only know in times to come. Perhaps. (Derrida, *Archive Fever* 36)

As the process through which ideas and styles are incorporated into the fabric of Canadian society and culture, translation plays a crucial but generally unacknowledged role. Often perceived as subservient or invisible (translators' names are frequently omitted from the covers and even title pages of books), translation is, on the contrary, a highly creative, influential, and serious art form. Translation has influenced canon formation and the revisiting of concepts of originality and rewriting in Canadian literary practices and institutions. For example, a controversy erupted over the appropriateness of Nancy Huston's 1993 Governor General's Literary Award in French language fiction for *Cantiques des plaines*, which she had self-translated from the English original, *Plainsong*. Huston has in fact self-translated several of her novels from French into English and vice versa. In this case, Quebec writers and intellectuals questioned whether a translated novel could be deemed an original work of fiction and argued that novels under consideration should be written in the language of the award.

The study and practice of translation have also drawn attention to minority/dominant culture dynamics, gender marking and bias, and cultural policies and cultural transfer.[1] Its mandate and impact go far beyond that usually assigned to it by official bilingualism and the subsequent traffic between French and English, institutionalized by the federal government in agencies such as the federal Translation Bureau, French immersion programs and schools, bilingual signage, and the translation grants section of the Canada Council. Since Canadian life involves interactions among a vast number of immigrant and First Nations languages, many of the books, performances, and films that make up Canadian culture are produced through or inflected by a transaction with another language, culture, or medium. These interactions include both conventional translation and the broader category of "cultural translation" through which languages and cultures are written into Canadian literary works. For a fuller picture of the making of modern Canadian culture and "the question of the future itself," it is therefore vital to record the variety as well as the vitality of these interactions, to analyze the wide range of cultural artifacts that are the product of translation, to explore the ways in which translations involve strategies of appropriation or distancing, and, finally, to develop and interpret an archive of Canadian translation activities.[2] These must be undertaken not only, as Derrida notes throughout *Archive Fever, A Freudian Impression,* as a record of our cultural memory and impressions but also as a promise and a responsibility for tomorrow.[3]

Experiments and bold initiatives in producing and theorizing Canadian feminist literary translation, postcolonial and minority literatures, and the politics of translation have drawn much international attention to Canadian literary translation practice and have influenced the direction of transnational translation studies. For example, in *Contemporary Translation Theories,* Edwin Gentzler acknowledges the contribution of Canadian translators to translation theory: "the complicated question of Canadian identity—problems of colonialism, bilingualism, nationalism, cultural heritage, weak literary system, and gender issues are involved—seems to provide a useful platform from which to begin raising questions about current translation theory" (184). In her critical introduction to *Comparative Literature,* Susan Bassnett referred to a Canadian school that conceptualizes translation as political activity. Comparing Brazilian and Canadian translation theorists, Bassnett observed that both groups are "concerned to find a translation practice and terminology that will convey the rupture with the dominance of the European heritage even as it is transmitted" (157). Both the *Encyclopedia of Literary Translation into English* (2000) and the *Routledge Encyclopedia of Translation Studies* (2008) feature substantial articles on translation in Canada. In *Introducing Translation Studies: Theories and Applications* (2000), Jeremy Munday's section on "Translation and Gender" acknowledges the vitality of feminist translation and focuses on the pioneering work of Barbara Godard, Susanne de Lotbinière-Harwood, and Sherry Simon. During the 1980s, an emerging dialogue between experimental feminist writers in Quebec with their counterparts in English Canada was both facilitated by and facilitated a specific feminist translation practice. For example, in its 1989 "La traduction au féminin/Translating Women" issue, the feminist journal, *Tessera,* whose mandate was to encourage just such a dialogue, signalled the synergy of translation, writing, and theory, grounded in a critique of patriarchal language and a revisioning of subjectivity.[4]

Because of Canada's unique history of two "founding" languages and increasing recognition of its Aboriginal peoples and cultures and its many ethnicities, Canadian translation practices thus offer models and theories that resonate with and contribute to postcolonial discourses. Understanding and tracking this international recognition of Canadian contributions to translation studies underscore the significance and urgency of the archive—of the recuperation and interpretation of memories, publications, documentation, and records in oral and print and digital forms.

A translated novel or film adaptation ensures the afterlife, the memory, the multiple manifestations of the source text. Thus, translation itself functions as a moveable archive. As a material archive it consists of a collection of drafts and versions of the novel translated into English or Cree and of the correspondence between author and translator, translator and publisher located in a physical site. As a conceptual archive, it enhances the hermeneutics of the source text, drawing attention to the contingencies and wellsprings of meanings and interpretations.

In the following discussion, the material and conceptual archive of a specific translation experience demonstrates how translation serves as an example both of a memory record and of a promise for the future. As a case in point of the role of small presses in the production and dissemination of Quebec literature in translation, we turn to the archives of Talonbooks, a small west-coast press—the Talonbook Fonds, Special Collections, Simon Fraser University. By delving into institutional dynamics, socio-political circumstances, and personal histories, such a study contributes to the creation of an archive of translation history and to our understanding of the making of modern culture in Canada, past and future.[5] That is, we learn what factors determine translation practices and how translation in turn affects the evolution of Canadian culture.

The physical site of the Talonbooks archives is a large storage room belonging to the Special Collections of the Bennett Library at Simon Fraser University, a labyrinth of boxes, papers, and overloaded carts; six long rows of metallic shelves covering four long walls are crammed with 707 neatly organized manuscript boxes and fifty-one banker boxes comprising the voluminous, still expanding Talonbook Fonds (Fig. 1).[6] The Fonds consist of typed manuscripts of poetry, plays, novels, memoirs; blue lines; galleys; annual catalogues; large flat files of production graphics; files and files of correspondence with published, prospective, rejected authors and translators; grant applications; and polite, enraged, or placatory correspondence with the Canada Council and other agencies

FIGURE 1. Talonbook Fonds, Bennett Library, Simon Fraser University. Photo courtesy of the author.

and institutions. With much of the material preceding electronic mail, desktop production, and the digital revolution, these archives represent a repository of information and offer memory retrievals of the volatile history of a small press, the drama of publishing in Canada between 1965 and the present, and trends in avant-garde poetry and drama and fiction. As Derrida notes, "the technical structure of the *archiving* archive also determines the structure of the *archivable* content even in its very coming into existence and in its relationship to the future" (*Archive* 17). Any reader or researcher delving into these archives is inevitably and inexorably subject to what is randomly retained and ordered in these files, to what is "remembered" in print, and to the cataloguing skills of a legion of assistants—the "technical structure" of files and banker boxes and of the filing system (by date, by correspondent), and their organization and location in a physical space. How can we know what is missing or concealed? What remains untold? What has been misplaced, lost, tossed, forgotten? Like memories, archives are constructions and interpretations of events shaped by the subjectivity of the donor and the archivist. In her study of Canadian women writers in and out of the archive, Barbara Godard reminds us that "[a] physical site, the archive is not only an institutional space enclosing the material traces of the past, but also an imaginative site and a conceptual space of changing limits" ("Contested" 66). And, therefore, "although the material traces are structured as the archive comes into existence and in its relationship to the future, the signs of this sifting and interpretation are often invisible" and "there are ... omissions, restrictions, repressions and exclusions" (66). Indeed, there is another history hidden among the omissions and exclusions—in the non-archived. Therefore, my "historical" study and excavation of Talonbooks relies on another moveable archive, a personal archive—the memory of Karl Siegler, what we might call the *Sieglerian signature* (à la *Freudian signature* [Derrida, *Archive* 5]). Siegler's recall of the trajectory of the translation history of the press, of all the players—the authors, the translators, their obsessions and foibles, and of the vagaries of funding by the BC government and by the Canada Council—is, without question, formidable.[7] His personal "archive" is often, but not always, corroborated by the files and the printed word in the Special Collections. Interviews, testimonies, and correspondence by other Talonbooks figures and editors, such as Jim Brown, David Robinson, Peter Hay, as well as their many authors and translators located in the Fonds or published in journals and little magazines (see below), of course, offer differently nuanced interpretations of events. Out of this accumulation and variety of archives we can *perhaps* construct an archive that digs into the past to recuperate and document the relationship between translation acts and Canadian cultural artifacts.

Small presses in the 1950s (Contact Press) and again in the '60s and '70s (Harvest House, House of Anansi, new press), along with established presses like McClelland and Stewart, which published Marie-Claire Blais' *Mad Shadows* (translated by Merloyd Lawrence in 1960),[8] began offering translations of experimental Quebec novelists and poets. Thus, although Talonbooks can claim neither the first English translation of a modern Quebec play[9] nor the first translation of a writer from Quebec's Quiet Revolution,[10] its unprecedented publication of four contemporary Quebec plays in 1974 signalled a pivotal moment in the history of literary translation in Canada. Not only was it publishing drama, a minor genre in the world of publishing but, remarkably, it was publishing Quebec drama from the far west edge of Canada. Within a space of a few months, this small Vancouver press had brought out Robert Gurik's *API 2967* (translated by Marc Gélinas), and his *The Trial of Jean-Baptiste M.* (translated by Allan Van Meer), followed swiftly by Michel Tremblay's controversial and popular *Hosanna* and *Les Belles-Soeurs* (translated by theatre producers John Van Burek and Bill Glassco). It signalled that it was time to ensure a wider availability of exciting, experimental Canadian and Quebec drama in the wake of successful and prize-winning productions of *API 2967* at the Venice Biennale, 1969; *The Trial* in Paris and Athens in 1974; and *Les Belles-Soeurs* (St. Lawrence Centre, 1972),[11] *Forever Yours, Marie-Lou* (Tarragon Theatre, 1972), and *Hosanna* (Tarragon, 1974) in Toronto. Unfortunately, Talonbooks omitted the translators from these cover pages.[12] As Talonbooks became the "official" English language publisher (according to Siegler) of Tremblay's plays, novels, and memoirs through negotiation and ongoing tactics and strategies of acquisition, it signalled that the field of literary production and the dominant producers could be challenged from the margins—the margin of size and the margin of location.[13] When Talonbooks achieved its "prise de positions" (Bourdieu 30) for its translations of Tremblay in attractively designed paperbacks, other translators began to approach them during the 1970s and '80s with suggestions: David Lobdell, Patricia Claxton, Linda Gaboriau, David Homel. Talonbooks then continued on to develop an impressive list of translations of experimental Quebec and francophone playwrights and novelists (e.g., Jovette Marchessault, Larry Tremblay, Michel Marc Bouchard, Marie-Claire Blais, Madeleine Gagnon, and Lise Tremblay). Observing the trajectory of this press, Kathleen Scherf remarked that "the life of Talonbooks closely documents and reflects the life of Canadian literary culture since 1967, with a west coast twist" (132). Embedded within this history of acquisition is the history of the cultivation of a specific canon of Quebec writers who resonate with Talonbooks' own stable of avant-garde writers for anglophone Canada. It is also the history of how cultural stereotypes and canons are created, in this case, of certain aspects of Quebec writing—humorous, carnivalesque, Montreal-centred, sometimes offering the perspective of homosexuals, sometimes that of children or working-class women.

Talonbooks' landmark publication of two Tremblay plays in 1974 had far-reaching consequences.[14] First, perched on the west coast, far from the publishing centres of Toronto and Montreal, this young, struggling press took a chance on publishing a playwright whose counter-discourse disrupted forever not only normative French speech in Quebec literature but also theatrical forms and conventions by writing in the vernacular about working-class women in Montreal's Plateau Mont-Royal. In the words of Toronto theatre critic, Urjo Kareda: "For some time last year, there was a dispute about which Canadian publishing house would acquire the English-language rights to the plays of Quebec dramatist Michel Tremblay.... Well, the battle was won by Talonbooks, a small but energetic publishing company in Vancouver" (F6).[15] In its introduction to the Winter 1986/Spring 1987 catalogue, Talonbooks boasted that the press is "well known for its translations of works from Quebec—notably, for bringing Michel Tremblay's plays and first novel into print in English." It was no mean feat to maintain this relationship, from the margins of Vancouver, with Quebec's most prolific and internationally renowned writer, while juggling Quebec publishing houses, barriers of language and customs, agents, translators, authors, and the Canada Council bureaucracy, all of which constituted "a cascade of challenges" (Siegler, Personal interview).[16]

Second, Talonbooks, which originated as a small press publishing poetry in 1967 under the editorship of Jim Brown, David Robinson, and Gordon Fidler, shifted its attention to contemporary Canadian drama with the arrival of Peter Hay in 1969 as drama editor: a risky but, in the end, profitable gamble.[17] The publication of drama, like that of translation, is a layered and complex process of production, involving scripts, notations, stage directions, agents, the variables of spectators and audience, playwrights, and directors. In his study of the press, Michael Hayward offers one reason for this venture: "Unable to locate Canadian play texts to teach [at Simon Fraser University], he [Peter Hay] eventually approached Talonbooks with the rights to two plays [James Reaney's *Colours in the Dark* and George Ryga's *The Ecstasy of Rita Joe*]" (4). Karl Siegler suggests another: "Canadian publishers such as Talonbooks, by continuing to publish poetry and drama titles into a marketplace too small to make such titles financially viable, are performing an important role in defining and maintaining Canadian culture" (qtd. in Hayward 12). In a number of communications, Siegler was adamant that Talonbooks become the "major play publisher in English Canada" (Letter to Naïm Kattan, 18 September 1972, Talonbooks Archives MsC 8.4.5.18).

In order, however, to begin to understand the felicitous conjunction of the emergence of small presses like Talonbooks with the turn to translation in the 1960s and '70s and the accompanying fields of forces and of struggles (Bourdieu 30), which invariably influence the potential cultural effects of translation on Canadian culture, we need to examine the cultural and institutional disposition of emerging small presses in Canada and their intricate connections and histories.

Cultural Conditions

> The discovery, among ourselves, that *we* have the writers—poets, playwrights, novelists, short story writers, even artists and film makers, *and* that they need books—as a service to *their* community and to the community at large.
>
> > – David Robinson in answer to George Woodcock's question: "What do you consider the principal reason (or reasons) for the rise of so many new publishing houses in Canada during the past five years?"[18]

Often started by writers and staffed by the writers and their (girl) friends,[19] small presses are ideological rather than profit-driven, often associated with modernism and the avant-garde (and seemingly justified by their lack of readership and mass audience!). In the 1960s and '70s, circumstances converged to create an explosion of small presses across Canada. Between 1965 and 1975 there were several dramatic changes in Canadian publishing. More and more, the major Toronto houses concentrated on mass-circulation titles and rejected books that lacked nation-wide sales appeal. Because many of these firms were evolving into public companies and/or subsidiaries of international corporations, publishing decisions often had more to do with the bottom line than the vision of one person. By contrast, small press owners maintained hands-on control over all aspects of publishing, from the manuscript to the finished book. The development of offset presses and computerized printing made possible the production of low-cost, attractively designed books, most of them in paper covers (Parker).

Bourdieu's observation about the effect of changes in power relations and the space of positions in *The Field of Cultural Production* is apposite here: "When a new literary or artistic group makes its presence felt in the field of literary or artistic production, the whole problem is transformed, since its coming into being ... modifies and displaces the universe of possible options; the previously dominant productions may, for example, be pushed into the status of outmoded (*déclassé*) or of classic works" (32). Thus, reacting against the tradition of realism in Canadian fiction and in the publishing sphere, writers like Dennis Lee and Dave Godfrey (Anansi), and Victor Coleman (Coach House Press) set up venues for experimental writers in adventurously designed and well-crafted books, independent of the editorial and marketing constraints of the big publishing houses. To that mix, Talonbooks added the desire to counter "the pan-Canadian, New Canadian Library, patriotic agenda in favour of articulating the local" (Scherf 137). As David Robinson remarked, "Talonbooks' impetus to begin publishing was local" (qtd. in Woodcock 57), and several emerging presses such as Talonbooks in Vancouver, Coteau Books in Regina, and Fiddlehead Books in the Maritimes defied the centrifugal pull and power of the centre, concentrating instead on the local and deliberately flaunting their peripheral status: "[I] try to bring new blood in, but also, to move things out" (qtd. in Woodcock 60). However, as its extensive drama list from 1969 on indicates, and its significant translation list further corroborates, Talonbooks, having accumulated substantial cultural capital, now perceives itself as a federalist press, a *Canadian* literary publisher (Siegler).[20]

Other small presses who pursued and published translations included Harvest House in Montreal, in operation from 1965 to 1995, with their French Writers in Canada series; House of Anansi, founded in 1967, which was persuaded by Sheila Fischman to produce the Roch Carrier trilogy; Michael Macklem's Oberon Press, 1966; and Coach House Press, 1965, which, under the direction of Barbara Godard and Frank Davey, created the Quebec Translation series (1975–89). Coach House, whose first translation was Victor-Lévy Beaulieu's *Jack Kerouac: a chicken-essay*, translated by Sheila Fischman in 1975, was instrumental in bringing Nicole Brossard's poetry, fiction, and feminist theory to the attention of English Canada. Ironically, Talonbooks declined to translate Brossard because she didn't have any reputation outside of Quebec.[21] Later, in the 1980s, the Women's Press, among the second wave of small presses, focused on feminist texts from Quebec.[22] By the mid-1970s, Talonbooks was including translations in fiction, and by the late 1970s, non-fiction. The flexibility and adventurousness of small presses, the hands-on (although sometimes testy) relationship between editors, designers, translators, and authors, along with attractive and accessible book designs and the continuing marketability of translations as course adoptions, appealed to authors and their translators. At the same time, translations of exciting new writing from Quebec enhanced the small anglophone presses' reputation as avant-garde and exploratory.

Further socio-political conditions influencing the appeal of translating Quebec literature included: the patriotism generated by centennial celebrations and Expo 67 in Montreal, the rise of Canadian nationalism, and the desire to discover and forge a "Canadian" identity, accompanied by anti-Americanism sentiments; the anti-Vietnam war protests, the peace and civil rights movements; campus activism and radicalism; and Paris 1968. Events in Quebec also conspired to attract the interest of writers and publishers: the Quiet revolution of the 1960s; the Quebec independence movement; the 1970 October Crisis, with its alarming crackdown on writers, artists, musicians, and performers; the close ties between leftist politics and culture; and the explosion of experimental writing in Quebec grounded in a radical sense of place and language.

The mounting interest in translations from French to English at least was thus linked to the desire of federal institutions and a coterie of anglophone writers, translators, and intellectuals (D.G. Jones, F.R. Scott,

John Glassco, Philip Stratford, Sheila Fischman, Ray Ellenwood) to bridge the cultural gap between the two solitudes and to understand the turbulent situation in Quebec. As Peter Hay chided in his "Introduction" to Gurik's *The Trial of Jean-Baptiste M.*: "[o]ne of the commonest commonplaces of Canadian culture is to remark about the absence of cross-fertilization between its two official languages.... Yet, there is only one thing rarer than a French Canadian play produced by an English Canadian theatre, and that's *vice versa*" (5). Describing Anansi's program of publishing French-Canadian books in translation, John Metcalf admitted that while "such translations or bilingual editions are usually pious exercises fuelled by government gold" and that "hardly anyone on either side of the divide actually *reads* them," the Carrier trilogy was a "genuine and popular success" (9). Indeed, Roch Carrier's *La Guerre, Yes Sir*, translated by Sheila Fischman, a bawdy and satirical portrait of rural Quebec during the Second World War, was widely taught in universities and high schools in the 1970s and '80s. In retrospect, however, these gestures of mediation and bridge building were nevertheless marked by an uncritical acceptance by anglophones of anglophone dominance and hegemony. For example, correspondence between Talonbooks and Leméac, Tremblay's French publisher, and between Talonbooks and the Quebec playwright Gurik, is entirely in English. Furthermore, many Quebec writers and intellectuals viewed translation and the bilingual project as a betrayal of Quebec's desire to promote and protect its French language and culture.

Another powerful incentive was envy of the vibrant and avant-garde cultural scene in Quebec and the propensity to embroider a narrative construction of Quebec as an eroticized and exoticized imagined community, as Frank Davey recalled:

> A frequently important element in the Anglophone desire for connection with Quebec was a romantic view of its Francophone culture as more passionate, violent, and creative than much of Anglophone culture—not only an FLQ Quebec where nationalists paraded with flags, planted bombs, kidnapped officials, and exploded themselves in parliamentary washrooms, but also a Gilles Vigneault–Pauline Julien Quebec where people were believed to care deeply about poetry, culture, and collective creativity ... and a site of libidinal excess. ("History" n.p.)

And, finally, there were timely and specific institutional dispositions emerging out of the volatile political climate and social context.

Institutional Factors

The late 1960s and the early '70s were a propitious time to embark upon translating the other solitude. In response to its Royal Commission on Bilingualism and Biculturalism, which had warned that Quebec's simmering discontent indicated that Canada was passing through the greatest crisis in its history (1965), the federal government enacted the Official Languages Act (1969), which was intended to enhance the status of French federally and implement bilingualism in parliament and federal institutions, and began to promote official bilingualism and biculturalism. On a smaller scale, literary translations received support through the Canada Council translation grant program that began in 1972,[23] which was also the year in which block publishing grants were inaugurated.[24] Publishers like Talonbooks also took advantage of federal programs like Opportunities for Youth and Local Initiatives Programs to hire assistants; these grants enabled theatrical troupes to produce and tour contemporary Quebec plays, as Allan Van Meer did throughout British Columbia in 1972, with his translated versions of Tremblay, Gurik, and Dominique de Pasquale (Talonbooks Fonds, MsC 8.4.13.14), versions of which then found their way to Talonbooks and other small presses.

A crucial boost to small presses and the publication of Quebec literature in translation was the educational capital created by the demand for course books, due to the rapid rise of new universities, the expansion of established ones, and the gradual development of courses in Canadian literature and Canadian Studies. In other words, course adoptions and the educational system conferred what Bourdieu would call a "legitimate mode of consumption" (37) and a more powerful position upon small presses, like Talonbooks, publishing translations.

An enduring effect, therefore, of the 1974 venture into translating Gurik and Tremblay is that 23–27 percent of Talonbooks' booklist now consists of translations, and that a corpus of Quebec playwrights are accessible and available for study in schools and universities and for mounting productions nationally and internationally. Consider, for example, that *Hosanna* played in Vancouver in the spring of 2008. Furthermore, like other presses, Talonbooks has expanded to include francophone literature outside Quebec (Jean Marc Dalpé) and translations from other languages. New emerging small presses—Broken Jaw Press in Fredericton, Butschek Books in Ottawa, Cormorant Books in Toronto, Ekstasis in Victoria—join older presses like Oberon, Véhicule (1973), Guernica (1970), and Exile Editions (1976) in publishing translations not only from French but from Spanish, Gallician, First Nations, German, Russian, Polish, Yiddish, Italian, and Arabic. In 2011/12, the Canada Council awarded ninety-seven translation grants.

By excavating deeply into the stored archive and its vast repository of materials and by tapping into the remarkable and detailed memories of the *Sieglerian signature*, we unearth evidence and corroboration of Talonbooks' instrumental role in publishing experimental Canadian drama; in defying the centre; in refiguring the cultural capital of Canadian literatures; and in pursuing, promoting, and repositioning the translation of Quebec avant-garde writing, or as Siegler puts it, postcolonial writing. Since Siegler continues to deposit and update the Talonbooks holdings, the archive extends from the past into the present. It also reveals that the rest of Canada's experience of writing in Quebec is worryingly contingent, for English Canada's exposure to the literature of Quebec remains limited by what gets translated, how and by whom it is translated, how adequately it is funded, and the necessity to attract readers and spectators. The canon of translated texts is eclectic and erratic, and even in the case of small, independent, ideologically driven presses, dependent less on any considered program of selection than on recommendations by translators who can be seen as taking up positions as gatekeepers of the "other" culture, the vagaries of the Translation Grant program, preferences of publishers, contracts and rights negotiations, the allure of prize winners, and marketability. "Name-stuff," as translator David Lobdell once admonished David Robinson (letter, January 25, 1977, MsC.8.a Box 21), tends to be published over lesser-known figures, thus ironically vitiating the more iconoclastic and experimental directions of the small press.[25]

And a "perhaps" haunts the archive, the archivist, and the intrepid researcher since "we will only know in times to come" (Derrida, *Archive* 36) the archive's significance and its effect on, and relationship to, the future. The archival experience and that unique visceral feel, smell, and sight of a now-almost-forgotten past of typewritten letters and manuscripts, carbon copies, and blue lines surely signal more than mere nostalgia for a seemingly simpler past. They evoke more than an understandable desire for a human-scaled and scalable technology, for a neighbourly clutch of small presses and bookstores, and a distaste for dizzying box bookstores and secretively conglomerate publishers. Instead, one might perceive ways in which the archival experience and the specific example given here of Talonbooks and other small adventurous presses beckon "the very question of a future" that could perhaps, still, cherish the local, the community, the collaborative and the collective, the periphery, the marginal, the small scale, and the defiant.

Is CanLit Lost in Japanese Translation?

Yoko Fujimoto

Introduction

The year 1983 was a turning point in the development of Canadian studies in Japan. This date coincides with the publication of *Komonwerusu no Bungaku*, an introductory guide in Japanese to commonwealth literature published by Kenkyusha, a company renowned for its dictionaries and scholarly and educational books on English language and literature. The book included a chapter on Canada, in which Keiichi Hirano, then professor of English at Tokyo University and co-editor of the book, offered a Frygian account of the history of Canadian literature that placed emphasis on the development of "Canadian" identity and the "Canadian" imagination. Given the fact that Hirano was one of the founders of the Canadian Literary Society of Japan (CLSJ), which was founded in 1982 as a salon for teachers and other aficionadas/os of Canadian fiction and poetry, *Komonwerusu no Bungaku* surely marked a rise in Japan of a more focused interest in Canadian literature than the long established appreciation and fame of L.M. Montgomery's *Anne of Green Gables*, first published in Japan in 1952.[1]

It was Hirano's chapter in *Komonwerusu no Bungaku* that brought Margaret Atwood to Japanese readers' attention. Hirano mentioned Atwood as a writer and critic of exceptional cultural and intellectual importance in Canada and identified *Survival* as "an epoch-making guide to Canadian literature" (38, my translation). Introducing Atwood's key concepts of victimization and survival, he stated in no uncertain terms that "[n]o discussion of Canadian literature in general and no attempt to write a history of Canadian literature in particular will ever be free from the influence of Atwood's *Survival*" (40). However, at that time, when few universities in Japan provided courses in Canadian literature, Atwood's *Survival*, a book apparently designed for classroom use, did not gain the same influential status it has enjoyed in Canada and other countries. This was the result of a relative indifference among the Japanese to the heated controversies over definitions of Canadianness, as well as the politics of defining it, controversies that largely characterized Canadian literary studies in the late 1970s and '80s in Canada. Moreover, Hirano's article, contrary to what might have been expected, had no apparent influence on generating interest, among Japanese publishers, in Canadian literature and its potential appeal to general readers. Indeed, despite the unequivocal terms through which Hirano established Atwood's importance, none of her books was translated or published in Japan until 1989, when the translation of *Dancing Girls and Other Stories* (*Danshingu Gaaruzu*)[2] appeared.

Today, over twenty years since the publication of *Komonwerusu no Bungaku*, the situation surrounding the reception of Canadian literature in Japan is significantly, if not dramatically, different. In 1995, *Sabaibaru*, the translation of *Survival*, finally appeared. Published as it was by a minor company and in a translation of doubtful quality, it did not achieve a sizable readership or substantial critical acclaim; nevertheless, the book, or more precisely its first chapter and the theory of victimization, has since come to be recognized and sometimes referred to as if it were the most authoritative account of Canadian culture. In the meantime, CLSJ, whose membership has grown to almost one hundred since its founding in 1982, is increasingly geared toward critical studies of a wider range of texts and issues, while the Japanese Association for Canadian Studies (JACS), claiming four hundred members, plays a central role in producing disciplinary and interdisciplinary research. At the same time, a growing number of specialists offer a wide variety of courses in Canadian studies, including culture and literature. It is still very unusual, however, for Canadian literary studies to comprise a part of the core curriculum of English or cultural studies departments. When Canadian texts are included in course materials, they are often taught as part of American or postcolonial literature and/or in the context of a language class where the focus is on close reading of only a few key texts per term that are rarely, if at all, taught in ways that would approximate survey courses.

Outside educational and academic institutions, Canadian literature has been gaining more lay readers in Japan in the past decade or so, as can be seen in the proliferation of the publication of Canadian novels in translation. This reflects, to a great extent, the success of contemporary Canadian writers in the global market, evidenced by their nomination for major international awards. The nomination of three Canadian writers for the Man Booker prize in 2002, which was awarded to Yann Martel, is one example of the growing global visibility of Canadian literary authors' works. The translation of Martel's *The Life of Pi* (*Pai no Monogatari*) was published in early 2004, while the other Canadian nominees, Rohinton Mistry and Carol Shields, whose names had already been widely circulating in global literary-prize markets, had been introduced to the Japanese reading public prior to 2002 through the translation of Mistry's *Tales from Firozshabaag* (*Bombei no Fushigi na Apaato*) and *Such a Long Journey* (*Kakumo Nagaki Tabi*), and Shields's *The Stone Diaries* (*Sutoon Daiarii*). Other translations into Japanese of Canadian authors since the 1990s include books by Barbara Gowdy, Anne Michaels, Alice Munro, Alistair MacLeod, and of course Margaret Atwood and Michael Ondaatje. Today, Canadian fiction is readily available in Japan, and it occasionally enjoys notable sales, especially when aided by the promotional capacity of major publishers, as I discuss later. Nevertheless, Canadian literature specialists in Japan are confronted with the uncanny fact that few readers associate these translations with Canada. When they do, "Canada" tends to become a sign deprived of and separated from the complex reality of the signified.

It is this phenomenon that I wish to focus on in this essay—namely, the slighting, or the loss of significance, of the national category that occurs in the process of reproducing and distributing Canadian literature in translation. Here I deal with translation not as linguistic process but as cultural "transplantation," a metaphor used by theorists, especially Lorna Hardwick, to stress the importance of "the cultural framework within which ... [texts are] embedded" (Hardwick 15). As Susan Bassnett and others "pleaded" in the early 1990s, translation studies, like other disciplines, have seen a "cultural turn" that brought a shift in focus "from a more formalist approach to translation to one that laid greater emphasis on extra-textual factors" (*Translation* 13). Following this vein of translation studies, and employing concepts of cultural translation theory introduced by such scholars as Itamar Even-Zohar and Gideon Toury, this essay explores the cultural contexts of Japan into which Canadian literature is transplanted, as well as the methods that facilitate this process. Specifically, I discuss the following aspects of the translation industry: the processes of selecting texts for translation; the publishers' practice of adding postscripts and other supplementary comments to books of foreign literature in translation; and, lastly, the involvement of contemporary Japanese writers in the publishers' promotional schemes.

What I hope to reveal in this study is how globalism affects the process of cultural transplantation in Japan. While globalism advances the commodification of culture and standardization of values, as a material process it occurs only in conjunction with the socio-historical conditions in the local context. My working premise, then, is that globalism and local conditions work in tandem to influence both the practice of transplantation and the reception of such cultural products as literary translations. Therefore, what seems lost or obscured in translation, the significance of a national label being the foremost example, is in fact the outcome of complex workings of cultural interaction. Thus my argument situates translation in the context of global and local interactions, while also pointing toward ways in which researchers and educators in Japan can contribute to "recovering" a more nuanced sense of reality from that constructed through the process of translation so that they can, hopefully, offer a balanced view of the current state of literary production and consumption, especially in relation to the translation of Canadian literary works.

I

To export or import literature entails transplanting books into a new territory where different social and cultural norms and practices are at work. When the texts are delivered in another language, the process of translation involves degrees of negotiation not simply with another language but also with a host of other elements that constitute the new environment for the transplanted text. Maintaining that literary values are inherent in a text, or assuming a text's international acclaim is adequate as the determining factor for its transplanting value, is of little use in understanding what enables or facilitates the transformation that a translated text undergoes. As a corrective to that approach, I trace the actual processes that mediate this transfer by taking the translation of Atwood's books as my example. In particular, I focus on the different kinds of rationales employed by Japanese publishers and editors in accounting for the importance of translating Atwood into Japanese.

As I have already mentioned, the first book by Atwood that appeared in Japanese translation was *Dancing Girls and Other Stories*, published in 1989. Of the more than a dozen of Atwood's books that have been translated since then, *The Handmaid's Tale* (*Jijo no Monogatari*) and *The Blind Assassin* (*Kuraki Me no Ansatsusha*) are by far the most successful in terms of sales figures. The translation of *The Handmaid's Tale*, published by Shinchosha in 1990, has sold 19,500 copies in hardcover and even more copies in the "bunko" (soft cover, pocket size) edition by Hayakawa-shobo.[3] Generally speaking, for a literary book in translation to be considered a bestseller in Japan its sales need to reach 100,000. Only in rare cases can foreign novels sell over a million copies, but this happens mostly in the category of popular literature (Kitamoto).[4] Indeed, *The Blind Assassin*, published by Hayakawa-shobo in 2002, has had a modest success: after its first print of 5000 copies sold out, an additional 3000 copies were published (Kagoshima). According to Yuri Kagoshima, then editor of literature at the Hayakawa Publishing Company, the fact that the translation of *The Blind Assassin* has gone into a second printing, despite its publication during the recession period that followed the bubble economy in Japan, was remarkable enough.[5] By comparison, during the time of the bubble economy in the 1980s, Hayakawa would have set 8000 copies as the minimum standard of success for the first printing of a novel in translation (Hayakawa).

Needless to say, for the publishers the bottom line is always sales. Nevertheless, their strategies for selecting texts for translation are not always clearly formulated. Some of the major factors that editors in Japan report bearing in mind when deciding which literary texts to translate include: (1) the book's content, particularly its presumed appeal to the general public; (2) any additional merits, such as major prizes won and film or television production; (3) the local socio-cultural context, that is, the state of Japanese society and readership at the time of publication; (4) the financial feasibility of the project; and (5) compatibility with the publishers' production and editorial policies.

Turning again to the translation of *The Blind Assassin*, we can begin to understand how each of these factors works at once independently and in relation to the others. More specifically, the launch of Atwood's book was announced in early 2000, coinciding with the period when the Hayakawa publishing company renewed its interest in, as well as emphasis on, the publication of literary works. Indeed, this was a time when this publishing house's editors were actively and enthusiastically engaged with preparations for their new line of products dubbed "epi-bunko," a paperback literature series in translation designed to create a new image for the press as well as increase accessibility to Hayakawa's (and at the same time other publishers') backlists that had sold well in other formats. While Graham Greene's *The Third Man* was chosen as the first title in the series, works by contemporary and internationally acclaimed writers such as Kazuo Ishiguro, J.M. Coetzee, and Toni Morrison also appeared in the same series. Atwood's *The Handmaid's Tale* was among the first thirteen titles published in this series in 2001. Still in continuous production, Hayakawa has characterized this series as a collection of "quality works of literature from abroad targeted at readers with a young sensibility."[6] In the pamphlet Hayakawa produced for advertising the "epi" series, the translated books' titles are accompanied by the list of "major literary awards of the world" that they won, including the Nobel prize, the Man Booker prize, America's National Book Award, and the Prix Goncourt and Prix Femina in France. The alignment of these translations with a globally recognized value system not only accounts for what exerted influence on this publishing house's editorial policy at the time when *The Blind Assassin* was being considered for publication but also reveals the self-evident assumptions of its editorial policy regarding what constitutes literary value.

Although there was ample evidence about the favourable reception of Atwood's book in the West (factor 1), its length of over five hundred pages in the English version was a major drawback. Translating such a long book in Japanese means incurring a severe financial burden; the estimated price of 3000 yen ($30–40 Cdn.) per copy, a minimum price for the publisher to break even, runs the risk of discouraging readers (factor 4). The cultural and economic climate at the time, with consumers showing preference for "keihakutansho,"[7] namely, anything "light-weight, thin, short and small," had a large impact on manufacturing in Japan, an impact also strongly felt in the publishing industry. The average price range of the books most widely circulated in that period was around 1500 yen ($15–20 Cdn.) (factor 3). Despite these adverse economic conditions, the proposal for publishing Atwood's novel of more than six hundred pages in Japanese translation was approved, and the price was set at slightly over 3000 yen. In my interview with him, Kagoshima, Hayakawa's editor, did not specify the rationale employed to approve the title for translation but suggested three additional factors as having played a crucial role at the final stage of the decision-making process: the novel had won the Dashiell Hammett prize in June 2000, which had special significance for Hayakawa, a publishing firm specializing in genre-specific literature such as mysteries and science fiction (factors 1, 2, and 5). Later that year, the book was also awarded the Man Booker Prize, which enhanced the publisher's prospects for success, especially in view of the recent commercial hit of another Booker winner, J.M. Coetzee's *Disgrace* (*Chijoku*), which they published in hardcover in November 2000 (factor 2).

The factors enumerated above are inevitably enmeshed in a complex web of relations. The financial circumstances that influence editorial policy about literary translations are specific to the local conditions; at the same time, however, as illustrated in the case of the "epi-bunko" series, publishing policies are not exclusively determined by local issues or by an individual company's trade trends. Rather, they are developed through a negotiation that involves internal as well as external factors. Noticeably, the factor of international prizes seems to outweigh most of the other factors initially considered to be major drawbacks. Indeed, the culture of celebrity that accompanies such prizes may well be the most important factor determining a publisher's decision to publish a translation. This reflects the extent to which the market value system of literary publications in the West is transplanted in Japan. Literary agents, individual translators, authors, and academics play the role of informants who communicate this value system to Japanese publishers. In this exchange system of knowledge and values, major companies such as Shinchosha come into direct contact with foreign publishers, often at international book fairs. For example, the book fairs in London, New York, and Frankfurt are key trade sites where publishing news is translated into terms that make the titles to be translated attractive marketing prospects (Sugai). This global marketing system suggests that the information and products the publishing industry's buyers have access to, when it comes to books published in European languages, are standardized and largely controlled by multinational publishing companies based in the West. The same can be said about prize-giving institutions, as is evident in the case of the Man Booker Prize, which operates on the basis of publishers' recommendations.[8]

At the same time, however, as the editors Sugai and Kagoshima have mentioned, Western publishers often make recommendations for translation that are tailored for specific buyers/publishers, based on their research on individual markets and past experience with selling foreign rights. In this respect, the global system within which the publishing industry operates does not simply enhance standardization; it is also responsive to local cultural and marketing differences. Moreover, Japanese publishers and editors do not yield easily to external pressures, as they have come to know that imported standards from the West do not always work well in Japan; instead, they have learned to invest significant effort in understanding the local contexts in which the translated texts are to be embedded. Thus the negotiations for securing the translation rights of a text and its successful marketing occur mostly within that space where the local and the global intersect. In other words, the main challenge publishers have to contend with in deciding which foreign texts to translate and invest in concerns the need to define Japanese cultural conditions in relation to the world—"the world" here meaning, more often than not, the West.

The imperative to "translate" a foreign text's relevance to the Japanese readership is a matter of understanding or, more specifically, anticipating the text's reception in Japan. Hayakawa's editor Kagoshima mentions gender as a factor that plays a role in reception. As she explains, female readers, the staple readers of foreign literature in Japan, have come to demonstrate greater tolerance for and deeper understanding of unconventional subjects and literary devices in novels. Thus she acknowledges these readers' readiness to accept and appreciate the irony, cynicism, and intellectual playfulness that characterize Atwood's writing. Coetzee's *Disgrace*, on the other hand, unexpectedly helped the publisher cultivate a new type of readership for foreign novels. The feedback the publishing firm received from high-income, well-educated, middle-aged male readers via the "readers' card," an insert often found in Japanese translations, showed that there was indeed a niche, at least among male readers, for a novel such as Coetzee's. Conversely, Sugai, an editor at Shinchosha Publishing, argues that, for her, it is Japanese writers, as well as the general reader, that are the targeted recipients of texts in translation. She hopes that "foreign authors, whose writing style is so different [from that of Japanese literature] and impressive," would "stimulate Japanese writers who threaten to become smaller and smaller [in their perspective] as long as they stay and write only within their own limited circles."

What is noticeable in these editors' statements is that their rhetoric resonates with Enlightenment ideas; that is, they seem to suggest that the dissemination of and exposure to "world literature" can result in eye-opening experiences, an advanced state of awareness otherwise not easily gained. Those familiar with Japanese history could also hear an echo of the West's intervention in Japan at the time of the Meiji Restoration period (circa 1868), which became the impetus for the construction of Japanese modernity. Westernization remained a driving force for the nation's development for decades, even long after the Second World War. In fact, the notions of "literature" and "novel" were themselves imported from the West and gradually incorporated into the cultural discourse concerning the production, reading, and studies of texts in Japan in the early twentieth century (de Bary 4).[9] As if to reiterate the effects of Japan's cultural encounter with the West, the editors I have interviewed have no reservation in employing a rhetoric that is interspersed with terms such as "immaturity" and "growth" with regard to the Japanese reader. Consider, for example, Kagoshima's remark that "Japanese readers were childlike in that they could not, until recently, accept the dark, grotesque, or sometimes disturbingly asocial elements of, say, Atwood's novels, but now they are able to read and enjoy literature of that sort." This comment is especially striking considering that these literary and cultural elements have long existed in Japan, where the eerie, the uncanny, and the grotesque are recurring themes in Japanese literature. Crucial here is the fact that the editors' comments are not meant to apply to Japanese society at large; instead, they are intended to profile the readership of translated literature. Nevertheless, their views may well reinforce the clichéd notion that accepting the values of a foreign culture holds the promise of progress and renewal in Japanese culture. This apparent anachronism is marked by the historical trajectory of modern Japan and its complicated relations with foreign cultures. Still, Kagoshima also spoke of influence in the reverse, namely, the thriving subculture in Japan today represented by the "manga" comics and animation films that have greatly influenced literary styles and tastes in different regions of the world. Either way, what emerged as a crucial point in my interviews with these editors, especially in relation to the cultural and marketing politics of literary translation, is the positioning of Japanese culture as the polar opposite of the West, or, to put this otherwise, positing "world" values as the norm that influences new trends in Japan's publishing industry.

Even today the East and West are configured as a set of powerful polarities that frame and inform the perception, interpretation, and evaluation of foreign literature, as well as the strategies of publishers. This is an issue that demands extensive analysis, but to pursue it further here would take me too far afield. Suffice it to say, within the binary construct of things literary—"world"/Western literature versus Japanese literature—Canadian literature is not recognized in and of itself, but only as part of the larger conception of "foreign literature." As far as the editors are concerned—and all of them made this point repeatedly when I interviewed them—they strive to evaluate each text they consider for translation as an independent work of art. Canada's cultural products are thus consumed in Japan simply as commodities or symbols of "Western," "foreign," or "world" culture in general; they belong to a vaguely defined, but paradoxically overdetermined, double cultural "order of things." More specifically, in the process of translating/transplanting Canadian books, the source culture does not reference Canada; it is not Canadian literature that is imported, but books circulating in the global market.

II

The editor's work, which plays an integral role in the process of transplanting foreign literature, as we have seen above, does not stop with the decision of which texts to translate. It covers a wide range of other activities, from describing and promoting a product in common parlance to choosing appealing images for book covers. Thus editors participate in a process that we can call, in Roman Jakobson's terms, "intralingual" and "intersemiotic" translation.[10] Similarly, the translators' task is not restricted to producing an interlinguistic translation, although they certainly mediate between languages and directly produce transferred texts. They also practise intralinguistic transfer by often producing new versions of previously translated works. It is, then, important that a study of Japanese translation of Canadian novels address multiple aspects of translation and not those simply concerning supposed differences between the two languages. Even when engaging in "interlingual" translation, translators do not or cannot merely position themselves in a neutral space between two texts or two languages. Unlike the model suggested by Jakobson's famous taxonomy, translation operates in a culturally nuanced field and involves constant negotiation with particular conventions, linguistic as well as non-linguistic. In short, Jakobson's three kinds of translation are not easily distinguished within the materiality of cultural production and the marketplace; indeed, his categorization of translation fails to take into consideration the contextual and extra-semiotic factors that shape the various conditions that make translation and its dissemination possible. As Umberto Eco and Siri Nergaard have argued, it is "too strictly bound to a linguistic point of view" (220).

A more potent model can be found in the "polysystem theory" that originated in the Russian Fomalists' ideas as developed by Itamar Even-Zohar in the 1970s. The polysystem is "a heterogeneous, hierarchized conglomerate (or system) of systems which interact to bring about an ongoing, dynamic process of evolution within the polysystem as a whole" (Shuttleworth 176). Even-Zohar mainly focuses on the literary system, which he regards as yet another polysystem. The literary system, he says, is "*the network of relations that is hypothesized to obtain between a number of activities called 'literary,' and consequently these activities themselves observed via that network,*" and "*the complex of activities, or any section thereof, for which systemic relations can be hypothesized to support the option of considering them 'literary'*" (28).

In this context, within the literary system, translated literature constitutes a polysystem in its own right. Moreover, translated texts occupy a peripheral or central position, "connected with innovatory ('primary') or conservatory ('secondary') repertoires, depend[ing] on the specific constellation of the polysystem under study" (Even-Zohar 46). As he argues, there are three cases in which translated literature as a polysystem becomes central to, and influences, the larger literary polysystem: when "a literature is 'young' and in the process of being established"; when "a literature is either 'peripheral' (within a large group of correlated literatures) or 'weak,' or both"; and when "there are turning points, crises, or literary vacuums in a literature" (47). The importance of "foreign literature" in Japan since the mid-nineteenth century, as I have already mentioned, can serve as a good example of the latter two cases. The way editors today speak of translated literature as a means of stimulating Japanese contemporary writers may imply the novel's "weak" position in the present Japanese literary system in relation to the strength of, say, "manga" or genres of non-fiction, but this is the subject for another essay. Suffice to say, while translation occurs between the polysystems of the source culture and target culture, it is best understood in relation to the polysystems of the target culture. A major implication of this is that the end product does not necessarily reflect, nor is it always intended to convey, an awareness of the specificity of the source culture, in this instance, the conditions informing Canadian culture or its literary polysystem.

Following Even-Zohar's theory that extends "the context of research ... in particular to include examining the evaluative writing on translation, for example, prefaces, reviews, reflective essays, and so on" (M. Baker 163), in what follows I examine how postscripts and other textual elements operate in Canadian novels translated into Japanese. The packaging of such texts reflects what Gideon Toury calls a "translation norm," a key concept in the influential "descriptive translation studies" that Toury, inspired by Even-Zohar's theory, developed (M. Baker 163). "Translation norms" are patterns of "translational behaviour" that can be identified by studying texts, for example by examining "relationships and correspondences between the S[ource]T[ext] and the T[arget]T[ext] segments"; they are also discernible from "explicit statements made by translators, publishers, reviewers and other participants in the translation act" (Munday 113). The postscript in Japanese literary translations can be understood as an "operational norm,"[11] for example, the omission of passages or the addition of textual material and footnotes (Munday 114). The idea of "translation norms" is especially pertinent for the present study, for it helps explain how Canadian literature becomes invisible or is represented in a particular, often distorted, way in Japanese translation. The examples from translations of Atwood's novels that I discuss below reveal as much an aspect of the literary system and translation in Japan as the specific ways in which Canadian literature is transferred and consumed in this particular cultural context.

For many Japanese readers, including undergraduate students in English studies, who often consult the translation of English texts they are assigned to read, the translator's postscript that accompanies the translation is one of the most "authoritative" and useful aids for making sense of a foreign text. It is standard practice that literary texts in translation include a postscript that is, more often than not, written by the translator, while no such postscripts are to be found in Japanese fiction. Such postscripts usually include basic information about the author, as well as information about the reception and evaluation of the work in question in places outside Japan. Moreover, they often provide explanatory comments on the work's content and its contexts that are designed to convey commonly accepted readings of the text, be they those of the translator him- or herself or those of critics. Postscripts, then, play a major role in steering students and other readers to consume translated texts based on what is presented as reliable and legitimate interpretation. In other words, readers come to see the postscript as having the "right answer." This particular function of the postscript as a reading aid is an integral part of the norm in the system of literary translation in Japan.[12]

The first translators of Atwood's books began their postscripts by introducing the author as a leading writer in Canada, whose reputation encompasses the English-speaking regions across the world. The translators of *Dancing Girls* (*Danshingu Gaaruzu*) and *Bluebeard's Egg* (*Aohige no Tamago*) both emphasize the "strange" atmosphere of the fictional world she constructs and her idiosyncratic perspective in terms of the "reality" she represents. Sachiko Kishimoto, the translator of the former work, while mentioning *Surfacing*, acknowledges the power of Atwood's stories to "peel off the deceptive outer skin of what we desperately believe is reality" (Kishimoto 210, my translation), a statement made without engaging with any of the issues or social contexts dealt with in either text. Yoshinori Ogawa, who translated *Bluebeard's Egg*, after a brief introduction of Atwood, concentrates on praising her insightful perceptions about the uncertainties characterizing the border separating the real and the unreal. He offers an appreciation of her writing style by attributing it to her preoccupation with the indeterminacies inherent in our world and what she calls "freedom of the present-tense" (qtd. in Yoshinori Ogawa 194). In both cases, what is communicated to the reader is Atwood's international status as a writer, her craftsmanship, and the uniqueness of her perception of "reality," but neither translator's postscript engages with the particularities of time and space in terms of how Atwood represents reality.

The translator of *The Handmaid's Tale* (*Jijo no Monogatari*), Eiji Saito, a professor of American literature, pays greater attention to the novel's contexts and form in the postscript he provides, relying on his extensive knowledge of American culture, history, and literature. He provides abundant background information for the novel's references to contemporary issues, historical events, and literary traditions, especially that of dystopia, while also commenting on the text's linguistic and literary devices. What is most characteristic about his postscript is the way he draws attention to the writer's strong American connection. As he writes, "[a]lthough Margaret Atwood is known as a leading Canadian writer, her education at the post-graduate level was in fact received in America" (567, my translation). Then, after mentioning Harvard as her *alma mater*, he goes on to reminisce about the place in a highly nostalgic tone, savouring his own sweet memories about the tranquility and beauty of the university town. "*The Handmaid's Tale*," he concludes, "is a dystopian novel, but I think it is also a love letter Atwood wrote for the town in which she spent a few years of her prime youth in her twenties" (567, my translation).

Operating as a norm that references the source culture, the postscript is designed to enhance and deepen the reader's understanding of the linguistic, cultural, and socio-political contexts that have shaped the source text. In other words, the postscript-as-norm is supposed to privilege the source system over the target system by resituating the translated text in its original location and conditions. This, however, is not the case with the examples I have just cited. Canadian literature specialists in Canada, as well as elsewhere, will immediately take notice of the problematic nature of the postscript to *The Handmaid's Tale*. It obscures, if it does not ignore entirely, both the novel's and Atwood's own ironic position in terms of American history—especially concerning the politics of colonial America, its parochial puritanism and oppressive enactments represented by the notorious witch trials. Atwood's equally ironic take on Canada's relationship with its neighbour in the past and present would also be lost to readers of the translation and its postscript. For example, there is no attempt to alert the reader that the despotic Gilead is set in the south of fictional Canada; as Professor Crescent Moon says at the end of the novel, Canada "did not wish to antagonize its powerful neighbor," and he wonders whether the protagonist had managed to escape to Britain by way of Canada (322–23). What is striking in the translator's postscript is the lack of any reference to the well-known anti-American sentiments in many of Atwood's books.[13]

In fact, when the Japanese translation of *The Handmaid's Tale* was reprinted as a paperback edition in 2001 by another publisher, Hayakawa, additional commentary was included. Written by Keiko Ochiai, a well-known feminist writer and social commentator, the second postscript draws attention in hindsight to how *The Handmaid's Tale* foreshadowed political developments in the world after 9/11 and how the exploitation of the female body is continuing. No matter how perceptive and relevant, this postscript, too, fails to situate the novel or Atwood within the local contexts of their source culture.

When a translation of *Surfacing* (*Ukabiagaru*) finally came out in 1994 from Shinsui-sha, a publishing company much smaller and far less known than any of the publishers I have already mentioned, it appeared in the press's "Women's Books" series, appropriately so, and was accompanied by a postscript that included pertinent information about the novel's literary and cultural contexts, including its feminist aspects. Translator Kaori Ohshima emphasizes the significance of the novel's historical background, stating that Canada was experiencing an identity crisis in the 1960s, the time frame of the novel, threatened as it was from inside by Quebec nationalism and from outside by American economic and cultural invasion. She writes, "Atwood is critiquing the Canadians' self-image by caricaturing it, while at the same time projecting it onto the protagonist's binary view of man as evil and woman as innocent victim" (282, my translation). The translator's sensitivity to the source culture is further evident in the acknowledgement she adds at the end of the postscript, where she expresses gratitude to a friend who has lived in Canada for an extended period of time for facilitating her understanding of "Canadian customs and expressions" (284). Nevertheless, this translation, released as it was by a small publishing house, has not reached a wide audience in Japan. Although it has not gone out of print, it is not available in major bookshops, nor online at Amazon.

The translation of *The Edible Woman* (*Taberareru Onna*), which was published in 1996 by Shinchosha, provided further evidence of the growing interest in the source culture in general and configurations of its literary systems in particular. The translator, Akio Oura, first summarizes the book's central issue as "a human individual's question of identity" (not restricting "human individual" to a woman), and offers an appreciation of the author's comical treatment of it (364, my translation). He then proceeds to connect this issue of identity with Canadian literature at large and includes *Survival* in his discussion, a translation of which had appeared the previous year. Oura argues that Atwood's perception of what characterizes Canadian literature is "excellent ... even though there may be views against it"; he also claims that Atwood's fiction may be read as a "respon[se] ... to Canada's need" to establish its own political, economic, and cultural identity (365). He does not elaborate on what the particularities of Canadian literature are at the time; nor does he mention the controversies resulting from *Survival*'s central thesis. Nevertheless, Oura's postscript appeared in a translation published by a major company, and could have then marked a significant turn in Atwood's reception in Japan, and thus potentially lead to an increased awareness of the problematics surrounding the construction of national literatures, but it did not reach a wide audience. The sales of this book stayed low, and as a consequence any impact it might have had on Japanese readership remained very limited.

It was only after *The Handmaid's Tale* was reissued in 2001, followed by the publication of *The Blind Assassin*, that Atwood began to attract public attention in Japan. At this point, her different publishers' strategies presented her to Japanese readers as a writer of international status who, along with other prize-winning writers, belonged to the rapidly growing global literary community. Her novels' stylistic and formal characteristics, as well as her particular vision, though already noted in the postscripts of her first translations in Japanese, now attracted greater attention in the translators' comments. In the postscript to *The Blind Assassin* (*Kuraki Me no Ansatsusha*) the translator, Yukiko Konosu, takes especial note of the elaborate use of various literary devices such as the unreliable narrator, the multiple framing of narratives in the novel's *mise en scène*, and the intertextuality and subtle tributes to other writers and literary traditions. Conversely, the novel's unmistakable Canadian context and its clear references to Canada's history are given only cursory attention.

Given the tendency in these postscripts to concentrate virtually exclusively on literary techniques and formal characteristics, Japanese readers relying on the material produced by major publishers and their translators are not provided with any guideposts as to the particular cultural and historical systems within which Atwood's texts operate. The ways in which particularities of place, time, and social dynamics are inscribed in her fiction are virtually erased, often reduced to a single, if not prescriptive, idea, such as her sophistication or advancement of various causes. At worst, in Atwood's Japanese translations Canada or Canadian literature is rendered invisible; at best, it is imagined as a largely self-contained, autonomous system that the writer, we are repeatedly told, "represents," the result being that Canada in this context functions as a floating signifier or synecdoche of a vaguely outlined world outside Japan.

III

To produce a descriptive study of translation norms in the Japanese literary system today, one would have to focus not only on the translators' postscripts but also on the publishers' promotional strategies, which include such things as cover design and blurbs on the dust jackets. These paratextual features, visually and otherwise, play a major role in the appeal the books hold for their potential buyers. For example, in Shinchosha's Crest Books series, book covers and dust jackets not only serve as a canvas for artistic expression but also convey various verbal messages, often overenthusiastic recommendations contributed by Japanese writers. The books' exteriors thus acquire significance as a space where what we might call cultural encounters take place. It is through such encounters between fervently endorsed foreign literature and its authors and Japanese fiction writers that the latter become part of the publisher's promotional packaging, while also, as Shinchosha's editor Rieko Sugai suggests, being exposed to what the Japanese publishing system considers to be positive influence on homegrown authors.

Launched in 1998, the Crest Books series is a new line of "high-quality" literature (mainly, but not exclusively, fiction) by contemporary authors from around the globe who are little known in Japan or who have had few of their books translated into Japanese ("Shincho"). Printed in soft cover and quality paper, with aesthetically appealing but not overly decorative design, the books in this series, according to the publisher, have a strong appeal as much to avid readers of foreign literature as to young readers who are interested in art or are conscious of fashion. Best sellers in the series so far include works by renowned contemporary writers, such as Ian McEwen, Graham Swift, Zadie Smith, Jhumpa Lahiri, Anita Shreve, Andrej Kurkow, and Bernhard Schlink. Canadian writers published in the series include Nancy Huston, Alice Munro, Alistair MacLeod, Frances Itani, David Bezmozgis, and Michael Ondaatje. Munro and MacLeod have been especially popular in recent years, their books listed among the most successful and best-selling in the Crest series.

MacLeod's short stories, published in a collection called *Island* (2000) in Canada, appeared in two volumes in 2002 and 2004 as *The Golden Gift of Grey* (*Haiiro no Kagayakeru Okurimono*) and *Winter Dog* (*Fuyu no Inu*) respectively, swiftly followed by his novel *No Great Mischief* in 2005. The novel's Japanese title, *Kanata naru Uta ni Mimi wo Sumase yo*, literally meaning "Hark the Song from Afar," has, in the way it signifies in Japanese, more abstract and romantic overtones than does the original title, which is intended to evoke particular historical episodes. Only three of Alice Munro's many books have been introduced to Japanese readers to date: *The Moons of Jupiter* (*Mokusei no Tsuki*); *Hateship, Friendship, Courtship, Loveship, Marriage* (*Irakusa*); and, most recently, *The View from Castle Rock*

(*Ringo no Ki no Shita de*). The back covers of the latter two, which are published in the Crest Books series, include endorsements from Japanese writers and quotations from book reviews that appeared in the West. The lower halves of their front dust jackets contain additional blurbs, sometimes repeating what appears on the back cover. While dustcovers and blurbs are commonly employed in Japan as a space of promotion, as is the case in the West as well, the number of endorsements provided by different famous authors that these texts display is rather unusual.

Blurbs and recommendations for MacLeod's books, often mentioning Canada or Cape Breton as the setting, share a tendency to emphasize how his construction of place allows for the long-lost history and lives of the past to survive in the present. Thus, the geographic specificity and particularities of MacLeod's subject matter become translatable via the nostalgic tropes employed in the blurbs. Here is an example from the recommendations printed on the back cover of MacLeod's *Haiiro no Kagayakeru Okurimono*: "The difference between the parents' and their children's lives, as they are delineated in this collection of stories from Canada, reminds us of Japan in the old days.... [F]ull of nostalgia and also slightly reminiscent of Saroyan, the collection struck me as traditional yet surprisingly refreshing" (my translation). The contributor of these words is Taichi Yamada, a famous playwright known as a chronicler of the changing images and values of the family in Japan. The back cover of MacLeod's *Fuyu no Inu* carries the words of a leading fiction writer and reviewer, Natsuki Ikezawa: "[O]ur daily lives today are made of aluminum and plastic, whereas in his [MacLeod's] world men are living surrounded by iron, evergreens, and rocks.... Until only 20 years ago people were able to live like this" (my translation). *Fuyu no Inu* also carries on its extra dust jacket a comment by the prize-winning novelist Yoko Ogawa: "This book tells a great tale of acceptance that every living thing on earth—human and animal—can only live its own life, and do so as a gift" (my translation).

In the case of Alice Munro, her exceptional skills as storyteller garner most of the attention in her translated books' appraisals, though the blurbs reflect the same emphasis I have noted above on her writing's timeless quality. For example, the statement "The way a moment is turned into eternity; the gaze that looks through months and years of time" is printed in large font and bold type at the top of the back cover of *Ringo no Ki no Shita de (The View from Castle Rock)*. On the book's cover, as well on the dust jacket, the reader finds yet another endorsement, this time written by poet and novelist Masayo Koike: "The force, which has brought different kinds of 'I' [in these stories] to 'the Here and Now,' will one day send this 'I' away towards yonder. Emotions buried deep in our blood become awakened, one by one. What a delicate and wild story" (my translation). Koike's affective words celebrate what is taken to be the universalist nature of Munro's characters, along with her writing's power to bring alive what are supposedly essential but forgotten elements of human experience. This discourse of the universal and timeless apparently seems to be compatible with the particular locality of the stories' setting that echoes Scotland both as a faraway, legendary place and as part of the characters' Canadian roots. This explains why Munro was "discovered" in Japan only recently and around the same time as MacLeod. *No Great Mischief* and *The View from Castle Rock* are family sagas, both set, in part, in Scotland centuries ago. Each book's narrative shows the characters' lives through layers of history linked with each other by means of repetitive patterns as their plots progress. Even though these books' translators, Kotake and Nakano, provide extended accounts in their postscripts concerning their respective historical and geographical settings, they do not fail to reassure the reader that these books are marked by values that transcend the particular (Nakano 262; Kotake 422). There is no doubt that the overall effect of the packaging of these books leans toward universality.

The publisher's strategy to promote the Crest Books series with Japanese writers' endorsements goes beyond the actual books and into another medium. *Nami*, the small magazine Shinchosha publishes monthly for advertisement purposes, carries an updated list of titles in the Crest Book series, each accompanied by a few lines of description and reprinted reviews of the most popular titles. It also carries articles and reviews, new and reprinted, as well as results of the polls that the company conducts to ask about various readers' favourite titles. *Nami* also provides a platform for round-table discussions by, and interviews with, Japanese literary figures of the younger generation, who are encouraged to respond to the Crest Books series. As the chief editor of the series Rieko Sugai confirms, the writers are responding with enthusiasm to the series as a whole and are particularly impressed by certain writers, including MacLeod and Munro.

In articles and discussions in *Nami*, a number of Japanese writers comment on the high literary quality of the featured Canadian texts. In one such article, reviewer Yumi Toyozaki maintains that MacLeod's books explore themes that Japanese writers have long stopped handling, such as "family," "roots," "poverty," and "the threat of nature" (my translation). Tamao Ariyoshi, a fiction writer and essayist, expresses her admiration at MacLeod's ability to "discover stories in the most elemental aspects of men's lives," as well as the "successful" way in which he renders the "earnestness found there. That is, he [MacLeod] constructs stories out of basic elements, so basic that it is difficult to turn them into stories" (4; my translation). What's more, Ariyoshi's encounter with MacLeod signals her initiation into "Canadian" literature; as she writes, "I did not know there was such an 'awesome' writer in Canada. It is a great credit [to the Crest Books series] to have introduced Canadian literature, so far unknown to Japanese readership, through this author." There are other Japanese writers who regard the regional and cultural diversity represented in the Crest Books series as its main virtue and strength. However, considering the lack of interest in the translation of Bezmozgis' *Natasha*, also published in the same series (Sugai), one may speculate that the depiction of Canada's increasingly multicultural society, rich in detail with unfamiliar (e.g., non-Western) cultural images, does not have as great an appeal to readers in Japan as what is taken to constitute universal human drama in terms of time and space.

The understanding and appreciation of Canadian literature in this context has the paradoxical effect of "othering" it. As implied in their comments, the writers' viewpoints situate Japan as here and now, as a perpetual present, whereas the foreign—Canada, in this case—is seen as a fixed site for the enactment of the past, where versions of distant pasts interact. The latter is often associated with things long lost to the "Japan" in this picture, things such as closely knit communities and intense human emotions. The past and its traditions are thus valorized over the present, idealized rather than disdained. If this is what marks current interest in Japan in world literature, then CanLit as a body of literature that has its own distinct history is lost in (Japanese) translation; its national signature, no matter how differently it may be conceived, is peeled off and forgotten. Instead, Canadian cultural products go through a process of transformation and reproduction in ways that fulfill the object of a particular Japanese desire, a nostalgic return to a lost and idealized past, a state reminiscent of both minoritized subjects' desire to have what they lack and the colonialist gaze turned voraciously to the other.

Conclusion

In this essay I have demonstrated aspects of importing Canadian literature into Japanese contexts. Through the examination of extratextual elements of translation norms and of the role of publishers, editors, translators, and Japanese authors involved in the dissemination of particular Canadian texts in Japan, it has become evident that Canadian cultural products are usually consumed as components of "Western" culture at large, imagined vaguely and idealistically, with faint awareness of the socio-historical backgrounds that inform it. The impact of globalization, as well as that of the prize-oriented literary culture that has emerged worldwide, is certainly evident in the publishers' selection and evaluation processes, as well as methods of advertisement. However, my case studies have also revealed the values that are shared and constructed in the local domain of literary translation, values that are also indicative of the publishers' and writers' hope for regenerating Japanese literature. What is discernible in this context is a strong desire to reassess international literature according to the rhetoric of diversity and universality, the desire to reconceptualize it, on one hand, as an avatar of foreignness, as the object of admiration and source of inspiration, while on the other hand accommodating and incorporating it as a part of a domestic literary system with gestures of transnational and translingual solidarity.[14] In this sentiment, some Canadian writers are put on a pedestal as the torchbearers for the future of literature and some as the guardians of lost traditions. Occasionally Canada is summoned as a signifier of innovation in style and perspective, or of continuity in humanity and tradition, or even as the combination of both tendencies.

I should make it clear at this point that my intention is not to criticize the current trends in translating literature in Japan. The cases I have dealt with do not provide a complete view of the manifold relationships between the Japanese and Canadian literary scenes. Rather, this study is intended as a preliminary step toward considering the role of Japanese scholars' research on Canadian literature, both in the context of Japanese cultural production and in the field of Canadian studies in general. Obviously this is a subject for another article, but my speculation constitutes a vital part of the conclusion drawn from the analyses I have attempted above. First of all, researchers can participate in processes of cultural translation by offering views and perspectives for critically reading cultures. Knowledge of local contexts of the source culture and critical comments and interrogation based on theoretical grounds can further stimulate the community of readers. Secondly, the main site of this interaction should be found in the field of education. Important critical studies and translations of Canadian texts have been conducted—and, in the case of translation, carefully annotated by researchers in Japan—but they can easily go out of print and be left unnoticed. For enhancing critical literacy and global awareness among young people, researchers and educators can co-operate in developing ways to deliver texts, creative and critical, supplemented with suggestions for different types of reading and interpretation. Study guides and teaching aids produced elsewhere will provide useful materials and methods, but formats and contents suited for the reality of Japanese universities and students are desperately required.

The Cunning of Reconciliation: Reinventing White Civility in the "Age of Apology"

Pauline Wakeham

On 22 September 1988, then Prime Minister Brian Mulroney delivered a formal apology and announced a compensation package for the internment, forced relocation, and seizure of property of Japanese Canadians during World War II. While Mulroney's Conservative government imagined this gesture of reconciliation to be a singular, exceptional event, the state's actions that day established a powerful precedent, spurring a diverse range of minoritized constituencies to either initiate or intensify redress campaigns for a variety of injustices.[1] Failing to anticipate the future that was approaching on the horizon, the federal government's responses to calls for redress were initially sporadic and haphazard, emerging in a series of fits and starts shaped by policy reversals and partisan rivalry. Over time, however, the government's reconciliatory gestures have begun to accumulate and proliferate with increasing rapidity, producing the semblance of a national commitment to addressing the injustices of an ostensibly past era. As Stephen Harper asserted in his 2006 apology for the Chinese head tax: "Even though the head tax, a product of a profoundly different time, lies far in our past, we feel compelled to right this historic wrong for the simple reason that it is the decent thing to do, a characteristic to be found at the core of the Canadian soul" (Office of the Prime Minister, *Address*). Rewriting a history of reluctant responses to marginalized constituencies' redress campaigns, Harper's statement reveals how the phenomenon of reconciliation has become naturalized as a product of the "core" of Canadian beneficence and integrated into a national mythology of magnanimous governance.

In this essay I analyze how, since the late 1980s, the proliferation of redress movements spearheaded by marginalized groups and the accumulation of gestures of rapprochement by the federal government have gradually been assimilated into a Canadian nationalist teleology, narrated as the latest stage in the country's supposedly long-standing tradition as a just and tolerant society. According to Daniel Coleman, the *grand récit* of Canada's beneficent governance is underpinned by the doctrine of white civility—a belief in Canada's successful domestication of the "gentlemanly code of Britishness" into a model of justice and equality ostensibly best fulfilled by a culture of English (male) whiteness (10). Applying Coleman's argument to a reading of the current moment, this essay argues that, over recent decades, the ideology of white civility has been reconfigured to frame the government's admission of wrongs against minoritized constituencies as, paradoxically, an indicator of beneficence, as further proof of the state's—and, more generally, Canadian society's—enlightened ability to reflect upon the past and to perform contrition in the present to produce national cohesion. Through transactions of conscience, wrongs are converted into evidence of national right. In the very process of purportedly promoting cultural rapprochement, an emerging dominant formulation of reconciliation works to secure a belief in a national imaginary of Canadian civility that overwrites ongoing power asymmetries and gross inequities. My critique of white civility's latest evolution thus builds upon Elizabeth Povinelli's compelling observation that "the ideals of liberalism are not about knowledge and its exposure to truth and revelation, but about the fantasies necessary to act in a liberal society and how these fantasies are protected and projected into social life through specific textual practices. The critique of liberalism does not begin with where it fails or where subjects know or do not know this failure, but rather where it seems to be succeeding" (155). The reinvention of white civility in the contemporary culture of redress—ostensibly a moment of reckoning with the failures of Canadian egalitarianism—has paradoxically become one of liberalism's considerable "successes" for sustaining a fantasy of national benevolence.

The second and integrally linked prong of this essay analyzes how the emergence of reconciliation relates to what Coleman argues is Canada's latest paradigm of civility: multiculturalism. Attending to the crucial overlaps and disjunctures between official multicultural policy and the federal government's developing approach to marginalized groups' calls for redress, I demonstrate that the latter is not entirely reducible to the former. Rather than suggesting a totalizing epochal shift from an era of multiculturalism to one of reconciliation, I argue instead that the emergence of reconciliation as a dominant social discourse has prompted a retooling of the logic of official multiculturalism of the 1980s and '90s in ways that have shifted and extended our understanding of how the idea of Canadian civility is instituted in state policy and constituted in and through social discourse. The sheer accretion of events of national contrition in recent years and the federal government's strategies for producing a semblance of national reconciliation have fomented a transformation in at least two significant areas that I trace in detail: (1) the management of national pasts, presents, and futures, and (2) the strategic positioning of Canada in relation to the global forum.

The reinvention of white civility in the current moment of reckoning with injustices is, however, still open to contestation and change. While it is possible to trace the emergence of a dominant version of reconciliation in Canada, it is important to note that the overarching culture of redress—the heterogeneous network of discourses and actors including the state and its apparatuses, corporations, the mass media, and citizen groups—is irreducible to a hegemonic state project and that multiple parties are engaged in the shaping of this discursive and political terrain. To trace the role of minoritized constituencies actively lobbying for apologies and compensation is not to suggest that such communities have necessarily begun to labour in the interests of power. Rather, the participation of marginalized groups in this culture of redress may diversify the shape of reckoning with injustices. Despite the fact that the dominant discourse of reconciliation is framed as the product of a united national vision, the question of what reconciliation putatively means and what it wants is, in fact, deeply contested terrain. Throughout this essay, I use the term "reconciliation" to signal an emerging dominant formulation of how differences between Canada's Anglo-Celtic establishment and its "others" might be negotiated. Without attempting to definitively fix the always shifting meaning of terms, it may be noted that "reconciliation," with its more nebulous connotations of the resolution of differences, lends itself to frequent invocations by a federal government seeking to sidestep material compensation and structural change with vague rhetorical gestures that pronounce national healing while maintaining entrenched power asymmetries. This dominant logic of reconciliation often takes recourse to the tool of the official apology—a tool that is amenable but not universally reducible to being used as a largely symbolic gesture. Minoritized constituencies, in contrast, more often invoke the idiom of redress to connote precisely the concrete reparations and socio-economic change that the state seems repeatedly to overwrite with its rhetorical approach. That said, in tracing a general distinction, it is important to note that the enunciation of these idioms across government and redress campaigns alike—among many other actors—is not mutually exclusive. With attention to such discursive cross-pollination, this essay traces the contours of the dominant formulation of reconciliation taking shape in Canadian society today in an effort to rupture the semblance of consensus and civility that power constructs around rapprochement and, in turn, to make space for a range of alternative vocabularies, concepts, and strategies for reckoning with both historical and ongoing injustices.

The Evolution of White Civility

In *White Civility: The Literary Project of English Canada*, Coleman outlines the development of white civility as a concept and practice in literary and cultural contexts from the mid-nineteenth century to the contemporary era. Transplanting the legacy of British civility and its purported model of peace, order, and good government from the imperial motherland to the colonial periphery, English-Canadian settlers sought to shore up their threatened sense of civilized refinement by emulating the administrative and social principles of England. Although the logic of white civility was initially utilized to emphasize English Canada's connections to Britain, and thus to differentiate Canada's distinguished heritage from that of the United States, English Canadians' anxieties regarding their subordinate status in relation to the imperial metropole took on, over time, a defensive twist in which Canada strategically reappropriated white civility from its British origins and framed its New World version as the most evolved instantiation. Refashioning their precarious position as settler-invaders subjugating Aboriginal people from a liability into an asset, English Canadians deflected culpability for imperial conquest back to the British metropole by reconstructing the work of settler colonists as bringing enlightenment and order to an uncivilized world. Beneath this veneer of benevolent governance, the practice of white civility developed with a crucial structural contradiction at its core: while the public sphere purported to be premised upon the tenets of equality and liberty, it was in actuality consolidated through the violent exclusion and exploitation of those "others" who could supposedly contaminate the body politic. Like the broader project of liberal modernity, of which Canadian white civility has constituted one particular national manifestation, the supposed universality of the principles of democracy and egalitarianism has always, in practice, been limited in its application to those subjects the civic sphere recognizes as appropriate political participants. Thus, "modern civility is, paradoxically, a limited or constrained universality that tends to proliferate and striate not only external but also internal differences" (Coleman 13). In Canada, racialized Aboriginal and diasporic populations have typically been cast as those "belated or primitive elements" that threaten the rational functioning of the civic domain—constituencies that the state, via a patronizing discourse of benevolence, claims to protect by mediating their access to the public sphere (Coleman 13). At the same time that white civility has excluded racialized others from full inclusion in Canadian society, it has consolidated white supremacy via a "conflation of whiteness with civility," so that, as Jennifer Henderson has noted (and, through her words, Coleman reminds us), "race" becomes "attached not just to bodies but also to forms of conduct" (Coleman 5; Henderson 18).

The most recent incarnation of white civility, according to Coleman, is "multicultural civility" (8), as promulgated by the discourse of official multiculturalism, which became federal policy under the Trudeau administration in 1971 and was subsequently buttressed by legislative developments in the Charter of Rights in 1982 and the Canadian Multiculturalism Act (or Bill C-93) in 1988 (Kamboureli 82).[2] Like the overarching logic of white civility to which it is articulated, multiculturalism deploys the guise of tolerating and even celebrating difference as a method for managing the white nation's others. Official multiculturalism thus mobilizes what Smaro Kamboureli calls a "sedative politics"—a "politics that attempts to recognize ethnic differences, but only in a contained fashion" in order to quell minority dissent and maintain "the conventional articulation of the Canadian dominant society," including its economic, cultural, and political capital (82). By the time that Kamboureli published *Scandalous Bodies: Diasporic Literature in English Canada* in 2000, she recognized that official multiculturalism was showing signs of age, noting the wearing out of this state paradigm. Kamboureli diagnosed Canadian society as foundering in "multicultural fatigue," a condition prompted by multicultural policy's inability to effectively "sedate" marginalized groups with the federal government's token gestures of lip service and funding for arts programs (81).[3] In the wake of anti-racist activists' and intellectuals' vocal critiques of multiculturalism's failure to materialize significant social change, the white nation's fantasy of benign diversity integrated harmoniously in a national mosaic began to chafe against the reality of social friction, growing atrophied in the process.

When, in his 2006 book, Coleman contends that white civility's latest incarnation is that of "multicultural civility," he does not address the wearing out of official multiculturalism that Kamboureli diagnosed several years prior. Instead, multicultural civility appears to be a durable and resilient logic of power throughout his text. While I concur with Coleman's assertion that multiculturalism has constituted a prominent reconfiguration of this ideology of Anglo-Celtic benevolence, I want to extend his compelling analysis further, arguing that white civility's most recent transmogrifications exceed the limits of the multiculturalism paradigm as we have previously "known," or at least analyzed, it. When the Government of Canada first began to express regret to minoritized groups during the heyday of multicultural policy-making in the late 1980s, apologies initially functioned as ancillary complements to the state's principal strategy of managing diversity through the co-optation of difference into a nationalistic cultural mosaic. Due to the temporal coincidence between multicultural policy and the period in which Canadian state apologies were first proffered as well as the fact that several of the government's expressions of contrition have "conveyed the group recognition characteristic of official multiculturalist affirmations," "redress politics" in Canada have frequently been considered "a species of multiculturalism" (James, "Do Campaigns?" 224). As a result, there are certainly important historical, conceptual, rhetorical, and policy orientation continuities and overlaps between redress politics and dominant multiculturalist discourse in Canada. And yet critiques such as those by Kamboureli reveal that Canadian multiculturalism has not remained static or internally consistent over time and that its utility for pacifying minoritized populations has diminished significantly, requiring alternative strategies. In response, I suggest that Coleman's analysis could be usefully extended to consider what is arguably the most compelling reinvention of white civility in recent years: the state's performance of apologies to marginalized constituencies and the emergence of a culture of redress in Canada.

Discussing the specific context of Australia—a former sister Commonwealth settler colony to Canada—Elizabeth Povinelli imagines the movement for national reconciliation with Aboriginal Australians to be an inextricable element of liberal multiculturalism's "cunning of recognition": its "injunction on indigenous subjects to stage for the nation ... [the] sublime scene of not too much and not too little alterity" (184). While inspired by Povinelli's stunning analysis, I am left feeling that the simultaneity and indistinguishability of the logics of multiculturalism and reconciliation that she traces in Australia might require some refinement for translation to the Canadian context. Such a translation would need to take account of the fact that while multiculturalism emerged as a policy directive in both settler states in the 1970s and 1980s,[4] the practice of apology and reconciliation connected—and yet, I contend, irreducible—to it has become a more widespread and diversified phenomenon in Canada. While Australia's program of reconciliation has been primarily focused upon Aboriginal peoples, Canada's culture of redress has been shaped by calls for redress from a wide range of minoritized constituencies consolidated around the "racial" or "ethnic" categories that were utilized to legitimate historical injustices against them. The push and pull of these diverse actors—and the complex intersections and unassimilable differences between Indigenous and diasporic experiences of injury and calls for reparation—have contributed to a re-mapping of the landscape of multiculturalism in Canada. In the process, what began as supplementary gestures under official multiculturalism have—via the proliferation of events and utterances of remorse both at home and across the globe—become consolidated as a powerful social paradigm. Thus, while multiculturalism constitutes a vital condition of possibility for the emergence of reconciliation, the latter has now retooled the former in significant ways. Appropriating Povinelli's apt phrase for describing the logic of multiculturalism—namely, the "cunning of recognition"—I want to suggest a new phrase to signal the hegemonic logic of the contemporary Canadian moment: the cunning of reconciliation, or the strategic co-optation of the ethical project of offering recompense for injustices by the political program of silencing resistance and manufacturing premature closure upon questions of power imbalances that continue to structure Canadian society. To borrow the words of Jacques Derrida, such a strategy is "aimed at producing a reconciliation ... favourable to a normalization": namely, the maintenance of an elite Anglo-Celtic power base under the banner of white civility (31).

The Apology Industry

The origins of the phenomenon of righting wrongs in Canada reveal the intricate intersections and divergences between official multiculturalism and reconciliation. In Canada, multiculturalism was a project initiated by the state for the complex motivations of "managing" diversity and diffusing the threat biculturalism posed to English-Canadian power by splintering cultural recognition into many shards of a cultural mosaic (Mackey 64).[5] The passage of the Charter of Rights and Freedoms in 1982—legislation largely understood as a cornerstone of multicultural policy-making—ignited minoritized constituencies' redress campaigns as Japanese, Chinese, and Ukrainian Canadian groups seized upon the Charter's equality rights to mount their claims relating to historical discrimination. Thus began what political scientist Matt James terms the "first major wave" of redress claims ("Permanent-Emergency" 325). While multiculturalism was an initiative "from above," the implementation of legislation under this program sparked a redress movement that was originally catalyzed "from below." Without the tireless lobbying of organizations such as the Chinese Canadian National Congress and the National Association of Japanese Canadians, the federal government would most likely never, of its own accord, have made the apologies it has.

In fact, the federal government failed to respond to calls for redress until a "second wave" of claimants—including Italian, German, and Jewish Canadians and Aboriginal peoples—entered the fray during the 1987–1992 debates surrounding the Meech Lake and Charlottetown Accords (James, "Permanent-Emergency" 326). As the state reluctantly began to issue apologies, its sporadic and tentative gestures led to a range of uneven responses, spanning a spectrum from apologies with and without fiscal compensation to commemorative initiatives that sidestep explicit statements of contrition with the funding of memorials. For instance, two years after the apology to Japanese Canadians, then Prime Minister Mulroney, speaking at a luncheon in 1990 for the Canadian Italian Business Professional Association and the National Council of Italian

Canadians, offered "a full and unqualified apology for the wrongs done to our fellow Canadians of Italian origin during World War Two," including the internment of seven hundred Italian Canadians for their suspected involvement in fascist organizations ("Notes for an Address"). In contrast to the lengthy consultation involved in the apology to Japanese Canadians as well as its formal declaration in Parliament, Mulroney's lunchtime statement to Italian Canadians appeared less ceremonial and official, a problem compounded by the fact that the prime minister's promise of financial reparations was later overturned by his own government.

Following the period of debates surrounding the Charlottetown Accord, a "third wave" of "redress politics" emerged that was typified by "relatively low-cost" strategies and cautiousness toward making full apologies that could render the government vulnerable to litigation (James, "Permanent-Emergency" 327). Such an approach was most forcefully articulated in a letter tabled in Parliament in 1994, signed by then Secretary of State for Multiculturalism, Sheila Finestone, which replied to requests for financial reparations from several advocacy organizations by firmly asserting the Mulroney Conservatives' patent rejection of all redress settlements.[6] By 1996, the Chrétien Liberal government in power attempted to impose closure upon grievances through limited concessions to particular groups. In that year, the federal government signed the High Arctic Relocation Reconciliation Agreement in an attempt to suppress Inuit calls for redress for the forced exile of approximately ninety community members to isolated areas in the High Arctic during the 1950s. While the reconciliation agreement provided $10 million in compensation, the fiscal reparations were used to buy the government's way out of making an apology—something it refused to do, rendering the agreement what James has called "an aggressively preemptive non-apology" ("Wrestling with the Past" 144). If the High Arctic Relocation Reconciliation Agreement constituted a categorical denial of apology, the Department of Indian Affairs' 1998 "Statement of Reconciliation," delivered by then Minister Jane Stewart at a January luncheon, was a more subtle evasion of a full apology in the guise of a declaration of "profound regret" for so-called historical actions affecting Aboriginal peoples, among which residential schools was foregrounded (Canada, Indian Affairs and Northern Development).

In the new millennium, as "multicultural fatigue" has taken its toll, the Canadian state's responses to redress claims have conversely begun to proliferate with increasing rapidity. On 25 November 2005, Bill C-331, recognizing the internment of Ukrainian Canadians, received royal assent, and roughly two years later, in October 2007, Prime Minister Paul Martin signed an agreement in principle, allocating $2.5 million toward commemorating the internment of Italian Canadians. On 22 June 2006, Stephen Harper issued a formal apology and compensation package for the Chinese head tax levied between 1885 and 1923 and the subsequent total ban on Chinese immigration until 1947. On 11 June 2008, Harper sought to resolve the shortcomings of the 1998 "Statement of Reconciliation" by issuing a formal apology in the House of Commons to First Nations, Inuit, and Métis constituencies for the government's role in residential schools. A few months later, spurred by the British Columbia government's own apology to the South Asian Canadian community for its role in the denial of entry to Indian passengers aboard the *Komagata Maru*, Stephen Harper offered a federal apology to South Asian Canadians from a Surrey park on 3 August 2008. The statement was promptly rejected by members of the South Asian Canadian community, which argued that the apology should have been declared in the House of Commons and thus made part of official parliamentary record (Hainsworth). Since that time, the federal government's list of apologies has lengthened to include a June 2010 apology to the families of the Air India bombing victims at the site of the memorial in Humber Bay Park in Etobicoke, Ontario. In the wake of the release of the Air India Inquiry final report, Harper apologized for the "institutional failings" of government intelligence and security agencies that might have prevented the tragedy as well as for the government's subsequent refusal to acknowledge that the perpetrators and most victims were Canadian citizens (Office of the Prime Minister, *PM Speaks*). In August that year, the new Minister of Aboriginal and Northern Affairs, John Duncan, flew to Inukjuak, Quebec (in the land claim settlement region referred to as Nunavik), to provide the long-awaited apology for the Inuit High Arctic Relocations of 1953 and 1955 that the government previously tried to bypass in 1996.[7] The federal government's reconciliatory return to the relocations reveals the anxious recursivity operative in Canada's culture of redress, a recursivity that, as we will see, undermines official efforts to impose closure upon the past.

In addition to the federal government's many apologetic speech acts, a range of associated state-funded programs have sought to produce reconciliation by other means. In the spring of 2008, the Department of Canadian Heritage announced that, under its Community Historical Recognition Program (CHRP), it would be offering grants to the South Asian Canadian community to commemorate the *Komagata Maru* case, to the Ukrainian Canadian Foundation of Taras Schevchenko to memorialize the internment of approximately five thousand Ukrainian Canadians during WWI, to the Chinese Canadian community to acknowledge discriminatory immigration policies, and to Jewish Canadians to memorialize Canada's role in turning away nine hundred German Jewish refugees aboard the *St. Louis* steamship in 1939. The clustering of multiple acts of remembrance and reconciliation under the provenance of the CHRP and the almost identical, fill-in-the-blank press releases posted on the Canadian Heritage website demonstrate the emergence of what might be called an "apology industry," an almost assembly-line approach to manufacturing reconciliation.[8] In other words, if the state's responses to marginalized constituencies initially began haphazardly, impacted by the contingencies of different government administrations and the play of partisan politics, there is mounting evidence to suggest that a more systematized, if still cautious, program of response is taking shape. Rather than straightforwardly evidencing heightened state reflexivity regarding the limits of Canadian tolerance and egalitarianism, however, the rise of an apology industry in the current moment reveals a more complex and layered contestation over interpretations of the past and their ramifications in the present, including the continuance of historically entrenched power asymmetries structuring Canadian society.

One of the key elements of the state's reconciliatory project is the policy orientation of "heritage redress." Since the dissolution of the Department of Multiculturalism and Citizenship and its absorption into the Department of Canadian Heritage in the mid-1990s, the federal government has begun to frame its program of reconciliation within what James identifies as a more "narrow 'heritage' approach" that focuses upon funding for commemorating past grievances with plaques, designated heritage sites, and museums, thereby emphasizing these grievances' status as "history" (James, "Do Campaigns?" 231). The term "heritage redress" was coined by the Conservative party for their election platform in 2004, but, as James suggests, it may be understood as a more generalized policy orientation over the past decade ("Do Campaigns?" 231). In 2005, Paul Martin's Liberals developed the Federal Acknowledgement,

Commemoration, and Education (ACE) program, administered by the Department of Canadian Heritage through its multiculturalism secretariat, as its institutionalized version of "heritage redress" policy. The ACE has now been superseded by the Conservatives' National Historical Recognition and Community Historical Recognition programs, launched in 2006 and operated through the Department of Citizenship and Immigration. While the NHRP distributes funds only to federal departments and agencies, the CHRP finances a select group of commemorative and education projects initiated by community-based organizations. In this way, the work of remembering injustices on behalf of the nation is frequently passed on to members of the aggrieved constituency while the federal government has the privilege of overseeing the process. Moreover, both the NHRP and CHRP limit funding to commemorative initiatives regarding "historical wartime measures and/or immigration restrictions applied in Canada" (Citizenship and Immigration Canada, *Community*). In so doing, these programs restrict the field of recognizable grievances to "a relatively small number of specific, temporally confined, and ... [ostensibly exceptional] events": while "wartime measures" are conveniently mitigated by the alibi of national security exigencies, the "group-based 'immigration restrictions'" deemed acknowledgeable by the Canadian government purportedly all ended by 1967 (James, "Neoliberal Heritage" 8).[9] Accordingly, these state programs profoundly shape what may be named as an injury while effecting the eventalization of grievances, or the reduction of redress claims to periodized and particularized occurrences rather than injustices contextualized within systemic histories of racist oppression. Moreover, "heritage redress" substitutes "serious negotiations over the dominant society's contemporary reparative responsibilities with scattered depoliticized acts of national 'commemoration' instead" (James, "Do Campaigns?" 233).

The collapse of First Peoples' redress movements into the assembly line of the apology industry has intensified these problems. While colonial injustices against Aboriginal groups are not eligible for commemorative funding under the National and Community Historical Recognition Programs and colonial injustices against Indigenous peoples have necessitated far more complex and multi-faceted processes of negotiation, a not dissimilar strategy of eventalization may be discerned in the state's management of First Peoples' redress claims. By attempting to contain the question of Aboriginal redress to the "event" of residential schools, the federal government seeks to manage unruly histories of colonial violence amongst which residential schools functioned as one prong of a diversified genocidal system—including the expropriation of Indigenous territory, armed military conquest, the forced relocation of Aboriginal peoples onto reserves, and the criminalization of cultural practices such as the potlatch. Although the NHRP and CHRP are significantly smaller initiatives in terms of scope and funding that do not broach the matter of residential schools, the emphasis upon commemoration and education prioritized in these programs bears some similarities to the mandate for the residential schools Truth and Reconciliation Commission of Canada (TRC). This commission is charged with the task, among other weighty responsibilities, of vetting community-based commemorative proposals as outlined under the Commemoration Policy Directive, or Schedule J, of the 2007 Indian Residential Schools Settlement Agreement. The emphasis upon commemoration in the TRC's mandate consequently risks reiterating the trope of "heritage," playing into discourses that might frame residential schooling as distant history, a policy of an era in which assimilationism was ostensibly construed as benevolence. That said, because the TRC's mandate extends far beyond Schedule J and because its commissioners are demonstrating a powerful ability to exercise agency in interpreting that mandate, the TRC is uniquely positioned to challenge the limits of "heritage redress" by exposing residential schooling as an all too recent problem for which the past continues in the present through the transmission of intergenerational trauma and the continuance of colonialism in Canada.[10]

The development of "heritage redress" policy points toward one of the overarching ways that the dominant discourse of reconciliation has transformed official multiculturalism: that of temporal orientation. While official multiculturalism in Canada has tended to be primarily focused upon managing difference in the national present, reconciliatory discourses stake a claim to a wider temporal spectrum, seizing the present to manage the national past and future. The Canadian state's multiculturalist project of managing diversity has pivoted upon a temporal logic of ongoing reiteration in the national present through which the government repeatedly performs its celebration of a modern cultural mosaic by funding cultural programs and arts festivals, seeking to "sedate" minoritized groups with token gestures of recognition and to defer addressing broader systemic issues of racist discrimination and socio-economic disparities. The repetitive temporality of continual social and fiscal transactions of acknowledging—or, more accurately, regulating—difference became a form of attrition fomenting the symptoms of "multicultural fatigue." As a remedy, the emerging reconciliation paradigm promoted by the federal government seeks to resolve the need for ongoing reiteration that has been a crucial factor in the withering of official multiculturalism. Instead of ongoing symbolic payouts, the financial compensation offered under the state's program of reconciliation is framed as reparations for the past, meant to memorialize so-called historical injustices precisely as "history," thereby foreclosing debate about ongoing injustices in the national present and future. Reconciling the past serves, therefore, as prophylaxis for the future. Such a shift from perpetual recognition to the production of an air of finality might be usefully described as a general, but not totalizing, transition from a politics of *recognition* to one of *reconciliation*—a transition in which the purportedly crippling condition of ongoing acknowledgment is replaced with discourses focused upon resolution, closure, and cure. In this context, the reconciliatory language of national healing reveals fraught new resonances regarding the biopolitical management of minoritized constituencies' collective injuries.

The logic of commemoration that constructs an event as distant is complemented in dominant discourses of reconciliation by the frequent reiteration of the trope of the "chapter" and its implicit organization of grievances into stories that have ended while the narrative of national life marches onward. This canonical book of the nation's past was referred to as early as Mulroney's apology to Italian Canadians in 1990, when he characterized the internment as "a particularly sad chapter of our history" ("Notes for an Address"). In more recent years, this trope has been invoked with increasing force, as it was foregrounded in Stephen Harper's 2006 apology for the Chinese head tax, when he declared the government's intent, via the performance of contrition, to "formally turn the page on an unfortunate period in Canada's past" (Office of the Prime Minister, *Address by the Prime Minister*). The reiteration of the trope of the chapter has been arguably most pervasive in media and governmental discourses surrounding the 2008 apology to Aboriginal peoples for residential schools. In the federal government's October 2007 speech from the throne, Governor General Michaëlle Jean prophetically declared the forthcoming statement of contrition an act that would "close this sad chapter in our history" (Government of Canada), a phrase that Stephen

Harper subsequently reiterated in his official apology.[11] Demonstrating the currency this trope has attained in recent discourses of reconciliation in Canada, Phil Fontaine, then Grand Chief of the Assembly of First Nations, similarly used the word "chapter" in his parliamentary response to the apology, albeit upgrading Harper's euphemistic modifier "sad" to the more decisive "dreadful" (qtd. in Glowacki). While these repeated references might be hastily dismissed as vacuous political clichés, the forceful recitation of the "chapter" trope functions as a crucial discursive strategy for the production of historical closure. Framing events of discrimination and oppression within the framework of a "chapter" suggests that history unfolds as a coherent, monologic narrative, easily segmented into distinct episodes that may be closed once read. The cunning of reconciliation consequently functions to contain wrongdoings to strictly delimited historical parameters and, in turn, to accentuate the current administration's enlightened reflexivity. In Coleman's terms, governmental gestures of apology serve as "performance[s] of civility" that seek to "manage" the nation's "traumatic history" by "mourning" it (29) and, in turn, framing racist ideology as, to quote Harper's head tax *mea culpa* once more, "a product of a profoundly different time" (Office of the Prime Minister, *Address by Prime Minister*).

The 2008 residential schools apology further demonstrates how such discursive attempts to inscribe closure upon the so-called wrongs of the past also seek to govern the national future. Toward the end of his House of Commons address, Harper suggested that the necessary components of national "resolution" had already been implemented with the 2007 Residential Schools Settlement Agreement, which provides students with financial compensation and offers them an opportunity to air their grievances through the Truth and Reconciliation Commission (TRC), which began its five-year term just days prior to the apology. In ostensibly rectifying the past, Harper's speech also attempted to foreclose further debate and dissent in the future—debate that, despite the Prime Minister's best efforts, has already begun in response to the limitations of government initiatives for "resolving" the matter of residential school abuse. While the Settlement Agreement has been criticized for the small amounts of compensation offered in comparison to individual civil suits as well as for its graphic approach to taxonomizing and assigning monetary value to a list of sexual and physical abuses for which additional compensation can be petitioned, the structure of the TRC and its lack of subpoena powers as well as its potential to place the burden of national catharsis on the shoulders of Aboriginal witnesses have also been the subject of debate.[12] In this light, Harper's apology attempts to write the future *avant la lettre* with a pre-emptive statement that arrives five years before the completion of the Commission and the publication of its final report.[13] The hasty acceleration of the apology's arrival also suggested the Conservatives' desire to lay claim to the event prior to the October 2008 election in an effort to bolster the appeal of a struggling minority government.

If, in one sense, the apology for residential schools may be judged as arriving too quickly and being rushed in its implementation, it is in other ways an apology freighted with a history of deferral and hesitation, haunted by the traces of previous failed attempts at imposing the very closure the cunning of reconciliation labours to produce.[14] To overwrite the history of its failures, the federal government presented June 2008 as a watershed moment, a profound historical turning point that eclipsed the state's previous failed attempts at producing resolution with Indigenous peoples. For example, the 1998 "Statement of Reconciliation" fell short of Aboriginal constituencies' expectations of a formal *mea culpa* due to its absence from official parliamentary and legal record and its failure to invoke the word "sorry." Moreover, the statement was subsequently compromised by the media's uncovering of a confidential government document written in late 1995 or early 1996 that advised federal officials to avoid uttering the word "apology" along with any direct acknowledgement of the government's liability for residential schools in order to protect the state from lawsuits in an era prior to the Settlement Agreement.[15] Similarly, although the federal government frames the commencement of the TRC as an unprecedented venture in rapprochement, an earlier version of documented residential school survivors' testimony was previously published as part of the 1996 findings of the Royal Commission on Aboriginal Peoples. Rather than allow the state's discourse of the present as a watershed moment to occlude the recent history of its unsuccessful efforts at rapprochement, it is crucial to critically revisit these past attempts and to learn from their possibilities and shortcomings. In the case of the Royal Commission's reports, many of the voices represented in the 1996 archives belong to residential school survivors who are no longer alive, and thus it is vital that these narratives not become buried beneath the events of 2008.[16]

Although the government's failed attempts to impose closure upon Aboriginal grievances have been the most pronounced and protracted, the need for repeated gestures of apology and compensation has also thwarted the state's success in silencing diasporic constituencies' calls for reparations. The Ministry of Canadian Heritage's recent announcement of another $5 million to the Chinese Canadian community on the heels of the 2006 redress compensation package suggest that the state's efforts to relegate injustices to the past is a faltering enterprise. The 2008 apology to the South Asian Canadian community for the *Komagata Maru* tragedy underscores how minoritized constituencies are refusing, in increasingly prompt and vocal terms, to accept the state's efforts to finalize debate on racist discrimination. Immediately upon the conclusion of Stephen Harper's apology speech in Surrey, Sikh community leaders denounced the gesture of contrition and polled the audience for a show of hands to reject the Prime Minister's statement (Hainsworth). Aggrieved communities are refusing the imperative of forgiveness that the state's apologies issue and, moreover, uncoupling the concept of forgiveness from that of forgetting. The accelerated refusal of the state's imposition of historical closure strikingly underscores how the temporal orientation of the cunning of reconciliation is faltering under the weight of minoritized constituencies' resistance, collapsing back into a logic of ongoing reiteration curiously reminiscent of that which fomented "multicultural fatigue" in the mid-1990s.

Canadian Civility and the "'Globalisation' of Forgiveness"

If an expansion of temporal management tactics is one aspect of the renovation of multiculturalism by the rise of discourses of reconciliation, another crucial area of transformation concerns the strategic positioning of Canada in relation to what Jacques Derrida has diagnosed as the "'globalisation' of forgiveness" (28). Since the end of WWII and the rise of decolonization movements, national and transnational communities have attempted to grapple with crimes against humanity by formulating new institutions charged with the mandate of restoring a sense of order—and, ostensibly, justice—to a world shaken by its propensity for violence. If the development of the UN and the International Court of Justice were among the first of such institutions, the mechanisms for addressing injustices have diversified over recent decades in the form of truth and reconciliation commissions and official apologies proffered by nation-states, imperial monarchies, and even corporations.[17] According to Derrida, such apparatuses of "repentance, confession, forgiveness, or apology" have proliferated in recent years (28), creating a world-historical phenomenon that Michel-Rolph Trouillot argues is historically unprecedented, emerging on the "global stage" as "the ultimate horizon of a new historicity" (173)—what many scholars have termed "the age of apology."[18] Trouillot posits that a crucial condition of possibility for the recent worldwide proliferation of apologies is the emergence of "a virtual yet global stage"—a mediated forum produced by communication technologies that "may be an illusion but, if so, it is an illusion through which an increasingly large part of humanity" engages with the world (181).

Although official multiculturalism's celebration of diversity has always in part been concerned with Canada's international reputation as a civil society, the focus of such international positioning during the 1970s and 1980s was arguably directed most concertedly toward differentiating the Canadian cultural mosaic from the so-called American "melting pot" as a check against US cultural encroachments. In recent years, the Canadian state's proliferation of reconciliatory gestures has been motivated by international pressures that have expanded beyond the threat of US cultural imperialism to a broader cluster of investments in the "virtual global gaze" (Trouillot 182). Since the end of the Second World War—the embryonic period of the "'globalisation' of forgiveness"—Canada has pursued "a doctrine of 'middle power' internationalism" that seeks to translate its national mythology of civility into a foreign policy predicated upon the "values of human rights, liberal democracy, and peacekeeping" (Abu-Laban and Nath 75). In the mid-1990s, however, the fallout of the Somalia affair tarnishing Canada's reputation as a peacekeeping force abroad coincided with increased scrutiny of Canada's human rights track record under the gaze of the UN Special Rapporteur on contemporary forms of racism, racial discrimination, xenophobia, and related intolerance and the development of forums such as the World Conference Against Racism in 2001. Following his mission to Canada in 2003, Special Rapporteur Doudou Diène published a report that pointed to the disjuncture between the Canadian mythology of civility, as espoused by federal officials, and the lived experience of minoritized communities. According to Diène: "A basic precondition for any credible effort to combat racial discrimination is the objective recognition that it really exists.... At [the] federal level, the representatives of the various departments showed a certain reluctance, if not actual hesitation, when it came to admitting the reality of racial discrimination in Canadian society" (21). In his conclusions and recommendations, Diène asserted that the "Canadian Government should add credibility, trust and recognition to its ... political commitment to combating racism, discrimination and xenophobia by recognizing, at the highest level, that such evils still persist" (24). For the Special Rapporteur, an important measure of the government's credibility in this arena—in addition to other legal and policy reforms—was the issuing of reparations to Chinese head tax payers and their families and to African Canadian communities in Nova Scotia, particularly former residents of Africville, whose homes were razed in the 1960s to make way for urban development (25). Under the surveillance of the virtual global gaze, therefore, the Canadian state has become pressured to repair its mythology of civility and jostle for position in the race toward reconciliation, seeking to outpace other settler colonies of the former British Commonwealth such as Australia and New Zealand in terms of their own domestic projects of rapprochement.[19] Canada seems to be "winning," if the measure of success is the sheer number of apologies proffered to the most diverse range of constituents—a diversity that reflects not only a domestic agenda but also a foreign policy bid to represent Canada as itself a globalizing entity that, through apology, forges ties with diasporic citizens and the international political spheres and economies to which they are articulated.

The "virtual global stage" (Trouillot 182) thus functions, in the words of Derrida, as "the theatrical space in which the grand forgiveness, the grand scene of repentance which we are concerned with, is played, sincerely or not" (29). This trend toward "theatricality" in the "'globalisation' of forgiveness" has prompted an intensification of the performative aspects of white civility in its latest incarnation. Coleman asserts that his invocation of the term "civility" in place of "tolerance" seeks "to emphasize ... [white civility's] dynamic or performative implication" (21). "Tolerance," he continues, "is passive, an endurance of difference, whereas civility involves manners and behaviours that must be learned and performed" (21). In the current moment, white civility as a performative practice of Canadian identity has moved beyond the floor of the House of Commons as affective performances that are disseminated and replayed across multiple cyberforums, from television to webcasts and

YouTube videos—thereby increasing the lifespan and circulation of these spectacles of purported Canadian altruism.

While official multiculturalism has always revelled in technicolour celebrations of the cultural mosaic, the enterprise of reconciliation has shifted the tenor of Canadian national performance in significant ways. Multiculturalism's spectacles tend to be focused upon what Sara Ahmed has called a "public fantasy of happiness" (121)—performances of cultural difference co-opted as national vibrancy where "happiness is promised as the reward for [a form of social] integration" that renders the non-white subject at once other to and yet compliant with white hegemony (132).[20] In contrast, the cunning of reconciliation has shifted national theatricality away from the spectacle of frenetic, compulsive happiness and towards the staging of remorse, grief, and contrition on national and global levels (and yet such performances of bad feeling are supposed, once purged, to become transformed into good feeling). While multiculturalism placed the demands of performance solely upon minoritized subjects to display superficial cultural signifiers for the national gaze, the turn to rapprochement has widened the spectrum of dramatis personae to include both aggrieved others and settler subjects, the latter who are ostensibly grief-stricken not by their own actions but rather by the burden of history they must carry. The cunning of reconciliation produces an affective economy in which state figureheads such as the Prime Minister demonstrate the depths of white civility through emotive displays of recompense which, in turn, seek to interpellate injured constituencies into an affective compact with the state. There has perhaps been no clearer example of this dynamic than the federal government's apology to Aboriginal communities for residential schools on 11 June 2008, the success of which seemed to hinge, in media and popular discourses, upon the perceived "sincerity" of Stephen Harper's delivery in the House of Commons (Curry, "Bill Curry on Residential Schools"). The apology's ability to effect closure upon the so-called wrongs of the past was staked on whether or not the media and the public deemed the apology "deeply moving" ("Canada's Expression of Sorrow"; "No Routine Apology Will Suffice"). Despite the logical impossibility of accurately calibrating the emotional sincerity of any state figurehead, the insistent reiteration of the emotive components of the apology as indices of its success reveals that one of the most potent elements of the cunning of reconciliation in the current era is its capacity to solicit the affective engagement of national and global publics in the drama of healing.

The symbolic value of such emotive performances of contrition are translatable into other currencies—ones that have calculated economic advantages. Participation in the age of apology has become crucial to a nation-state's involvement in neoliberal economic globalization. In an ironic twist, the performance of rapprochement is often the elite passport into a system of global finance built on the foundations of colonial oppression that is now thematized as the subject of many calls for redress. According to the rationality of neoliberal economic globalization, the symbolic capital accrued by performing rapprochement frequently transmogrifies into financial capital, either through the lifting of economic sanctions by which the international community has at times penalized states for human rights abuses, or through more diversified processes in which multinational corporations are enticed to invest in nation-states with political and social stability. The link between the symbolic capital of rapprochement and its economic rewards under neoliberal globalization has resulted in a strategic overlapping of discourses of human rights and discourses of economic prosperity and capital accumulation, effecting what Jodi Melamed calls a "rhetorical transference" through which concepts such as "liberty" become collapsed into "economic liberty" while human security is conflated with economic security, or capitalist prosperity (16–17).[21] Nation-states are thus able to seamlessly conflate the project of reconciliation with interests in global economic competition, legitimating motivations for enticing foreign investment under the rhetoric of protecting the security and liberty of its citizens. In this way, the cunning of reconciliation recalibrates official multiculturalism's "intercalation of the politics of culture with the culture of capital" (Povinelli 17) for the "'globalisation' of forgiveness."

Dominant formulations of reconciliation in Canada, therefore, are proving immensely amenable to the production of a semblance of social cohesion—that catchphrase of neoliberal rationality signifying acquiescent communities through which global flows of money and commodities may travel with minimal friction. The Canadian government and the mainstream media have certainly attempted to publicize the nation's ostensibly renewed political stability with Quebec—for which the appointment of Michaëlle Jean as Governor General serves as one symbolic assurance—in order to paint the threat of secession that deterred foreign investors as a resolved matter of the past. Reconciliation with Aboriginal peoples is of even greater concern to Canada's transnational economic development due to the perceived threat Indigenous constituencies pose to disrupting resource extraction. In a June 2009 report published by the Canadian Defence and Foreign Affairs Institute and sponsored by Nexen Incorporated—a "Canadian-based global energy company" with oil interests in West Africa, the Middle East, and the Canada's Athabasca oil sands—First Nations and Métis communities were identified as one of the key "threat groups" that could jeopardize the oil industry in the Canadian west.[22] The dominant logic of reconciliation formulated by the Canadian government seeks to neutralize this so-called threat by interpellating Aboriginal peoples into "renew[ed] ... partnership[s]" (Canada, Indian Affairs and Northern Development), or what Stephen Harper referred to in his residential schools apology as a strategically vague "new relationship" with the Canadian government. Less than a year later, however, Harper's Conservatives announced their new funding strategy for Aboriginal reserves, defining this "new relationship" as one that privileges communities willing to bend to the will of the federal government and that of the market. The $1.4 billion earmarked for spending on Aboriginal peoples in the Harper administration's 2009 budget was announced as being allocated in greater amounts to those bands willing to "partner" with the "federal government and the private sector on economic development and infrastructure" (Ivison, "Chuck Strahl"). As then Minister of Indian Affairs and Northern Development Chuck Strahl asserted with regard to Aboriginal communities: "if you don't develop healthy working relations and partnerships with other levels of government and your neighbours, you will suffer because you lack opportunities" (qtd. in Ivison "Chuck Strahl"). In this way, the reconciliatory language of partnership (which, in the words of Strahl sounds more like a veiled threat: "you will suffer") becomes a way of disciplining First Peoples as good neoliberal subjects who earn their place in the nation through furthering the state's economic goals. Such a system, as Phil Fontaine has observed, redefines "partnership" as "the imposition of government will" (qtd. in Ivison "Rewards").

The alibi that hegemonic discourses of reconciliation have provided for the furtherance of a neoliberal agenda and the maintenance of colonial power asymmetries in Canadian society, however, has become subject to scrutiny under the virtual global gaze and the strategic lobbying of that gaze by marginalized constituencies in Canada. Africville redress campaigners made a presentation to the 2001 UN World Conference Against

Racism, drawing international attention to their then unresolved claim. Aboriginal groups have similarly aired their grievances at the UN, calling attention to the Canadian government's longstanding opposition to the UN Declaration on the Rights of Indigenous Peoples as evidence of the state's failure to substantiate its symbolic performances of rapprochement with concrete actions. In so doing, Aboriginal organizations refused the 2008 apology's narrative of closure, using the *mea culpa* instead to hold the state accountable to future change while recruiting the virtual global stage as a watchdog for government behaviour. Lobbying for the government to make good on its apologetics has borne fruit, as the Canadian government reluctantly endorsed the UN Declaration in November 2010.[23] Such resistance strategies demonstrate that the cunning of reconciliation is not totalizing. As much as Canada's domestication of the "'globalisation' of forgiveness" may aid and abet the nation-state's participation in neoliberal economic globalization, it may also open new possibilities for minoritized constituencies' goals—from soliciting the international court of public opinion to press for concrete reparations rather than symbolic gestures, to utilizing the state's economic motivations as leverage in policy negotiations.

Rethinking "Reconciliation"

By tracing the logic of the cunning of reconciliation as it has taken shape in recent years, I have sought to demonstrate how the project of redressing injustices has been co-opted by the power bloc as a performance of white civility, an index of the supposed enlightenment of the Euro-Canadian establishment. While some might wish to defend the philosophical ideals embedded in liberal humanism and differentiate their intellectual intent from their historical implementation in troubling social formations like white civility, I call for a more extended critique of liberal ideology's relation to colonial reckoning. Throughout his book, Coleman holds out hope for recuperating what he refers to as a "real project" of civility—one that, caught in a strange tension between sincerity and irony, is "wryly" self-conscious of the violent history of civility in Canada even as it continues to believe in the reparative possibilities of the "prodigious effort to create a civil society" and the "degrees of justice and equality that have been achieved within the [Canadian] civil sphere" (9). I argue for a different approach. Rather than considering the

Western concept of the civil sphere as the principal, albeit flawed, model upon which to base a conceptualization of future society in Canada, a reckoning with the histories and presents of racist oppression and colonization calls for an effort to think beyond the hegemony of Eurocentric philosophical and political ideals and to imagine transcultural forms of social justice and redress. This is nothing less than a profoundly challenging task—one that requires serious engagement with the work of activists and intellectuals who challenge Eurocentric epistemologies and work beyond their boundaries. At the same time, as a Euro-Canadian scholar, I want to remain cognizant of the risks of appropriating or representing such promising intellectual work in caricatured fashion. It is imperative to guard against attempts by the state to co-opt transculturalism into its own hegemonic program of apology in ways that reinvigorate Eurocentric logics with the occasional "exotic" Aboriginal garnish, the nod to alterity that, not unlike earlier strategies of official multiculturalism, appropriates difference on behalf of a firmly entrenched Euro-Canadian establishment.[24]

Alternative transcultural conceptualizations of redress and reconciliation are being formulated in compelling terms in the field of Indigenous legal studies. Several scholars working in this field have expounded arguments regarding the power of Indigenous legal traditions within the Canadian legislative and judicial system. James (Sákéj) Youngblood Henderson, Research Director of the Native Law Centre of Canada, implicitly refuses the vague universalization of the term "reconciliation"—as well as the semblance of consensus that hegemonic discursive formations construct around this concept—by theorizing a specific vision for "constitutional reconciliation between the *sui generis* Aboriginal orders or treaty federalism and the governmental powers" (430). Henderson seizes upon the legal term *sui generis* which, from the Latin, means "'forming a kind by itself; unique, literally of its own particular kind' or class" (Borrows 9) that was first invoked by the Supreme Court in the *R. v. Van der Peet* decision of 1996 to characterize the distinctive role of Aboriginal rights in Canada. Strategically redeploying Western juridical discourse to uphold the unassimilable and inalienable quality of Aboriginal epistemologies and legal traditions, Henderson demonstrates in detail how Aboriginal law and rights are "*sui generis* to the Canadian order" and yet "protected by Canadian constitutional law" ("Sui Generis" 424). In this context, Henderson argues that "constitutional reconciliation"—a more specific appellation than the free-floating term that is often unmoored from material apparatuses such as the courts or the law—hinges upon the full recognition of Aboriginal peoples' *sui generis* rights in policy-making and treaty land negotiations (Battiste and Henderson 213). In this vein, Henderson's "constitutional reconciliation" insists on something far more specific—namely, a precise political and legal relationship that acknowledges Aboriginal peoples' historical precedence on the lands that constitute "Canada"—than the state's token gestures and lip service to a future of "mov[ing] forward together."[25]

Henderson and Anishinabe scholar John Borrows' work on the concept of *sui generis* Aboriginal rights might serve as a broader conceptual model for reimagining Aboriginal relations with the Canadian nation-state. As Borrows further explains, the term *sui generis* suggests that Aboriginal rights "do not wholly take their source or meaning from the philosophies that underlie the Western canon of law" (9). Rather, "[t]he existence of this doctrine suggests the possibility that Aboriginal rights stem from alternative sources of law that reflect the unique historical presence of Aboriginal peoples in North America" (9). At the same time, "[w]hile the sui generis doctrine of Aboriginal rights places significant emphasis upon Aboriginal difference, it does not ignore the similarities between Aboriginal and non-Aboriginal peoples" that have taken shape over centuries of asymmetrical co-habitation in Canada (9). Accordingly, "[t]he sui generis doctrine reformulates similarity and difference and thereby captures the complex, overlapping, and exclusive identities and relationships of the parties" (10). The concept of *sui generis* rights consequently offers a framework for thinking about transcultural versions of redress and reconciliation by marking out a space for Indigenous legal traditions that intersects with and yet also exists beyond and independently of Western juridical discourse. Such a model might be useful not only for rethinking the relations between Indigenous peoples and the Canadian state in its current formation but also for conceptualizing the productive forms of coalition that might continue to develop between different redress movements led by Aboriginal and diasporic constituencies, while resisting the collapsing of differences between such marginalized groups. In this context, the *sui generis* doctrine points to a more flexible form of articulation between aggrieved parties that allows for both linking and separation, or points of affiliation and divergence, in the struggle for social change.

The Long March to "Recognition": Sákéj Henderson, First Nations Jurisprudence, and *Sui Generis* Solidarity

Len Findlay

I aim to accomplish three things in this essay. First, I seek to enhance the profile among Canadianists of the work of Sákéj Henderson, Director of the Native Law Centre at the University of Saskatchewan and advisor to the Assembly of First Nations, the Four Directions Council of the United Nations Working Group on Indigenous Peoples, and to innumerable groups of First Nations litigants, students, and interdisciplinary scholars. Second, I offer a reading of Henderson's recent rerouting of his citizenship studies through a sustained reflection on and reassertion of First Nations jurisprudence and Aboriginal rights in his book so titled by the same phrasing, and his claim that these issues are essential (in the words the book's subtitle that deliberately echo Pierre Trudeau and Harold Cardinal) to defining a just society. It is an effort that Henderson locates explicitly within a knowledge "ecology" placed in critical relation to the current knowledge economy that connects Canada through state policies and institutions to a world still taking its cues, or taking its lumps, from the white Enlightenment. Third, I wish briefly to illustrate how literary and cultural producers, educators, and activists can make use of such insurgent, indigenous-humanist work as Henderson's in their own projects, especially through new configurations and inflections of recognition and redistribution capable of nourishing new (and much needed) pedagogies, new research agendas, new modes of consultation and collaboration on the dialectical interplay of literature broadly defined, citizenship generously but critically construed, and institutions that understand and effectively advance Aboriginal and treaty rights as invaluable forces within confederation, forces from which *all* Canadians continue to benefit.[1]

The Indigenous Intellectual

James (Sákéj) Youngblood Henderson is a major "public intellectual" and an arrestingly indigenous exemplar of that variously problematic expression (see Collini). The label "indigenous intellectual" is not Henderson's self-description but my attempt to capture a distinctive dynamic in his thinking and strategic appropriation of Eurocentric terminology and knowledge systems in Canadian and international contexts, both within and beyond fresh understanding and recognition of "Indigenous intellectual property."[2] Henderson's intellectual work derives from the rootedness of indigenous knowledge communities and the invasive swagger of imperialist ideas, but it is not confinable within the public–private distinction on which much writing about the public intellectual rests. Nor does allegiance to particular places allow the indigenous intellectual to be himself or herself exilic, at least not in the celebrated manner of Eric Auerbach or Edward Said. Henderson has not gravitated like Said to an iconically diasporic figure like Auerbach, nor to Said's effort from the relative safety and marked liminality of Istanbul "virtually *to see* the development of Western culture at almost the last moment when that culture still had its integrity and civilizational coherence" (*Orientalism* 258). Nor would Henderson follow Auerbach and Said in looking to Hugh of St. Victor for a sense of his path: "The man who finds his homeland sweet is still a tender beginner; he to whom every soil is as his native one is already strong; but he is perfect to whom the entire world is as a foreign land" (qtd. in *Orientalism* 259). Henderson would not be surprised that a twelfth-century articulation of a Christian transcendental knowledge system (Taylor, *Didascalicon*) could be used by two very different diasporic comparativists in the twentieth century to similarly personal ends. The flight from the Nazis and expulsion of Palestinians from their homeland in 1948 became occasions for the command performance of humanism as a wounded universal, a locus of transcendence and reimmunization against bad territoriality and the ruthless pursuit of cultural and "racial" purity. The implacable intellectual strengthens his resolve by appealing to a saintly precursor in Hugh, and in so doing creates a touchstone for his own embrace of homelessness as vocation. This is not to deny that Said would exercise a right of "returning again and again" to what he would later term this "hauntingly beautiful passage" (Said, *Culture* 335). However, beyond the opportunities it affords to detoxify notions of homeland (*patria*), soil (*solum*) and wholeness (*totus*), particularly after the fascist appeals to *Blud und Boden* and *Gleichschaltung* and the experience of *al naqba* on the ground and in the Occupied Territories, and to allude to the productivity of exile (*exilium*) by echoing Ovid, Hugh's prose remains awkwardly aligned with an ascetic *contemptus mundi* and silent about imperial and colonial violence.[3] This resonant and influential figuration of the cosmopolitan intellectual therefore needs indigenizing and re-territorializing, in the interests of a different politics and poetics of attachment, before it can be set to decolonizing work in North America. Cosmopolitanism is not the answer to contested land claims and the assertion of Aboriginal and treaty rights.

Accordingly, Henderson as indigenous intellectual has worked the interface between native and newcomer legal orders linked to the land to help clear and travel for decades old and new roads toward human rights and treaty justice for indigenous peoples, roads that always cross somebody's territory and implicate a particular ecology. Rather than a diasporic citizen of the world, he is more of a Turtle Island amphibian or resident of the "in-between lodge" (Henderson qtd. in I. Findlay, xii) where indigenous legal scholars function as neither traditional knowledge keepers nor practitioners working exclusively with the civil and common law codes and their nervous federal convergences in "the" law of Canada. The ongoing challenges of such work remain clear even in the new Citizenship and Immigration Canada *Study Guide* for potential citizens of this country, a text which reasserts allegiance to the tainted discourse of "discovery" while remaining entirely silent on the matter of Aboriginal law.[4] The *Guide*'s welcome shift from two to three founding peoples clearly shows the influence of John Ralston Saul's *A Fair Country*, but the influence of Henderson is nowhere to be seen within the document, and he was not included in its massively Euro-Canadian list of consultants. The long march continues.

But this march, for the indigenous intellectual, is serially terrestrial rather than cumulatively transcendental. Henderson's career has criss-crossed the US–Canada border because it is not only the buffalo that tastes the same on both sides (as Sitting Bull said), but the racist bullshit and state obstructionism, too (as later Aboriginal leaders have said in so many words). Henderson pursues collaborations in the areas of Aboriginal law, Aboriginal science, and the indigenous humanities. His intellectual reach is internationalist, transcultural, multilateral, with a grounding in Mi'kmaw based on his partnership with Marie Battiste and his work on the Mi'kmaw Concordat for the community in Eskasoni, Cape Breton, and for the Mi'kmaw Nation more generally. Radicalized by his Chickasaw boyhood and residential school in Oklahoma, and by his experiences at Harvard where he successfully sued the university for repayment of his fees after searching the Native American obligations attached to Harvard's title to the land it stands on, he taught at Berkeley with Russel Barsh and Vine Deloria Jr. among others, co-authoring a key contribution to Native American emancipation (*The Road: Indian Tribes and Political Liberty* [1980]) in a United States much more receptive to radical thought and practice than it has been recently (until the presidency of Barack Obama raised the hopes of progressives only to frustrate many of them).[5] Then Henderson came to Canada.

Henderson's search for justice for Aboriginal peoples has led him to affirm Aboriginal and treaty rights at the UN (a compelling narrative recounted in his *Indigenous Diplomacy*) and at the Circumpolar Conference where he had to set Marilyn Albright and her Canadian peers right (at least for a season in the political cycle) about the nature and implications of the indigenous Arctic for those increasingly committed to a shamelessly neo-colonial scramble for Arctica. For more than a decade now, he has been based in Saskatoon, city of "starlight tours" for Aboriginal men conducted by the city police (Hubbard); city also of centennial celebrations and the discreet rewhitening of history, opportunity, and institutional practice in the name of "western development" and the heroic pioneers (Bell 157–59). At times, he tells me, the RCMP have had an unmarked car parked outside the Henderson family front door, intimidatingly hidden in plain view because the force disapproves of his research on the treatment of Aboriginal men and women, boys and girls, in RCMP custody. In sum, Henderson's career reminds us of the need to look beyond the predictable circuits of disciplinary celebrity and to find excellence and inspiration in new forms and places. Moreover, Canadianists need to indigenize their practice in ways that recognize their own privileges and limits, and the pressing need for an end to appropriation and plundering of indigenous knowledge and the ecologies that sustain it (Battiste and Henderson).

Henderson's life and works bear witness also to the possibility for new coalitions across difference that will keep on exposing Canada's dirty little colonial and neo-colonial secrets and the state apparatus of chilling surveillance, serial litigation sustained by deep pockets, abiding greed, a massive legal bureaucracy, and strategic misrecognition.

For Henderson, gaining recognition as a scholar has been important primarily for the opportunity it has afforded him to interrogate and change dominant understandings of what knowledge is and of the notion of recognition itself. His academic practice is a form of passing or strategic simulation and compliance—but with a larger, collective purpose. The temporality of recognition is for him crucial and tied to prior occupancy and the flourishing pre-encounter indigenous legal orders, orders not reducible to that Eurocentric presence and presentism according to which the indigenous "Other" exists only in the eye of the dominant. Recognition by Canadian courts of Aboriginal rights was not the recognition of something adumbrated in the Calder decision and formalized in 1982 in section 35 (1) of the Constitution Act. No, it was the recognition and affirmation of "*existing* aboriginal and treaty rights" (Henderson, *Jurisprudence* 33; emphasis added) that preceded the Royal Proclamation of 1763 and have continued independent of elite edicts and their uneven implementation. For Henderson, the stories of the First Peoples cannot be reduced to enabling or diverting episodes punctuating the spread of empire. Nor can the arrow of "progress" or "civilization" puncture the membrane of the indigenous circle, no matter how powerful the pricks that impel it. Aboriginal rights preceded and have survived Canada's transition from colony to sovereign state, in which the state tried to remake Aboriginal peoples as its own dwindling and deficient wards recognizable only as exotic traces of prehistory and residues of the primitive to be assimilated in the name of the modern. However, while this history is being disrupted, rewritten, and re-performed in a concerted "Aboriginal renaissance" (Battiste and Henderson 13–14; Battiste 83), the doctrine of constitutional rather than parliamentary supremacy has given the courts renewed interest in recognition, and in reparation, but with redistribution a predictably weak third. Yet in the past twenty-five years, the discourse of the "primitive" (Battiste and Henderson 8) has been slowly expunged from litigation and judicial opinions, replaced by the idea of Aboriginal and treaty rights as a "golden thread" (123; citing Justice McLachlin's phrase from her dissenting judgment in Van der Peet [1996]) running through Canadian history, and the recognition and fuller interpretation of the fact acknowledged in the Supreme Court of Canada's Sparrow decision as "the culmination of a long and difficult struggle in both the political forum and the courts" (qtd. in Henderson, *Jurisprudence* 16). And this protracted and hugely encumbered process, this long march, is not yet over for Henderson, because there is residual Eurocentrism, paternalism, sexism, and obtuseness in the judiciary; because the political battles are far from won, both inside and outside Aboriginal communities and organizations, as evidenced by the Harper government's refusal to sign the United Nations Declaration on the Rights of Indigenous Peoples, by the re-privileging of white authority in Citizenship and Immigration Canada's new *Guide*, and the Prime Minister's astonishing statement at the G8 meetings in Pittsburgh that "Canada has no history of colonialism" (Walia par. 1); and because educators and cultural producers still too often ignore or misrecognize indigenous rights and capacities while resenting any talk of redistribution that they think, often with good reason, may occur at their own expense. It is worth remembering that constitutional entrenchment of "existing aboriginal and treaty rights" occurred only because of the efforts of Canada's First Nations. Moreover, those who benefit most from the current distribution of opportunity and reward have fought fiercely, like their predecessors in this country, to maintain their largely "white privilege" (McIntosh 165) while blaming the victim and using media ownership, corporate clout, academic accomplices, and now the remilitarization of our economy and national self-understanding,[6] to work for the election, and re-election, of administrations eager to incarcerate where they cannot assimilate representatives of Canada's "Indigenous difference" (Macklem 10). Afro-American scholar and activist Angela Davis argues for a "clear relationship between the rise of the prison-industrial-complex in the era of global capitalism and the persistence of structures in the punishment system that originated with slavery" (*Abolition* 35)—and therefore originated with colonialism, one might add.

Recognizing Recognition Plus

Having mentioned the word "recognition" a couple of times, I will turn now to what that term means for those, like Sákéj Henderson, who pursue recognition at the constitutional table, in the courts, at the United Nations, in the academy, and in various communities and public spheres.

What this pursuit reveals is a critical engagement with recognition as key to the presumptions and practices of the rights-bearing individual as citizen of the modern liberal state. The work of Nancy Fraser is probably better known to Canadianists than the work of Henderson. And I for one certainly feel indebted to Fraser for recoupling recognition and redistribution at a time when economic and class concerns were being replaced by the fetishization of identity in the human sciences and when, as a consequence, groups seeking recognition or combating misrecognition were being reified by their academic supporters as well as their enemies. Fraser turned to the category of "status" from that of identity in order to retain gains made in the name of identity politics while also articulating those gains together with a renewed recognition of the importance of capital and class in determining social and cultural outcomes for individual and collective agents ("Rethinking Recognition" 31–32). Like Fraser, Patchen Markell and a number of fine Canadian scholars (well assessed by Angus 68ff.) have struggled to recouple recognition, as arguably a good in itself, with recognition as a lever of redistribution, and many of their insights can be mapped onto Henderson's foundational jurisprudential model (no *terra nullius* here!) in ways that can advance the causes of decolonization. And I now turn to examples of the challenges involved in this endeavour and where collaboration might most usefully occur.

Broadly put, Henderson works in two registers, one Euro-legal and the other Aboriginal-ecological, one black-letter and the other "poetic." Accordingly, the signing of the constitution into law on Parliament Hill on 17 April 1982 is seen by him not only as a piece of constitutional history about which he continues to write indefatigably (as in his recent and longest textual march of nearly one thousand pages in his *Treaty Rights*) but also as an early spring day of changing light and weather conditions leading to the following account of events at sunset:

> These sounds [of the Aboriginal drummers] unfolded the durable jurisprudence of the Life-giver's covenants. The embodied spirits enraptured the stationary dancers. It was a silent realm, full of mystery. Some say experiencing it is like being in the oldest time. In a breath, the dancers belonged to all things, again—with the first sun, after the long rain, the morning star, the sweet earth—and the old teachings were renewed. Their spirits reached out to the Great Silence and the teachings, together. In honour of that unity, the singers' voices joined together. They began to rearrange the mysteries.

> A complicated and split-head consciousness [Henderson himself] listened. Unaware, his body began to sway in time with the teaching rhythms and the other dancers. He began to perceive the comforting clarity of the teachings in many nourishing languages. He was learning again the teachings of the Life-giver. These sounds belonged to another realm. They were generated by the sacred realm.
>
> Gradually, a constitutional negotiator forgot the whispers of the postcolonial ghost-dancing. He began praying once more, learning, again. He was merging with the ancient messages of First Nations jurisprudences in the beginning song of the Gourd Dance. (*Jurisprudence* 3–4)

At first blush, this passage from Henderson's "Prologue" to his *Jurisprudence* book would seem to pose huge difficulties—and not only for legal scholars who expect and demand something very different from someone with a juris doctorate from Harvard. For a non-Aboriginal materialist like me the challenges are equally huge. For instance, language, culture, and ceremony are prominent in the passage I quoted, but there appears to be no sign of economic production in the midst of cultural performance. Contradiction there is, to be sure, but that contradiction is not located in the commodity form but in the "split head" consciousness (Cajete 189) of Henderson as observer and then participant who lives in two worlds, "red" and "white," living their contradictions in a very particular way. And, rather than mergers and acquisitions vulnerable to left critique, there is the merging of an embodied and somatically responsive subject with some mystical plenum. What on earth does smashing capitalism have to do with "rearranging the mysteries"? How can those committed to redistributive justice work effectively together, coming as they seem to do from mutually *un*recognizable places? How can they recognize themselves in each other's projects? How can the Aboriginal activist and the historical materialist get beyond Pierre Trudeau's categorical dismissal of 1969: "We can't recognize aboriginal rights because no society can be built on historical 'might have beens'" (qtd. in Henderson, *Jurisprudence* 5)?

Let's begin a response to such questions with the "problem" of spirituality for the non-Aboriginal supporter of Aboriginal causes. For Henderson, spiritual allegiance is an inalienable Aboriginal right and tradition, exercised differently over time and according to the protocols governing particular situations of self-renewal, encounter, and exchange. This right must be recognized and respected rather than appropriated or dismissed. Its importance is evident in the history of attempts to suppress its every vestige through state prohibitions of sun dance and ghost dance, potlatch and powwow, and via the ideological state apparatus of the residential schools. A left critic may view the sentiments often expressed as a coda to a death sentence—"May God have mercy on your soul"—as the opiate of the masses dispensed formulaically from the indefensibly complicit judicial bench: in other words, law dispensing capital(ist) punishment. However, that critic may also find that Aboriginal spirituality cannot be so readily demystified. Its durability is in part political, which is why it has been so often refused or travestied by state functionaries who choose to be bemused or offended by its independence from Eurocentric textualism and combative hermeneutics, rooted instead in the embodied performance of a desire for and the achievement of consensus in a territory and ecology. On Parliament Hill in Ottawa, this spirituality asserts itself in Henderson in a way as invasive as, but far more nourishing than, the biopolitics of the Canadian state and its only too durable creation, now the Department of Aboriginal Affairs and Northern Development, which continues to seek to travel along the streams of Aboriginal blood and spittle, tears and semen, in its mapping and management of indigenous difference that continues in relation to AIDS and H1N1 influenza. So much for the medicine chest provisions of the treaties.

Second, the Aboriginal appeal to spontaneous orders of ecology as a gift to be held in trust and attended to for their "teachings," the topic Henderson elaborates in his fourth chapter, is, as he points out (116–17), no more naïve than mainstream appeals to the spontaneous orders of the self-regulating market fuelled by the competitive pursuit of self-interest and marked by the unsustainable fictions of sub-prime lending rates, the tenacious facts of toxic assets, and the spurious agency of a global "reset" button and highly politicized "stimulus packages." Nor are these ecological orders any more vulnerable to scepticism and critique than the spontaneously "just" order produced in democratic societies, or indeed, the spontaneously "egalitarian" order of the social relations of production in post-revolutionary worker states (as Deborah Simmons bluntly reminds us). Henderson may seem to build this idea of ecological orders into an implausibly holistic schema: "In the continent known to Europeans as North America, First Nations knowledge and jurisprudence are organized around *four insights*: the insights of covenants of creation, embodied spirits, implicate order, and dynamic transformation" (128–29; emphasis added). But this is no more or less compelling than, for example, Hugh of St. Victor's *four-fold* division of knowledge in the *Didascalicon*, cited admiringly by Auerbach and Said; or William Blake's claim to "see the *Four-fold* Man, the Humanity in deadly sleep / And its fallen Emanation, the Spectre and its cruel Shadow" (*Jerusalem* I. Plate 15; emphasis added); or Northrop Frye's revisioning of Blake's claim in the *four-fold* essays of his *Anatomy of Criticism* and much else in his massive oeuvre. Modalities of the four-fold, like articles of faith and idioms of aspiration more generally, characterize *all* versions of our national (or transnational) imaginary, and the response to that fact is not to deny the validity of one or some but to learn how to learn from them all.

Moreover, the legitimating force of cultural ceremony is not a feature of Aboriginal societies alone. Think of the British monarchy (Nairn), for instance, or think of Canadian state occasions like the one Henderson describes through an indigenous lens. Think even of that Inukshuk logo for the athletic extravaganza staged in 2010 in Vancouver and the federal government's intent via the Department of Canadian Heritage "to invest $20-million toward the opening ceremony of the Olympic Winter Games in order to ensure that the event adequately reflects the priorities of Government and helps to achieve domestic and international branding goals" (official memo qtd. in Matas A1). This missive came after the Harper administration's loud complaints about the politicization of the opening ceremony at the Beijing Olympics (including the Chinese invocation of another version of the long march!). In the neo-colonial play of home and away, politicians who spout democratic freedoms abroad as the guaranteed result of free markets simultaneously practise at home semiotic thuggery euphemized as spin and controlled messaging from the Prime Minister's Office. So much for self-recognition.

There are other bridges and strategic affinities between Aboriginal difference and the demystification and displacement of capital in the passage quoted and throughout the book it introduces, most notably in the imbrication of *collective* rights with *class* politics, but I cannot develop them adequately here.[7] However, if we allow that left politics and First Nations agency are more mutually *recognizable* than might at first be thought, despite their difficult history in Canada (see e.g., Bedford and Irving; and Simmons), then maybe the coded, wary culturalism of the one and socially inflected economism of the other can be used together to advance redistributive justice. Here is where socialism and indigenous practice differ from other—individualist and identitarian—value systems, political projects, and social imaginaries; here is where "all my relations" and the social relations of production can work together to counter the manic uncoupling of consumption from the conditions and consequences of production, the moment in the mall or in shopping online apparently disconnected from the story of the world; here is where stewardship and sustainability can come together in the coalition of indigenous interests and organized labour (see ILO covenant 169, reprinted as Appendix VI in Henderson's *Indigenous Diplomacy*), which colonial and neo-colonial capital has been at such pains to prevent. The alibis of overeager bemusement at Aboriginal "gobbledygook" (Judd Buchanan, Minister of Indian Affairs in 1975, in response to the Dene *Manifesto*; qtd. in Henderson, *Jurisprudence* 230) or the scandalously sanguine, deeply ahistorical assurance of globalizing capitalists that eventually all boats will rise, even canoes and kayaks, and that patience in your marginal place is more "constructive" or "productive" than embarking on or persisting with a long march to recognition—these and many other manifestations of vehement but vulnerable capitalist hegemony ought to be fought with every instrument socially progressive intellectuals have, including the hegemonic discourse of "the" law and "private" property used against themselves. It is not only Latin America that had and continues to have "open veins" (Galeano). Yet the indigenous and the indigenizing intellectual are more than capable of developing together a new politics and poetics of collective attachment to the land.

Sui Generis Solidarity and Trans-Systematics

"We" therefore need a new political economy of citizenship and/as knowledge production linked emphatically to redistribution as well as recognition. As Said put it in one of his final reflections on public intellectual work, "there needs to be a component to our engagement that stresses the need for the redistribution of resources, and that advocates the theoretical imperative against the huge accumulations of power and capital that so distort human life" ("Public Role" 38). Meanwhile, the history and current realities of indigenous struggles for both recognition and redistribution comprise a social and intellectual treasury on which we might all respectfully seek to draw. Let me name this mutually dependent, convergent movement provisionally as *sui generis* solidarity, broadly understood as a radical and radicalizing counter to divide and rule (including the capitalist division of labour) and the fast rapacity of information capitalism. I would advise retaining the expression *sui generis* in order to honour and learn more from the progress that has been made by Canada's First Peoples under the alien yet serviceable aegis of rigorous Latinity, as Henderson and his Aboriginal colleagues have embraced the notion of the *sui generis* only to shift it from signifying concealment and anomaly into the uniqueness of the treaties themselves and thence beyond "interpretative monopolies" and the conventions of "statutory interpretation" to a new "fair, large and liberal" hermeneutic (Henderson, "Interpreting" 49; 58; 62; 81; 88); and then moving the category on from treaties to citizenship (Henderson, "*Sui Generis*"). True to this expansive and supple understanding of the *sui generis*, I recommend the shifting of its emphasis from recognition to redistribution, in a "rearrangement of the mysteries" but also a transformation of the relations and objectives of production that will develop socially and ecologically sustainable trans-Canadian and planetary practices.

If this latter proposal sounds much too grand, even "hopelessly utopian" as so many wealthy fatalists might say, then I would urge you to place *trans-systematics* alongside trans-Canadas on all occasions in a preparatory act of *sui generis* solidarity. *Trans-systematics* is an area of academic innovations with strong roots at McGill University's Faculty of Law in the work especially of H. Patrick Glenn, and now with major commitments from the Native Law Centre of Canada, run by Sákéj Henderson in a strategic rearrangement of the academic mysteries. If colonization works always at least bifocally, home and away, then seriously decolonizing work needs to do the same. And trans-systematics has for about ten years now been engaged with Canada's *three* founding legal orders and jurisprudences while at the same time embarking on major transnational mappings of legal traditions and practices—not looking for the next First World Justinian to arrive on the beleaguered scene of international law mouthing the neo-imperialist phrase *civis Americanus sum*, but seeking instead the forms of social relations and distinctive stewardship that will recognize difference outside the "colonial calculus" (Henderson, *Jurisprudence* 229) but within new regimes of redistribution and consumption. Thanks to the brilliant work of Glenn, especially his chapter on "chthonic legal tradition" (59–91) where the linkages to land are most prominent, and the unyielding tenacity of Henderson, the tunnel vision of legal positivism is giving way to the authority (and humility) of tradition, both within the common law (which Glenn calls "chaos with an index" [350]) and in all versions of legal systems vainly insulating themselves against domestic and global change.

And literary scholars and cultural workers need to know as much about this legal-jurisprudential *turn* as they do about linguistic and cultural and ethical turns. From such ongoing self-education and receptivity to difference, *sui generis* solidarity may arise, and with it new distributions of authority and responsibility, indeed new knowledge systems, within and beyond the Canadian academy. At a time when "the duty to consult" (Newman) seems to be understood by governments as a licence to insult the first and ongoing residents of Indian country, and while many political and legal theorists can't see beyond the end of their own positivist norms, a new generation of scholars needs with due modesty and in good faith to consult their Aboriginal colleagues and host communities as to how best to join the long march to recognition and redistribution, lest we all take the short step into catastrophe.

bush/writing: embodied deconstruction, traces of community, and writing against the state in indigenous acts of inscription

peter kulchyski

how did they get so rich?/how did we get so poor?
— emma larocque, *my hometown northern canada south africa*

the blind man's walk

it is mid-august of the year 2005 and i am in a small boat crossing westward across cumberland sound in nunavut. my daughter, at that time a mere three-year-old, is with me, along with three children of the metuq family and my friend alookie and her partner noah. i am slowly getting to know noah, learning to trust his remarkable range of capabilities and also finding his broader cultural knowledge to be strong. he shows me old graves that i would have missed, old camping sites, historical sites, all in casual conversation to break the monotony of travel. as we pass a cliff, sheer out of the ocean, he points to the angular line made by a ledge that traverses the face of the rock, his finger etching the line until he reaches about halfway to a spot where the line is broken, a kind of gap created by the ledge disappearing for a moment behind a rock and reappearing upwards of it: a cave, open on both ends. offhandedly he says, "there, right there, that's where the blind man walked and when he passed through that cave he could see again." what is written on the land, what is written especially in the rocks, says more to me than i can speak, defies me and embraces me, fills me with questions and longings the effect of which can be summed up in the expression "haunts me."

it is mid-august of the year 2006 and i am at a wide shallow river, again with my daughter, the metuq family, and two student friends. we are catching arctic char with our bare hands or with small metal hooks fastened with tape or rope onto broken hockey sticks. that time, that place, those people, together combine to make a moment too fragile to touch. the water is bitter cold, but the pleasure of pulling out a splashing *ikaluk* leads us to forget the numbness in our hands and feet. again noah shows me something, this time an old fish cache, a kind of giant barrel made of piled rocks and stones, all but invisible in the arctic landscape unless you know what to look for. but this time it is the action, the catching and gutting and carrying of fish for food, that compels my attention even more than does the site and what haunts the site.

inuit are hunting peoples. hugh brody, among many others in a vibrant canadian tradition of anthropological inquiry, has done a great deal to illustrate and dramatize the difference between hunting and farming cultures, both forms of social relations that preceded capitalism. the extraordinary difference between them is elided by such phrases as "traditional," "tribal," "pre-capitalist," or even "indigenous," though the latter remains tactically and legally useful in the struggle for land rights. one of marx's great conceptual insights is that the broadest level of social categorization can be understood as a difference in the forms of productive activity, the forms in which people socially organize their productive activity, and the forms of technology they use. inuit hunters have created a variety of the gathering and hunting modes of production that suit their arctic ecological context and their social temperament or character.

the extraordinary reach or value or purchase of the concept mode of production can barely be overestimated. one small but important example from the realm of postcolonial studies will suffice here. in his indispensable study, *postcolonialism: an historical introduction*, robert young discusses the difference between franz fanon's and amilcar cabral's views of "tradition." fanon is suspicious of the political, emancipatory value of tradition and situates himself as an enlightenment thinker determined to bring into being an "enlightened" man in all his abstract glory. cabral, by contrast, draws extensive inspiration from local tradition and is a particularist and culturalist. although young knows the notion mode of production, he never suggests colonialism and the resistances it inspires might take a different form depending upon the social structure of the colonized—whether they are egalitarian hunters or hierarchical and patriarchal farmers. hence there is no way for him to recognize or adduce that fanon's and cabral's differences might be related to the substantive differences between the "traditions" that provide context to their revolutionary practice. the islamic context within which fanon worked in algeria, like the christian, judaic, and buddhist contexts, involves deep structural hierarchies of gender and wealth because those religious contexts institutionalize spirituality in the service of the tithe-based or the agricultural mode of production. the saharan context of cabral's work involves a dramatically different substantive set of traditions, especially where gathering and hunting as a mode of production is prevalent. fanon and cabral could have roughly the same values, dreamed the same dream of emancipation, while taking entirely opposite approaches to "tradition" because the traditions they engaged with were substantively different.

the activity of our little group, catching fish—and the reminder that this activity took place in this site for a long time, as the stone fish cache attests—leads me to a twofold conclusion about contemporary indigenous sociality. although jean-luc nancy's influential philosophical reflection on community specifically rejects a notion that community is tied to production,[1] in the context of an inuit fishing and hunting camp it is hard not to be persuaded that the strength of the social bond derives in part from the coordinated activities, the shared success and frustration, the mutual sense of accomplishment or discouragement, that come from socially shared production. the dominant culture, a homogenizing set of values and way of seeing that can be found in europe, north america, japan, and enclaves of every city in the world, is now so steeped in communities of consumption—punkers dress as punkers, left liberals watch the daily show and sometimes wear the t-shirt, perhaps a small group of music devotees are the only three in their building who listen to m.i.a.—that the ephemeral nature of such social collectivity eludes even students of the social, since most people are always in one or another of these communities. the cultural logic of spectacle, a social form critically diagnosed by guy debord[2] in which mass passivity is inculcated through the very logic of the image and the underlying structure of possessive individualism, a legal and economic structure delineated by c.b. macpherson[3] in which the individual unit defined as owner grounds a whole social and cultural structure, both relentlessly work to dissolve communities that deserve the name. communities of lasting social bonds would clearly stand in the way of processes conducive to capital accumulation, an insight that marx in his early years developed and elaborated throughout his intellectual career.[4] a shared productive activity establishes, in my view, a more durable social bond than that provided by collectives based on spectacle logic or possessive individualism, a social bond in which trust becomes possible.

the sight of the stone cache at the site of our production reminds me, secondly, that these communities are intergenerational. the labour, the creative activity,[5] of past generations is embodied not only in the careful, resilient pile of stones but in the discovery of the site itself, and the techniques used to catch fish at the site, and the knowledge of the time of year when the fish will be running at this site, and so on. the metuq children are the latest incarnation and descendents of generations of previous children who fished at this spot. philosophies of community are impoverished precisely because they often take the present and presentist reality of community as its sole mode of existence.[6] rarely has any human attribute been so debased and commodified in our era as that of community itself—as a given rather than a (de)construct that echoes a deeply individualized set of cultural and social processes. the stone cache is a gamble with history, a casting of labour into the future, a hope that descendents will benefit from the labour of ancestors, and a trust that descendents will exist. there are two facts, then, the fact of production and the fact of intergenerational temporality, inscribed in bodies and in stone, that to my mind deserve attention and emphasis in thinking community.

intergenerational communities of production are incarnated by contemporary indigenous hunting peoples (though there remain peasant communities with similar, though less egalitarian, features). the rapidly disappearing knowledge and memory of such social forms, a disappearance associated with the still growing hegemony of capitalist social relations, has impoverished social life and the philosophies that reflect it in our times. one wonders if hardt and negri could be as confident in their pronouncement that "there is no outside" of empire if they were standing in this water rather than drinking from the bottles that get delivered to their homes in the imperial centres.[7] as our world races from the possibility of nuclear catastrophe to the possibility of ecological disaster, all in the context of spreading banality and blandness over a culture of suspicion that possessive individualism must necessarily steep itself in,[8] perhaps it is not unfair to suggest that many people in contemporary times may need to see a certain light, not the light of enlightened reason but the embodied newness of the world that can be rediscovered in its freshness and vitality (what michael taussig calls the "re-enchantment of the world") when negotiating the passage through the cave halfway up the blind man's walk.

the state is a certain kind of writing

if, as fredric jameson suggests, the "other sees the totality as a skin," which we living inside it are dangerously unaware of, perhaps the viewpoint of some of these "others" calls forth a whole host of conceptual refigurings. the capitalist state—variously theorized as the management arm of the ruling classes, the repressive and ideological tools of the capitalist system, a relatively autonomous structure ruling in the interests of the whole, or even as one link in a decentred chain of productive powers in a network of micropolitical fields—takes on different dimensions when looked at in colonial context. a theory of the state is demanded that recognizes the agency of the state as a totalizing structure: it acts culturally, working against a range of resistances to ensure that time, space, and subjectivity are reconfigured in a manner conducive to the expansion of the commodity form and the accumulation of capital.[9]

writing is one of the key mechanisms that the state deploys in this field of activity. the state calculates, observes, measures, reports through the medium of writing. writing creates its own referent. that is, state inscriptions play a significant though contested role in positioning bodies. the gap between what the inscription enunciates and the flow of materiality and bodies creates a space in which domination and subversion alike may operate. the oldest joke in the north has to do with the oft-commented-upon disjuncture between what the reports say and what the "on the ground" actualization embodies. but what is "on paper" often gets the last laugh. linear, phonetic notation, individualized through the guarantee of the signature, is the form of writing associated with state power and becomes defined as the only form of writing that exists. training in its protocols is so culturally embedded that not to do so is inconceivable. here we might say that supplementing a violence of the letter—as when the constitutional status of inuit is determined in a 1939 supreme court of canada case that involved no direct consultation or contact with inuit whatsoever[10]—there is a violence in the letter, in the fact of the letter itself. this violence establishes the precondition of state involvement and action: "we" from western culture have writing: "they" from other cultures do not; "our" writing authorizes our presence: "they" have none; "our" writing proves our cultural superiority: "they" lack.

perhaps the state is no more nor less than a certain kind of writing. the expression "a certain kind of writing" can be deployed to mark an alternative understanding of inscription, to emphasize that while the state deploys and can be at least in part defined by writing, it does not enjoy a monopoly over the form. the writing that marks the state can be found in laws, in state reports, and in official documents, but is also found in academic writing, in writing produced within the corporate sector, in writing that circulates around the arts, and even in the very bowels of literature itself.

a certain kind of writing allows for abstraction, for universalization. these processes ensure that a certain kind of writing is complicit in social hierarchy. a certain kind of writing is separate from the bodies of the people and the land and works insistently and insidiously to inscribe an alien power. a certain kind of writing insistently authorizes individualism. a certain kind of writing traces new names on bodies and lands (colonial nominalism) as if none previously existed. a certain kind of writing, in its instrumentality and bureaucratic banality, covers over the people and the world, gives them dog tags and maps so they may be linked to the great chain of commodities. a certain kind of writing reminds us that the politics of form pervasively inhabits indigenous political struggles. perhaps the state is no more nor less than a certain kind of writing.

the racial distribution of wealth, part one: manitoba hydro

the modern period, broadly conceived as inaugurated by columbian encounters in 1492, is marked by a massive global redistribution of wealth. wealth from southern, "brown" countries has been appropriated by european, northern, white countries. where the "brown" peoples were agricultural, the redistribution took the form of direct appropriation. where they were hunters, something more dramatic was demanded. wealth had to be reconfigured in order to be redistributed. wealth had to change its very form, from time to commodity, in order then to be linked to the great chain. the wealth of hunters was not measured through the things they produced (and carried as a burden) or as the monuments they expended energy and lives to produce. the wealth of hunters was measured as time, the extraordinary quality and quantity of leisure time they enjoyed as people whose work on average demanded less labour time.[11] marshall sahlins has argued that stone-age hunters had needs that were easily met ("the zen road to affluence," he called it) and shorter average work days than those of contemporary working people. a structural implication of nomadicism is that things become burdens: less is better. the character of the labour of hunters itself—again as the boundary mode of production is crossed all concepts and binaries fall into disarray—in contemporary times might be hard to distinguish from leisure. the vibrancy of the cultures that indigenous peoples have produced is a direct result of the extraordinary time for philosophical reflection and symbolic labour their material circumstances have nurtured. the radicality of sahlins's insight, now nearly four decades old, is still being mined.

on a world scale, the racial distribution of wealth is moderated only somewhat and as a specifically racialized process by the relatively recent emergence of non-european capitalist powers. "browns" may now enjoy the dubious pleasures of dominating other "browns" or even whites. however, a mere sidelong glance at patterns of consumption in the contemporary world tells us that wealth remains largely in the hands of a privileged few, the majority of whom are of european origin. this story is told compellingly by amiya kumar bagchi in his magisterial study of global capitalism *perilous passage: mankind and the global ascendancy of capital,* in which he writes of how the "footloose rich of the world provide a major support for the ongoing process of further enrichment of the wealthy and the further marginalization of the poor" (303). his discussion of "twentieth century differentials between rich and poor countries," focusing on infant mortality rates in a chapter on "capitalism and uneven development in the twentieth century," makes for sobering reading indeed.

although globally this process took and takes place among nations, it also takes place within nation-states, such as canada, where settler colonies have succeeded in establishing dominance over indigenous peoples. reconfiguration and redistribution of wealth are the economic facts of canadian history and contemporary canadian reality. my own beloved home province, manitoba, serves as one forceful reminder of a possible ten (or thirteen, if we include the territories).

two early hydro dam developments in manitoba, at saukgeen on the winnipeg river (1951, the pine falls dam) and at grand rapids on the saskatchewan river (1965), emboldened the public utility manitoba hydro to dream greater dreams about the rivers in northern manitoba. this eventually lead to the churchill river diversion and lake winnipeg regulation projects, a complex set of dams and dredges that would restructure the hydrology of northern manitoba. the projects involved a dam built at the north end of south indian lake that in 1976 raised the water level of that lake by three metres, forcing relocation of one cree community, south indian lake, and diverting water from the churchill river through artificial trenches and an existing river into the nelson river. sections of northeastern lake winnipeg were dredged to improve water flow, and a control dam, called jenpeg, that regulates water levels of the big lake, was completed in 1979 near where the nelson river begins at the lake's north end. finally, a major production dam, the limestone dam (1990), was built farther north on the nelson river, joining the earlier kelsey (1960) and kettle (1970) dams on that river and benefiting from the massively increased flow created by all the other developments. five cree communities—norway house, nelson house, cross lake, split lake, and york landing—were seen to be affected by the project and allowed to seek compensation where they could prove a tangible impact (south indian lake was a part of the nelson house band at the time). several provincial governments, both ndp and conservative, were in power during the various phases of the project. the five communities organized a "northern flood committee" in the seventies and, under the duress of seeing actual construction taking place, in 1977 signed a modern treaty, the "northern flood agreement," which established a compensation regime and an arbitration regime.

this story is not as widely known as the more famous hydro project conflicts that took place in quebec at nearly the same time.[12] nor is the conflict over expansion of the current system—a dam on the burntwood river called wuskwatim is now being constructed, while another on the nelson river, called keeyask, is being proposed—receiving the national attention that similar expansion provoked in northern quebec. however, there is a struggle over the future of these rivers, and the battle is not by any means over.

in effect what is involved is a reconfiguration of wealth. wealth in the form of time, enjoyed by hunting peoples, is being restructured to take the form of wealth as a commodity. the rivers are being transformed from hunting and fishing territories, which allowed the wealth of a way of life, into a source of energy that can be bought and sold: the process thought of in cultural studies and in marxist theory as commodification. once reconfigured as commodity, the wealth produced is available for redistribution. the benefits are spread among southern non-aboriginal peoples, who in winnipeg pay among the lowest north american prices for electricity and on whose behalf super profits are generated (disproportionately supporting the salaries and activities of a fragment of the social elites—the lawyers, consultants, politicians, engineers, and bureaucrats who benefit from the activity—in the province). very small expenditures are grudgingly paid out to the *inwewin* communities most affected. the newer proposed developments are to be based on a "partnership" model whereby communities can use the meagre funds they receive for the purpose of compensating and alleviating problems created and invest them in newer projects in the hopes of some day convincing hydro accountants to "give" them a share in profits. it is enough to make the recent "peace of the braves" agreement in quebec look good.[13]

the end results of this reconfiguration and subsequent redistribution of wealth are the creation of small pockets of wealth and large pockets of poverty. northern hunting communities, once based on an incalculable wealth in the form of time, are immiserated. the pockets of poverty are "brown." the pockets of wealth, from suburban winnipeg to the financial centres that underwrite the whole process, are white. the same story can be told about mineral "development" in canada. the same story can be told about logging "development" in canada. the same story can be told about oil and gas "development" in canada. the code words are "progress," "civilization," "modernization," and "development," but their meaning is clear: the racial distribution of wealth.

dissidents: camping with ovide mercredi and robbie buck

the processes associated with the racial reconfiguration and redistribution of wealth were and are opposed.[14] from the nature of that opposition we can learn vital lessons. grand rapids is one of the communities most affected by hydro development. the dam, built in the mid-sixties, involved first connecting the first nation to the south by road, then silencing the sacred rapids that gave the place its name. the site of the community itself bespeaks a manichean colonial divide straight out of the pages of fanon: a manicured suburban paradise for hydro employees, with paved roads and all the amenities modern infrastructure can provide, including a lovely playground and a single-employees unit tellingly called by locals "the taj mahal" in honour of its amenities. nearby, the reserve is built on gravel roads, with the usual substandard housing, and there are people living there who do not have electrical power because they cannot afford their hydro bills. it must be galling to know that in the suburban houses just down the road, electricity rates are subsidized for the mostly white hydro employees.[15]

former grand chief of the assembly of first nations ovide mercredi returned from years at the national political level—to seek a "lower" political office in the interest of serving one's small community rather than looking for an elite sinecure is both honourable and to my mind courageous—and courageously ran for and won the position of chief in his own home community of grand rapids. as well as a first nation, there was also a municipality of grand rapids largely occupied by non status *inwewin* and metis, as well as a few non-aboriginal people. the mayor of the municipality was robbie buck, who had been involved in frustrating negotiations with the public utility over compensation for the dam. when the chief received an imperious fax from the utility announcing that within a few days the spillway would be opened to allow excess water to flow over the dried former river bed—this after the community repeatedly expressed interest in the local importance of the issue—it was enough. mercredi and buck set up a small camp on the river bed, defying the utility.

the immediate concern was that the river bed had not been "brushed," cleared of willows that would then run into the river and lake when the spillway was opened. this debris would often end up in fishermen's nets, creating a considerable problem. however, the occupation soon became a focal point for a whole litany of complaints, including the meagre amounts of overall compensation paid. within weeks, both the chief executive officer of manitoba hydro and the premier made visits to the occupation. what will come of the negotiations that followed remains to be seen. on a dry river bed of a formerly great river, two leaders camped where they as children had swum or fished. their camping is an ancient custom or practice, but in the newly engineered ecology and political context, they positioned their bodies in an old way on a new place, writing a new river story of resistance. other forms of resistance, in other communities, preceded and followed these striking events.

although the five communities most affected by the churchill river diversion had begrudgingly signed a deal, the northern flood agreement (nfa), in the late seventies, the public utility had found its provisions too generous (or "ambiguous") to implement. for example, the nfa had a provision that referred to studies that would work toward the "eradication of mass poverty and unemployment" in the communities. so the utility got the communities, one at a time, to sign what it called "implementation agreements," replacing the nfa with single cash payments. only four of the five communities agreed. the fifth, at cross lake, marked its refusal to sign by passing a "first written law" and unilaterally transforming its internal governance from an indian act band council model to a traditionalist, four-council governance structure. they marked the transformation by changing their name to pimicikamak. they also passed a "hydro payments law," which lead to citizens paying their hydro bills to the first nation, which in turn used the funds to support its opposition to hydro (one example: hydro had a prominent billboard in winnipeg with a smiling blond baby and the logo "it's your future"; pimicikamak responded with a billboard of a crying *ineniw* infant and the logo "what about our future?"). the struggle continues, with lobbying in the united states against expanding the hydro dam development system in manitoba, with court engagements restricting use of pimicikamak's hydro generated war chest; with a march of power that i was able to attend in spring of 2007. these writings—from the first written law as document, to the billboard of a crying child, to the walking bodies—are all versions of what i am calling bush writings: resistant, embodied, creative texts out of the bush that sometimes document the racial reconfiguration and redistribution of wealth.

it is spring, 2007, and i am with my daughter and a research assistant, agnes pawlowska, in a cabin at poplar river. poplar river, on the northeast side of lake winnipeg, is only indirectly affected by hydro; there is no dam on this river, and as a result it is a river from which one can safely drink. i meet and have tea with sophia and ray rabliaskas, who happily show me the video that was made in connection with sophia's recently awarded goldman prize for environmental stewardship. poplar river, in alliance with four other anishnabwe communities, managed to leapfrog a now defunct city of winnipeg proposal for world heritage site status. instead of the heavily funded, provincially supported plan to gain recognition for the "exchange district" in the city, the bush of northeastern manitoba was given the nod, made the shortlist for world heritage site status in the latest round of competition. the province eventually, though begrudgingly, came on side and by now actively supports the proposal. but one could almost hear the gnashing of teeth in the corporate boardrooms of manitoba hydro, which had big plans for transmission lines down the east side of lake winnipeg in conjunction with its newest expansion plans. now they will have to build a more expensive, less efficient, longer route down the west side. sophia was one of several community leaders who realized that, if they waited, development would soon be coming to their traditional territory, so they made the proactive move of deciding to find the strongest form of protection that was available. this, too, is a form of bush writing, writing a new narrative of possibility, of movement on the land, of laws and lines on maps, that may help a people pass their values on to their children.

there are both "proactive" and "reactive" resistances to hydro's plan for more reconfigurations and redistributions of wealth. the north is a site of struggle. the totalizing expansion of the commodity form and capital accumulation processes is not inevitable but is hotly contested on the social margins, the outskirts, of the settler colony. deep traces that inscribe the ancient repetition of practices and occupations of and on the landscape that mark the community's past and continued existence; movements of bodies in ancient ways for new purposes; billboards and alternative laws and new treaties: these all circulate in the bush in northern manitoba, hurling themselves against the concrete, the turbines, the high tension wires, trying to inscribe another story. canada carefully traces a linear-phonetic writing of progress, development, and modernity. the bush writings tell another story in an other way. some small part of that is a story of dissidents.

the racial distribution of wealth, part two: the mackenzie gas project

it is june 2006, and i am the only non-native in a meeting in the small community of colville lake in denendeh (the northwest territories) between leaders there and leaders from the slightly larger community of fort good hope.[16] fort good hope is on the deh cho (mackenzie river), not far to the south of the arctic circle; colville lake is north and west inland. the people call themselves *kaschogotine*. using traditional speaking protocols and their own language, the people are trying to resolve issues around presenting a united front in negotiations (always, endless negotiations, with canada, with the government of the northwest territories, with imperial oil), about gas royalty distributions and self-government.

the meeting unfolds rather quickly, without a chair or robert's rules of order. the two chiefs open the meeting with formal welcomes. slowly through the day, everyone in the room takes a turn, making shorter or longer speeches touching on the issues. both women and men speak passionately about their community's interests, their love of the land, important historical moments in their evolving relationship (colville lake was once a sub-band of fort good hope), and so on. a lunch has been prepared and at the due time there is a break.

the meeting in colville lake has had a profound impact on me, teaching me that the abstraction processes structured into the modern state form effectively deskill citizens in their ability to communicate and make judgments. where such state forms do not prevail, have not asserted themselves over more sophisticated systems, people can talk and listen ethically without the support of an outside regime of rules. so people talked through the day. they did not repeat themselves. they did not interrupt each other. they did not go on at too great a length. they did not need to "go around the circle" or use any other form of predetermined organization. everyone had the protocols they needed as a skill, a capability.

the larger question at issue at that point in time in the mackenzie valley was whether the territorial government would collect royalties directly from the pipeline or continue to rely on the federal government, which would be responsible for direct taxation. communities like fort good hope did not support the territorial regime, which they saw with some good reason as a largely colonial structure. they wanted whatever resources might come to them to come through their own tax, rent, and royalty regime. rather than having a distant government dole out to them targeted funds, they wanted to directly access those funds from the source and decide for themselves where to allocate what they got. there is also a knowledge at the community level, not widely reported by canada's cheerleaders of capitalism like *the globe and mail*, that if they ask for too much and as a result no mackenzie gas pipeline is built they are not doing themselves in. in twenty years, or thirty, another proposal will be advanced. sooner or later, if a pipeline will come, they will get the jobs then, and hopefully the project, on their own terms. the hope is that sooner or later, in one generation or the next, they can rewrite the narrative of the racial distribution of wealth.

writing against the state

let me now refer to an image, not so easily assimilated, which many are familiar with, as no doubt it is used at the beginning of so many introductory canadian literature classes. the image is called the "teaching rocks," though it is also known as the peterborough petroglyphs. the teaching rocks involve an indeterminate set of carved out figures in an unbounded rock face located near the current curve lake first nation in southern ontario. how do you teach about these images on the teaching rocks? do you tell the story implied in one image? do you "read" from one discrete symbol to the next? if so, in what order? can you "read" as your fancy takes you? what kind of literature inscribes itself on rock, so that instead of taking it with you on your holiday travels, you have to travel to it to read it? the images are now contained, with an imposed structure and an imposed name; the images are categorized and labeled (overwritten by another form of state writing) so readers may know how many of each type exist in various known locations; but the teaching rocks have not yet been assimilated. and so these rocks retain a power to disturb the very being of literature, as do the teaching rocks in south eastern manitoba, known as petroforms, less contained, even fragile to the predations of any unethical teenager's boots.

these writings are embodied; their embodiment overrules their powers of abstraction. they still retain what walter benjamin calls an "aura," their singularity, their attachment to place and role in ceremony. whatever is "taught" from them will depend a great deal on the situation the teaching is embedded in. the teaching rocks have been compared to visual art. i here attempt to assimilate them instead to the category of literature, because i think they retain a stronger destabilizing power in that realm, and because they point to the possibility of a different being of writing than that which is normally encountered, which is normally read: a writing in stone.

but the state knows of this counter power. in northern manitoba, on the nelson river, were two sites: the chair and the footprints. the chair was a bum-shaped hollowing of rocks where the trickster weesawkeejak sat. the footprints were human-sized and -shaped indentations in the rock, arranged as if walking straight up a sheer rock cliff beside the river. there was nothing to be done about the chair. it is now under water, flooded by the imperious demands of the commodity in its manitoba incarnation as manitoba hydro. the footprints have another story. they were blasted out of context with dynamite, moved, i am told,[17] first to the manitoba museum of man and nature in winnipeg. but the footprints were neither those of man nor of nature, and elders protested, so they were moved back up north, placed next to a restaurant. no doubt they were able to sell "foot long" hot dogs. elders again protested, so they were moved back to the river, laid flat near where they had so long stood on their own. i am told by elders that what lies by the river is a copy, a cast, of the original. the footprints have lost their power. this resonates with the fact that their destruction was the clearest sign that the people had somehow lost their power: nothing to do but helplessly watch as their hearts were ripped out of the land. nothing to do, that is, but either sign on to an agreement of collaboration or pick yourself up and start fighting.

this was probably the most sacred site in northern manitoba. the nelson river is part of a huge chain of waterways that connects bush cree *ineniw* from opaskweyak to tataskwayak and further; the footprints were one of its most striking, unworldly features. while we canadians robustly protested the talibans' blowing up of two ancient buddhist statues—how illiberal and unenlightened of them to take their gods seriously—and that event no doubt "softened" us for the war that we pretend is not a war so we can be in it in all our peace-loving glory, we have no moral compunctions about blowing up aboriginal sacred sites. how many still, spiritual places are at this moment being crushed by bulldozers in north-eastern alberta? in the name of the commodity, no sacredness can hold sway. in the united states, the blackfoot were able to use the doctrine of religious freedom to save sacred lands in the mountains from mining development. here in canada, the much praised notions of aboriginal rights have little purchase when it comes to aboriginal spiritual places. canadians might as well call it all "paganism," since that is how we continue to treat it. "not another burial ground," "not another sacred site"— you can hear the developers groan.

these places have something, some things, to teach. they are sacred places and speak of deeply spiritual and social matters. they are sites of art, of the expressive power of images. they are sites of remembrance, of social being, of reflection. they recall the expressive powers and inspirations of generations past. they are writings and stories. they are inscribed on rock. not to be reproduced, we eagerly reproduce them. they offer meaning tripping over meaning, but it is a meaning that just cannot quite be grasped. they are there: sometimes tolerated and even celebrated by the state (oh! a tourist site! economic development!!); sometimes dynamited or flooded into oblivion with the seriousness of purpose granted by state sanction. they challenge not only the grammatical structure that underlies our literature—the form by which an inscription contains and expresses its meaning, the framing devices and internal rules of order that ensure self-consolidation, totality, and coherence—but the very mode of inscription that founds the being of euro-western writing, what foucault once called linear, phonetic (and, i would add, individualized) notation. they demand remembrance of the ethical charge of embodied writing, that subjects make their own interpretations and retain their powers of situational judgment, all within a strong social context. they are so much more, but they are as well in these dimensions a writing against the state.

three words that cannot be spoken

what is it that cannot be said? here, in this middling country, surviving in the shadow of imperial powers, land of bland, nice people and widespread politeness, where when we—canadians—travel we sport our flags to show we are decidedly not those other, too patriotric, inhabitants of north america; here, as we—canadians—grapple for our "identity," our sense of purpose, our defining *raison d'être*, there are words that we do not speak and that we do not ever hear. who can say these words? not aboriginal political or cultural leaders, who must toe the line to ensure credibility in the "mainstream." not scholars or even activists from outside of the country, whose opportunities to be listened to here might instantly evaporate if their criticisms were to reach such a thorough level. the afghani rebels who experience our brute, repressive force will express these sentiments but their expressions will never reach a canadian public. so it is left for that subset of canadians who are also comfortable, white, activist-scholars to enunciate: it is left for some with privilege to spend that privilege.

it may also be at this moment of canadian "national" development, of canada coming into being as a nation, that we—canadians—must cross the hurdle of this particular unspoken. speaking it may give a new kind of national self-awareness, may open new possibilities of dialogue, may most importantly raise the bar, the standard, on what it is that makes our canadian country deserve our canadian affection. perhaps it is a call in ethical terms to be what we canadians can be rather than what we canadians settle for. the die is cast, the email has been sent: i, who grew up almost "in the bush," rural, northern, manitoban, born in and of the boreal forest and canadian shield, lumpenproletarian by origin in social class terms, attender of a government-run residential school, wanderer across the far reaches of the subarctic and arctic, now privileged professor whose career is firmly attached to canadian universities, i will whisper these words so fast that you might not catch them, i will hurl them into the whirlwind of your consciousness and let them stand fast or dissolve as your caprice allows, i will shape an event in the form of the enunciation of three words that cannot be spoken: "i hate canada."

i hate canada: because "canada" is the most powerful ideological tool deployed historically and still deployed in the interests of a settler colony's colonial project. "canada" is what prevents the emergence or re-emergence of innu-aschee, of denendeh, of nunavut, of nitassinan, of manitou-baa, of n'dakie menan, of haida gwai. "canada" is the ideological structure that is intimately tied to and supportive of the continued racial distributions of wealth within this part of the world. "canada" is the nexus of exclusions and appropriations of indigenous acts of culture, the site of cultural legitimation or delegitimation. "canada" is the bulldozer, the dynamite, the clear cut, the open pit, the flood, the transmission line, the cut line, the urban sprawl, the arrests, the long monotonous nightmare of real deprivation, the condescending compassion of social workers, the liberal guilt of court workers, the culturally blind care of health industry officials, the rules of life handed down by insurance companies and lawyers, the two-lane, four-lane, six-lane, eight-lane expressways, the violence of the letter in st. catherine's milling, in the indian act, in the british north america act, in the natural resources transfer acts, the brutal structure of so many repressions piling over each other: the smashing of the drum, the beating of a young girl for the sin of speaking her language, the destruction of the footprints, the tearing apart of families, the prison cell where heroin rather than pot must be the drug of choice if the guards are not to find out, and, finally, its most triumphant expression, the perfect shopping mall so carefully built upon this mountain of pain that its benign brightness lulls us into pleasant daydreams of finding the authentic indian commodity. canada is measured in the dignity it doles out through eyedroppers to those who are so miserable they must avail themselves of its assistance.

i hate canada because my studies of history have come to convince me that nations, in our modern times, are responsible for too many deaths.[18] nations equal the possibility of national war, the calamity of our epoch. there will be more wars as long as there are nations. for my part, i am as happy if a working family finds fair employment whether they live in ontario or oaxaca. it is, paradoxically, the people most tied to specific areas of land—indigenous peoples in our hemisphere—who are most concerned to develop an ethical awareness of global ecological linkages. the nation contains dissent, dissolves difference, divides peoples, and serves the interests of capital accumulation very well. we cannot begin a thoroughgoing critique of nations and nationalism without starting with the one our accidents of birth tie us to. the three words not to be spoken must be spoken: i hate canada.

embodied deconstruction

another way in which the notion of writing against the state can be articulated is through the concept of "embodied deconstruction." "embodiment" here serves to mark the movement of meaning away from universal abstraction toward situation, context, the body of land and people, individual or social. "deconstruction" here is deployed in something of its philosophical rigour and not in the loose, as in "take apart for analysis," sense that the term has popularly gained. deconstruction refers to a writing that insistently displaces certain hierarchical dualisms associated with a metaphysics of presence that ground western philosophical thought and practice. in the inuit community of pangnirtung on baffin island in nunavut, people do not mark their lawns with fences. the town as a result has an unkempt look, and tourists often prefer the nice greenlandic inuit villages with their bakeries and white picket fences. but every lawn in pangnirtung is also a potential short cut, and many a public path cuts across a private property. hence as i walk through town, i pry apart the binary opposition between public and private that grounds western property relations. with and through the very motion of my walking body, i write a new script, i join the community in inscribing a different relation between public and private: embodied deconstruction.

colville lake is a kaschogotine community located slightly north of the arctic circle on the lake that gives it its name. in the mid-eighties, the community had no electricity; it was a small group of houses in a rough semicircle looking out onto the lake, with an area for a church and fishing lodge off to the side. it has gained separate band status, some government housing, and some newer structures in the decades since my first visit. it sits right on an enormous reservoir of natural gas: billions of dollars' worth of value to hundreds of millions of people. you can drill a well from the middle of town. some of the newer structures are provided by oil companies eager to get on the good side of the village burghers.

there are not more than 120 people in colville lake. they fish. they hunt. they work on hides. they tell stories. they speak their language. they know they are sitting on massive wealth. they want some, a share, a fair share. is it right, ethical, that a hundred-odd (and they are odd!) people should decide about a resource of value to millions? here, ethical questions fold over each other: do the millions really need this energy source? should there be an end to the demands of the millions? is there something of incalculable value in the unique way of life practised by a small number of people? these are not questions that can be "answered," but they must be grappled with; if we do not grapple with them at all but rather surrender to the comfort and familiarity of our lockean mythology, we abdicate any claim to ethics. my small contribution is to try to show that the colville lakes of the world actually do have compelling cases to make.

canada does, of course, allow very small minorities to make decisions that will affect millions of people. but only if those few people sit in the grammatical structure of boardrooms, apparently. ultimately, "canada" gets to decide what happens to colville lake. "canada" is the boardroom. in its current being, colville lake stands as a reproach to contemporary social being; in its very being it represents a different kind of wealth, wealth in the form of time. in its very being it has inherited from previous generations and works to pass on to succeeding generations the inscription of a different possibility of configuring the written and the spoken, the public and the private, the male and the female, the rich and the poor. this mode of inscription is a kind of bush/writing: embodied deconstruction.

NOTES

Introduction Shifting the Ground of a Discipline

1. I am not suggesting here that formalism has been a dominant mode of reading Canadian literature. But it is worth noting that attention to the literariness associated with formalism need not be exclusively understood as an approach that refutes the relevance of the externality of literary texts associated with mimetic approaches. As Mihai Spariosu, among other scholars, notes in his "Editor's Introduction" to *Mimesis in Contemporary Theory. Vol. 1. The Literary and Philosophical Debate* (Amsterdam: John Benjamins, 1984), "'objective,'" that is, formalist, theories of literature, such as that of structuralism, are "ultimately based on mimetic assumptions." His example of Tzvetan Todorov, an "influential theorist with a non-mimetic reputation," is a case in point. Todorov "postulates a continuity between literary and non-literary language, which enables him to reintegrate literary structures into larger social structures through ... the 'verbal function' of literature" (xx). I return to this point later.

2. TransCanada project is an expedient way of referring to the serial conference TransCanada: Literature, Institutions, Citizenship, which I co-organized in collaboration, chiefly, with Roy Miki (TransCanada One, at Simon Fraser University, 2005, and TransCanada Two, University of Guelph, 2007) and Christl Verduyn (TransCanada Three, Mount Allison University, 2009), as well as to the various events and projects sponsored by TransCanada Institute (TCI), University of Guelph, which was founded in 2007 (see TCI's website for full information). A selection of the plenary talks presented at TransCanada One has appeared in *Trans.Can.Lit: Resituating the Study of Canadian Literature*, co-edited by Smaro Kamboureli and Roy Miki.

3. As we said in our call for papers for TransCanada Two: Literature, Institutions, Citizenship, "it has become apparent to many scholars that its [Canadian literature's] study can no longer take place in isolation from the larger forces that shape the nation, global relations, and the corporatization of higher education. The pressures of multiculturalism on the Canadian state ... put more emphasis upon discourses of citizenship and security. At the same time, market-driven factors increasingly shape the publication, dissemination, and reception of Canadian writing. These are just some of the factors that have caused a subtle yet palpable shift in the critical and cultural paradigms that inform the study and teaching of Canadian literature." See the TransCanadas website.

4 Though this project has been collaborative, I do not purport to speak for others here. As the TransCanada Two conference's call for papers states, "[t]he task of identifying the implications of these shifts and, above all, of devising constructive ways of responding to them involves a long-term and multilateral project that can only be a shared endeavour, undertaken in interdisciplinary and collaborative terms."

5 Concern with the nation, of course, is not necessarily synonymous with adopting a nationalist position; in fact, it often critiques nationalism. As far as Canadian nationalism is concerned, this is not the place to examine or distinguish between its different and often contradictory manifestations across time. In this context I have in mind mostly the tenor and effects of the Massey Report (see Royal Commission 1951), as well as those reports that appeared immediately after the Centennial, A.B. Hodgetts' *What Culture? What Heritage?* (1968), Robin Mathews and James Arthur Steele's *The Struggle for Canadian Universities* (1969), and T.H.B. Symons's *To Know Ourselves: The Report of the Commission on Canadian Studies* (1975). The intensification of nationalist sensibilities in the late 1960s and early '70s had a direct impact on introducing Canadian studies programs in universities and on the formation of the Association of Canadian Studies (1973). My interest here lies not in Canadian Studies as such, what one of the anonymous readers of this book assumed, but rather on Canadian *literary* studies. While both of them are institutionalized, the first is a formal entity that has followed a distinct trajectory since its inception; though some of their concerns overlap, the second is not identified with a single administrative body.

6 Obviously I have in mind here Jonathan Kertzer's *Worrying the Nation: Imagining a National Literature in English Canada* (Toronto: U of Toronto P, 1998).

7 For my formulation of *ex*tensive and *in*tensive readings I am indebted to David Damrosch's *What Is World Literature?* He writes that "world literature is not an immense body of material that must somehow, impossibly, be mastered; it is a mode of reading that can be experienced *intensively* with a few works just as effectively as it can be explored *extensively* with a large number" (299). For a similar formulation, also deriving from Damrosch, see David Ferris, "Indiscipline," in Haun Saussy, ed., *Comparative Literature in an Age of Globalization* (Baltimore: Johns Hopkins UP, 2006), 78–99, especially 86.

8 Regarding the term "situational" see Adele Clarke, *Situational Analysis: Grounded Theory after the Postmodern Turn* (Thousand Oaks, CA: Sage, 2005), where it is employed as a method of qualitative analysis in the social sciences. While my use of the term is akin to hers in some respects, chiefly, in referring to an emphasis on and questioning of relations among different methods and foci and an interest in investigating heterogeneous discourses,

she applies it specifically to "*both* data gathering and analysis/interpretation" as they pertain to "historical discourse materials" (xxii–xxiii).

9 Jakobson further elaborated on literariness, especially in the context of poetry, in subsequent essays. See also, "On Realism in Art," "The Dominant," and "Linguistics and Poetics," in Krystyna Pomorska and Stephen Rudy, eds., *Roman Jakobson: Language in Literature* (Cambridge: Belknap, 1987), 19–27, 41–46, and 62–94, respectively.

10 See, for example, Antoine Compagnon, *Literature, Theory, and Common Sense*, trans. Carole Cosman (1998; Princeton: Princeton UP, 2004) and Adrian Pilkington, *Poetic Effects: A Relevance Theory Perspective* (Amsterdam: John Benjamins, 2000), for two studies that specifically address the complexity of literariness as a concept, and Derek Attridge, *The Singularity of Literature* (London: Routledge, 2004), as a recent example of the interrogation of what constitutes the literary.

11 This editorial introduction also appears as the opening chapter in his book *Revisionary Interventions into the Americanist Canon* (Durham: Duke UP, 1994).

12 In this discussion I use "events" in the sense in which Foucault describes an event or statement as that which "*emerges* in its *historical irruption*; what we try to examine is *the incision* that it makes, the irreducible—and very often—*tiny emergence*. However banal it maybe, however unimportant its consequence may appear to be, however quickly it may be forgotten after its appearance, however little heard or badly deciphered we may suppose it to be, a statement is always an event that neither the language ... nor the meaning can quite exhaust.... [I]t is linked to the gesture of writing.... [I]t opens up to itself a residual existence ... *in the materiality of manuscripts, books, or any other form of recording*; ... it is unique, yet subject to repetition, transformation, and reactivation." See *The Archaeology of Knowledge and The Discourse on Language* (New York: Pantheon, 1972), 28; my emphasis.

13 This point is somewhat akin to Raymond Williams' argument in his *Marxism and Literature* (Oxford: Oxford UP, 1977) that culture develops through relations between what he calls dominant, residual, and emergent forms.

14 According to Rüsen's logic, a normal crisis binds a "collective identity" together, while a catastrophic crisis, because of its "traumatic character," "remains a permanent threat to collective identity" (258). Perhaps it is because he is interested in the formation and "duration" of collective identities via crisis events and memory (his case study is the Holocaust) that he writes that "[t]he concept of continuity in the two modes of crisis differs substantially. A normal crisis binds past, present, and future together into an unbroken unity of self; the wounds contingency makes in historical identity heal in the course of time. In the case of a catastrophic crisis,

however, unity becomes precarious at its core; the wounds to historical identity remain open" (255).
15 See Maracle, "Moving Over," *Trivia* 14 (Spring 1989): 9–10. See also Julia Emberley's *Thresholds of Difference: Feminist Critique, Native Women's Writing, Postcolonial Theory* (Toronto: U of Toronto P, 1993), where she calls this event "a watershed in Canadian feminist cultural politics" (79). For an example of how important this "moment" was for Aboriginal women writers and academics, see Jo-Ann Episkenew's dialogue with Deanna Reder, "Tâwaw cî?: Aboriginal Faculty, Students, and Content in the University English Department," published as "Web Exclusive Article" in *Academic Matters*, dated 23 March 2011. As Episkenew comments in this interview, "It has been twenty years since the 1988 International Feminist Book Fair in Montreal, when Sto:lo and Métis author Lee Maracle demanded that non-Aboriginal writers and academics 'Move Over.' My Aboriginal colleagues and I are here as a result of this famous directive—and to give credit where it is due, we are also here because of those who have made space. That being said, has enough changed?"
16 There were other emergent moments of this kind that contributed to this debate, notably Lenore Keeshig-Tobias's intervention at the 1989 Annual General Meeting of the Writers' Union of Canada and her co-founding, with Daniel David Moses and Tomson Highway, of the Toronto-based Committee to Re-Establish the Trickster. See her "Stop Stealing Native Stories," *The Globe and Mail* 26 January 1990: A7. See also Maracle's interview with Jennifer Kelly, "Coming Out of the House: A Conversation with Lee Maracle," *Ariel: A Review of International English Literature*, 25.1 (January 1994): 73–88, where Maracle draws a distinction between the "'appropriation' debate" and "moving over" (82–83).
17 Cultural exhibits and events like the group exhibit *Yellow Peril: Reconsidered* (1990), curated by Paul Wong; *Self Not Whole: Cultural Identity and Chinese-Canadian Artists* (1991), and *Racy Sexy* (1993), along with *Desh Pradesh*, created different fora for discussions about race and racialization that, along with other things, prepared the ground for the Writing Thru Race conference; many of the artists and writers involved in these events were also active lobbying the Canada Council, the result being fundamental changes in its structure and support of artistic and literary production in Canada. For a study that records and analyzes some of these events and changes in the cultural sphere, see Monika Kin Gagnon, *Other Conundrums: Race, Culture, and Canadian Art* (Vancouver: Arsenal Pulp, 2000), with a Foreword by Larissa Lai (15–20); see also my book *Scandalous Bodies: Diasporic Literature in English Canada* (2000; Waterloo: Wilfrid Laurier UP, 2009), where I discuss at different points the important interventions some of these events have made.

18 That Makeda Silvera raised the question of race and racist practices in the publishing and cultural scenes in Canada at the 1983 Women and Words conference, and that Maria Campbell drew attention to the plight of Native women writers and invited younger and still unpublished Native women authors to share the stage with her at the same event are clear instances of emergent moments, interventional gestures that, along with other things, gradually created the conditions that made possible ground-breaking events like the Writing Thru Race conference and changes in the field at large, including its curricular and pedagogical delivery.

19 In keeping with my attempt in this Introduction to understand and theorize the significance of emergent events, I place emphasis on how such events impact on the field; dealing with the full implications of the function of emergent events, especially with regard to how they shape the communities from within which they emerge, is a project I intend to address elsewhere.

20 I am alluding here to the Social Sciences and Humanities Research Council of Canada (SSHRC)'s "transformation" process; see *From Granting Council to Knowledge Council: Renewing the Social Sciences and Humanities in Canada. Consultation Framework on SSHRC's Transformation*, vol. 1 (Ottawa: SSHRC, January 2004), and *From Granting Council to Knowledge Council: Renewing the Social Sciences and Humanities in Canada*, vol. 3 (Ottawa: SSHRC, 2005).

21 See the first call for papers for the TransCanada conferences. Along with planning the TransCanada conferences, TransCanada Institute also organized, early in its formation, a workshop on the humanities that resulted in *Retooling the Humanities: The Culture of Research in Canadian Universities* (Edmonton: U of Alberta P, 2011), Daniel Coleman and Smaro Kamboureli, eds. For how the notions of the public and research accountability are configured in this climate, see our Preface (xiii–xxiv) and "Introduction: Canadian Research Capitalism: A Genealogy of Critical Moments" (1–39).

22 Though not occurring as frequently, the concern with the Canadianness of Canadian authors and literature continues today; see John Barber, "Are Canadian Writers 'Canadian' Enough?" *The Globe and Mail* 29 October 2011. Web.

23 Though de Certeau's study focuses on the discipline of history and historiography, it is equally relevant in this context as he shows disciplinary formations to be contiguous with colonialism and imperialism, but I do not have the space to discuss his work in detail.

24 The meaning of "others" in this context deliberately slides from that of "other" topics to that of "other" human subjects to capture what I believe belongs to the same resistance that the field-imaginary has historically displayed—and in some respects continues to do so—against topics that posed/pose challenges to its political unconscious, as well as against writers

and critics who have been marginalized or otherwise contained because of race, gender, cultural difference, and/or their methodological approaches and scholarly politics.

25 I am appropriating here Gayatri Chakravorty Spivak's poignant phrase, "The ventriloquism of the speaking subaltern is the left intellectual's stock-in-trade" (255). See her book, *A Critique of Postcolonial Reason: Toward a History of the Vanishing Present* (Cambridge, MA, and London: Harvard UP, 1999), a study pertinent to my discussion of disciplinary formations as well as to notions of representation and accountability. Jacques Derrida's *Of Hospitality: Anne Dufourmantelle Invites Jacques Derrida to Respond* (Stanford: Stanford UP, 2000) is also relevant to my formulation here. See also Spivak's "Responsibility," *boundary 2* 21.3 (Fall 1994): 19–64.

26 Given its occasion, Foucault's speech announces his future study themes and tasks, and so its argument unfolds through a series of "musts" and "must nots." Thus when talking about how we might avoid a discipline's fear of otherness, he says: "we must call into question our will to truth, restore to discourse its character as an event, and finally throw off the sovereignty of the signifier" ("Order" 66); and as he is approaching his conclusion, he articulates four "methodological requirements" for addressing discourse as event: the "principle of reversal"; the "principle of discontinuity"; the "principle of specificity"; and the "rule … of exteriority" (67).

27 Deleuze draws a distinction between Foucault's two sets of terms, exteriority/interiority and outside/inside, but dealing with this distinction here would take me too far afield.

28 Judith Bulter's argument about the outside and inside of discourses would be highly relevant to my discussion here had I the space to engage with it. In talking about the erasures and exclusions that construct subjects, and influenced by Foucault, Butler writes that "there is an 'outside' to what is constructed by discourse, but this is not an absolute 'outside'"; it is "a constitutive 'outside'" in that it is created as such by the production mechanisms of a discursive regime. Intent on eluding the "kind of discursive monism … that refuses the constitutive force of exclusion, erasure, violent foreclosure, [and] abjection" (8), she calls for a "refigur[ing of] this necessary 'outside' as a future horizon, one in which the violence of exclusion is perpetually in the process of being overcome" (53). See her *Bodies That Matter: On the Discursive Limits of "Sex"* (New York and London: Routledge, 1993).

29 See Brydon's similar point (4), and Blodgett (*Five Part* 189).

30 See also Karl R. Popper, *Logic of Scientific Discovery*, trans. by Popper, with the assistance of Julius Freed and Lan Freed (1959; 1992; London: Routledge, 2002), in which he argues for a gradual progress from one model to another.

31 It would be pertinent to consider here Jürgen Habermas's distinction, in his *Legitimation Crisis* (trans. Thomas McCarthy [Boston: Beacon, 1975] 148), among cultural crises whereby "the normative structures change, according to their inherent logic, in such a way that the complementarity between the requirements of the state apparatus and the occupational system, on the one hand, and the interpreted needs and legitimate expectations of members of society, on the other, is disturbed"; legitimation crises that "result from a need for legitimation that arises from changes in the political system (even when normative structures remain unchanged) and that cannot be met by the existing supply of legitimation"; and motivational crises that "are the result of changes in the socio-cultural system itself."

32 Here "Poetics" stands for thematics as Cameron's critical lexicon distinguishes between "poetics," which "tends to constitute itself solely through empiricism," and "criticism," which "is concerned primarily with what is supposedly unique and particular to a given text" (125).

33 See Moss's "Bushed in the Sacred Wood," *The Paradox of Meaning: Cultural Poetics and Critical Fictions* (Winnipeg: Turnstone, 1999), 13–28.

34 Consider, for example, Frank Davey's "Surviving the Paraphrase" (*Surviving* 13–28), as well as my essay that deals with this work, "Frank Davey and the Method of Cool"; Barry Cameron and Michael Dixon, "Mandatory Subversive Manifesto: Canadian Criticism vs. Literary Criticism," *Minus Canadian: Penultimate Essays on Literature*, ed. Cameron and Dixon. Spec. issue of *Studies in Canadian Literature* 2 (1977): 137–45; Russell M. Brown, "Critic, Culture, Text: Beyond Thematics," *Essays on Canadian Writing* 11 (1978): 151–83, and his most recent take on the topic (2001); and Rosmarin Heidenreich's introduction to her study *The Postwar Novel in Canada: Narrative Patterns and Reader Response* (Waterloo: Wilfrid Laurier UP, 1989).

35 "Four Windows on to Landscapes" and "The House Repossessed" are the respective subtitles of his essay's two parts.

36 "Canada" does not appear in either part of Tallman's essay, while "Canadian" is employed only once to refer to "André, the guilt-haunted Canadian artist" in Mordecai Richler's *The Acrobat* (Part Two, 44).

37 For a recent example of this, see Emily Apter, *The Translation Zone: A New Comparative Literature* (Princeton: Princeton UP, 2006).

38 See Donna Palmateer Pennee's essay, "'Après Frye, rien'? Pas du tout! From Contexts to New Contexts" (202–19), as well as Ajay Heble's, "New Contexts of Canadian Criticism: Democracy, Counterpoint, Responsibility" (78–97), both in *New Contexts of Canadian Criticism* (Peterborough: Broadview, 1997). This important anthology, which includes both new and reprinted essays, is dedicated to Mandel.

39 To this list, which reflects Mandel's eclecticism, or, if you prefer, his strategic use of different theories, one could add poststructuralism and postmodernism, especially in relation to his later work.

40 The majority of the essays collected in Mandel's *The Family Romance* were published or delivered in the early 1980s.

41 One could, of course, furnish other examples that challenge the predominance of the thematic paradigm around that period, such as Robin Mathews' *Canadian Literature: Surrender of Revolution* (Ottawa: Steel Rail, 1978) that, though fiercely nationalist, adopts a Marxist approach.

42 One of the anonymous readers of this book wondered what exactly "belatedness" refers to here. Clearly I have in mind the general conditions and signs of anxiety that various arguments about the institutionalization of Canadian literature have been addressing for a while now. See, for example, my introduction to *Making a Difference: Canadian Multicultural Literatures in English* (Toronto: Oxford UP, 2000), ix–xvii; Coleman, "From Canadian Trance to TransCanada: White Civility to Wry Civility in the CanLit Project," *Trans.Can.Lit* (35); and Szeman's *Zones of Instability* (178).

43 See Lewis S. Feuer, *Ideology and the Ideologists*, with a new introduction by Irving Louis Horowitz (1975; New Brunswick, NJ: Transaction, 2010).

44 Harold Bloom, *The Anxiety of Influence: A Theory of Poetry* (1973), 2nd ed. (New York: Oxford UP, 1997).

45 That this conference was part of the annual Canadian Literature Symposium at the University of Ottawa that was inaugurated with a conference on Grove in 1973, and that the book came out in the publication series of these symposia, Reappraisals: Canadian Writers, certainly reinforces this. My thanks to Cynthia Sugars, who helped me confirm the inaugural date of this annual event.

46 The cross- and intra-generational nature of that conference is evident by the presence of, for example, George Bowering, Sherrill Grace, Robert Kroetsch, Shirley Neuman, Stephen Scobie, along with Heather Murray, Susan Rudy Dorscht, and Richard Cavell.

47 Fredric Jameson, "Third-World Literature in the Era of Multinational Capitalism," *Social Text* 15 (1986): 65–88. See Aijaz Ahmad's *In Theory: Class, Nations, Literature* (London: Verso, 1992) 95–122 for one of the most famous critiques of Jameson's argument, as well as Imre Szeman's revisiting of this debate, "Who's Afraid of National Allegory? Jameson, Literary Criticism, Globalization," *The South Atlantic Quarterly* 100.3 (Summer 2001): 803–27.

48 I realize that the argument I am making here is too condensed, but unpacking it would take me too far afield. While I expand on these issues in my introduction to the forthcoming *Critical Collaborations: Indigeneity, Diaspora, and Ecology in Canadian Literary Studies*, I have already addressed some of these or related issues elsewhere as well. See "The Limits of the Ethical Turn:

Troping Towards the Other, Yann Martel, and *Self*," in Marlene Goldman and K. Kyser, eds., *The Ethical Turn in Canadian Literature and Criticism*, Spec. issue of *University of Toronto Quarterly* 76.3 (Summer 2007): 937–61; "The Politics of the Beyond: 43 Theses on Autoethnography and Complicity," in Eleanor Ty and Christl Verduyn, eds., *Asian Canadian Writing beyond Autoethnography* (Waterloo: Wilfrid Laurier UP, 2008) 31–53; and "Introduction: Discourses of Security, Peacekeeping Narratives, and the Cultural Imagination in Canada" in Kamboureli and Heike Härting, *Discourses of Security, Peacekeeping Narratives, and the Cultural Imagination in Canada*, Spec. issue of *University of Toronto Quarterly* 78.2 (Spring 2009): 659–86. See also Coleman and Kamboureli.

49 Werner Sollors, too, attributes positivism to thematic criticism. "Thematics," he writes, "by necessity misses what makes literature exciting; it is a positivist misunderstanding of what constitutes literary texts and their specificity and uniqueness" ("Thematics" 217). This is a slightly different version of his earlier essay on the topic cited below.

50 Robert Kroetsch, "The Exploding Porcupine" in *The Lovely Treachery of Words* (Toronto: Oxford, 1989): 108–16.

51 Further on this point, regarding the "monoculture of interdisciplinarity" and interdisciplinarity in the corporate world, see chapter six in Alan Liu's book, especially 177–78.

52 Another permutation of thin interdisciplinarity would involve cases where interdisciplinarity is simply synonymous with what we might call name-dropping, or strategic citation, that is, calling upon another discipline for validation but without engaging extensively with what is at stake methodologically.

53 My statement here is not based on systematic research but rather on my observation as a result of reading extensively in other disciplines. For example, we find an array of references in Canadian literary scholarship to philosopher Charles Taylor, but his work on multiculturalism and Canadian modernity does not draw at all from literary or cultural studies. The same applies to Will Kymlicka; while many literary scholars writing about multicultural, diasporic, and postcolonial issues are aware of and cite his work, he seems to be oblivious to discussions of these topics in our field.

54 I think it is crucial to distinguish between works that practise interdisciplinarity—the writerly level—and, say, edited collections where one may encounter different essays that reflect the parameters of their particular disciplines but that, when read sequentially, might produce an inter- or transdisciplinary understanding of the topics at hand—the readerly level.

55 See also Basarab Nicolescu, *Manifesto of Transdisciplinarity*, trans. Karen-Claire Voss (Albany: State U of New York P, 2002), which offers a history of the concept, and Margaret A. Somerville and David J. Rapport, eds., *Transdisciplinarity: Recreating Integrated Knowledge* (Oxford: EOLSS, 2002).

National Literatures in the Shadow of Neoliberalism

1 I'm picking up on Len Findlay's question of "What might strategic interdisciplinarity look like in the future?" ("Always Indigenize!" 313). But I am also referring to Smaro Kamboureli's caution in "Frank Davey and the Method of Cool" that interdisiplinarity is not necessarily an index or mark of nonconformist knowledge and has recently become more central in the funding strategies and research imperatives in Canadian universities.

2 See Antonio Negri, *Insurgencies: Constituent Power and the Modern State*, trans. Maurizia Boscagli (Minneapolis: U of Minnesota P, 1999).

3 For a longer and more systematic analysis of the shifts and mergers of cultural theory that accumulate into a problematic notion of the global, see Timothy Brennan's chapter "Globalization's Unlikely Champions" in his study *Wars of Position* (126–44).

4 In *Fear of Small Numbers* (Durham: Duke UP, 2005) Appadurai writes: "Although many debates surround the extent to which globalization has eroded the contours of the system of nation-states, no serious analyst of the global economy over the past three decades would deny that whatever may have been the initial fictions and contradictions of the nation-state, these have been brought into sharper view through the deeper integration of world markets and the extensive spread of ideologies of marketization worldwide, especially after 1989" (21). He follows up with this statement: "The virtually complete loss of even the fiction of a national economy … leaves the cultural field as the main one in which fantasies of purity, authenticity, orders, and security can be enacted" (22–23). National economies are much more flexible than this, but if they are conceived of as being held in the container of the nation-state, then they appear brittle. Only by radically reducing a national economy to a brittle process contained within an absolute space can it be declared a fiction—and to do so then leaves us with no mode of address for the very real economic and cultural transformation of neoliberalism. One other point here: once the economic has been delinked and diminished, culture is held up as the field at which the state wields its monopoly of oppression. Yet, this move to elevate culture to step into the space abandoned by the erosion of a national economy with any effect again elides the actions of real social actors who see national-scale politics aimed at economic justice. What is actually striking in the calls for economic justice and social transformation in Latin America at the moment is the lack of the cultural. Venezuela, for example, is only now turning to the cultural aspects of what it calls "the Bolivarian revolution." Unlike Canada, it has only in the last two years created a national museums foundation and begun to institute a form of CanCon (Ven Con?) that assures that Venezuelan music is played on the radio. In contrast, the state project of countering the

national effects of overlapping neo-colonialism and neoliberalism has been largely *economic*, aiming first at the transformation of the national economy and then stretching out to form regional trade pacts and global alliances. Here, the cultural is belated and was not even particularly mobilized for the earlier educational, health, democratic, and property rights reforms.

5 So smoothed over are the contradictions of the city, particularly in its representation of homelessness, that the Vancouver Public Library sponsored a "Sleepover Stanley Park Trivia Contest" that asked, "Have you ever wondered what it might be like to spend an evening in Stanley Park?" To enter, contestants had to read *Stanley Park* and answer ten trivia questions based on the novel. Successful contestants would sleep over in Stanley Park (as the homeless characters in the novel do): "Winners and their guests will be treated to an overnight adventure in Stanley Park ... complete with horse-drawn carriage ride through the trees, a sumptuous candlelight dinner at Prospect Point, a lantern-lit forest walk, music and storytelling by the campfire with Vancouver artists, and a refreshing breakfast" (One Book). The summer population of homeless people in the park ranges between three hundred and five hundred, although the number is hard to verify as no real census can be taken.

6 For more information on Jeff Luers see his Jeff Free Luers page on the website myspace. For information on the OPM, check out the Eco-Action website.

7 For work specifically addressing neoliberalism by some of these authors, see Jeff Derksen, ed., "Poetry and the Long Neoliberal Moment" in *West Coast Line* 51 (2006). Also, in the introduction, I initiate some of the ideas I elaborate in this essay.

"Beyond CanLit(e)": Reading. Interdisciplinarity. Transatlantically.

I would like to sincerely thank my colleagues Dr. DeNel Rehberg Sedo and Dr. Anouk Lang for a series of productive discussions about our research methods, as well as for the huge amount of time, energy, and intellectual effort that they have committed to Beyond the Book. The primary funder of Beyond the Book was the Arts and Humanities Research Council (2005–8, grant number 121166). Funding for the pilot study was provided by the British Academy, the Canadian government via Department of Foreign Affairs and International Trade, the Foundation for Canadian Studies in the UK, and by Mount Saint Vincent University.

1 The project was conceived in late 2002 and designed in mid-2003 by myself, a British North American Studies scholar with a humanities training in literary studies, and DeNel Rehberg Sedo, an American who works

at Mount Saint Vincent University in Canada as a communications scholar and who trained as a social scientist. The Beyond the Book core team also included Dr. Anouk Lang (Postdoctoral Research Fellow) and Anna Burrells (part-time Administrative Assistant). For an overview of the project, visit the Beyond the Book project website.

2 Thanks to Marjorie Stone for a stimulating e-mail dialogue in February 2007 and for her ongoing support of my work, and to Julie Rak and Lynette Hunter for their intelligent comments about method, particularly during the Beyond the Book conference (31 August–2 September 2007).

3 In addition to the core team, the project employed temporary fieldworkers local to the research sites as well as several research assistants (in both Canada and the UK) who have been graduates in a range of disciplines, including education, international development, theology, psychology, and cultural studies; and various transcribers and translators who were graduates of American and Canadian studies, Hispanic studies, and French studies.

4 Our research sites/selected mass reading events are: (Canada) Kitchener-Waterloo-Cambridge One Book, One Community; One Book, One Vancouver; *Canada Reads*; (USA) One Book, One Chicago; One Book, One Huntsville; Seattle Reads; (UK) Great Reading Adventure (Bristol); Birmingham Book Festival; *Richard & Judy's Book Club* (Channel 4 – TV); Liverpool Reads.

5 There are, of course, many scholars investigating both contemporary readers and historical readers. A good cross-section of those working on contemporary cultures of reading was represented at the Beyond the Book conference (see the website's "resources/archives" for the program). SHARP's website gives an insight into those working on historical reading and readers, as does its Canadian sister organization Canadian Association for the Study of Book Cultures. The work of Janice Radway and Elizabeth Long has influenced my own methods and theories profoundly. Within Canada very interesting work is being undertaken by, among others, Margaret Mackey, education/library science (how reading competencies develop across media); David Miall, literary studies (empirical—lab work—studies of reading); Julie Rak, cultural studies/literary studies (how readers negotiate genres in various spaces including bookstores); Paulette Rothbauer, library and information science (rural teens and LGTB urban teen readers).

6 Get Into Reading is a project that was begun by Jane Davis, who is also founder-editor of *The Reader*. For more information about this community activist project, see the Get Into Reading website.

7 See, for example, the research projects connected to The Reader organization, at its website. These include "An investigation into the therapeutic benefits of reading in relation to depression and well-being," a two-year

project about GIR's version of bibliotherapy, which involves health care professionals, academic psychologists, and a literary critic.

8   I am deliberately evoking the title and focus of the seminar organized by Smaro Kamboureli and Daniel Coleman, The Culture of Research: Retooling the Humanities, 20 October 2006 at the University of Guelph (see the Transcanadas website). See also Daniel Coleman and Smaro Kamboureli, eds., *Retooling the Humantities: The Culture of Research in Canadian Universities* (Edmonton: U of Alberta P, 2011).

9   See also Fuller and Rehberg Sedo, "Mixing It Up: Using Mixed Methods to Investigate Contemporary Cultures of Reading" in Anouk Lang, ed., *From Codex to Hypertext: Reading at the Turn of the Twenty-First Century* (Amherst: U of Massachusetts P, 2012), 234–51.

10 If you attempt transformative interdisciplinarity, you intend to generate not only new knowledge about the subject of investigation but also new methodologies—and thus to "transform" the methods and theories that each team member learned within their original disciplines. Some meditations on "interdisciplinarity" from the perspective of the humanities that I have found useful include: Linda Hutcheon and Micheal Hutcheon, "A Convenience of Marriage"; Renée Hulan, "Blurred Visions: The Interdisciplinarity of Canadian Literary Criticism" in *Essays on Canadian Writing* 65 (1998): 38–55; and Joe Moran, *Interdisciplinarity* (London: Routledge, 2002).

11 I recognize that some literary scholars, especially feminist critics, employ self-reflexive strategies in their analytical writing, for example, the creative-critical practices developed by the *Tessera* collective in Canada (see, for example, Godard, *Collaboration in the Feminine: Writing on Women and Culture from Tessera* (Toronto: Second Story, 1994), as a means of interrogating the relationships between language, gender, and power. However, here I am focusing on the epistemological frameworks that are brought to bear on decisions regarding research methods as opposed to the status of the end products of research, that is, the textual accounts of analysis and interpretation.

12 Some of the practical limitations within fieldwork help to make visible formal and informal networks through which culture is made and evaluated. For instance, the difficulties of recruiting to focus groups also indicated to us which groups have most cultural capital within particular cities and who has the time, leisure, and social confidence to participate in cultural activities (as well as our focus groups!).

13 See, for example, Sandra Harding, "Rethinking Standpoint Epistemology: What Is 'Strong Objectivity'?" in Linda Alcoff and Elizabeth Potter, eds., *Feminist Epistemologies* (New York: Routledge, 1993) 49–82; and her study, *Whose Science? Whose Knowledge? Thinking from Women's Lives* (Milton Keynes: Open UP, 1991).

White Settlers and the Biopolitics of State Building in Canada

This research was supported by the Canada Research Chair Program, in which I hold a Tier 1 Chair in Political Economy and Social Governance. I also thank Drs. Isabel Altamirano-Jimenez and Malinda Smith for their insightful reading of an earlier draft of this chapter.

1. See, for example, Iris Marion Young, "Polity and Group Difference: Critique of the Ideal of Universal Citizenship" in *Ethics* 94 (1989): 250–74; Lisa Swartzman, *Challenging Liberalism: Feminism as Political Critique* (University Park, PA: Pennsylvania State UP, 2006); David Theo Goldberg, *The Racial State*; and Charles W. Mills, *The Racial Contract* (Ithaca, NY: Cornell UP, 1997).

2. While in the contemporary era it would be inaccurate to refer to Canadians of Anglo-Celtic heritage as a diaspora, the term does resonate among the early white settlers. Similar to other diasporic communities, these early immigrants were dispersed from an original centre (Imperial Britain) to two or more peripheral regions, retained a collective memory of homeland, and derived a collective consciousness and solidarity from a relationship with the homeland. Although the term diaspora is now often used to define minority ethnic groups in relation to the dominant group within contemporary national social formations, this practice tends to obscure the disasporic underpinnings of white settler societies and reproduces dominant representations of national belonging and especially fragile distinctions between founding peoples and immigrant populations. See, for example, Robin Cohen, *Global Diasporas: An introduction* (London: Routledge, 1997).

3. For example, a recent collection of essays on Canadian multiculturalism concludes that "one is inevitably struck by the persistent disadvantage of Black and Aboriginal individuals on many of the dimensions of inclusion examined in this book ... it would seem to be time for a national debate on the bluntness of categories such as 'visible minority'" ("Conclusion" in Banting, Courchene, and Seidle 682).

4. See, for example, Lentin, "From Racial State to Racist State"; Goldberg, *The Racial State*; Valverde, "Society must be defended"; and McWhorter, "Sex, Race and Biopower."

5. Elsewhere I have used Speeches from the Throne to track shifting definitions of the iconic Canadian associated with laissez-faire, social liberal, and neoliberal governing paradigms: "Citizenship and Solidarity: Reflections on the Canadian Way," in *Citizenship Studies* 6.4 (2002): 377–95; "Three Stories of Canadian Citizenship" (Adamoski, Chun, and Menzie 43–68); and "The Social in Social Citizenship."

6 The term "citizen" appears in the form of "citizen-soldiers," who helped quell the Riel Rebellion ("1885" 19) or the potential usefulness of immigrants as "citizens of the dominion" ("1900" 18).

7 The Royal Northwest Mounted Police was founded in 1873, largely in response to the Cypress Hills Massacre of the same year. Alleging the theft of horses, a group, comprised mostly of American whiskey-traders, entered the Cypress Hills area of present-day Saskatchewan and murdered twenty-three Nakota (Assiniboine) peoples. The RNWMP was established as a mark of Canadian sovereignty and to police the territories.

"Some Great Crisis": Vimy as Originary Violence

This research was undertaken with the support of a SSHRC doctoral fellowship, and facilitated by TransCanada Institute. My thanks to Smaro Kamboureli and David Williams, who offered helpful critiques of earlier drafts of the essay, and to the members of the TransCanada/TransQuebec Workgroup, with whom its key concerns were workshopped.

1 As the paradox of a nation trying to construct its mythic past so that it has something to deconstruct—of writers who, as she writes, "must return to their history ... in order to discover (before they can contest) their historical myths" (6)—the empty origin is central to Linda Hutcheon's argument in *The Canadian Postmodern*. John Moss complained Canadians "have not the mythology of a revolution" to give it a history (*Sex* 11), while Robert Kroetsch worried that "in Canada we cannot for the world decide when we became a nation or what ... might have been the originary moments" (27). More recently, Cynthia Sugars notes that "the moment when the nation (as a white nation-state) was catalyzed into being (even in proto-national form) is impossible to pinpoint" ("Disinheriting" 178), while Stephanie McKenzie warns that "to accept, or make archetypal, the 'lack of a traditional, mythological foundation' spells defeat if one is looking for a mythological base similar to that which has *traditionally* served other nations" (25). Finally, David Williams's recent study on the Great War raises the myth wearily: "Must we link it to 'the birth of the nation,' our national myth of origins that Canadians might otherwise lack?" (*Media* 271).

2 Daniel Coleman (8), Jonathan Kertzer (133–34), Diana Brydon ("Canada" 74), and David Williams (*Imagined* 73), to name but a few, all trace the idea of the national forgetting back to Renan's essay. Moreover, it is a central passage for Benedict Anderson's now ubiquitous *Imagined Communities*, which extends Renan's suggestion that the nation is founded on "forgetting" to the idea that we are called to "remember/forget" (201).

3 Max Weber, for example, defines a state as "a human community that (successfully) claims the monopoly of the legitimate use of physical force within a given territory" (78). Similarly, Charles Tilly defines states as "coercion-wielding organizations that are distinct from households and kinship groups and exercise clear priority in some respects over all other organizations within substantial territories" (1).

4 For a recent engagement on the status of the "ethical turn" in Canadian criticism, see the September 2007 *University of Toronto Quarterly* special issue on the topic (76:3).

5 Tim Cook outlines how the war archives were closed to all except the country's official historian, Colonel Archer Fortescue Duguid, who, while clearly overwhelmed by its immensity, kept the 135 tons of archival material closed to all save himself (507). As a result, few historians ventured extensive writing on the war (510), and "memoirs and war novels were the history of the masses and they did not rely on the archival record" (513–14). For an exhaustive survey on the way in which public opinions of the war were shaped by cultural productions of all kinds, see Jonathan Vance's study, *Death So Noble: Memory, Meaning, and the First World War*.

6 For critical reappraisals of the position of Vimy in the national memory, see Jonathan Vance's *Death So Noble* and Hayes, Iarocci, and Bechthold's *Vimy Ridge: A Canadian Reassessment*.

7 I turn to Benjamin's "Critique of Violence" because of the implicit attention Benjamin pays to the cultural or symbolic nature of the nation-state's authority. While there are much more commonly cited accounts of state formation, such as those by Weber or Tilly, I worry, along with Mara Loveman, that "the cultural dimension ... is all but lost in such accounts" (1660).

8 Confederation, of course, can be understood as a culmination of the violence of colonial settlement, but Benjamin's understanding of a "founding violence" that can be invoked for its symbolic power demands an act that is immediately bloody and widely recognized in terms of its violence. For more on Derrida's complex reading of Benjamin's essay, see my essay "'And Yet': Derrida on Benjamin's Divine Violence," *Mosaic* 40:2 (June 2007): 103–16.

9 Apparently Allward did not initially design the monument with either a particular site or even a particular battle in mind but simply to "commemorate the wartime co-operation between Canada and France" (Atherton).

10 The pamphlet includes both French and English versions of this text, and the differences between them are significant. The French passage, which reads, "Cette victoire à la crête de Vimy a uni les Canadiens et a donné un sentiment de fierté à ce jeune pays," considerably softens the English version's unequivocal claim that "the victory ... established their country

as a proud young nation" into the suggestion that the victory simply gave Canadians "a sense of pride in the young country."

11 Papineau attempts to soften his stance, but the threat remains: "We shall inflict upon them the punishment they deserve—not by physical violence—for we shall have had enough of that ... but by the invincible power of our moral influence" (22).

12 See Vance, 229–45.

Amplifying Threat: Reasonable Accommodations and Quebec's Bouchard-Taylor Commission Hearings (2007)

All translations in parentheses are by Monika Kin Gagnon. We wish to acknowledge the research assistance of Vivian Tabar, Erin Despard, and Angela Wilson. Parts of this essay were originally published as Gagnon, "Making (Non)Sense of L'Affaire Hérouxville: Citizenship, Culture and Belonging in Quebec," and Jiwani, "Editorial Focus from Quebec," in *Racelink, a quasi-journal of RACE*.

1 See, for instance, Tim Nieguth and Aurélie Lacassagne, "Contesting the Nation: Reasonable Accommodation in Rural Quebec," *Canadian Political Science Review* 3.1 (2009): 1–16, and Lori Beaman's analysis in Is Religious Freedom Impossible in Canada? (unpublished paper, Department of Classics and Religious Studies, U of Ottawa, 2009).

2 See, for instance, "Muslim Council of Montreal condemns attack on Muslim school: Attack comes after unbalanced 'reasonable accommodation' discussion and poll suggesting racism in Quebec," Muslim Council of Montreal 17 January 2007.

3 See Frances Henry and Carol Tator, *Discourses of Domination: Racial Bias in the Canadian English-Language Press* (Toronto/London/Buffalo: U of Toronto P, 2002); Augie Fleras and Jean Lock Kunz, *Media and Minorities, Representing Diversity in a Multicultural Canada* (Toronto: Thompson Educational Pub., 2001); Gada Mahrouse, "Update on the Taylor Bouchard Commission on 'Reasonable Accommodation,'" *RACElink*; Yasmin Jiwani, *Discourses of Denial: Mediations of Race, Gender and Violence* (Vancouver: U of British Columbia P, 2006); and Minelle Mahtani, "Representing Minorities: Canadian Media and Minority Identities," *Canadian Ethnic Studies* 33.3 (2001): 93–133.

4 Owned by the Asper family, Canwest has been noted to exercise considerable influence on the coverage its papers afford to particular issues and political ideologies. See Robert Everton, "Israel Asper and the Israeli Propaganda" in Jeffery Klaehn, ed., *Filtering the News* (Montreal: Black Rose, 2005) 3–94; and Leslie Regan Shade, "Aspergate: Concentration, Convergence and Censorship in Canadian Media" in David Skinner, James Compton, and

Mike Gasher, eds., *Converging Media, Diverging Politics: A Political Economy of News in the United States and Canada* (Lanham, MD: Lexington Books, 2005) 101–16. At the time of writing, Calgary's Shaw Communications has recently purchased controlling shares in Canwest at a cost of two billion dollars, saving it from its creditors when it went into bankruptcy protection in December 2009.

5 See Jiwani, "Gendering Terror: Representations of the Orientalized Body in Quebec's Post–September 11 English-Language Press," *Critique: Critical Middle Eastern Studies* 13.3 (2004): 265–91; and Sharon Todd, "Veiling the 'Other,' Unveiling Our 'Selves': Reading Media Images of the Hijab Psychoanalytically to Move Beyond Tolerance," *Canadian Journal of Education* 23.4 (1998): 438–51.

6 See Sunera Thobani, *Exalted Subjects, Studies in the Making of Race and Nation in Canada* (Toronto: U of Toronto P, 2007); and Sherene Razack, *Looking White People in the Eye: Gender, Race, and Culture in Courtrooms and Classrooms* (Toronto: U of Toronto P, 1998).

7 This "clash of civilizations" thesis, articulated by Samuel Huntington, has distilled and simplified a larger conflict into a rudimentary cultural framework. Huntington argues that Islam and Confucianism are the two biggest threats to the West on the grounds that these cultures are mobilized by religious convictions and further that their values are antithetical to Western values of democracy, rule of law, and so on. Huntington's thesis falls short on various accounts in that it fails to consider the heterogeneity within countries governed by Muslim rulers and further discounts the historical, economic, and political motives that have led the USA to put many of these rulers in place. Further, as Tariq Ali makes clear, the clash of civilizations thesis basically uses religion and culture as explanatory tools, masking the fact that the real "threats" to the West are economic in nature—oil and the mass export of cheap Chinese goods. He advances the view that what we are witnessing in the world today is a "clash of fundamentalisms."

8 See Stéphane Baillargeon, "Accommodements raisonnables—L'égalité des sexes en tout temps et en tous lieux, plaide le CSF," *Le Devoir* 28 September 2007: A4; Marie-Andrée Chouinard, "Position extrême." *Le Devoir* 1 October 2007; Christiane Pelchat, "Le port du voile, d'hier à aujourd'hui," *Le Devoir* 10 October 2007: A7; Pearl Eliadis, "Quebec Status of Women's position is an attack on minority rights," *The Gazette* (Montreal) 4 October 2007.

9 See Joan Wallach Scott, *The Politics of the Veil* (Princeton: Princeton UP, 2007).

10 Stuart Allan, *News Culture*, 2nd ed. (Maidenhead: Open UP, 2004); Lance W. Bennett, *News, the Politics of Illusion*, 5th ed. (White Plains: Longman, 2003); and Stuart Hall, "Media Power: The Double Bind," *Journal of Communications* 24.4 (1974): 19–26.

11 See Ian Connell, "Television News and the Social Contract," in Stuart Hall, ed., *Culture, Media, Language* (Britain: Hutchinson in association with the Centre for Contemporary Cultural Studies, Birmingham, 1980): 139–56; Nancy Murray, "Anti-Racists and Other Demons: The Press and Ideology in Thatcher's Britain," *Race & Class* 27.3 (1986): 1–19.
12 The stories analyzed in *The Gazette* (Montreal) spanned from 8 September 2007 to 2 November 2007.
13 See Jiwani, "Helpless Maidens and Chivalrous Knights: Afghan Women in the Canadian Press," *University of Toronto Quarterly* 78.2 (2009): 728–44; and "War Talk—Engendering Terror: Race, Gender and Representation in Canadian Print Media," *International Journal of Media & Cultural Politics* 1.1 (2005): 15–21. See also Razack, *Casting*, and Jasmin Zine, "Unsettling the Nation: Gender, Race and Muslim Cultural Politics in Canada," *Studies in Ethnicity and Nationalism* 9.1 (2009): 146–93.
14 See Floya Anthias and Nira Yuval-Davis, *Racialized Boundaries, Race, Nation, Gender, Colour and Class and the Anti-Racist Struggle* (London, UK: Routledge, 1992).
15 See Sedef Arat-Koç, "Hot Potato: Imperial Wars or Benevolent Interventions? Reflections on 'Global Feminism' Post September 11th," *Atlantis* 26.2 (2002): 433–44; Miriam Cooke, "Saving Brown Women," *Signs* 28.1 (2002): 468–70; Mary Ann Franks, "Obscene Undersides: Women and Evil between the Taliban and the United States," *Hypatia: A Journal of Feminist Philosophy* 18.1 (2003): 135–56; and Jiwani, "Helpless."
16 See Jiwani, "War Talk"; "Helpless."
17 This intervention occurred at the International Workshop on Cultural Dialogues, Religion and Communication, Ottawa, 22 October 2009.
18 Rachad Antonius's comments were made at a conference hosted by L'Observatoire international sur le racisme et les discriminations, entitled *Médias et processus de racisation: quelles approches pour quelles actions?* at l'Université du Québec à Montréal, 12 June 2008.

The Time Has Come: Self and Community Articulations in *Colour. An Issue* and *Awakening Thunder*

1 I argue that subjectivities are produced in the act of writing, publication, reading, and circulation of texts; that if, as Benedict Anderson says, nations are imagined communities, then the imaginative work of its citizens necessarily reproduces them, sometimes as identical to what they were before but more often, as Judith Butler has taught us, with a difference.
2 A fully historicizing paper, which goes beyond the scope of this essay, would go back to the progressive periodicals of the 1970s—*The Asianadian* and *Inalienable Rice*, or even further back to look at the histories of community

newspapers, which still proliferate in many marginalized communities at the present time. Paul Yee's *Salt Water City* (Vancouver: Douglas and McIntyre, 2006) documents some of these publications, as does my article with Jean Lum in the catalogue for the 1990 film, video, and photo exhibition, *Yellow Peril: Reconsidered*.

3   To consider the different stances taken by the wide range of special issues produced at that time, certainly in terms of historical moment but also in terms of political and critical location, would warrant a book-length study.

4   While I argue for the "specialness" of *Awakening Thunder* and its production of a special and different present, as I have already suggested, its moment of publication was just one among other groundbreaking anti-racist cultural texts and events that filled the lives and imaginations of many racialized cultural workers in that moment. In the late 1980s and early '90s, it was possible—not without great personal cost but nonetheless possible—to speak about race and racialization in public Canadian fora that simply were not available to racialized cultural workers until that point. Beyond SKY Lee's *Disappearing Moon Café* (Vancouver: Douglas and McIntyre), published in 1990, the same year as *Awakening Thunder*, other texts attesting to repressed histories began to emerge. For example, in 1989 in Vancouver, Zainub Verjee and Lorraine Chan put on *In Visible Colours*, a women-of-colour and First Nation women's film and video festival, while in 1991 Paul Wong launched *Yellow Peril: Reconsidered*, an exhibit featuring twenty-five Asian Canadian artists working in contemporary media. These, and other events and publications too numerous to list here, all contributed to the production of a particular kind of anti-racist present that, to my mind, offered a distinct break from the past, even as it built on it.

5   Interestingly, the Koma Gata Maru incident of 1914 is not invoked in the Introduction to *Awakening Thunder* as a founding trauma for Asian Canadian identification. In that year, approximately 376 Punjabi migrants (the number is disputed) were denied entry into Canada on the basis of the fact that their journey from the Punjab was not continuous. They were turned back, and many died on the return voyage. Twenty were killed on their arrival in Calcutta during a skirmish with police. Insofar as more radical Asian Canadian identities are imagined (in Benedict Anderson's sense) as founded in uprooting and exclusion as traumas that place us in a fraught relationship to the Canadian state, the Koma Gata Maru incident has been of great importance for Asian Canadians who identify specifically as South Asian Canadian. At the Anniversaries of Change conference organized at SFU Harbour Centre by Chris Lee and Henry Yu in 2007, for instance, the Koma Gata Maru incident was recognized along with other moments of violence against Asian Canadians, specifically, for that conference, the 1907

anti-Asiatic riots in Vancouver, as well as the Japanese Canadian internment and the Chinese Head Tax and Exclusion Acts. What I would like to recognize here is not so much an act of intentional exclusion from what Gagnon, in the *Yellow Peril: Reconsidered* catalogue, has called "Belonging in Exclusion," but rather to note that the early 1990s were a moment in which the recognition of community and kinship through shared experiences of trauma was itself at a moment of formation. Subsequent work in racialized trauma and memory solidifies this recognition over the course of the 1990s and into the new millennium. There is a full essay, if not a book, to be written, I think, on the movement through imaginings of community in relation to histories of trauma as they evolve through this period.

6   Here I acknowledge that I feel tempted to read a kind of progress into the motion from one special issue to the next. However, in the final instance, I note that there is a discursive moment to which each issue belongs, not necessarily in a linear or progressive relation to other special issues but certainly in relation to a particular way of thinking about race, class, gender, and sexuality.

7   These "posts" are, of course, relative, and depend on acceptance of the linear trajectory of Western philosophy. Given the diverse and fragmented backgrounds of the editors and contributors, I argue that there are many possible ways of situating this special issue in terms of time and tradition. To explore this multi-pronged temporality would, in fact, make a very interesting project.

8   In *Broken Entries*, Miki explains the problem of self-knowledge and articulated subjectivity for Canadian artists and writers of colour growing up in assimilationist Canada. He suggests that, for such subjects, subjective interiority is rendered speechless and devoid of content, so much so that the racialized subject does not even recognize the absence (110).

Archivable Concepts: Talonbooks and Literary Translation

1   See for example Denise Merkle, Jane Koustas, Glen Nichols, et/and Sherry Simon, eds., *Traduire depuis les marges/Translating from the Margins* (Montreal: Éditions Nota Bene, 2008); Sherry Simon, *Gender in Translation: Cultural Identity and the Politics of Transmission* (London/New York: Routledge, 1996); Luise Von Flotow, *Translation and Gender: Translating in the "Era of Feminisim,"* (Manchester: St. Jerome, 1991); Barbara Godard, "Gender and Gender Politics in Translation," in *Encyclopedia of Literary Translation into English*, vol. 1. A-L., Olive Classe, ed. (London: Fitzroy Dearborn, 2000): 501–11; Godard, *Gender and Translation: A Bibliography* (Ottawa: CRIAW, 2001); and "La Traduction au féminin/Translating Women," Spec. issue of *Tessera* 6 (Spring/printemps 1989).

2. This article forms part of an ongoing collaborative research project and network, Translation Effects: The Making of Modern Canadian Culture, organized by Kathy Mezei, Sherry Simon, and Luise von Flotow. One of the outcomes of this project will be a "Companion" of literary translation and translation artifacts in Canada. These introductory remarks reflect our collaborative thoughts.

3. Derrida suggests that the meaning of archive comes from the Greek *arkheion*, a house, a domicile, "the residence of the superior magistrates; the *archons*, those who commanded ... it is at their home, in that *place* which is their house ... that official documents are filed" (*Archive Fever* 2). Thus he alerts us to how deeply the archive is implicated by power, the law, memory, privacy, secrecy, the death drive, modern technologies of record-keeping, as well as by its specific physical space.

4. For further discussion of this example, see Alessandra Capperdoni, "1989: *Tessera's* Spring issue on 'La traduction au féminin comme réécriture' marks the heyday of feminist translational poetics in Canada," forthcoming. And as evidence of the impact of feminist translation theory, see Luise von Flotow, ed., *Translating Women* (Ottawa: U of Ottawa P, 2011).

5. For invaluable assistance and information, I gratefully and warmly thank Karl Siegler, Ian Chunn, Michael Hayward, and the Special Collections at SFU, in particular, Eric Swanick, Tony Power, Keith Gilbert, and Judith Polson.

6. Talonbooks Fonds is part of the Contemporary Literature Collection within the larger Special Collections and Rare Books Division, Bennett Library, SFU; accession number MsC 8. It measures 129.6 square metres.

7. Talonbooks Fonds, Special Collections. Karl Siegler joined Talonbooks in January 1974 as business manager and in 1984, with his wife, Christy, took over as owner and publisher. In 2008, Kevin and Vicki Williams became majority shareholders in the press, while Karl continued as editor and publisher and Christy as production manager. In September 2011, after four dedicated decades, they turned over their shares to Kevin and Vicki and left the press.

8. David Lobdell had hoped to retranslate *Mad Shadows* for Talonbooks (Letter to David Robinson, 25 January 1977, Talonbooks Fonds, MSC.8.a Box 21).

9. Gratien Gélinas, *Bousille and the Just* (*Bousille et les justes*), trans. Kenneth Johnson and Joffre Miville-Dechêne (Toronto: Clarke Irwin, 1961).

10. new press, run by former Anansi publisher David Godfrey, along with James Bacque and Roy MacSkimming, created the short-lived New Drama series (new press was taken over by General Publishing in 1974), which offered several Quebec plays in translation in 1972, including Marcel Dubé's *The White Geese* (translated by Jean Remple, 1972) and Robert Gurik's *The*

Hanged Man (translated by Philip London and Laurence Bérard, 1972). These plays lie within a more traditional realist tradition than Tremblay's oeuvre, and for this reason they, along with the two Gurik plays published by Talonbooks, have not been in demand as course adoptions and therefore are no longer in print.

11 *Les Belles-Soeurs* "set off a storm of controversy, firstly because of the language (a particularly raucous—some say vulgar—*joual*), and then because it dared to portray working class women doing working class things. Also, it went after men. None of this sounds particularly special today, but in 1968, theatre in Quebec was just releasing itself from religious and morality plays and joining (late) in the Quiet Revolution; although Marcel Dubé and Gratien Gélinas had been writing about 'normal' folk for years, they had not been doing it quite like this" (see the Canadian Theatre website). For the translation history of *Les Belles-Soeurs* and for an analysis of issues such as the translation of *joual*, see Louise Ladouceur, *Making the Scene: la traduction du théâtre d'une langue officielle à l'autre au Canada* (Montreal: Nota Bene, 2005); Louise Ladouceur, "Recently Canadian: versions franco-québécoises du théâtre canadien-anglais," in *Tendances actuelles en histoire littéraire canadienne* (Quebec: Éditions Nota bene, 2003) 131–48; Vivien Bosley, "Diluting the Mixture: Translating Michel Tremblay's *Les Belles-Sœurs*," in *TTR : traduction, terminologie, rédaction* 1.1 (1988): 139–45.

12 See Louise Ladouceur, "Le 31 mars au 28 avril 1973: La production anglaise des *Belles-Soeurs* de Michel Tremblay au St-Lawrence Center de Toronto connaît un succès éclatant," in *Translation Effects: The Making of Modern Canadian Culture*, ed. Kathy Mezei, Sherry Simon, and Luise von Flotow (forthcoming, University of Ottawa Press).

13 For invaluable assistance and information, I gratefully and warmly thank Karl Siegler, Ian Chunn, Michael Hayward, and the Special Collections at SFU, in particular, Eric Swanick, Tony Power, Keith Gilbert, and Judith Polson.

14 Beginning in 1963 as the poetry magazine *Talon*, by 1967 it had morphed into Talonbooks and was publishing poetry collections.

15 Kareda comments on the popularity of Tremblay's plays at the Tarragon Theatre and St. Lawrence Centre in Toronto; he also notes that there was a demand for making translations available for the "expanding Canadian drama courses at high schools and universities" (F6).

16 14 April 2008, Vancouver. Hereafter referred to as "Siegler."

17 Siegler claims that Talonbooks sells five hundred to a thousand copies of *Les Belles-Soeurs* annually (Interview).

18 Woodcock, "New Wave in Publishing," in *Canadian Literature* 57 (1973): 52.

19 For a concise history of small presses in Canada, see George Parker, "Small Presses," at the Canadian Encyclopedia website. See also David McKnight,

"Small Press Publishing," in Carole Gerson and Jacques Michon, eds., *History of the Book in Canada, 1918–1980*, vol. 3 (Toronto: U of Toronto P, 2007) 302–18; Roy MacSkimming, *The Perilous Trade: Book Publishing in Canada, 1946–2006* (Toronto: McClelland and Stewart, 2007). Jim Brown recalled: "I remember my girlfriends got stuck with the job of typing it—I always had girlfriends who were good typists," Barry McKinnon with Jim Brown, "Vancouver Writing Seen in the 60s," in *line* (1986): 105.

20   Robinson's emphasis on the local may refer to the preponderance of BC and Vancouver poets published by Talonbooks in the 1960s and early '70s (bill bissett, Lionel Kearns, George Bowering, Frank Davey, Phyllis Webb, Jamie Reid, Peter Trower).

21   Letter, David Lobdell to David Robinson, 28 November 1977, Talonbooks Fonds, MsC.8.a, Box 21, 82.

22   Susanne de Lotbinière-Harwood, *Re-belle et infidèle: la traduction comme pratique de réécriture au féminin / The body bilingual: translation as a re-writing in the feminine* (Toronto/Montreal: Women's Press/Éditions du Remue-ménage, 1991); Lise Gauvin, *Letters from an other*, trans. Susanne de Lotbinière-Harwood (Toronto: Women's Press, 1989); Nicole Brossard, *The aerial letter*, trans. Marlene Wildeman (Toronto: Women's Press, 1988).

23   In 1977, aid to translations included grants for the translation of plays for production. Translation grants were awarded as subsidies to publishers, not to translators; the publisher then paid the translator.

24   Correspondence in the Talonbooks Fonds reveals an edgy, cantankerous relationship in the late 1960s and '70s with Canada Council officials like Naïm Kattan (who claims to have initiated the translation grant program), Robert Fink, and Robin Farr, as Talonbooks continually renegotiates its position in relation to "institutionalized cultural authority" (Bourdieu 39). Jim Brown recalls concerns about the Council's role in determining what should be published and "the question of autonomy," noting that the Vancouver scene tended to be paranoid about central Canadian and federal interference: "The Canada Council is going to become the editor for small presses—and it did happen," in *Line* 1986: 118.

25   For example, prizewinners, especially Governor General's Literary Award for Fiction or Drama prizewinners, tend to have priority.

Is CanLit Lost in Japanese Translation?

1   For an account and analysis of the reception of *Anne of Green Gables*, see Yoshiko Akamatsu, "Japanese Reading of *Anne of Green Gables*," in Irene Gammel and Elizabeth Epperly, eds., *L.M. Montgomery and Canadian Culture* (Toronto: U of Toronto P, 1999), 201–12.

2 Japanese titles appear in parentheses throughout the essay.
3 All sales figures, as well as comments attributed to the publishers Takeshi Kitamoto and Hayakawa, were provided by them in the course of my interviews with them in the summer of 2007.
4 Such writers as Stephen King and Dan Brown are considered to represent the "entertainment" or "popular" category of literature.
5 The bubble economy in Japan is usually considered to have started in 1986 and ended in 1991 or '92.
6 See the Hayakawa website for its history.
7 "Keihakutansho" is the term first used in the journal *Nikkei Business* to mark the trend of stable and gradual, as opposed to rapid, growth of the economy. See the journal's website for a reprint of their first article about this trend (30 November 1981). The term, sometimes in a slightly derogatory sense, is still used to describe continuing economic trends in Japan today.
8 For details about the procedure for entering a title for this prize, see the Man Booker website.
9 See also Hisaaki Yamanouchi, *The Search for Authenticity in Modern Japanese Literature*, in which he writes, "[t]he first twenty years after the Meiji Restoration was the period of the Japanese Enlightenment, which was characterized by the espousal of individual freedom, belief in progress, and an empirical, utilitarian and pragmatic tendency" (21–22). I dealt with this issue in "Contexts and 'Con-textuality' of Minae Mizumura's Honkaku-Shosetsu," where I discussed the novelist Mizumura's position-taking in relation to the tradition of modern Japanese literature.
10 Jakobson (*Linguistic*) classified translation into three types: intralingual translation or rewording, meaning "an interpretation of verbal signs by means of other signs of the same language"; interlingual translation or translation proper, that is, "an interpretation of verbal signs by means of signs of some other language"; and intersemiotic translation or transmutation, which means "an interpretation of verbal signs by means of signs of nonverbal sign systems" (139).
11 Gideon Toury discusses three types of norms: "initial norms," involving the translator's choice between the norms of the ST and source culture and those of the TT and target culture; "preliminary norms," which concern "translation policy" and "directness of translation"; and "operational norms," concerning decisions made in the actual process of translation (57–59).
12 Although such postscripts are not unique to Japanese translation, a translator's foreword or afterword does not constitute a typical feature of the publication of foreign literature in the US, the UK, or Canada. For example, the English translations of Haruki Murakami's books do not have introductions or postscripts by their translators or other critics.

13 Compare the "critical" commentary in this postscript to how the East German translation of *Surfacing*, which came out in 1979, was situated. As Stefan Ferguson argues, the novel's "anti-Americanism was the foremost feature of the book highlighted for readers in East Germany by means of the translator's afterword. The West German version by the same translator has no equivalent to this 'interpretative' text; the readers are left to decide for themselves" (109).

14 Natsuki Ikezawa, who has been editing a highly acclaimed series of his own of world literary classics, mentions, though jokingly, the possibility of secretly publishing his own text as a Crest Book, disguised as a translation from a foreign language ("round-table" 14).

The Cunning of Reconciliation: Reinventing White Civility in the "Age of Apology"

A shorter version of this paper was originally presented at the TransCanada II Conference at the University of Guelph in October 2007. I'd like to thank Cheryl Suzack and Len Findlay for inviting me to be part of that conference panel and for inspiring me with their own work. Since that time, my thinking has benefited greatly from colleagues who read drafts of this essay and have been important interlocutors: Jennifer Blair, Jennifer Henderson, Matt James, Erica Kelly, Smaro Kamboureli, and Robert Zacharias. Thanks are also due to my research assistant, Sally Fuentes, for locating some of the archival documents discussed in the paper and for checking the bibliographic citations.

1 As part of the Japanese Canadian Redress Settlement, the federal government established the Canadian Race Relations Foundation (CRRF)—an organization with a mandate "to support and promote the development of effective policies and programs for the elimination of racism and racial discrimination" (Canadian Race Relations Foundation). Ironically, the federal government intended that the creation of such an organization would serve as a symbol of reparation for all minoritized groups, thereby serving as a prophylactic against additional redress claims. According to the CRRF, "the government established the [organization] ... instead of paying reparations to other groups seeking redress" in a bid to launch "a preemptive strike against the settlement of further redress claims" (Canadian Race Relations Foundation). In practice, however, the CRRF has complicated attempts to quash additional redress movements, lending support to minoritized constituencies advocating for reparations.

2 Eva Mackey has invoked the phrase "official multiculturalism" to refer to the state-implemented program in Canada. For another incisive critique of

the limits of this policy, see her book *The House of Difference: Cultural Politics and National Identity in Canada*.

3 For a discussion of a series of cultural events during the 1990s (e.g., the "Writing Thru Race" conference in 1994 and the anti-racist policy developed by the Women's Press) through which minoritized writers and anti-racist activists challenged the "sedative politics" of official multiculturalism and, in turn, to which the mainstream media articulated anxiety regarding "ethnic" resistance to the hegemonic status quo, see Kamboureli, 81–92.

4 The Australian Minister of Immigration from 1972 to 1974, Al Grassby, is credited with putting the term "multiculturalism" into circulation in Australia, while government policy on multiculturalism was developed substantially in the Galbally Report of 1978.

5 In contrast to the Canadian context, multiculturalism in the United States arguably developed more as a movement from "below," spurred by "ethnic" or minoritized groups' calls for recognition (Phu 117). In her critique of neoliberal multiculturalism in the United States, Jodi Melamed contends that "[t]he conventional usage history of the term *multiculturalism* begins in the 1970s, when it denoted grassroots movements in primary and secondary education for community-based racial reconstruction.... Since the 1990s, *multiculturalism* has become a policy rubric for business, government, civil society, and education. Those who continue to use it to describe movements for justice on the part of historically marginalized groups often lean on modifiers to emphasize an idea of 'strong' or 'transformative multiculturalism'" (15).

6 The groups seeking redress for discriminatory treatment to which the letter was addressed were: the Canadian Jewish Congress, the Chinese Canadian National Council, the National Congress of Chinese Canadians, the German Canadian Congress, the National Association of Canadians of Origins in India, the National Congress of Italian Canadians, the Ukrainian Canadian Congress and the Ukrainian Canadian Civil Liberties Association.

7 In addition to the many national apologies that have been proffered by the federal government, many provincial and municipal apologies have also been announced over the past two decades, including the Halifax Regional Municipality's apology and compensation package for the razing of Africville.

8 I borrow the phrase "the apology industry" from Barbara Yaffe's 2 June 2008 editorial in the *Vancouver Sun*. While I disagree with many of Yaffe's contentions, the phrase she deploys is suggestive for my critique of the state's project of reconciliation.

9 James notes that despite the supposed end of group-based immigration restrictions, "informal class and gender biases in the points-based immigration regime remain" ("Neoliberal Heritage" 21).

10 The final residential school in Canada ceased to operate in 1996 and was located on the Gordon Reserve in Saskatchewan (Younging 177).

11 In his House of Commons address on 11 June 2008, Harper referred to residential schools as both a "sad episode in our history" and a "sad chapter in our history."

12 The expected average payment for each applicant is $28,000 (Glowacki). See also Katherine O'Neill's article "Graphic List of Abuse to Settle Claims."

13 Only months before Harper's statement, then Minister of Indian Affairs Jim Prentice asserted that the federal government's apology for residential schools would not occur until the end of the TRC. The Conservatives' minority government was criticized for this move and the other parties utilized their day of opposition in the House of Commons on 2 May 2007 to pass a motion for the House to issue a collective apology to residential school survivors.

14 Willie Blackwater, residential school survivor and petitioner of the civil case in which the Supreme Court, in 2005, ruled that both the federal government and the churches were liable for abuse committed at these institutions, was invited to be one of the Aboriginal representatives seated on the floor of the House of Commons on 11 June 2008. Blackwater has been quoted in *The Globe and Mail* as remarking that the plans for and implementation of the apology were rushed. He asserts: "There should have been a lot more time to plan and prepare" (Curry "Lengthy Battle"). Although Aboriginal groups have been calling for an apology for years, the government's implementation of the apology was rushed and disorganized, with sparse details about the plans for the day publicly released only at the last minute.

15 For media coverage of this government report, vaguely entitled "Residential Schools Discussion Paper," refer to the article "Compensating Natives Cheaper" and Wendy Cox's "Who's Sorry Now?"

16 Dale Turner made this important point at "Breaking the Silence: International Conference on the Indian Residential Schools Truth and Reconciliation Commission of Canada" at the Université de Montréal in September 2008.

17 In 2000, the insurance company Aetna Inc. made an official apology for issuing insurance policies on the lives of slaves that made slave owners the beneficiaries in the case of death. J.P. Morgan Chase and the Wachovia Corporation subsequently issued apologies in 2005 for their links to former banks now owned by the companies that accepted slaves as collateral for loans and mortgages made to slave owners.

18 *The Age of Apology: Facing Up to the Past* is the title of a 2008 anthology discussing the proliferation of apologies on the global stage. Paul Gilroy has also recently invoked this phrase (5), while Deena Rymhs has used the term "age of forgiveness" (105).

19 The Australian government made its first official apology on 13 February 2008, expressing regret to Aboriginal and Torres Strait Islander groups for the assimilative policy of removing Aboriginal children from their families that has become known as the "Stolen Generations." On 16 November 2009, the prime minister offered a formal apology to the "home children"—children from poor families or wards of the state who were forcibly sent from England to various colonial colonies between 1920 and 1967 to work as labourers. In 2002, the government of New Zealand apologized to the nation of Samoa for colonial subjugation during the early twentieth century and to the Chinese community in New Zealand for racist immigration policies during the late-nineteenth and early-twentieth centuries. The Queen of England offered an apology to the Tainui tribe of New Zealand in 1995. Since that time, the New Zealand government has apologized to additional Maori tribes such as the Ngai Tahu in 1998 and the Te Uri a Hau in 2004 (Gibbs 154).

20 In her critique of British multiculturalism, Ahmed charts a shift in social discourses surrounding multiculturalism—namely, its decline from a policy that once provided "an image of happy multiculturalism that has now been given up" in the wake of its failure and a loss of social faith in its ability to promote social "integration" (132)—that parallels Kamboureli's assessment of multicultural fatigue in Canada.

21 The latter example regarding the conflation of "human security" with "economic security" is my own addition to Melamed's argument. The concept of "economic security" has, in the wake of the American and international financial crises of 2008, become more resonant than ever.

22 For more information about Nexen Incorporated, refer to their website: http://www.nexeninc.com. The Canadian Defence and Foreign Affairs Institute describes itself as "a charitable, independent, non-partisan, research institute with an emphasis on: Canadian Foreign Policy; Defence Policy; and International Aid." The report mentioned above was authored by Tom Flanagan, Professor of Political Science at the University of Calgary and titled "Resource Industries and Security Issues in Northern Alberta." Flanagan has long been a conservative critic of Indigenous rights issues in Canada and is the author of the book *First Nations? Second Thoughts* (McGill-Queen's, 2000).

23 Beverley Jacobs, then President of the Native Women's Association of Canada utilized the spotlight provided at a reception following the 2008 apology to assert that the government's performance of recompense required action, including endorsement of the UN Declaration (O'Neill, "Aboriginal Leaders").

24 Thanks to Jennifer Blair for pointing out the potential for state co-optation of transcultural formulations of reconciliation and the similarities such tactics might share with multiculturalist strategies.

25 In his apology of 11 June 2008, Stephen Harper concluded his address with the assertion that the TRC "will be a positive step in forging a new relationship between aboriginal peoples and other Canadians" fuelled by "a desire to move forward together with a renewed understanding that strong families, strong communities and vibrant cultures and traditions will contribute to a stronger Canada for all of us."

The Long March to "Recognition": Sákéj Henderson, First Nations Jurisprudence, and *Sui Generis* Solidarity

1 This point was forcefully made by John Ralston Saul in his 2008 book, *A Fair Country*. In the course of his argument for three founding peoples and a "métis civilization" Saul has this to say about Canadian universities: "This is not the sort of argument you are likely to hear at school or university. In fact, our universities are marching resolutely toward an ever more written, Euro-USA derivative, footnoted, theoretically fact-based future. Not even at the height of the British and French empires was there so much cringing here, so much defining of an inferiority complex as respect for meritocracy" (72).
2 For a useful enumeration of the UN-sponsored declarations relating to indigenous intellectual property see the Wikipedia entry. See also Battiste and Henderson (especially 173–200).
3 For the classical allusions in this passage, see Jerome Taylor 216.
4 See *Discover Canada: The Rights and Responsibilities of Citizenship*, a "Study Guide," where Aboriginal and treaty rights are recognized but where instead of autonomous legal traditions and notions of citizenship, Aboriginal peoples are accorded "cultures … rooted in religious beliefs" and "significant achievements in agriculture, the environment, business, and the arts." This paternalism and silence are intellectually indefensible and politically ominous.
5 During his presidential campaign, Obama was honoured with a Native American name. Since election he has encouraged nation-to-nation relations with the federal government and welcomed Aboriginal leaders and now a tribal embassy to Washington. For details see Capriccioso. That said, Obama has been increasingly forced to compromise with power brokers inside the Beltway and to use up energy and political capital in fending off the Tea Partiers.
6 See, for example, Rick Hillier's *A Soldier First: Bullets, Bureaucrats, and the Politics of War* (Toronto: HarperCollins, 2009).
7 Such an account would have to map the burgeoning activities and institutional presence of indigenous intellectuals in Canada and engage at length with

the remarkable rise of indigenous anti-capitalism in the Wasáse movement deriving from the book of that name by Taiaiake Alfred: *Wasáse: Indigenous Pathways of Action and Freedom* (Peterborough, ON: Broadview, 2005).

bush/writing: embodied deconstruction, traces of community, and writing against the state in indigenous acts of inscription

1 nancy argues that "the community cannot arise from the domain of work" (*the inoperative community* 31).
2 among many other references, debord refers to "the passive acceptance it [the spectacle] demands" (section 12, 3).
3 see *political theory of possessive individualism*.
4 marx wrote of the estrangement from other human beings in his 1844 *economic and philosophical manuscripts* (see the chapter on estranged labour) and frequently wrote of the dissolution of communities in *capital* (1867); see, for example, chapter 27 on the expropriation of the agricultural population from the land. the section of his notebooks, the *grundrisse*, pertaining to pre-capitalist social formations are also interesting in this regard.
5 for marx, labour was an activity that lead to a creation; hence, "creative activity" in this sense does not necessarily imply artistic endeavour, though i prefer to maintain that resonance.
6 this is not the place for a lineage that might go back to thomas hobbes. i am thinking particularly of work in the last few decades, from benedict anderson's critically useful *imagined communities* through hardt and negri's work on *multitude* and nancy's work. even though jean-paul sartre, especially in his work on flaubert, has a strong sense of generational change, and in his two *critiques* offers both a productivist grounding of community and a critical distinction between alienated, serial collectives and temporary but more meaningfully fused groups, he does not think intergenerational communities. of course althusser and others emphasized social reproduction but did so in terms of strategies of domination rather than strategies of emancipation.
7 by "imperial centres" i am reverting to an older sense of imperialism than that enunciated in their concept of empire. for a slightly more sustained critique of their work, see my *like the sound of a drum* (71).
8 i deploy the phrase "culture of suspicion" in my essay "six gestures" as a way of contrasting the embodied practices reflective of trust still operating in inuit communities (166); the phenomenon of "gated communities" (discussed by, among many others, mike davis in his *city of quartz*) can be taken as an architectural emblem of the culture of suspicion, where the dominant culture's premise of possessive individualism implies strict protection of private property.

9   while there is an extensive literature documenting the crucial role the capitalist state plays in colonialism, the emphasis of this is on the repressive nature of state interventions. under the influence of foucault's turn away from critical analysis of the state as a locus of power, a good deal of postcolonial cultural studies has tended to ignore the specific role of the state as cultural agent. to develop an approach that looks at the role of the state as a specifically cultural and totalizing agent, i have tended to draw on the work of jean-paul sartre in the *critique of dialectical reason*, hannah arendt's analysis of the relation of colonialism to totalitarianism in *the origins of totalitarianism*, and especially nicos poulantzas (who also focuses on writing) in *state, power, socialism*. anthony giddens has also engaged in work along these lines in *the nation-state and violence*.

10 see *re:eskimos*, supreme court of canada, 1939. the federal and quebec provincial governments referred to the court a question of who had jurisdiction over inuit (each wanted the other to pay bills for relief/welfare of quebec-residing inuit), since indians were a federal responsibility. the court decided that for constitutional purposes inuit were indians. see kulchyski and tester, *tammarniit*, chapter one, and kulchyski, *unjust relations*. inuit were not in any way consulted, as also was the case with st. catherine's milling, a key case determining the nature of aboriginal title in canada, in which the treaty three nations were not involved in any extent (see also *unjust relations*).

11 here marshall sahlins's great essay "the original affluent society" in *stone age economics* still resonates; but see also hugh brody's *maps and dreams*. I have an extended critique of sahlins in *like the sound of a drum* (46–49).

12 these are dealt with in boyce richardson's *strangers devour the land*, and comparisons with manitoba can be found in martin and hoffman's more recent *power struggles*. in quebec, the main conflict started in 1970 with an announcement that dams were about to be built in cree territory. most cree found out by listening to the radio (that is, they were not consulted). a series of struggles lead to a court case in 1973, a land claim in 1975, a renewed proposal for developments in the late eighties, and the more recent "peace of the braves" agreement in 2002.

13 two books deal with the past hydro projects in northern manitoba: james waldram's *as long as the rivers run,* and jean-luc chodkiewicz and jennifer brown's collection *first nations and hydro electric development in northern manitoba*. more recent developments can be followed through *power struggles* (in which I have an article on the wuskwatim project). a film, *green green waters*, was produced dealing with recent developments, and the manitoba wildlands website and manitoba hydro's website are both good sources of information.

14 with regard to hydro developments in manitoba, the chodkkiewicz and brown collection contains useful statements from indigenous opponents.

my own *the red indians* contains some history of indigenous dissidence in canada, as does boyce richardson's collection *drumbeat*. on the global front, robert young's *postcolonialism*, prashad's *the darker nations*, and bagchi's *perilous passage* all provide formidable historical accounts of global colonialism and resistance to it.

15 this description is based on personal observation. my guide to the community was gerald mckay, at that time a municipal councilor. i've written, with ramona neckoway, a study of the community called "the town that lost its name" in *doing community economic development* (loxley, silver, and sexsmith, eds.). the article contains photos that demonstrate this description.

16 i was invited as a researcher and friend of the fort good hope delegation; i took notes that became the "official record" of the meeting. there were no industry or government representatives or, as noted, any other non-natives of any sort, in attendance. my best contribution to the meeting, apart from taking detailed notes, was to stay entirely quiet.

17 this information comes from meetings with the justice seekers of nelson house, ably lead by carol kobliski, and my research assistant and sometimes co-author ramona neckoway, also from nelson house. since my discussions with elders in nelson house were not sshrc funded, ethically stamped, and approved formal interviews, but rather engaged political conversations as an element of my own ethical "giving back" to the community, i sadly cannot name my sources here.

18 here i echo a long line of marxist social critics from lenin's *imperialism* through to bhabha's *nation and narration*; anderson's *imagined communities* and poulantzas's *state, power, socialism* have been particularly important to my work.

WORKS CITED

Abu-Laban, Yasmeen, and Nisha Nath. "From Deportation to Apology: The Case of Maher Arar and the Canadian State." *Canadian Ethnic Studies* 39.3 (2009): 71–98. Print.

Adamoski, Robert, Dorothy E. Chunn, and Robert Menzie, eds. *Contesting Canadian Citizenship: Historical Readings*. Peterborough: Broadview, 2002. Print.

Ahmed, Sara. *The Cultural Politics of Emotion*. New York: Routledge, 2004. Print.

———. "Multiculturalism and the Promise of Happiness." *New Formations* 63 (Winter 2007/2008): 121–37.

Ali, Tariq. *The Clash of Fundamentalisms: Crusades, Jihads and Modernity*. London: Verso, 2002. Print.

Altamirano-Jimenez, Isabel. "Neoliberalism and Social Investment: Reconstructions of Women and Indigeneity." *Women and Public Policy in Canada: Neoliberalism and After*. Ed. Alexandra Dobrowolsky. Toronto: Oxford UP, 2009. 125–44. Print.

Althusser, Louis. "Ideology and Ideological State Apparatuses." Trans. Ben Brewster. *Lenin and Philosophy*. New York: Monthly Review, 1971. 127–86. Print.

Anderson, Benedict. *Imagined Communities: Reflections on the Origin and Spread of Nationalism*. Rev. ed. New York: Verso, 1991. Print.

Angus, Ian. *Identity and Justice*. Toronto: U of Toronto P, 2008. Print.

Appadurai, Arjun. "Grassroots Globalization and the Research Imagination." *Globalization*. Ed. Arjun Appadurai. Durham: Duke UP, 2001. 1–21. Print.

———. *Modernity at Large: Cultural Dimensions of Globalization*. Minneapolis: Minnesota UP, 1996. Print.

"Apology and Reconciliation: A Timeline of Events." *Response, Responsibility, and Renewal: Canada's Truth and Reconciliation Journey*. Ed. Greg Younging, Jonathan Dewar, and Mike DeGagné. Ottawa: Aboriginal Healing Foundation, 2009, 176–77.

Arendt, Hannah. *The Origins of Totalitarianism*. New York: Harcourt Brace Jovanovich, 1973. Print.

Aristotle. *Poetics*. Book Ten. *Classic Writings on Poetry*. Ed. William Harmon. Trans. S.H. Butcher. New York: Columbia UP, 2003. 33–62. Print.

Ariyoshi, Tamao. Review of *Haiiro no Kagayakeru Okurimono*, by Alistair MacLeod. *Nami* 416 (August 2004): 16. Print.

Asian Pacific Authors on the Prairies. Spec. issue of *Prairie Fire* 18.4 (1997): 1–40. Print.

Atherton, Tony. "Finding Vimy amid the Hype." *Ottawa Citizen* 7 April 2007. Web.

Atwood, Margaret. *Danshingu Gaaruzu*. Trans. Sachiko Kishimoto. Tokyo: Hakusuisha, 1989. Trans. of *Dancing Girls and Other Stories*. Toronto: McClelland and Stewart, 1978. Print.

———. *Jijo no Monogatari*. Trans. Eiji Saito. Tokyo: Shincho-sha, 1990. Trans. of *The Handmaid's Tale*. Toronto: McClelland and Stewart, 1985. Print.

———. *Jijo no Monogatari*. Trans. Eiji Saito. Tokyo: Hayakawa-shobo, 2001. Trans. of *The Handmaid's Tale*. Toronto: McClelland and Stewart, 1985. Print.

———. *Kuraki Me no Ansatsusha*. Trans. Yukiko Konosu. Tokyo: Hayakawa-shobo, 2002. Trans. of *The Blind Assassin*. Toronto: McClelland and Stewart, 2000. Print.

———. *Sabaibaru*. Trans. Kayoko Kato. Tokyo: Ochanomizu-shobo, 1995. Trans. of *Survival: A Thematic Guide to Canadian Literature*. Toronto: McClelland and Stewart, 1972. Print.

———. *Taberareru Onna*. Trans. Akio Oura. Tokyo: Shinchosha, 1996. Trans. of *The Edible Woman*. Toronto: McClelland and Stewart, 1969. Print.

———. *Ukabiagaru*. Trans. Kaori Ohshima. Tokyo: Shinsui-sha, 1994. Trans. of *Surfacing*. Toronto: McClelland and Stewart, 1972. Print.

Auerbach, Eric. *Gesammelte Aufsätze Zur Romanischen Philologie*. Ed. Fritz Schalk. Bern/Munich: Francke Verlag, 1967. Print.

Bagchi, Amiya Kumar. *Perilous Passage: Mankind and the Global Ascendancy of Capital*. Toronto: Rowman and Littlefield, 2005. Print.

Baker, Houston A. *Blues, Ideology, and Afro-American Literature: A Vernacular Theory*. Chicago: U of Chicago P, 1984. Print.

Baker, Mona. "Norms." *Routledge Encyclopedia of Translation Studies*, 1998. 163–65. Print.

———, ed. *Routledge Encyclopedia of Translation Studies*. New York: Routledge, 1998. Print.

———, and Gabriela Saldanha, eds. *Routledge Encyclopedia of Translation Studies*. 2nd ed. London: Routledge, 2008. Print.

Bal, Mieke. *Travelling Concepts in the Humanities: A Rough Guide*. Toronto: U of Toronto P, 2002. Print.

Bannerji, Himani. *The Dark Side of the Nation: Essays on Multiculturalism, Nationalism and Gender*. Toronto: Canadian Scholars' Press, 2000. Print.

Banting, Keith, Thomas Courchene and Leslie Seidle, eds. *The Art of the State, Volume III: Belonging? Diversity, Recognition and Shared Citizenship in Canada*. Montreal: Institute for Research in Public Policy, 2007. Print.

Barbour, Douglas. *Lyric/Anti-Lyric: Essays on Contemporary Poetry*. Edmonton: NeWest, 2001. Print.

Barris, Ted. *Victory at Vimy: Canada Comes of Age: April 9–12, 1917*. Toronto: Thomas Allen, 2007. Print.

Barsh, Russel Lawrence, and James Youngblood Henderson. *The Road: Indian Tribes and Political Liberty*. Berkeley, California: U of California P, 1980. Print.

Bassnett, Susan. *Comparative Literature: A Critical Introduction*. Oxford: Blackwell, 1993. Print.

———. *Translation Studies*. London: Routledge, 1991. Print.

Battiste, Marie. "Constitutional Reconciliation of Education for Aboriginal Peoples." *Systemic Discrimination Against Aboriginal Peoples*. Ed. Marie Battiste. Spec. issue of *Directions* 5.1 (2009): 81–83. Print.

———, and James (Sákéj) Youngblood Henderson. *Protecting Indigenous Knowledge and Heritage: A Global Challenge*. Saskatoon: Purich, 2000. Print.

Bedford, David, and Danielle Irving. *The Tragedy of Progress: Marxism, Modernity, and the Aboriginal Questions*. Halifax: Fernwood, 2001. Print.

Bell, Lynne. "The Post/Colonial Photographic Archive and the Work of Memory." *Image and Transcription: An Anthology of Contemporary Canadian Photography*. Ed. Robert Bean. Toronto: Gallery 44 and YYZ Books, 2005. 151–65. Print.

Benjamin, Walter. "Critique of Violence." 1921. Trans. Edmund Jephcott. *Reflections: Essays, Aphorisms, Autobiographical Writings*. Ed. Peter Demetz. New York: Schocken Books, 1986. 277–300. Print.

Bennett, Donna. "Criticism in English 5(c)." *The Oxford Companion to Canadian Literature*. 2nd ed. Ed. Eugene Benson and William Toye. Toronto: Oxford UP, 1977. 251–52. Print.

———. "English Canada's Postcolonial Complexities." *Essays on Canadian Writing* 51–52 (1993–94): 164–211. Print.

Berton, Pierre. *Vimy*. Toronto: McClelland and Stewart, 1986. Print.

Bessai, Diane, and David Jackel. Preface. *Figures in a Ground: Canadian Essays on Modern Literature Collected in Honor of Sheila Watson*. Ed. Diane Bessai and David Jackel. Saskatoon: Western Producer Prairie Books, 1978. Print.

Bhabha, Homi. "Anxious Nations, Nervous States." *Supposing the Subject*. Ed. Joan Copjec. London: Verso, 1994. 201–17. Print.

———. *The Location of Culture*. London: Routledge, 1994. Print.

———, ed. *Nation and Narration*. New York: Routledge, 1990. Print.

Blake, William. *Jerusalem: The Emanation of the Giant Albion*. Ed. Morton D. Paley. Princeton: William Blake Trust/Princeton UP, 1991. Print.

Blodgett, E.D. "The Canadian Literatures as a Literary Problem." *Configuration*. 13–38. Print.

———. Preface. *Configuration: Essays on the Canadian Literatures.* Downsview: ECW, 1982. 6–10. Print.

———. *Five Part Invention: A History of Literary History in Canada.* Toronto: U of Toronto P, 2003. Print.

Borrows, John. *Recovering Canada: The Resurgence of Indigenous Law.* Toronto: U of Toronto P, 2002. Print.

Bourdieu, Pierre. *The Field of Cultural Production: Essays on Art and Literature.* Trans. Claud Du Verlie. Ed. Randal Johnson. Cambridge: Polity, 1993. Print.

Boyden, Joseph. *Three Day Road.* Toronto: Viking Canada, 2005. Print.

Bradford, Richard. *Roman Jakobson: Life, Language, Art.* London: Routledge, 1994. Print.

Brand, Dionne. *Inventory.* Toronto: McClelland and Stewart, 2006. Print.

Brennan, Timothy. *Wars of Position: The Cultural Politics of Left and Right.* New York: Columbia UP, 2006. Print.

Brenner, Neil, and Nik Theodore. "Cities and the Geographies of 'Actually Existing Neoliberalism.'" *Antipode* 34.3 (2002): 349–79. Print.

Breton, Brigitte. "Saine introspection." *Le Soleil* 15 December 2007: 42. Print.

Brodie, Janine. "An Elusive Search for Community: Globalization and the Canadian National Identity." *Review of Constitutional Studies* 7.1–2 (2002): 155–78. Print.

———. "The Social in Social Citizenship." *Recasting the Social in Citizenship.* Ed. Engin Isin. Toronto: U of Toronto P, 2008. 20–43. Print.

Brody, Hugh. *Maps and Dreams: Indians and the British Columbia Frontier.* Harmondsworth: Penguin Books, 1983. Print.

Bromberg, Ava, Gregory D. Morrow, and Deidre Pfeiffer. "Editorial Note: Why Spatial Justice?" *Critical Planning* 14 (2007): 1–3. Print.

Brown, E.K. "The Problem of a Canadian Literature." 1944. *E. K. Brown: Responses and Evaluations: Essays on Canada.* Ed. David Staines. Toronto: McClelland and Stewart, 1977. 1–23. Print.

Brown, Russell M. "The Practice and Theory of Canadian Thematic Criticism: A Reconsideration." *University of Toronto Quarterly*, 70.2 (Spring 2001): 653–89. Print.

Brydon, Diana. "Canada and Postcolonialism: Questions, Inventories, and Futures." *Is Canada Postcolonial? Unsettling Canadian Literature.* Ed. Laura Moss. Waterloo: Wilfrid Laurier UP, 2003. 49–77. Print.

———. "Dionne Brand's Global Intimacies: Practicing Affective Citizenship." *University of Toronto Quarterly* 76.3 (2007): 990–1006. Print.

———. "Metamorphoses of a Discipline: Rethinking Canadian Literature within Institutional Contexts." Kamboureli and Miki 1–16.

Buitenhuis, Peter. *The Great War of Words: British, American and Canadian Propaganda and Fiction, 1914–1933.* Vancouver: U of British Columbia P, 1987. Print.

Bullock, Katherine H., and Gul Joya Jafri. "Media (Mis)Representations: Muslim Women in the Canadian Nation." *Canadian Woman Studies* 20.2 (2000): 35–40. Print.

Cain, Stephen. *American Standard/Canada Dry.* Toronto: Coach House, 2005. Print.

Cajete, Gregory. "Indigenous Knowledge: The Pueblo Metaphor of Indigenous Education." *Reclaiming Indiginous Voice and Vision.* Ed. Marie Battiste. Vancouver: U of British Columbia P, 2000. 181–91. Print.

Cameron, Barry. "English Canadian Discourse in/on Canada." *Studies on Canadian Literature: Introductory and Critical Essays.* Ed. Arnold E. Davidson. New York: Modern Language Association of America, 1990. 124–43. Print.

Campbell, Wilfred. "At the Mermaid Inn." *The Globe* 10 December 1892. *Canadian Poetry.* Canadian Poetry Press. Web.

Canada. Aboriginal Affairs and Northern Development. "Statement of Reconciliation." *Notes for an Address by the Honourable Jane Stewart Minister of Indian Affairs and Northern Development on the occasion of the unveiling of* Gathering Strengths – Canada's Aboriginal Action Plan. 7 January 1998. Web.

———. Canadian Charter of Rights and Freedoms. 1982. Web.

———. Citizenship and Immigration Canada. *Agreement-in-Principle to Highlight Ukrainian Canadian Contribution to Building Canada.* 24 August 2005. Web.

———. Citizenship and Immigration. *Discover Canada: The Rights and Responsibilities of Citizenship.* 2009. Web.

———. Citizenship and Immigration Canada. "Community Historical Recognition Program." 5 June 2009. Web.

———. *The Constitution Act, 1982.* Schedule B to the *Canada Act 1982.* 1982, c.11. Web.

———. House of Commons. *Apology to Former Students of Indian Residential Schools,* 11 June 2008. 39th Parl., 2nd sess., No. 110. Ottawa: Public Works and Government Services of Canada, 2008.

———. House of Commons. *Visible Minorities: Japanese Canadians Interned during World War II – National Redress.* 22 September 1988. 33rd Parl., 2nd sess. Ottawa: Canadian Government Publishing Centre, 1988.

———. *The Indian Act, 1876.* Web.

———. Indian Affairs and Northern Development. *Statement of Reconciliation.* 7 January 1998. Web.

———. Office of the Prime Minister. *Address by the Prime Minister on the Chinese Head Tax Redress.* 22 June 2006. Web.

———. Parliament. House of Commons. *Apology to Former Students of Indian Residential Schools.* 39th Parl., 2nd sess. 2008. Web.

———. *Report of the Royal Commission on Aboriginal Peoples.* Vol. 1. Ottawa: Indian and Northern Affairs, 1996. Print.

———. *Report of the Royal Commission on National Development in the Arts, Letters, and Sciences 1949–1951.* Web.

———. *Speech from the Throne: Strong Leader, a Better Canada.* 16 October 2007. Web.

———. *Speeches from the Throne.* 1867–2009. Web.

———. *Speeches from the Throne and Motions for Address in Reply.* 28 November 2008. Web.

———. Supreme Court of Canada. *Re: Eskimos.* 1939. S.C.R. 104. Web.

———. Veterans Affairs. "The Canadian National Vimy Memorial." 1990. Print.

———. *Visible Minorities: Japanese Canadians Interned during World War II – National Redress.* 33rd Parl., 2nd sess. Ottawa: Canadian Government Publishing Centre, 1988. Print.

"Canada's Expression of Sorrow." *Globe and Mail* 12 June 2008. Web.

Canadian Race Relations Foundation. "Background Paper on the CRRF's Policy on Redress and Reparations." *CRRF-FCRR.CA.* Web.

Cappriccioso, Rob. "Tribal Embassy Opens to Great Fanfare." *Indian Country Today* 17 November 2009. Web.

Castells, Manuel. *The Urban Question: a Marxist Approach.* London: Edward Arnold, 1977. Print.

Charest, Jean. "Open letter from Jean Charest, Quebecers must remain open; The province must not allow fear and intolerance to triumph, premier says." *The Gazette* (Montreal) 30 October 2007: A21. Print.

Cheyne, Ria. "Theorising Culture and Disability: Interdisciplinary Dialogues." *Journal of Literary and Cultural Disability Studies* 3.1 (2009): 101–4. Print.

Chodkiewicz, Jean-Luc, and Jennifer Brown, eds. *First Nations and Hydroelectric Development in Northern Manitoba.* Winnipeg: Centre for Rupert's Land Studies, 1999. Print.

Chow, Rey. *The Age of the World Target: Self-Referentiality in War, Theory, and Comparative Work.* Durham: Duke UP, 2006. Print.

———. *Ethics after Idealism: Theory-Culture-Ethnicity-Reading.* Bloomington: Indiana UP, 1998. Print.

Christie, Norm. *For King and Empire: The Canadians at Vimy, April 1917.* Ottawa: CEF Books, 2002. Print.

Classe, Olive, ed. *Encyclopedia of Literary Translation into English.* Vol. 1. London: Fitzroy Dearborn, 2000. Print.

Cliché, Jean-François. "Accommodements raisonnables: Quel malaise? demande Louis Balthazar." *Le Soleil* 27 November 2007: 8. Print.

Code, Lorraine. *What Can She Know? Feminist Theory and the Construction of Knowledge.* Ithaca: Cornell UP, 1991. Print.

Coetzee, J.M. *Chijoku.* Trans. Yukiko Konosu. Tokyo: Hayakawa-shobo, 2000. Trans. of *Disgrace.* London: Secker and Warburg, 1999. Print.

Coleman, Daniel. *White Civility: The Literary Project of English Canada.* Toronto: U of Toronto P, 2006. Print.

———, and Smaro Kamboureli, eds. *Retooling the Humanities: The Culture of Research in Canadian Universities.* Edmonton: U of Alberta P, 2011. Print.

Coleman, William D., Imre Szeman, and Petra Rethmann. Introduction: "Cultural Autonomy, Politics, and Global Capitalism." *Cultural Autonomy: Fictions and Connections.* Ed. Petra Rethmann, Imre Szeman, and William D. Coleman. Vancouver: U of British Columbia P, 2010. 1–27. Print.

Collini, Stefan. *Absent Minds: Intellectuals in Britain.* Oxford: Oxford UP, 2006. Print.

Collins, H.M., and R.J. Evans. "The Third Wave of Science Studies: Studies of Expertise and Experience." *Social Studies of Sciences* 32.2 (2002): 235–96. Print.

"Compensating Natives Cheaper: Report." *Globe and Mail* 27 July 1998: A5. Print.

Cook, Tim. "Quill and Canon: Writing the Great War in Canada." *American Review of Canadian Studies* 35.3 (2005): 503–30. Print.

Cox, Wendy. "Who's Sorry Now?: Secret Report on Canada's 'Apology.'" *Canadian Press* 10 June 2008. *Settlers in Support of Indigenous Sovereignty (SISIS).* Web.

Creswell, John W. *Research Design: Qualitative, Quantitative and Mixed Methods Approaches.* London: Sage, 2003. Print.

Croteau, Martin. "Face au 'malaise identitaire' des Québécois, Jean-François Lisée lance *Nous.*" *La Presse* 15 November 2007: A25. Print.

Curry, Bill. "Bill Curry on Residential Schools." *Globe and Mail* 10 June 2008. Web.

———. "Lengthy Battle for Public Apology." *Globe and Mail* 11 June 2008. Web.

Damrosch, David. *What Is World Literature?* Princeton: Princeton UP, 2003. Print.

Davey, Frank. "A History of the Coach House Press Translation." N.d. MS.

———. *Post-National Arguments: The Politics of the Anglophone-Canadian Novel Since 1967.* Toronto: U of Toronto P, 1993. Print.

———. *Surviving the Paraphrase: Eleven Essays on Canadian Literature.* Winnipeg: Turnstone, 1983. Print.

Davies, Kevin. *Comp.* Washington, DC: Edge Books, 2000. Print.

Davis, Angela Y. *Abolition Democracy: Beyond Empire, Prisons, and Torture*. Toronto: Publishers Group Canada, 2005. Print.

Davis, Lennard J. "A Grand Unified Theory of Interdisciplinarity." *Chronicle Review* 53.40 (2007): B9. Print.

Davis, Mike. *City of Quartz*. New York: Vintage Books, 1992. Print.

de Bary, Brett. Introduction. *Origins of Modern Japanese Literature*. By Kōjin Karatani. Durham, NC: Duke UP, 1993: 1–10. Print.

de Certeau, Michel. *The Writing of History*. Trans. Tom Conley. New York: Columbia UP, 1988. Print.

de Man, Paul. *The Resistance to Theory*. Minneapolis: U of Minnesota P, 1986. Print.

Debord, Guy. *The Society of the Spectacle*. Trans. Ken Knabb. Detroit: Black and Red, 2002. Print.

Deleuze, Gilles. *Foucault*. Trans., with an introduction, Seán Hand. London: Continuum, 1999. Print.

Denning, Michael. *Culture in the Age of Three Worlds*. London: Verso, 2004. Print.

Derrida, Jacques. *Archive Fever: A Freudian Impression*. Trans. Eric Prenowitz. Chicago: U of Chicago P, 1995. Print.

———. "Force of Law." Trans. Mary Quaintance. *Acts of Religion*. Ed. Gil Anidjar. New York: Routledge, 2002. 230–98. Print.

———. "Interpretations at War." Trans. Mary Quaintance. *Acts of Religion*. Ed. Gil Anidjar. New York: Routledge, 2002. 137–88. Print.

———. *On Cosmopolitanism and Forgiveness*. Trans. M. Dooley and M. Hughes. New York: Routledge, 2001. Print.

Diène, Doudou. "Racism, Racial Discrimination, Xenophobia, and All Forms of Discrimination: Mission to Canada." *United Nations Economic and Social Council, Commission on Human Rights*, 60th session, 1 March 2004. Web.

Dolbec, Michel. "Hérouxville mène une croisade xénophobe, titre Libération." *Le Devoir* 17 February 2007: A4. Print.

Dölling, Irene, and Sabine Hark. "She Who Speaks Shadow Speaks Truth: Transdisciplinarity in Women's and Gender Studies." *Signs* 25.4 (2000): 1195–98. Print.

Dougherty, Kevin. "'Here, It Works like This': Accommodation Hearings in Beauce. Newcomers must conform, mayor insists." *The Gazette* (Montreal) 2 November 2007: A8. Print.

Durflinger, Serge. "Safeguarding Sanctity: Canada and the Vimy Memorial during the Second World War." Hayes, Iarocci, and Bechthold 291–305.

Dutrisac, Robert. "Les musulmans de Québec se plaignent de discrimination. Les politiciens se font aussi égratigner." *Le Devoir* 30 October 2007: A3. Print.

Dybek, Stuart. *The Coast of Chicago*. London: Picador, 2004. Print.

———. Personal interview with Danielle Fuller. October 2004.
Eagleton, Terry. *How to Read a Poem*. Malden, MA: Blackwell, 2007. Print.
Eco, Umberto, and Siri Nergaard. "Semiotic approaches." Mona Baker, *Routledge* 218–22.
Eliadis, Pearl. "How do you avoid cultural conflicts in a multicultural society?" *CBC Cross Country Checkup*. 25 Feruary 2007. Web.
Even-Zohar, Itamar. "Polysystem Theory." *Polysystem Studies*. Spec. issue of *Poetics Today* 11 (1990): 27–94. Print.
Fanon, Franz. *Black Skin, White Masks*. Trans. Charles Lam. New York: Grove, 1967. Print.
Farr, Roger. *Surplus*. Burnaby, BC: LINEBooks, 2006. Print.
Ferguson, Stefan. "Margaret Atwood in German/y: A Case Study." *Translating Canada*. Ed. Luise von Flotow and Reingard M. Nischik. Ottawa: U of Ottawa P, 2007. 93–110. Print.
Fernandez, Sharon, et al., eds. *Awakening Thunder: Asian Canadian Women*. Spec. issue of *Fireweed* 30 (1990): 1–140. Print.
Fernandez, Sonya. "The Crusade over the Bodies of Women." *Patterns of Prejudice* 43.3–4 (2009): 269–86. Print.
Findlay, I.M. Foreword. Battiste, *Reclaiming Indigenous Voice and Vision*. Ed. Marie Battiste. Vancouver: U of British Columbia P, 2000. ix–xiii.
Findlay, Len. "Always Indigenize! The Radical Humanities in the Postcolonial Canadian University." *Ariel: A Review of International English Literature* 31.1, 2 (2000): 307–26. Print.
———. "TransCanada Collectives: Social Imagination, the Cunning of Production, and the Multilateral Sublime." Kamboureli and Miki 173–86. Print.
Flanagan, Tom. "Resource Industries and Security Issues in Northern Alberta." *Canadian Defence and Foreign Affairs Institute*. June 2009. Web.
Fleury, Robert. "Accommodants, dites-vous?" *Le Soleil* 21 October 2007: 24. Print.
Foucault, Michel. *Language, Counter-Memory, Practice: Selected Essays and Interviews*. Trans. Donald F. Bouchard and Sherry Simon. Ed., with an introduction, Donald F. Bouchard. Ithaca: Cornell UP, 1977. Print.
———. "The Order of Discourse." Trans. Ian McLeod. *Untying the Text: A Post-Structuralist Reader*. Ed. Robert Young. Boston: Routledge and Kegan Paul, 1981. 48–77. Print.
———. *Society Must Be Defended: Lectures at the Collège de France 1975–76*. Trans. David Macey. New York: Picador, 2003. Print.
Fraser, Nancy. "Reframing Justice in a Globalizing World." *New Left Review* 36 (November–December 2005): 69–88. Print.

———. "Rethinking Recognition: Overcoming Displacement and Reification in Cultural Politics." *Recognition Struggles and Social Movements: Contested Identities, Agency and Power.* Ed. Barbara Hobson. Cambridge: Cambridge UP, 2003. 21–32. Print.

Freeman, Alan, and Doug Saunders. "Queen, French, Leader Echo PM's Link to Vimy." *Globe and Mail* 10 April 2007: A1, A5. Print.

Frye, Northop. *Anatomy of Criticism: Four Essays.* Princeton: Princeton UP, 1957. Print.

———. "Conclusion." *Literary History of Canada.* 1965. *The Bush Garden: Essays on the Canadian Imagination.* Concord, ON: Anansi, 1995. 215–53. Print.

Fujimoto, Yoko. "Contexts and 'Con-textuality' of Minae Mizumura's *Honkaku-Shosetsu*." *Bulletin of the Graduate Division of Letters, Arts and Sciences of Waseda University* 52.2 (2007): 19–37. Print.

Fuller, Danielle. "Critical Friendships: Reading Women's Writing Communities in Newfoundland." *Women's Studies International Forum* 25:1 (2002): 247–60. Print.

———, and DeNel Rehberg Sedo. "A Reading Spectacle for the Nation: CBC and 'Canada Reads.'" *Journal of Canadian Studies* 40/1 (Winter 2006): 5–35. Print.

———, and Susan Billingham. "CanLit(e): Fit for Export?" *Essays on Canadian Writing* 71 (2000): 114–27. Print.

Gagan, David P. "The Relevance of 'Canada First.'" *Journal of Canadian Studies* 4 (November 1970): 36–44. Print.

Gagnon, Monika Kin. *Other Conundrums: Race, Culture and Canadian Art.* Vancouver: Arsenal, 2000. Print.

Galabuzi, Grace-Edward. *Canada's Economic Apartheid: The Social Exclusion of Racialized Groups in the New Century.* Toronto: Canadian Scholars' Press, 2006. Print.

Galeano, Eduardo. *Open Veins of Latin America: Five Centuries of the Pillage of a Continent.* New York: Monthly Review, 1997. Print.

Garber, Marjorie. "'What's Past Is Prologue': Temporality and Prophecy in Shakespeare's History Plays." Trans. James Strachey. *Renaissance Genres: Essays and Theory, History and Interpretation.* Ed. Barbara Lewalski. Cambridge: Cambridge UP, 1986. 301–31. Print.

Gentzler, Edwin. *Contemporary Translation Theories.* London: Routledge, 1993. Print.

Gibbs, Meredith. "Apology and Reconciliation in New Zealand's Treaty of Waitangi Settlement Process." *The Age of Apology: Facing Up to the Past.* Ed. Mark Gibney et al. Philadelphia: U of Philadelphia P, 2007. 154–70. Print.

Giddens, Anthony. *The Nation-State and Violence.* Berkeley: U of California P, 1987. Print.

Gilroy, Paul. *Between Camps: Nations, Cultures and the Allure of Race*. New York: Routledge, 2004. Print.

Glenn, H. Patrick. *Legal Traditions of the World: Sustainable Diversity in Law*. 2nd ed. Oxford: Oxford UP, 2004. Print.

Glowacki, Wayne. "Residential School Payout a 'Symbolic' Apology: Fontaine." *CBC News* 19 September 2007. Web.

Godard, Barbara. "Contested Memories: Canadian Women Writers In and Out of the Archive." *Annual Review of Canadian Studies/La Revue Annuelle d'Etudes Canadiennes* 27.59 (2007): 59–88. Print.

———. "Structuralism/Post-Structuralism: Language, Reality, and Canadian Literature." 1987. *Canadian Literature at the Crossroads of Language and Culture*. Ed. Smaro Kamboureli. Edmonton: NeWest, 2008. 53–82. Print.

Goldberg, David Theo. *The Racial State*. Oxford: Blackwell, 2002. Print.

Goodspeed, D.J. *The Road Past Vimy: The Canadian Corps 1914–18*. Toronto: Macmillan, 1969. Print.

Gordon, Todd. "Towards an Anti-Racist Marxist State Theory: A Canadian Case Study." *Capital and Class* 91 (2007): 1–29. Print.

Griswold, Wendy. *Regionalism and the Reading Class*. Chicago: U of Chicago P, 2008. Print.

Habermas, Jürgen. *The Structural Transformation of the Public Sphere, an Inquiry into a Category of Bourgeois Society*. Trans. Thomas Burger, with the assistance of Frederick Lawrence Burger. Cambridge: MIT P, 1989. Print.

Hage, Ghassan. *White Nation: Fantasies of White Supremacy in a Multicultural Society*. New York: Routledge, 1998. Print.

Hage, Rawi. *De Niro's Game*. Toronto: Anansi, 2007. Print.

Hainsworth, Jeremy. "Sikhs Don't Accept Apology for Komagata Maru." *Globe and Mail* 31 March 2009. Web.

Hall, Stuart. "Culture, the Media and the 'Ideological Effect.'" *Mass Communication and Society*. Ed. James Curran, Michael Gurevitch, and Janet Woollacott. London: E. Arnold in association with The Open UP, 1979. 315–47. Print.

———. "Media Power and Class Power." *Bending Reality: The State of the Media*. Ed. James Curran, Jake Ecclestone, Giles Carley, and Alan Richardson. London: Pluto, 1986. 5–14. Print.

———. "The Treatment of Football Hooliganism in the Press." *Football Hooliganism: The Wider Context*. Ed. R. Ingham. London: Interaction, 1978. Print.

———, and Chas Critcher, Tony Jefferson, and Brian Roberts. *Policing the Crisis: Mugging, the State, Law and Order*. London: Macmillan, 1978. Print.

Hardt, Michael, and Antonio Negri. *Empire*. Cambridge: Harvard UP, 2000. Print.

———. *Multitude: War and Democracy in the Age of Empire*. New York: Penguin, 2005. Print.

Hardwick, Lorna. *Translating Words, Translating Cultures*. London: Duckworth, 2000. Print.

Harlow, Barbara. *After Lives: Legacies of Revolutionary Writing*. London: Verso, 1996. Print.

Harvey, David. *A Brief History of Neoliberalism*. Oxford: Oxford UP, 2005. Print.

———. *Spaces of Capital: Towards a Critical Geography*. London: Routledge, 2001. Print.

Hay, Peter. Introduction. *The Trial of Jean-Baptiste M*. Vancouver: Talonbooks, 1974. Print.

Hayakawa. *Book Planet: Hayakawa epi <Bukku Puranetto> Sokan*. Tokyo: Hayakawa-shobo, n.d. Print.

———. *World Literature Super Best: Kaigai Bungaku Suupaa Besuto*. Tokyo: Hayakawa-shobo, n.d. Print.

Hayes, Geoffrey, Andrew Iarocci, and Mike Bechthold, eds. *Vimy Ridge: A Canadian Reassessment*. Waterloo: Laurier Centre for Military Strategic and Disarmament Studies and Wilfrid Laurier UP, 2007. Print.

Hayward, Michael. "Talonbooks: Publishing from the Margins." 1991. MS. Talonbook Fonds, Vancouver. Print.

Heinrich, Jeffrey. "Media stir up storm over 'accommodation.'" *The Gazette* (Montreal) 3 February 2007: A9. Print.

———. "Much Ado about What People Wear; Longueuil Residents Sound Off. 'We Shouldn't Concede Anything to Fanatics like That—Not One Thing,' Man Says of Sikhs." *The Gazette* (Montreal) 18 October 2007: A8. Print.

Henderson, James (Sákéj) Youngblood. *First Nations Jurisprudence and Aboriginal Rights: Defining a Just Society*. Saskatoon: Native Law Centre, U of Saskatchewan, 2006. Print.

———. *Indigenous Diplomacy and the Rights of Peoples: Achieving UN Recognition*. Saskatoon: Purich, 2008. Print.

———. "Interpreting *Sui Generis* Treaties." *Alberta Law Review* 36.1 (1997): 46-96. Print.

———. "*Sui Generis* and Treaty Citizenship." *Citizenship Studies* 6.4 (2002): 415-40. Print.

———. *Treaty Rights in the Constitution of Canada*. Toronto: Thomson Carswell, 2007. Print.

Henderson, Jennifer. *Settler Feminism and Race-Making in Canada*. Toronto: U of Toronto P, 2003. Print.

Henigham, Stephen. *When Words Deny the World: The Reshaping of Canadian Writing*. Erin: Porcupine Quill, 2002. Print.

Hillier, Rick. *A Soldier First: Bullets, Bureaucrats, and the Politics of War*. Toronto: HarperCollins, 2009. Print.

Hirano, Keiichi. "Kanada no Bungaku no Haikei." Hirano and Tsuchiya 14–50.

———, and Satoru Tsuchiya, eds. *Komonwerusu no Bungaku*. Tokyo: Kenkyusha, 1983. Print.

Hitchcock, Peter. *Imaginary States: Studies in Cultural Transnationalism*. Urbana: U of Illinois P, 2003. Print.

Hjartarson, Paul. "Culture and the Global State: Postcolonialism, Pedagogy, and the Canadian Literatures." Sugars 101–16.

Hodgetts, A.B. *What Culture? What Heritage? A Study of Civic Education in Canada*. Toronto: Ontario Institute for Studies in Education, 1968. Print.

Hogan, Patrick Colm. *Philosophical Approaches to the Study of Literature*. Gainesville, FL: U of Florida P, 2000. Print.

Hubbard, Tasha, dir. and screenplay. *Two Worlds Colliding*. Prod. Bonnie Thompson. National Film Board of Canada, 2004. Film.

Hucker, Jacqueline. "After the Agony in Stony Places." Hayes, Iarocci, and Bechthold 279–90.

Huntington, Samuel P. *The Clash of Civilizations*. New York: Simon and Schuster, 1996. Print.

Hutcheon, Linda. *The Canadian Postmodern: A Study of Contemporary English-Canadian Fiction*. Toronto: Oxford UP, 1988. Print.

———, and Michael Hutcheon. "A Convenience of Marriage: Collaboration and Interdisciplinarity." *PMLA* 116.5 (2001): 1364–76. Print.

———, with Stephen Scobie, George Bowering, and Robert Kroetsch. "Present Tense: The Closing Panel." *Future Indicative: Literary Theory and Canadian Literature*. Ed. John Moss. Ottawa: U of Ottawa P, 1987. 239–45. Print.

"If you don't stand behind our troops … feel free to stand in front of them." Web. <http://www.supportsticker.ca>

Ikezawa, Natsuki, Toshiyuki Horie, and Yumi Toyozaki. Back cover. *Fuyu no Inu*. Trans. of *Island* by Alistair Macleod. Tokyo: Shinchosha, 2004. Print.

———. "The round-table on the occasion of the 6th anniversary of the Shincho Crest Books: Kofuku na Dokusha ga Mieru Shiriizu." *Nami* 416 (August 2004): 10–19. Print.

"Indigenous Intellectual Property." *Wikipedia*. Web.

Isin, Engin. *Recasting the Social in Citizenship*. Toronto: U of Toronto P, 2008. Print.

Ivison, John. "Chuck Strahl Takes a Risk on First Nations." *National Post* 4 June 2009. Web.

———. "'Rewards' for Reserves: Tories to Unveil Native Funding Strategy." *National Post* 4 June 2009. Web.

Jakobson, Roman. "On Linguistic Aspects of Translation." 1959. *The Translation Studies Reader*. Ed. Lawrence Venuti. 2nd ed. New York: Routledge, 2004. 138–44. Print.

James, Matt. "Do Campaigns for Historical Redress Erode the Canadian Welfare State?" *Multiculturalism and the Welfare State: Recognition and Redistribution in Contemporary Democracies*. Ed. Keith Banting and Will Kymlicka. Oxford: Oxford UP, 2006. 222–46. Print.

———. "Neoliberal Heritage Redress." *Reconciling Canada: Critical Perspectives on the Culture of Redress*. Ed. Jennifer Henderson and Pauline Wakeham. Toronto: U of Toronto P, forthcoming.

———. "The Permanent-Emergency Compensation State: A 'Postsocialist' Tale of Political Dystopia." *Critical Policy Studies*. Ed. Michael Orsini and Miriam Smith. Vancouver: U of British Columbia P, 2006. 321–46. Print.

———. "Wrestling with the Past." *The Age of Apology: Facing Up to the Past*. Ed. Mark Gibney, Rhoda E. Howard-Hassmann, Jean-Marc Coicaud, and Niklaus Steiner. Philadelphia: U of Pennsylvania P, 2008. 137–53. Print.

Jameson, Fredric. "Third-World Literature in the Era of Multinational Capitalism." *Social Text* 15 (1986): 65–88. Print.

Jensen, Klaus B., ed. *A Handbook of Media and Communication Research: Qualitative and Quantitative Methodologies*. London: Routledge, 2005. Print.

Jenson, Jane. "Building Citizenship: Governance and Service Provision in Canada." Ottawa: Canadian Policy Research Network Discussion Paper F (2001): 17. Print.

———. "Social Citizenship in the 21st Century: Challenges and Options." Timlin Lecture. University of Saskatchewan, Regina. February 2001. Web.

———, and Martin Papillon. "Challenging the Citizenship Regime: The James Bay Cree and Transnational Action." *Politics and Society* 28.2 (2000): 245–64. Print.

Jiwani, Yasmin. "Mediations of Domination: Gendered Violence Within and Across Borders." *Feminist Interventions in International Communication, Minding the Gap*. Ed. Katherine Sarakakis and Leslie Regan Shade. Plymouth, UK: Rowman and Littlefield, 2008. 129–45. Print.

Justice, Daniel Heath. "The Necessity of Nationhood: Affirming the Sovereignty of Indigenous National Literatures." *Moveable Margins: The Shifting of Canadian Literature*. Ed. Chelva Kanaganayakam. Toronto: Tsar, 2005. 143–59. Print.

Kagoshima, Yuri. Personal interview with Yoko Fujimoto. 1 August 2007.

———. *Scandalous Bodies: Diasporic Literature in English Canada*. 2000. Waterloo: Wilfrid Laurier UP, 2009. Print.

———. Preface. Kamboureli and Miki vii–xv.

Kamboureli, Smaro, and Roy Miki, eds. *Trans.Can.Lit: Resituating the Study of Canadian Literature*. Wilfrid Laurier UP, 2007. Print.

Kareda, Urjo. "Small publisher wins play rights." *Toronto Star* 19 September 1974: F6. Print.

Kertzer, Jonathan. *Worrying the Nation: Imagining a National Literature in English Canada*. Toronto: U of Toronto P, 1998. Print.

Keshen, Jeff. "The Great War Soldier as Nation Builder in Canada and Australia." *Canada and the Great War: Western Front Association Papers*. Ed. Briton C. Busch. Montreal: McGill-Queen's UP, 2003. 203–15. Print.

Kishimoto, Sachiko. Translator's Postscript. *Danshingu Gaaruzu*. Trans. of *Dancing Girls and Other Stories* by Margaret Atwood. Tokyo: Hakusuisha, 1989. 208–11. Print.

Kitamoto, Takeshi. Personal interview with Yoko Fujimoto. 2 August 2007.

Klarer, Mario. *An Introduction to Literary Studies*. 2nd ed. London: Routledge, 2004. Print.

Klein, Julie Thompson. *Interdisciplinarity: History, Theory, and Practice*. Detroit: Wayne State UP, 1990. Print.

Knowles, Valerie. *Forging Our Legacy: Canadian Citizenship and Immigration, 1900–1977*. Ottawa: Public Works and Government Services, 2000. Print.

Koike, Masayo. Back cover. *Ringo no Ki no Shita de*. Trans. of *The View from Castle Rock* by Alice Munro. Tokyo: Shinchosha, 2007. Print.

Konosu, Yukiko. Translator's Postscript. *Kuraki Me no Ansatsusha*. Trans of *The Blind Assassin* by Margaret Atwood. Tokyo: Hayakawa Shobo, 2002. 669–78. Print.

Korski, Tom. "Vimy Ridge Observance Edging into Weirdness." *Hill Times* 9 April 2007: 13. Print.

Kotake, Yumiko. Translator's Postscript. *Irakusa*. Trans. of *Hateship, Friendship, Courtship, Loveship, Marriage* by Alice Munro. Tokyo: Shinchosha, 2006. 438–45. Print.

Kroetsch, Robert. "A Canadian Issue." *boundary 2* 3.1 (Fall 1974): 1–2. Print.

———. "Disunity as Unity." *The Lovely Treachery of Words: Essays Selected and New*. Toronto: Oxford UP, 1989. 21–33. Print.

———. "The Exploding Porcupine." *The Lovely Treachery of Words: Essays Selected and New*. Toronto: Oxford UP, 1989. 108–16. Print.

Kuhn, Thomas S. *The Structure of Scientific Revolutions*. 3rd ed. 1962. Chicago: U of Chicago P, 1996. Print.

Kulchyski, Peter. *Like the Sound of a Drum*. Winnipeg: U of Manitoba P, 2005. Print.

———. *The Red Indians*. Winnipeg: Arbieter Ring Press, 2007. Print.

———. "six gestures." *Critical Inuit Studies*. Ed. Pamela Stern and Lisa Stevenson. Lincoln: Nebraska UP, 2006. 155–67. Print.

———, and Frank Tester. *Tammarniit (Mistakes)*. Vancouver: U of British Columbia P, 1994. Print.

———, ed. *Unjust Relations: Aboriginal Rights in Canadian Courts*. Toronto: Oxford UP, 1994. Print.

Kymlicka, William. "Ethnocultural Diversity in a Liberal State: Making Sense of the Canadian Model(s)." Banting, Courchene, and Seidle 39–86.

———. "Multiculturalism and Citizenship-Building in Canada." *Building Citizenship: Governance and Service Provisions in Canada*. Vol. F/17. Ottawa: Canadian Policy Research Network Discussion Paper, 2001. 47–70. Print.

Lachapelle, Guy. "Assez, c'est assez!" *Le Devoir* 5 November 2007: A7. Print.

Lai, Larissa. "Community Action, Global Spillage." *Citizenship and Cultural Belonging*. Ed. David Chariandy and Sophie McCall. Spec. issue of *West Coast Line* 59 (Fall 2008): 116–28. Print.

———. "Strategizing the Body of History: Anxious Writing, Absent Subjects and Marketing the Nation." *Asian Canadian Writing Beyond Autoethnography*. Ed. Eleanor Ty and Christl Verdun. Waterloo: Wilfrid Laurier UP, 2008. 87–114. Print.

Lampman, Archibald. "Two Canadian Poets: A Lecture, 1891." *Masks of Poetry: Canadian Critics on Canadian Verse*. Ed. A.J.M. Smith. Toronto: McClelland and Stewart, 1962. 26–44. Print.

LaRocque, Emma. "My Hometown Northern Canada South Africa." 1992. *Native Poetry in Canada: A Contemporary Anthology*. Ed. Jeannette C. Armstrong and Lalage Grauer. Peterborough: Broadview, 2001. 154–59. Print.

Lebowitz, Michael. "Ideology and Economic Development." *Monthly Review* 56.1 (2004). Web.

Lee, Benjamin. "Critical Internationalism." *Public Culture* 7 (1995): 559–92. Print.

Lefebvre, Henri. *La Production de l'Espace*. Paris: Editions Anthropos, 1981. Print.

———. *State, Space, World: Selected Essays*. Trans. Gerald Moore, Neil Brenner, and Stuart Elden. Ed. Neil Brenner and Stuart Elden. Minneapolis: U of Minnesota P, 2009. Print.

Lenin, V.I. *Imperialism, the Highest Stage of Capitalism*. New York: International Publishers, 1939. Print.

———. *The State and Revolution*. 1917. London: Penguin, 1992. Print.

Lentin, Ronit. "From Racial State to Racist State: Ireland on the Eve of the Citizenship Referendum." *Variant* 20 (2004): n. p. Print.

Lenk, Helle-Mai. "The Case of Emilie Ouimet, News Discourse on Hijab and the Construction of Quebecois National Identity." *Anti-Racist Feminism*. Ed. Agnes Calliste and George J. Sefa Dei. Halifax: Fernwood, 2000. 73–88. Print.

"Les Québécois disent non." *La Presse* 27 October 2009: A1. Print.

Lévesque, Kathleen. "Un exercice «de Blancs pour des Blancs» : Des immigrants s'inquiètent de la tournure de la commission Bouchard-Taylor." *Le Devoir* 6 September 2007: A1. Print.

Lighthall, W.D. *Canadian Poets of the Great War*. Ottawa: Royal Society of Ottawa, 1918. Print.

Liu, Alan. *Local Transcendence: Essays on Postmodern Historicism and the Database.* Chicago: U of Chicago P, 2008. Print.

Lloyd, David. "Nationalisms against the State." *Politics of Culture in the Shadow of Capital.* Ed. Lisa Lowe and David Lloyd. Berkeley: U of California P, 1987. 173–96. Print.

Long, Elizabeth. *Book Clubs: Women and the Uses of Reading in Everyday Life.* Chicago: Chicago UP, 2003. Print.

Loveman, Mara. "The Modern State and the Primitive Accumulation of Symbolic Power." *AJS* 110.6 (May 2005): 1651–83. Print.

Loxley, John, Jim Silver, and Kathleen Sexsmith, eds. *Doing Community Economic Development.* Winnipeg: Fernwood, 2007. Print.

Mackey, Eva. *The House of Difference: Cultural Politics and National Identity in Canada.* New York: Routledge, 1999. Print.

Macklem, Patrick. *Indigenous Difference and the Constitution of Canada.* Toronto: U of Toronto P, 2002. Print.

MacLean, K. Seymour. "Education and National Sentiment." 1881. *The Search for English-Canadian Literature: An Anthology of Critical Articles from the Nineteenth and Early Twentieth Centuries.* Ed. Carl Ballstadt. Toronto: U of Toronto P, 1975. 98–107. Print.

MacLeod, Alistair. *Fuyu no Inu.* Trans. Etsuko Nakano. Tokyo: Shinchosha, 2004. Vol. 2. Trans. of *Island.* Toronto: McClelland and Stewart, 2000. Print.

———. *Haiiro no Kagayakeru Okurimono.* Trans. Etsuko Nakano. Tokyo: Shinchosha, 2002. Vol. 1. Trans. of *Island.* Toronto: McClelland and Stewart, 2000. Print.

———. *Kanata naru Uta ni Mimi wo Sumase yo.* Trans. Etsuko Nakano. Tokyo: Shinchosha, 2005. Trans. of *No Great Mischief.* Toronto: McClelland and Stewart, 1999. Print.

MacPherson, C.B. *Political Theory of Possessive Individualism.* Toronto: Oxford UP, 1964. Print.

MacSkimming, Roy. *Making Literary History: House of Anansi Press, 1967–1997.* Concord, ON: Anansi, 1997. Print.

Mahrouse, Gada. "Update on the Taylor Bouchard Commesion on 'Reasonable Accommodation.'" *Racelink, a quasi-journal of RACE* (2008): 18–21. Web.

Mair, Charles. "The New Canada." 1875. *The Search for English-Canadian Literature.* Toronto: U of Toronto P, 1975. 151–54. Print.

Maira, Sunaina. "'Good' and 'Bad' Muslim Citizens: Feminists, Terrorists, and U.S. Orientalisms." *Feminist Studies* 35.3 (2009): 631–56. Print.

Mandel, Eli. Introduction. *Contexts of Canadian Criticism: A Collection of Critical Essays.* Ed. Eli Mandel. Chicago/Toronto: U of Chicago P/U of Toronto P, 1971. 3–25. Print

———. Preface. *Contexts of Canadian Criticism: A Collection of Critical Essays.* vii. Print.

———. *Criticism: The Silent-Speaking Words*. Toronto: CBC, 1966. Print.

———. *The Family Romance*. Winnipeg: Turnstone, 1986. Print.

Manning, Erin. *Ephemeral Territories: Representing Nation, Home, and Identity in Canada*. Minneapolis: U of Minnesota P, 2003. Print.

Marcum, James A. *Thomas Kuhn's Revolution: An Historical Philosophy of Science*. London: Continuum, 2005. Print.

Markell, Patchen. "Recognition and Redistribution." *The Oxford Handbook of Political Theory*. Ed. John S. Dryzek, Bonnie Honig, and Anne Phillips. Oxford: Oxford UP, 2006. 450–69. Print.

Marshall, T.H. *Citizenship and Social Class*. Cambridge: Cambridge UP, 1950. Print.

Marston, Sallie A. "A Long Way from Home: Domesticating the Social Production of Scale." *Scale and Geographic Inquiry*. Ed. Eric Sheppard and Robert B. McMaster. London: Blackwell, 2004. 170–91. Print.

———, Paul Jones, and Keith Woodward. "Human Geography without Scale." *Transactions of the Institute of British Geographers* 31.1 (2006): 416–32. Print.

Martel, Yann. *Pai no Monogatari*. Trans. Noriyuki Karasawa. Tokyo: Take-shobo, 2004. Trans. of *Life of Pi*. Toronto: Knopf Canada, 2001. Print.

Martin, Thibault, and Steven M. Hoffman, eds. *Power Struggles: Hydro Development and First Nations in Manitoba and Quebec*. Winnipeg: U of Manitoba P, 2008. Print.

Marx, Karl. *Capital. Volume 1*. 1867. Trans. Ben Brewster. Toronto: Penguin Classics, 1990. Print.

———. *Economic and Philosophic Manuscripts of 1844*. Trans. Martin Milligan. New York: Prometheus Books, 1988. Print.

———. *Grundrisse*. 1939. Trans. Martin Nicolaus. Toronto: Penguin Books, 1993. Print.

Matas, Robert. "Ottawa Aims to Put Its Stamp on the 2010 Games." *Globe and Mail* 22 August 2008: A1, 3. Print.

Mathews, Robin, and James Arthur Steele. *The Struggle for Canadian Universities: A Dossier*. Toronto: New Press, 1969. Print.

Mathur, Ashok, ed. *Race Poetry, Eh?* Spec. issue of *Prairie Fire* 21.4 (2001). Print.

Mbembe, Achille, and Janet Roitman. "Figures of the Subject in Times of Crisis." *Public Culture* 7.2 (1995): 323–52. Print.

McIntosh, Peggy. "'White Privilege': Unpacking the Invisible Knapsack." *Race, Class, and Gender in the United States: An Integrated Study*. Ed. Paula S. Rothenburg. New York: St. Martin's, 1998. 165–69. Print.

McKenzie, Stephanie. *Before the Country: Native Renaissance, Canadian Mythology*. Toronto: U of Toronto P, 2007. Print.

McWhorter, Ladelle. "Sex, Race and Biopower: A Foucauldian Geneology." *Hypatia* 19.3 (2004): 38–54. Print.

Melamed, Jodi. "The Spirit of Neoliberalism: From Racial Liberalism to Neoliberal Multiculturalism." *Social Text* 24.4 (2006): 1–24. Print.

Miki, Roy. *Broken Entries: Race, Subjectivity and Writing.* Toronto: Mercury, 1998. Print.

———. "Globalization, (Canadian) Culture, and Critical Pedagogy: A Primer." Sugars *Home-Work*. 87–100. Print.

———. *In Flux: Transnational Shifts in Asian Canadian Writing.* Edmonton: NeWest, 2011. Print. Writer as critic series.

———, ed. *Meanwhile: The Critical Writings of bp nichol.* Vancouver: Talonbooks, 2002. Print.

———, ed. *Pacific Windows: Collected Poems of Roy K. Kiyooka.* Burnaby: Talonbooks, 1997. Print.

———. *Random Access File.* Red Deer: Red Deer CP, 1995. Print.

———. *Saving Face: Poems Selected 1976–1988.* Winnipeg: Turnstone, 1991. Print.

Miki, Roy, and Cassandra Kobayashi. *Justice in Our Time: The Japanese Canadian Redress Settlement.* Vancouver: Talonbooks, 1991. Print.

Miki, Roy, and Fred Wah. *Colour. An Issue.* Spec. issue of *West Coast Line*. 28.1–2 (1994). Print.

Mistry, Rohinton. *Bombei no Fushigi na Apaato.* Trans. Takayoshi Ogawa. Tokyo: Bungeishunju, 1991. Trans. of *Tales from Firozsha Baag*. Markham: Penguin, 1987. Print.

———. *Family Matters.* Toronto: McClelland and Stewart, 2002. Print.

———. *Kakumo Nagaki Tabi.* Trans. Takayoshi Ogawa. Tokyo: Bungeishunju, 1996. Trans. of *Such a Long Journey*. Toronto: McClelland and Stewart, 1991. Print.

Mittelstrass, Jürgen. "On Transdisciplinarity." *Science and the Future of Mankind.* Bloomington: Indiana UP, 1964. 495–99. Print.

Morton, Desmond, and J.L. Granatstein. *Marching to Armageddon: Canadians and the Great War 1914–1919.* Toronto: Lester and Orpen Dennys, 1989. Print.

Moss, John. Introduction. *Future Indicative: Literary Theory and Canadian Literature.* Ed. John Moss. Ottawa: U of Ottawa P, 1987. 1–4. Print.

———. *Sex and Violence in the Canadian Novel.* Toronto: McClelland and Stewart, 1977. Print.

Mouffe, Chantal. *On the Political.* London: Routledge, 2005. Print.

Munday, Jeremy. *Introducing Translations Studies: Theories and Applications.* New York: Routledge, 2001. Print.

Municipalité Hérouxville. "Normes de vie." 2007. Web.

Munro, Alice. *Irakusa.* Trans. Yumiko Kotake. Tokyo: Shinchosha, 2006. Trans. of *Hateship, Friendship, Courtship, Loveship, Marriage*. Toronto: McClelland and Stewart, 2001. Print.

———. *Mokusei no Tsuki*. Trans. Kazuko Yokoyama. Tokyo: Chuo-Koron-sha, 1997. Trans. of *The Moons of Jupiter*. Toronto: Penguin, 1982. Print.

———. *Ringo no Ki no Shita de*. Trans. Yumiko Kotake. Tokyo: Shinchosha, 2007. Trans. of *The View from Castle Rock*. Toronto: McClelland and Stewart, 2006. Print.

Murray, Heather. "Reading for Contradiction in the Literature of Colonial Space." *Northrop Frye's Canadian Literary Criticism and Its Influence*. Ed. Branko Gorjup. Toronto: U of Toronto P, 2009. 216–31. Print.

Nadasday, Paul. *Hunters and Bureaucrats*. Vancouver: U of British Columbia P, 2003. Print.

Nairn, Tom. *The Enchanted Glass: Britain and Its Monarchy*. London: Pan Books, 1990. Print.

Nakano, Etsuko. Translator's Postscript. *Fuyu no Inu*. Trans of *Island* by Alistair McLeod. Tokyo: Shinchosha, 2004. 256–62. Print.

Nancy, Jean-Luc. *The Inoperative Community*. Ed. Peter Connor. Trans. Peter Connor, Lisa Garbus, Michael Holland, and Simona Sawhney. Minneapolis: U of Minnesota P, 1991. Print.

Narayan, Uma. *Dislocating Cultures/Identities, Traditions and Third World Feminism*. New York: Routledge, 1997. Print.

National Endowment for the Arts. *The Big Read*. Washington, 2005. Web.

Newman, Dwight G. *The Duty to Consult: New Relationships with Aboriginal Peoples*. Saskatoon: Purich, 2009. Print.

Nieguth, Tim, and Aurélie Lacassagne. "Contesting the Nation: Reasonable Accommodation in Rural Quebec." *Canadian Political Science Review* 3:1 (2009): 1-16. Web.

"No Routine Apology Will Suffice." *Globe and Mail* 10 June 2008. Web.

"No Stoning: Don't stone women to death, burn them or circumcise them, immigrants wishing to live in the town of Hérouxville in Quebec, Canada, have been told." *BBC News* 29 January 2007. Web.

"Notes for an Address by Prime Minister Brian Mulroney. National Congress for the Italian Canadians and the Canadian Italian Business Professional Association." 4 November 1990. Document on file with and courtesy of Matt James.

Office of the Prime Minister of Canada. "Address by the Prime Minister on the Chinese Head Tax Redress." 22 June 2006. Web.

———. "PM speaks at the Commemoration Ceremony for Air India Flight 182." 23 June 2010. Web.

O'Loane, L. "Our Chances for a Literature." 1890. *The Search for English-Canadian Literature: An Anthology of Critical Articles from the Nineteenth and Early Twentieth Centuries*. Ed. Carl Ballstadt. Toronto: U of Toronto P, 1975. 83–85. Print.

O'Neill, Juliet. "Aboriginal leaders hope apology will curb prejudices." *Ottawa Citizen* 13 June 2008.
O'Neill, Katherine. "Graphic List of Abuse to Settle Claims." *Globe and Mail* 25 February 2008. Web.
Ochiai, Keiko. "Kinmirai, Hannkako, aruiwa Riarutaimu no Disutopia." Postscript. *Jijo no Monogatari*. Trans. of *The Handmaid's Tale* by Margaret Atwood. Tokyo: Hayakawa-shobo, 2001. 569–73. Print.
Ogawa, Yoko. Back cover. *Fuyu no Inu*. Trans. of *Island* by Alistair MacLeod. Tokyo: Shinchosha, 2004. Print.
Ogawa, Yoshinori. Translator's Postscript. *Aohige no Tamago*. Trans. of *Bluebeard's Egg* by Margaret Atwood. Tokyo: Chikuma-shobo, 1993. 192–95. Print.
Ohmae, Kenichi. *The End of the Nation State: The Rise of Regional Economies.* New York: Free Press, 1995. Print.
Ohshima, Kaori. Translator's Postscript. *Ukabiagaru*. Trans. of *Surfacing* by Margaret Atwood. Tokyo: Shinsui-sha, 1994. 280–84. Print.
One Book, One Vancouver. Vancouver Public Library. Web.
Ong, Aihwa. *Neoliberalism as Exception: Mutations in Citizenship and Sovereignty.* Durham: Duke UP, 2006. Print.
———. "Neoliberalism as a Mobile Technology." *Transactions of the Institute of British Geographers* 32.1 (2007): 3–8. Print.
Oura, Akio. Translator's Postscript. *Taberareru Onna*. Trans. of *The Edible Woman* by Margaret Atwood. Tokyo: Shinchosha, 1996. 362–66. Print.
Owen, Stephen. "National Literatures in a Global World?—Sometimes—Maybe." *Field Work: Sites in Literary and Cultural Studies.* Ed. Marjorie Garber, Paul B. Franklin, and Rebecca L. Walkowitz. New York: Routledge, 1996. 120–28. Print.
Panitch, Leo. "Globalization and the State." *The Globalization Decade: A Critical Reader.* Ed. Leo Panitch, Colin Leys, Alan Zuege, and Martijn Konings. Halifax: Fernwood Press, 2004. 9–43. Print.
Papineau, Talbot. "An Open Letter from Capt. Talbot Papineau to Mr. Henri Bourassa (1916)." *Canadian Nationalism and the War.* Montreal: 1916, 15–23. *Thomas Fisher Rare Books Library.* Web.
Parker, George L. "Small Presses." *The Canadian Encyclopedia.* Web.
Pearson, David. "Theorizing Citizenship in British Settlers Societies." *Ethics and Racial Studies* 25.6 (2002): 989–1012. Print.
Pease, Donald E. "New Americanists: Revisionist Interventions into the Canon." Special issue, *boundary 2* 17 (Spring 1990): 1–37. Print
Peck, Jamie, and Adam Tickell. "Neoliberalizing Space." *Antipode* 34.3 (2002): 380–404. Print.
Péloquin, Tristan. "Nous avons perdus nos repères: Gérard Bouchard et Charles Taylor sentent clairment qu'il y a un malaise au Québec à l'égard des immigrants." *La Presse* 18 August 2007: A6. Print.

Pennee, Donna Palmateer. "'Après Frye, rien?' Pas du tout! From *Contexts* to *New Contexts*." *New Contexts of Canadian Criticism*. Ed. Ajay Heble, Donna Palmateer Pennee, and J.R. Struthers. Peterborough: Broadview, 1997. 202–19. Print.

———. "Literary Citizenship: Culture (Un)Bounded, Culture (Re)Distributed." Sugars 75–86. Print.

Perrault, Laura-Julie. "Pour un islam à la québécoise: Astrolabe prêche en faveur d'un dialogue entre les grands organismes musulmans." *La Presse* 10 December 2007: A4. Print.

Phu, Thy. "Photographic Memory, Undoing Documentary: *Obasan*'s Selective Sight and the Politics of Visibility." *Essays on Canadian Writing* 80 (2003): 115–40. Print.

Plante, Louise. "Commission Bouchard-Taylor Islamistes et journalistes vertement critiques." *La Presse* 24 October 2007: A9. Print.

Poulantzas, Nicos. *State, Power, Socialism*. Trans. Patrick Camiller. London: Verso, 1980. Print.

Povinelli, Elizabeth. *The Cunning of Recognition: Indigenous Alterities and the Making of Australian Multiculturalism*. Durham: Duke UP, 2002. Print.

Prashad, Vijay. *The Darker Nations*. New York: New Press, 2008. Print.

Pratte, André. "Du kirpan à Saku." *La Presse* 1 November 2007: A20. Print.

"Prime Minister Stephen Harper commemorates the 90th Anniversary of the Battle of Vimy Ridge." 9 April 2007. Web.

Quebec Charter of Human Rights and Freedoms. 1975. Web.

Racial Minority Writers' Committee. *Writing thru Race Final Report*. Toronto: Writers' Union of Canada, 1995. Print.

Radway, Janice. *Reading the Romance: Women, Patriarchy and Popular Literature*. 1984. London: Verso, 1987. Print.

Rajchman, John. "Diagram and Diagnosis." *Becomings: Exploration in Time, Memory, Futures*. Ed. Elizabeth Grosz. Ithaca: Cornell UP, 1999. 42–54. Print.

Razack, Sherene. *Casting Out: The Eviction of Muslims from Western Law and Politics*. Toronto: U of Toronto P, 2008. Print.

———. *Race, Space and the Law: Unmapping White Settler Society*. Toronto: Between the Lines, 2002. Print.

Renan, Ernest. "What Is a Nation?" *The National Reader*. Ed. Omar Dahbour and Micheline R. Ishay. New York: Humanity Books, 1999. 143–55. Print.

Ricci, Nino. *Lives of Saints*. Dunvegan, ON: Cormorant, 1990. Print.

Richardson, Boyce. *Drumbeat*. Toronto: Summerhill, 1990. Print.

———. *Strangers Devour the Land*. Toronto: Macmillan, 1977. Print.

Roberts, Susan, Anna Secor, and Matthew Sparke. "Neoliberal Geopolitics." *Antipode* 35 (2003): 886–97. Print.

Rule, Jane. *The Young in One Another's Arms*. 1977. Vancouver: Arsenal, 2005. Print.

Rüsen, Jörn. "Holocaust Memory and Identity Building: Metahistorical Considerations in the Case of (West) Germany." *Disturbing Remains: Memory, History, and Crisis in the Twentieth Century*. Ed. Michael S. Roth and Charles G. Salas. Los Angeles: Getty Research Institute Publications Program, 2001. 252–70. Print.

Rymhs, Deena. "Appropriating Guilt: Reconciliation in an Aboriginal Canadian Context." *English Studies in Canada* 32.1 (March 2006): 105–23. Print.

Sahlins, Marshall. "The Original Affluent Society." *Stone Age Economics*. Chicago: Aldine-Atherton, 1972. Print.

Said, Edward W. *Culture and Imperialism*. New York: Alfred Knopf, 1993. Print.

———. *Orientalism*. New York: Vintage, 1979. Print.

———. "The Public Role of Writers and Intellectuals." *The Public Intellectual*. Ed. Helen Small. Oxford: Blackwell, 2002. 19–39. Print.

Saito, Eiji. Translator's Postscript. *Jijo no Monogatari*. Trans. of *The Handmaid's Tale* by Margaret Atwood. Tokyo: Shincho-sha, 1990. 563–67. Print.

Sartre, Jean-Paul. *Critique of Dialectical Reason*. Vol 1. Trans. Alan Sheridan-Smith. London: New Left Books, 1978. Print.

———. *Critique of Dialectical Reason*, Vol. 2. Trans. Quintin Hoare. New York: Verso, 1991. Print.

Sassen, Saskia. *Territory, Authority, Rights: From Medieval to Global Assemblages*. Princeton: Princeton UP, 2006. Print.

Saul, John Ralston. *A Fair Country: Telling Truths about Canada*. Toronto: Viking Canada, 2008. Print.

———. *Reflections of a Siamese Twin: Canada at the End of the Twentieth Century*. Toronto: Penguin, 1977. Print.

Saunders, Doug. "From Symbol of Despair to Source of Inspiration." *Globe and Mail* 10 April 2007: A5. Print.

Schagerl, Jessica. "Taking a Place at the Table." *Retooling the Humanities: The Culture of Research in Canadian Universities*. Ed. Daniel Coleman and Smaro Kamboureli. Edmonton: U of Alberta P, 2011. 95–111. Print.

Scherf, Kathleen. "A Legacy of Canadian Cultural Tradition and the Small Press: The Case of Talonbooks." *Studies in Canadian Literature* 25.1 (2000): 131–49. Print.

Scott, Joan Wallach. *The Politics of the Veil*. Princeton: Princeton UP, 2007.

Sharma, Nandita. *Home Economics: Nationalism and the Making of 'Migrant Workers' in Canada*. Toronto: U of Toronto P, 2006. Print.

Sheffield, Gary. "Vimy Ridge and the Battle of Arras: A British Perspective." Hayes, Iarocci, and Bechthold 15–29.

Shields, Carol. *Sutoon Daiarii*. Trans. Keiko Ojima. Tokyo: Shogakkan, 1996. Trans. of *The Stone Diaries*. Toronto: Random House, 1993. Print.

"Shincho Crest Books towa." *Shinchosha Publishing Corporation*. Web.

Shklovsky, Viktor. "Art as Technique." *Russian Formalist Criticism: Four Essays.* Trans. Lee T. Lemon and Marion J. Reis. Nebraska: U of Nebraska P, 1965. 3–24. Print.
Shuttleworth, Mark. "Polysystem Theory." Mona Baker, *Routledge* 176–79.
Siegler, Karl. Personal interview with Kathy Mezei. 14 April 2008.
Siemerling, Winfried. "Rereading the Nation: Cultural Difference, *Transculture*, and Literary History in Canada and Quebec." *Literature and the Nation.* Ed. Brook Thomas. Tübingen: Gunter Narr Verlag, 1998. 183–204. Print.
Simmons, Deborah. "Socialism from Below and Indigenous Resurgence: Reclaiming Traditions." *New Socialist* 15 July 2009. Web.
Smith, Dorothy E. *The Everyday World as Problematic: A Feminist Sociology.* Boston: Northeastern UP, 1987. Print.
———. *Texts, Facts and Femininity: Exploring the Relation of Ruling.* London: Routledge, 1990. Print.
Smith, Malinda. "Race Matters and Race Manners." *Reinventing Canada: Politics of the 21st Century.* Ed. Janine Brodie and Linda Trimble. Toronto: Prentice-Hall, 2003. 108–30. Print.
Smith, Neil. *The Endgame of Globalization.* New York: Routledge, 2005. Print.
———. *The New Urban Frontier: Gentrification and the Revanchist City.* New York: Routledge, 1996. Print.
———. "Scale Bending and the Fate of the National." *Scale and Geographic Inquiry.* Ed. Eric Sheppard and Robert B. McMaster. London: Blackwell, 2004. 193–211. Print.
———, and Jeff Derksen. "Urban Regeneration: Gentrification as Global Urban Strategy." *Stan Douglas: Every Building on 100 Block West Hastings.* Ed. Redi Shier. Vancouver: Arsenal/Pulp, 2002. 62–95. Print.
———, and Cindi Katz. "Grounding Metaphor: Towards a Spatialized Politics." *Place and the Politics of Identity.* Ed. Michael Keith and Steve Pile. London: Routledge, 1993. 67–83. Print.
Solidarity South Pacific. "Background to West Papua." Web.
Sollors, Werner. Introduction. *The Return of Thematic Criticism.* Ed. Werner Sollors. Cambridge, MA: Harvard UP, 1993. ix–xxv. Print.
———. "Thematics Today." *Thematics: Interdisciplinary Studies.* Ed. Max Louwerse and Willie van Peer. Amsterdam: John Benjamins, 2002. 217–36. Print.
Soyinka, Wole. *Myth, Literature and the African World.* Cambridge: Cambridge UP, 1976. Print.
Stanley, Liz, and Sue Wise. "Methodology and Epistemology in Feminist Research Processes." *Feminist Praxis: Research, Theory and Epistemology in Feminist Sociology.* Ed. Liz Stanley. London: Routledge, 1990. 20–60. Print.
Steiner, Peter. *Russian Formalism: A Metapoetics.* Ithaca: Cornell UP, 1984. Print.

Stewart, J.D.M. "In the Political Trenches, Vimy Ridge Fights for the Issue of the Day." *Globe and Mail* 3 April 2007. Web.

Stone, Marjorie. "The Research Matrix, the Metropolis Project, and Multiculturalism Program Critiques: Bridging for Knowledge Mobilization in the Humanities." 2007. MS.

Strong-Boag, Veronica. "The Citizenship Debates." Adamoski, Chunn, and Menzie 69–94.

Sugai, Rieko. Personal interview with Yoko Fujimoto. 13 September 2007.

Sugars, Cynthia. "(Dis)Inheriting the Nation: Contemporary Canadian Memoirs and the Anxiety of Origins." *Movable Margins: The Shifting Spaces of Canadian Literature*. Ed. Chelva Kanaganayakam. Toronto: Tsar, 2005. 177–202. Print.

———, ed., *Home-Work: Postcolonialism, Pedagogy, and Canadian Literature*. Ottawa: Ottawa UP, 2004. Print.

Swyngedouw, Eric. "Neither Global nor Local: 'Glocalization' and the Politics of Scale." *Spaces of Globalization: Reasserting the Power of the Local*. Ed. Kevin R. Cox. New York: Guilford, 1997. 137–66. Print.

Symons, T.H.B. *To Know Ourselves: The Report of the Commission on Canadian Studies*. 2 volumes. Ottawa: AUCC, 1975. Print.

Szeman, Imre. "Poetics and the Politics of Globalization." *Studies in Canadian Literature* 32.2 (2007): 148–61. Print.

———. *Zones of Instability: Postcolonialism and the Nation*. Baltimore: Johns Hopkins UP, 2004. Print.

Tabb, William. "After Neoliberalism?" *Monthly Review* 55.2 (2003). Web.

Tallman, Warren. "Wolf in the Snow. Part One: Four Windows on to Landscapes." *Canadian Literature* 5 (Summer 1960): 7–20; "Part Two: The House Repossessed." *Canadian Literature* 6 (Autumn 1960): 41–48. Print.

Tanke, Joseph. "Michel Foucault at the Collège de France." *Philosophy and Social Criticism* 31 (2005): 687–97. Print.

Taussig, Michael. *Shamanism, Colonialism, and the Wild Man: A Study in Terror and Healing*. Chicago: U of Chicago P, 1987. Print.

Taylor, Jerome, trans. and introduction. *The "Didascalicon" of Hugh of St. Victor: A Medieval Guide to the Arts*. New York: Columbia UP, 1961. Print.

Taylor, Timothy. *Stanley Park*. Toronto: Vintage Canada, 2001. Print.

Tilly, Charles. *Coercion, Capital, and European States, AD 990–1990*. Cambridge: Blackwell, 1990. Print.

Toury, Gideon. *Descriptive Translation Studies and Beyond*. Amsterdam: John Benjamins, 1995. Print.

Toyozaki, Yumi. "Kuresuto Bukkusu Mittsu no Miryoku." *Nami* 463 (July 2008): 64–65. Print.

Trouillot, Michel-Rolph. "Abortive Rituals: Historical Apologies in the Global Era." *Interventions* 2.2 (2000): 171–86. Print.
Turner, Bryan. "Conceptual Problems in the Theory of Citizenship." *Citizenship and Social Theory*. Ed. Bryan Turner. London: Sage, 1993. 1–23. Print.
Urquhart, Jane. *The Stone Carvers*. Toronto: McClelland and Stewart, 2001. Print.
Valpy, Michael. "The Making of a Myth: Michael Valpy on How a Minor Battle for a French Hill Morphed into Canada's Defining Moment." *Globe and Mail* 7 April 2007: A1, F4. Print.
———. "Setting Legend in Stone." *Globe and Mail* 7 April 2007: F5. Print.
Valverde, Mariana. "Society Must Be Defended: Lectures at the Collège de France 1976–77." *Law, Culture and Humanities* 1 (2005): 119–28. Print.
van Dijk, Teun A. *Elite Discourse and Racism*. Vol. 6, *Race and Ethnic Relations*. Newbury Park, CA: Sage, 1993. Print.
———. *Racism and the Press*. London: Routledge, 1991. Print.
Vance, Jonathan. *Death So Noble: Memory, Meaning, and the First World War*. Vancouver: U of British Columbia P, 1997. Print.
"Vimy, 90 Years Later." *Canada.com* 3 April 2007. Web.
Wah, Fred. *Faking It: Poetics and Hybridity. Critical Writing 1984–1999*. Edmonton: NeWest, 2000. Print. Writer as critic series VII.
———. *Waiting for Saskatchewan*. Winnipeg: Turnstone, 1985. Print.
Waldram, James. *As Long as the Rivers Run*. Winnipeg: U of Manitoba P, 1988. Print.
Walia, Harsha. "Really Harper, Canada Has No History of Colonialism?" *The Dominion* 28 September 2009. Web.
Warley, Linda, John Clement Ball, and Robert Viau. Introduction: "Mapping the Ground." *Writing Canadian Space*. Ed. Warley, Ball, and Viau. Spec. issue of *Studies in Canadian Literature* 23.1 (1998): 1–7. Print.
Weber, Max. "Politics as Vocation." *Max Weber: Essays in Sociology*. Ed. Hans Heinrich Gerth and Charles Wright Mills. London: Routledge, 1991. 77–128. Print.
Weech, Terry L., and Marina Pluzhenskaia. "LIS Education and Multidisciplinarity: An Exploratory Study." *Journal of Education for Library and Information Science* 46.2 (2005): 154–64. Print.
Weis, Linda. *The Myth of the Powerless State*. Ithaca: Cornell UP, 1998. Print.
West, Cornel. "The New Cultural Politics of Difference." *Out There: Marginalization and Contemporary Cultures*. Ed. Russell Ferguson, Martha Gever, Trinh T. Minh-ha, and Cornel West. Cambridge: MIT Press, 1990. 19–38. Print.
Williams, David. *Imagined Nations: Reflections on Media in Canadian Fiction*. Montreal: McGill-Queen's UP, 2003. Print.

———. *Media, Memory, and the First World War*. Montreal: McGill-Queen's UP, 2009. Print.

Williams, Raymond. "Culture Is Ordinary." 1958. *The Raymond Williams Reader*. Ed. John Higgins. Malden: Wiley-Blackwell, 2001. 10–24. Print.

Witoszek, Nina, and Lars Trägårdh, eds. *Culture and Crisis: The Case of Germany and Sweden*. New York: Berghahn Books, 2002. Print.

Wood, Ellen Mieksin. *The Origin of Capitalism: A Longer View*. London: Verso, 2002. Print.

Wood, Patricia K. "Aboriginal/Indigenous Citizenship: An Introduction." *Citizenship Studies* 7.4 (2003): 371–78. Print.

Woodcock, George. "New Wave in Publishing." *Canadian Literature* 57 (1973): 50–64. Print.

Yaffe, Barbara. "The Apology Industry." *Vancouver Sun* 2 June 2008. Web.

Yamada, Taichi. Back cover. *Haiiro no Kagayakeru Okurimono*. Trans. of *Island* by Alistair Macleod. Tokyo: Shinchosha, 2002. Print.

Yamanouchi, Hisaaki. *The Search for Authenticity in Modern Japanese Literature*. New York: Cambridge UP, 1978. Print.

Yeğenoğlu, Meyda. *Colonial Fantasies: Towards a Feminist Reading of Orientalism*. Cambridge: Cambridge UP, 1998. Print.

"You Can Stay in Canada as Long as You Don't Stone Your Women." *New Zealand Herald* 1 February 2007. Web.

Young, Robert. *Postcolonialism: An Historical Introduction*. Oxford: Blackwell, 2008. Print.

Zine, Jasmin. "Unsettling the Nation: Gender, Race and Muslim Cultural Politics in Canada." *Studies in Ethnicity and Nationalism* 9.1 (2009): 146–93. Print.

Žižek, Slavoj. "Multiculturalism, or, the Cultural Logic of Multinational Capitalism." *New Left Review* 225 (September/October 1997): 28–50. Print.

CONTRIBUTORS

JANINE BRODIE holds a Canada Research Chair in Political Economy and Social Governance and Trudeau Fellowship at the University of Alberta. She has written numerous books and book chapters on many of the core challenges in Canadian politics and public policy, including gender equality, citizenship, social policy, continental integration, and transformations in governance and is broadly published in national and international scholarly journals.

JEFF DERKSEN works with an interdisciplinary view of culture and globalization in the twentieth century. His research deals with the relationship of cultural production (what Raymond Williams called "creative practices") and the nexus of social, political, economic, and cultural forces that constitute globalization. His areas of special interest are national cultures and the role of the state in the era of globalization; cultural imperialism and the politics of aesthetics; the poetry and poetics of globalized cities; the emergent global cultural front (in a general cultural context and in avant-gardes); culture and gentrification in global-urban spaces; architecture and urbanism; cultural poetics, cultural studies, and cultural geography.

LEN FINDLAY is Director of the Humanities Research Unit at the University of Saskatchewan and member of the Indigenous Humanities group. Among his many publications are "Always Indigenize! The Radical Humanities in the Postcolonial Canadian University" (*Ariel*) and "Extraordinary Renditions: Translating the Humanities Now" (*Re-Tooling the Humanities*).

DANIELLE FULLER is Senior Lecturer in Canadian Studies at the University of Birmingham (UK). Her chief research areas are contemporary Canadian writing, particularly Atlantic Canadian literary culture; the politics of cultural production in Canada, and reading communities in present-day North America and the UK. She is also committed to interdisciplinary research methods that combine empirical and textual strategies. Her many publications include *Writing the Everyday: Women's Textual Communities in Atlantic Canada* (McGill-Queen's UP, 2004), which explores how and why communities form around texts that record women's everyday realities, histories, and traditions. She is currently completing a monograph, with DeNel Rehberg Sedo, entitled *Reading Beyond the Book: The Social Practices of Contemporary Literary Culture*.

YOKO FUJIMOTO taught literatures in English and critical theory at Waseda University, Tokyo. Her research interests included contemporary Canadian literature, cultural translation, and the novel as a form of representing knowledge. Her recent publications include "Arts and Other Worlds: Representations of Knowledge in Michael Ondaatje's *Anil's Ghost*," included in *Kanada Kenkyu Nempo*. Yoko passed away in May 2011, during the development of this book.

MONIKA KIN GAGNON is Associate Professor in the Department of Communication Studies at Concordia University. Author of *Other Conundrums: Race, Culture and Canadian Art* (2000) and, with Richard Fung, *13 Conversations About Art and Cultural Race Politics* (2002), she has published extensively on culture, media, the visual arts, and film. She recently completed the DVD collection *Charles Gagnon: 4 Films* (2009) and the Korsakow film *Archiving R69* (2011). Her current research includes an anthology on Canadian multi-screen films at Expo 67 and the intermedia practice of Theresa Hak Kyung Cha.

YASMIN JIWANI is an Associate Professor in the Department of Communication Studies at Concordia University, Montreal. Her publications include: *Discourses of Denial: Mediations of Race, Gender and Violence*, as well as a co-edited collection titled *Girlhood, Redefining the Limits*. Yasmin is also a co-founder of Researchers and Academics of Colour for Equity (RACE), a Canadian-based organization. Her work has appeared in various journals and anthologies. Her research interests include mediations of race, gender, and violence in the context of war stories, femicide reporting in the press, and representations of women of colour in popular television programs.

SMARO KAMBOURELI is Professor and Canada Research Chair, Tier 1, in Critical Studies in Canadian Literature at the University of Guelph, and Director of TransCanada Institute. She has edited and co-edited many volumes, most recently with Daniel Coleman, *Retooling the Humanities: The Culture of Research in Canadian Universities* and, with Roy Miki, *Trans.Can.Lit: Resituating the Study of Canadian Literature*, the first volume of the TransCanada project (Transcanadas.ca). She is also the author of *Scandalous Bodies: Diasporic Literatures in English Canada* and the editor of the two editions of the anthology *Making a Difference: Canadian Multicultural Literature*.

PETER KULCHYSKI is a professor in the Department of Native Studies at the University of Manitoba. His research interests include Aboriginal cultural politics; political development in the NWT and Nunavut; contemporary critical theory; land claims and self-government; Inuit history; and performance studies. His many publications include *Kiumajuk [Talking Back]: Game Management and Inuit Rights in Nunavut 1900 to 1970*, with Frank Tester (2007); *Like the Sound of a Drum: Aboriginal Cultural Politics in Denendeh and Nunavut* (2006); and *The Red Indians* (2007).

LARISSA LAI is a poet, novelist, critic, and Assistant Professor in the Department of English at the University of British Columbia. Her publications include *Salt Fish Girl* (2002), *sybil unrest* (with Rita Wong, 2008), and *When Fox Is a Thousand* (1995). She has been the writer-in-residence at the University of Calgary, Simon Fraser University, and, most recently, the University of Guelph. Her first solo full-length poetry book, *Automaton Biographies* (2009), was a finalist for the Dorothy Livesay Poetry Prize.

KATHY MEZEI is Professor Emeritus in the Department of Humanities at Simon Fraser University. Recent and forthcoming books include *Domestic Modernism, the Interwar Novel, and E.H. Young* (2006), co-written with Chiara Briganti; *The Domestic Space Reader*, edited with Chiara Briganti (2012); and *Translation Effects: The Shaping of Modern Canadian Culture*, edited with Luise von Flotow and Sherry Simon (2012). She was a visiting fellow at Clare Hall, Cambridge, in 2011.

PAULINE WAKEHAM is an Associate Professor in the Department of English at the University of Western Ontario, where she teaches and researches in the fields of Canadian and indigenous literary and cultural studies. She is the author of *Taxidermic Signs: Reconstructing Aboriginality* (University of Minnesota Press, 2008) and is currently co-editing, with Jennifer Henderson, a volume of essays titled *Reconciling Canada: Critical Perspectives on the Culture of Redress*.

ROBERT ZACHARIAS is a SSRHC Postdoctoral Fellow at the University of Toronto, where he works out of the Centre for Diaspora and Transnational Studies. His research interests include Canadian literature, Mennonite writing, critical theory, and migration fiction. He has recent publications in *Mosaic* and *Studies in Canadian Literature*, as well as in the edited collections *Embracing Otherness* (2010) and *Narratives of Citizenship* (2011).

INDEX

Aboriginal peoples and communities, 91, 93, 95, 103, 105–8, 128, 138, 142, 144, 155, 175, 212–13, 215–17, 220–22, 224–25, 228–33, 235–47, 263–64, 272n15, 282n3, 296n14, 297n19, 298n25, 298nn4–5, 300n10; aboriginality, 31, 35–36, 107; aboriginalization, 95, 106–7; jurisprudence, 4, 235, 243–46; law, 106, 232–38; rights, 91–92, 95, 105, 231–33, 235–40, 244, 263, 298n4; spiritual allegiances, 241–43. *See also* apology: to Aboriginal peoples in Canada; "Indian"; Indian Act; Indigeneity; land claims; residential schools
absinthe, 153
Affaire Hérouxville, 129–38, 144–45, 149
Africville, 227, 230, 295n7
Aggarwal, Pramila, 163
Ahmed, Sara, 169, 228, 297n20
Albright, Marilyn, 238
Ali, Tariq, 286n7
Allward, Walter, 122–23, 125–26, 284n9
Altamirano-Jimenez, Isabel, 95
Althusser, Louis, 53, 299n6
American and Afro-American literary studies, 8, 25–26
amnesia, national, 111, 114, 127, 128
Anderson, Benedict, 108, 114, 117–19, 283n2, 287n1, 288n5, 299n6, 301n18
anti-racism and anti-racist politics, 10, 51–52, 61, 151–54, 161, 171–72, 214, 288n4, 295n3

apology, 93, 209, 212–19, 226–27, 232, 296n14, 297n19; to Aboriginal Australians, 297n19; to Aboriginal peoples in Canada, 217–18, 220–24, 296nn13–14, 297n3, 298n25; to Chinese Canadians, 209, 218; industry, 216–25, 295n8; to Italian Canadians, 217, 222; to Japanese Canadians, 209, 216; to South Asian Canadians, 225. *See also* reconciliation
Appadurai, Arjun, 13, 42, 46, 278n4
archives and archiving, 12, 60, 173–78, 185–86, 224, 284n5, 290n3
Arendt, Hannah, 300n9
Armstrong, Jeannette, 11
Ariyoshi, Tamao, 206
Asian Canadians, 92, 94, 154–72, 288n5; literature and studies, 14, 152–72
Assembly of First Nations, 223, 235, 258
Association of Canadian Studies, 270n5
Atwood, Margaret, 20–21, 187–95, 198–202; *The Blind Assassin*, 191–93, 202; *Bluebeard's Egg*, 199; *Dancing Girls and Other Stories*, 188, 191, 199; *The Edible Woman*, 201–2; *The Handmaid's Tale*, 191–92, 199–200, 202; *Surfacing*, 199–201, 294n13; *Survival*, 20, 187–88, 201
Auerbach, Eric, 236, 244
Australia, 69, 93; apology to and reconciliation with Aboriginal Australians, 215, 227, 297n19; term multiculturalism in, 295n4
Austro-Hungarian Canadians, 100

Bacque, James, 290n10
Bagchi, Amiya Kumar, 255, 301n14
Baker, Houston, 24, 25–26
Ball, John Clement, 20–21
Bannerji, Himani, 12, 154
Bannerji, Kaushalya, 163
Barbour, Douglas, 168
Barris, Ted, 117
Barsh, Russel, 238
Bassnett, Susan, 174–75, 189
Battiste, Marie, 238
Beaulieu, Victor-Lévy, 182
Benjamin, Walter, 118–20, 262, 284nn7–8
Bennett, Donna, 21, 23–24
Berton, Pierre, 117, 122–23
Bessai, Diane, 2
Beyond the Book, 65, 70–71, 74–75, 78–84, 280n1, 280n2, 280n5
Bezmozgis, David, 203, 206; *Natasha*, 206
Bhabha, Homi, 42, 114, 158, 301n18
bilingualism: official, 174, 184
Billingham, Susan, 67–68
biopolitics, 4, 88, 96–107, 243
Blais, Marie-Claire, 178, 179
Blake, William, 244
Blodgett, E.D., 20, 21–22, 23, 26
Bloom, Harold, 23, 25
book clubs, 4, 54, 69
Borrows, John, 233
Bouchard, Gérard, 129, 130, 140
Bouchard, Michel Marc, 179
Bouchard-Taylor Commission, 129–30, 133, 135, 137–45, 148–49
Bourdieu, Pierre, 181, 184
Boyden, Joseph, 128
Brand, Dionne, 42, 56, 59–60; *Inventory*, 59–60
Brennan, Timothy, 38, 47
British Empire, 99, 100, 101, 103, 112–13, 121, 298n1

British North America Act, 91, 109, 265
Brody, Hugh, 250, 300n11
Broken Jaw Press, 185
Brossard, Nicole, 182
Brown, E.K., 110
Brown, Jennifer, 300n13
Brown, Jim, 177, 179, 292n19, 292n24
Brown, Russell, 20
Brydon, Diana, 5, 60, 85, 283n2
Buck, Robbie, 258
Bullock, Katherine H., 144
Burke, Edmund, 10
Burnham, Clint, 59
bush writings, 4, 259, 260, 267
Butler, Judith, 274n28, 287n1
Butschek Books, 185

Cabral, Amilcar, 250–51
Cabri, Louis, 59
Cain, Stephen, 42, 59, 60
Cameron, Barry, 19–20, 275n32
Campbell, Maria, 273n18
Campbell, Wilfred, 110
Canada Council for the Arts, 153, 174, 176, 177, 179, 184, 185, 272n17, 292n24
Canada Reads, 69, 70, 73–74, 82
Canadian Battlefield Memorials Commission, 122
Canadian Broadcasting Corporation (CBC), 69, 133
Canadian Charter of Human Rights, 133–34
Canadian Defence and Foreign Affairs Institute, 230, 297n22
Canadian government. *See* Government of Canada
Canadian Islamic Congress, 135
Canadian Italian Business Professional Association, 216

Canadian Jewish Congress, 295n6
Canadian Literary Society of Japan, 187, 188
Canadian Literature (journal), 153
Canadian literature and literary studies, 53, 59, 61–63, 73, 75, 84–85, 151, 184, 187–90, 196, 198, 200–202, 206–8, 262, 269n1, 269n3, 276n42, 276n44; disciplinary formation and contexts, 2–36, 43, 44; ethical turn in, 114–15, 284n4; as institution, 15, 19–20, 30, 62, 68–69, 120, 128, 270n5, 276n42
Canadian Multiculturalism Act, 213
Canadian nation: colonial and imperial logics of, 4, 39, 87–108, 120, 151–72, 212, 220–21, 229–31, 239–40, 249–67, 284n8; cultural constructs of, 43; originary violence and, 109–12, 114–16, 118–20, 122, 128; sovereignty and, 120
Canadian Nationals Act, 102
Canadian Race Relations Foundation, 294n1
canon and canonicity, 12, 18, 173, 179, 185
Cardinal, Harold, 235
Carrier, Roch, 182, 183
Castells, Manuel, 38
Cavell, Richard, 1, 276
celebrity, culture of, 193, 238
Centre culturel islamique de Québec, 144
Chan, Kim-Man, 164–69
Charest, Jean, 129, 132, 133, 137–38
Charlottetown Accord, 216, 217
Charter of Rights and Freedoms, 213, 216
Cheyne, Ria, 34
Chinese Canadians, 92, 102–3, 155, 216, 219, 225, 289n5

Chinese Canadian Head Tax and Exclusion Act, 10, 91, 103, 115, 155, 157, 209, 218, 222, 227, 289n5
Cho, Lily, 1
Chow, Rey, 47, 168
Christie, Norm, 124
citizen and citizenship, 31, 35, 50, 52, 56–58, 61, 87–99, 107–8, 118, 137, 165–66, 172, 229, 235–37, 241, 245–46, 259, 283n6, 287n1, 298n4; in Canada, 88–93, 98–99, 218; conditional forms of, 146–47; as field of study, 87–88, 96; as legal status, 87, 90; normative, 144–46; in Quebec, 133, 137; rights, 87–92; settler conceptions of, 94–96, 98, 106
"Citizen's Code" (Hérouxville), 132–33
Citizenship and Immigration Canada, 237
civility, Canadian, 23, 147, 210–12, 225–31. *See also* white civility
Claxton, Patricia, 178
Coach House Press, 181, 182
Coetzee, J.M., 192, 193, 194; *Disgrace*, 193, 194
Coleman, Daniel, 23, 114–15, 210, 212–15, 223, 227, 231, 283n2
Coleman, Victor, 181
collaboration and collaborative work, 4, 32, 65–66, 68–69, 75–78, 84–85, 186, 235, 238, 263
Collis, Stephen, 59
colonialism: theory and discourse, 44, 45, 167, 240, 273n23, 300n9; colonial logic, 4, 39, 96; in North America, 92, 93. *See also* neo-colonialism; post-colonialism
commemoration, 122, 124, 221, 222
commodification, 257; commodity culture and, 51, 56, 265; of culture and history, 59, 190, 254, 260

community, 12, 19, 108, 118–19, 151, 155–56, 163, 166, 186, 251–52, 258, 289n5; claims of ownership, 55; formation, 52; global literary, 202; imagined, 51, 55, 58, 183; in modern nation-state, 114; of readers, 69–70, 72, 74, 208
Community Historical Recognition Program, 219, 220, 221
comparative literature and studies, 21–22
cosmopolitanism, 42, 50, 51, 55, 59, 133, 237
cosmopolitics, 42, 50
Coteau Books, 181
Creswell, John W., 76
crisis, 4, 8, 9, 11, 19, 36, 41, 43, 52, 63, 109–20, 128, 201, 271n14
critical race theories and theorists, 87, 89, 96
Culleton, Beatrice, 11
cultural appropriation, 10
cultural theory, 37–38, 41, 45–50, 66, 78, 278n3

Daily Star, 125–26
Dalpé, Jean Marc, 185
Damrosch, David, 270n7
Davey, Frank, 12, 24, 43, 182, 183, 275n34, 292n20
Davies, Kevin, 59
Davis, Angela, 240
Davis, Jane, 74, 280n6
Davis, Mike, 299n8
Debord, Guy, 251, 299n2
de Certeau, Michel, 15, 273n23
Declaration on the Rights of Indigenous Peoples, 231, 240
defamiliarization, 7, 10, 77. See also making strange
Deleuze, Gilles, 16, 160, 274n27
Deloria, Vine, Jr., 238

de Lotbinière-Harwood, Susanne, 175
de Man, Paul, 7
Denning, Michael, 38
de Pasquale, Dominique, 184
Derrida, Jacques, 28, 119–20, 128, 152, 174, 177, 216, 225–26, 227, 274n25, 284n8, 290n3
de-territorialization, 38, 40, 46, 47, 59
Le Devoir, 135, 137, 141, 143, 144
diasporic populations and subjectivities, 36, 68, 91, 213, 215, 225, 227, 233, 236–37, 277n53, 282n2
Diène, Doudou, 226–27
disciplinarity, transing, 32–37. See also interdisciplinarity; transdisciplinarity
discipline(s), 1–36, 78, 85, 274n26, 277nn52–54; disciplinary formations, 18, 24, 26, 274n25; history as, 63, 273n23; undisciplining the, 8–14
diversity, ethnic and cultural, 88–93, 107–8, 139, 163, 214–16, 221, 227
drama, Canadian, 177–81, 185, 290–91n10
Dubé, Marcel, 290n10, 291n11
Durflinger, Serge, 125
Dybek, Stuart, 74

Eagleton, Terry, 6
Eco, Umberto, 197
economy and economics, 1, 11, 13, 37–63, 100, 108, 191–92, 229–31, 235, 242, 254–62, 267, 278–79n4, 286n7, 293n7, 297n21
editorials and editorial introductions, 23, 117, 126, 142, 151, 153–54, 159, 163–64, 170–71, 181, 191–93, 271n11, 295n8
Ekstasis, 185
Eliadis, Pearl, 133, 134

Ellenwood, Ray, 183
Emberley, Julia, 1, 272n15
emergence, 5, 8–13, 15, 17; emergent discourses, events, 3, 8–18, 24–30, 31, 272n16, 273nn18–19
empire, 42, 43, 60, 162, 239, 252, 299n7. *See also* British Empire
Episkenew, Jo-Ann, 272n15
epistemological shifts and changes, 7, 24, 26, 77, 281n11
ethnic and ethnicity, 15, 90–94, 96, 134, 142, 152, 165, 175, 213, 282n2, 295n3, 295n5; categories of, 94, 215; hierarchies of, 87–88, 93, 99, 101
Even-Zohar, Itamar, 189, 197–98
Exile Editions, 185
experimental literature, 171–72, 175, 178–79, 181–82, 185
*ex*tensive readings, 5, 270n7

Fanon, Franz, 95, 146, 250–51, 258
Farr, Roger, 42; *Surplus*, 56–58
Farrell, Dan, 59
feminism and feminist discourse and theories, 11, 24–25, 81, 83, 87, 89, 115, 153, 154–57, 174–75, 182, 201, 281n11; feminist-standpoint theory, 71, 84
Ferguson, Stefan, 294n13
Fernandez, Sharon, 153–54, 155–56, 158–59, 164–65, 171
Fernandez, Sonya, 146
Feuer, Lewis, 25
Fiddlehead Books, 181
Fidler, Gordon, 179
field-imaginary, 6–18, 28, 32–33, 35–36, 273n24. *See also* Canadian literature and literary studies: disciplinary formation and contexts
Findlay, Len, 6, 10–11, 39, 63, 278n1; multicultural sublime, 10–11

Finestone, Sheila, 217
Fireweed, 152, 153, 171
First World War, 100, 110, 116–17, 120–24, 126, 219
Fischman, Sheila, 182, 183
Flanagan, Tom, 297n22
Fleury, Robert, 142
(f)lip, 11
Fontaine, Phil, 223, 230
formalism, Russian, 2, 6–7, 197, 269n1
Foucault, Michel, 8–9, 14, 15, 16, 28–29, 96–98, 100, 108, 264, 271n12, 274nn26–28, 300n9
francophone or French Canadians, 90–91, 99–100, 137, 141, 147–48. *See also* Quebec history and culture
Fraser, Nancy, 49–50, 241
Frye, Northrop, 23, 31, 112–13, 244

Gaboriau, Linda, 178
Gagan, David P., 109
Gagnon, Madeleine, 179
Gagnon, Monika Kin, 151, 157, 160
Garber, Marjorie, 157–58
Gazette, 131, 135, 137, 139, 141, 145, 287n12
Gélinas, Gratien, 291n11
Gélinas, Marc, 178
gender, 9, 14, 15, 25, 70, 89, 131, 132, 144–48, 163, 170, 172, 174, 194, 251, 274n24, 281n11, 289n6
generational shifts, cross- and intra-, 24–30, 276n46, 299n6
Gentzler, Edwin, 174
German Canadian, federal apology, 216
Get Into Reading, 74, 280n6
Giddens, Anthony, 300n9
Gilroy, Paul, 296n18
Glassco, Bill, 178
Glassco, John, 183

Glenn, H. Patrick, 246–47
globality, 38–39, 47
globalization, 3, 37–51, 55–57, 60–63, 87, 207, 229, 231
Globe and Mail, 110, 126, 127, 261, 296n14
Godard, Barbara, 11, 26–27, 28, 29–30, 175, 177, 182
Godfrey, David, 181, 290n10
Goldberg, David Theo, 96
Goodspeed, D.J., 117
Government of Canada, 55, 98, 123, 133, 136, 174, 184, 209–12, 214, 216–31, 240, 244, 261, 294n1, 295n7, 296n13, 296n14; Dept. of Aboriginal Affairs and Northern Development, 243; Dept. of Canadian Heritage, 219, 220, 225, 244; Dept. of Citizenship and Immigration, 220, 237, 240; Dept. of Foreign Affairs and International Trade, 67, 131; Dept. of Indian Affairs and Northern Development, 217, 230, 245, 296n13; Dept. of Multiculturalism and Citizenship, 219; Dept. of Veterans Affairs, 124. See also *Speeches from the Throne*
Governor General's Literary Awards, 161, 173
Gowdy, Barbara, 189
Gramsci, Antonio, 48
Granatstein, J.L., 117
Greene, Graham, 192; *The Third Man*, 192
Griswold, Wendy, 75
Guernica, 185
Gurik, Robert, 178, 183, 184, 290n10

Habermas, Jürgen, 136, 275n31
Hage, Rawi, 128; *De Niro's Game*, 128
Hall, Stuart, 135–36

Handa, Amita, 153–54, 155, 158–59, 164–65, 168
Hardt, Michael, 42, 43, 50, 60, 252, 299n6
Hardwick, Lorna, 189
Harlow, Barbara, 59
Harper, Stephen, 52, 126–27, 209, 218, 222–25, 228, 230, 240, 244, 296n11, 296n13, 298n25
Harvest House, 178, 182
Harvey, David, 40, 41, 52–53
Hay, Peter, 177, 179–80, 183
Hayakawa Publishing, 191–93, 194, 200, 293n3
Hayward, Michael, 180
head tax. See Chinese Canadian Head Tax and Exclusion Act
Heinrich, Jeffrey, 131, 141
Henderson, James (Sákéj) Youngblood, 6, 232–33, 235–47; *Jurisprudence*, 241–42
Henderson, Jennifer, 213
Henighan, Stephen, 43–44
Hérouxville affair. See Affaire Hérouxville. See also "reasonable accommodation"
High Arctic Relocation Reconciliation Agreement, 217
Highway, Tomson, 272n15
Hillier, Rick, 298n6
Hirano, Keiichi, 187–88
history, 5, 8, 37, 45, 60–61, 91–92, 108, 111–13, 156, 159–61, 162, 164, 170–71, 177, 200, 219, 221–24, 228, 239, 245, 252, 288n4; colonial, 113, 140, 167, 168, 170, 221; literary and critical, 19–20, 24, 68–69, 83, 178–80, 187–88, 291n19; military, 121–22; national and of nation, 48, 59, 63, 90, 91, 92, 115, 118, 124, 169, 175, 202, 206, 209, 231, 239–40, 255, 296n11;

patriarchal, 156, 158; of present, 160–61; of Quebec, 137–38, 147, 149; racist and of racism, 140, 152, 169, 171, 238; of white settler societies, 93, 94–95
Hitchcock, Peter, 63
Hjartarson, Paul, 44
Hogan, Patrick Colm, 17
Homel, David, 178
House of Anansi, 178, 181, 182, 183
Hucker, Jacqueline, 123–24
Huntington, Samuel P., 286n7
Huston, Nancy, 173, 203
Hutcheon, Linda, 12, 27, 78, 283n1
Hutcheon, Michael, 78

Ikezawa, Natsuki, 204, 294n14
Immigration Act (1910), 101–2
immigration and immigrants, 29, 35, 90–91, 95, 96, 100–101, 137–43, 282n2; legislation, policies, and practices of, 91–92, 94, 99–103, 105, 107, 108, 129–32, 155, 218, 219, 220, 283n6, 295n9, 297n19. *See also* Affaire Hérouxville
imperialism, 58, 60, 103, 226, 273n23, 299n7
"Indian" and "tribes," 90, 95, 99, 103–6, 300n10. *See also* Department of Indian Affairs and Northern Development; residential schools
Indian Act (1876), 91, 104, 105, 259, 265
Indian Residential Schools Settlement Agreement, 221, 223 24
indigeneity, 6, 9, 93–95
Indigenous peoples, 91–93, 95–96, 98, 99, 103–8, 215, 220–21, 224, 229–30, 244–45, 249–55, 265–66, 297n22, 298–99n7, 300n14;

intellectual(s), 235–40, 298n7; legal traditions, 232–33, 237, 239. *See also* Aboriginal peoples and communities; Declaration on the Rights of Indigenous Peoples; residential schools
Innis, H.A., 23
*in*tensive readings, 5, 270n7
interdisciplinary work and interdisciplinarity, 23, 31, 32–35, 37, 65–66, 75–85, 188, 235, 270n4, 277n52, 277n54, 281n10; "*thin*" and "*thick*," 33–35
International Court of Justice, 225
internment: of Italian Canadians, 217, 218, 222; of Japanese Canadians, 155, 157, 209, 288n5; of Ukrainian Canadians, 218, 219
Inuit, 90, 217, 218, 250, 251, 253–54, 266, 299n8, 300n10; apology to, 218
Ishiguro, Kazuo, 192
Islam and Islamic faith, 132, 135, 139, 144, 146, 147, 151, 286n7. *See also* Canadian Islamic Congress; Centre culturel islamique de Québec; Muslim
Islamophobia, 132, 133, 141, 149
Italian Canadians, 216–18, 222, 295n6
Itani, Frances, 203

Jackel, David, 2
Jacobs, Beverley, 297n23
Jafri, Gul Joya, 144
Jakobson, Roman, 6, 196–97, 271n9, 293n10
James, Matt, 216, 217, 219, 295n9
Jameson, Fredric, 29, 55, 253, 276n47
Japan, translation of Canadian literature in, 187–207
Japanese Association for Canadian Studies, 188

Japanese Canadians, 92, 216. *See also* internment: of Japanese Canadians; redress claims, movements, politics
Japanese Canadian Redress Movement, 12, 155, 161
Japanese Canadian Redress Settlement, 294n1
Jean, Michaëlle, 107, 222, 229
Jenson, Jane, 89, 90
Johanssen, Reg, 59
Jones, D.G., 20, 182
Le Journal de Montréal, 135, 137, 141
Justice, Daniel Heath, 44

Kagoshima, Yuri, 191, 192–95
Kamboureli, Smaro, 11, 152, 165, 213–14, 269n2, 278n1, 297n20
Karasick, Adeena, 59
Kareda, Urjo, 179, 291n15
Katz, Cindi, 46
Keeshig-Tobias, Lenore, 272n16
Kenkyusha, 187
Kertzer, Jonathan, 111, 270n6, 283n2
Keshen, Jeff, 120–21
Kishimoto, Sachiko, 199
Kiyooka, Roy, 161
Klein, Julie Thompson, 35
knowledge: disciplinary, 33–35; First Nations and indigenous, 236, 238, 243; keepers, 237; nonconformist, 39, 62, 278n1; power and, 9, 71, 155
Kobayashi, Cassandra, 161
Kogawa, Joy, 12
Koike, Masayo, 205
Konosu, Yukiko, 202
Kotake, Yumiko, 205
Kroetsch, Robert, 21, 32, 276n46, 283n1
Kuhn, Thomas S., 17–18, 26
Kurkow, Andrej, 203
Kymlicka, William, 90–91, 277n53

Lacan, Jacques, 28
Lachapelle, Guy, 143
Lahiri, Jhumpa, 203
Lai, Larissa, 51–52, 59, 61–62
Lampman, Archibald, 110
land claims and rights, 36, 50, 237, 250
Lang, Anouk, 81, 82, 280n1
Lawrence, Merloyd, 178
League of Nations, 120
Lecker, Robert, 12
Lee, Dennis, 181
Lee, SKY, 11, 153, 288n4; *Disappearing Moon Café*, 153, 288n4
Lefebvre, Henri, 38, 49
Leméac, 183
Lighthall, W.D., 116, 128
literariness, 2, 6–8, 269n1, 271n9–10
literary theory, 24–30
Liu, Alan, 33–35
Livesay, Dorothy, 23
Lloyd, David, 41
Lobdell, David, 178, 185, 290n8
Local Initiatives Program, 184
Loveman, Mara, 284n7
Lowther, Pat, 59
Luers, Jeff, 57–58
Lusk, Dorothy, 59

Mackey, Eva, 294n2
Macklem, Michael, 182
MacLean, K. Seymour, 109–10
MacLeod, Alistair, 189, 206; *Island*, 203, 204; *No Great Mischief*, 203, 205
MacPherson, C.B., 251
MacSkimming, Roy, 290n10
Mahrouse, Gada, 135
Mair, Charles, 119–20, 125
Maira, Sunaina, 147
making strange, 6–8, 19
Mandel, Eli, 22–24, 26, 275n38, 276n39–40
Maracle, Lee, 10, 11, 272n16

Marchessault, Jovette, 179
marginality and marginalization, 23, 41, 152, 156, 161, 167, 170–71; communities and groups, 74, 79, 209–11, 214–15, 219, 230, 233, 287n2, 295n5; subjects and voices, 151, 165, 168, 172, 274n24
Markell, Patchen, 241
Marlatt, Daphne, 11
Marois, Pauline, 137, 143
Marshal, T.H., 88–89
Marston, Sallie A., 39
Martel, Yann, 189; *The Life of Pi*, 189
Martin, Paul, 52, 218, 219–20
Marx, Karl, 37, 62, 250, 252, 299nn4–5
Massey Report, 270n5
Mathews, Robin, 270n5, 276n41
Mathur, Ashok, 151
McClelland and Stewart, 178
McEwen, Ian, 203
McKenzie, Stephanie, 283n1
McLuhan, Marshall, 23
Meech Lake Accord, 127, 216
Melamed, Jodi, 229, 295n5, 297n21
memory: of First World War, 125; Vimy Ridge as, 120–24
Mercredi, Ovide, 258
Metcalf, John, 183
methodological approaches and questions, 13, 72, 75–85
Métis, 218, 230
Mezei, Kathy, 11, 290n2
Michaels, Anne, 189
Miki, Roy, 30–31, 44, 59, 62, 63, 161–62, 168–71, 269n2, 289n8
Mistry, Rohinton, 128, 189; *Family Matters*, 128; *Such a Long Journey*, 189; *Tales from Firozshabaag*, 189
Mittelstrass, Jürgen, 33
modernity, 23, 52, 60, 96, 147, 195, 213, 260, 277n53

Montgomery, L.M., 110, 116, 187; *Anne of Green Gables*, 187, 292n1
Montreal Massacre, 155
Morrison, Toni, 192
Morton, Desmond, 117
Moses, Daniel David, 272n16
Moss, John, 20, 21, 27–28, 29, 283n1
Mouffe, Chantal, 50, 54
Mulroney, Brian, 52, 127, 209, 216–17, 222
multiculturalism, multicultural, 12, 35, 41, 68, 90–92, 94, 96, 133, 141, 159, 206, 210–16, 221–22, 225–29, 232, 269n3, 277n53, 282n3, 294–95nn2–3, 297n20; in Australia, 295n4; in Britain, 297n20; in USA, 295n5
Munday, Jeremy, 175
Munro, Alice, 189, 203–5; *Hateship, Friendship, Courtship, Loveship, Marriage*, 203–4; *The Moons of Jupiter*, 203–4; *The View from Castle Rock*, 203–5
Murray, Heather, 20, 276n46
Muslim citizens and culture in Canada, 132, 141–43, 149
Muslim Council (Montreal), 134–35

Nakada, Mark, 59, 166–69
Nakano, Etsuko, 205
Nancy, Jean-Luc, 23, 251, 299n1, 299n6
nation, 39, 44–47, 49, 94, 98, 270n5; national literature(s), 37–44, 50–51, 53, 59–63, 110, 202; national narrative(s), 21, 37, 45, 88, 90, 93–94, 96, 108, 113, 115–17, 119, 122, 126, 128; nation building, 52, 90, 101, 102, 98–99, 102, 107, 108, 120. *See also* Canadian nation; nationalism; population building

National Association of Canadians of Origins in India, 295n6
National Association of Japanese Canadians, 216
National Congress of Chinese Canadians, 295n6
National Congress of Italian Canadians, 295n6
National Council of Italian Canadians, 216–17
National Endowment for the Arts, 71
National Historical Recognition Program, 220, 221
nationalism, 5, 42, 45, 60, 63, 107; discourses of, 49; history of, 48; investment in, 110, 270n5; in relation to neoliberalism, 50, 52. *See also* transnationalism; settler nationalism
Native Law Centre of Canada, 232, 235, 246
Native Women's Association of Canada, 297n23
Naturalization Act (1914), 102
Negri, Antonio, 38, 42, 43, 50, 60, 252, 299n6
neo-colonialism, 31, 170, 239, 244, 245, 279n4
neoliberalism, 31, 37, 40–42, 45, 47, 50–63, 89
Nergaard, Siri, 197
Neuman, Shirley, 11
new press, 178, 290n10
New York Times, 117
New York Tribune, 117
nodes and nodal points, 11–12, 19, 26
Northern Flood Agreement, 256, 259

Obama, Barack, 238, 298n5
Oberon Press, 182, 185
Ochiai, Keiko, 200
Official Languages Act (1969), 184
Ogawa, Yoko, 204
Ogawa, Yoshinori, 199
Ohmae, Kenichi, 43
Ohshima, Kaori, 201
Oikawa, Mona, 153–54, 155, 158–59, 163, 164–65, 168
Ondaatje, Michael, 189, 203
One Book, One Community programs, 54, 69, 70–71, 73, 83, 280n4; Chicago, 71, 74; Kitchener-Waterloo-Cambridge, 54, 70, 72–73; Vancouver, 54
Ong, Aihwa, 43
Osborn, Bud, 59
Oura, Akio, 201
Owen, Stephen, 42

Panitch, Leo, 43
Paredes, Milagros, 153–54, 155, 158–59, 164–65, 168
Parks Canada, 127
patriotism and patriotic, 109–10, 116, 124, 182, 264
Pearson, David, 93–96, 99, 103
Pearson, Lester, 127
Pease, Donald E., 8
Peck, Jamie, 40–41, 43
pedagogy and pedagogical, 10, 44, 67, 78, 235, 273n18
Pennee, Donna Palmateer, 24, 44, 49
Philip, M. NourbeSe, 12
Pluzhenskaia, Marina, 35
polysystem theory, 197–98
Popper, Karl R., 274n30
postcolonial theory and postcolonialism, 10, 21, 42, 43–44, 113, 115, 127, 163, 174, 175, 185, 188, 250, 277n53, 300n9
Poulantzas, Nicos, 300n9, 301n18
Povinelli, Elizabeth, 210, 215
Prairie Fire, 151, 153
Prashad, Vijay, 301n14

Pratte, André, 143
La Presse, 130, 135, 139, 141, 143–44, 148

Quebec: First World War and, 121, 125; history and culture, 91, 129–32, 141, 182; literature in translation, 175, 178–79, 182–85; mainstream print media in, 136–37; national identity of, 133, 138, 147; perceived Other in, 131; as sovereign nation, 137–38, 141, 148
Quebec Charter of Human Rights and Freedoms, 132
Quebec Council on the Status of Women, 139
Quiet Revolution, 138, 178, 182, 291n11

"race," 152, 157, 159–62, 168–69, 213
racialization and racialized subjectivities, bodies, discourse, experience, 4, 9, 31, 36, 89–108, 130–36, 141, 144–49, 151–53, 159, 161–72, 213, 215, 255, 272n17, 288n4–5, 289n8; critical race theories and theorists, 35, 36. *See also* anti-racism
racism: elite, 140–41; as form of governance, 96; "reverse racism," 160; state, 92–93, 96–98, 103, 105–6. *See also* biopolitics
Radway, Janice, 77, 280n5
Rajchman, John, 160
Rancière, Jacques, 63
Reaney, James, 180
"reasonable accommodation," 129–34, 138–39, 141, 143, 147–49. *See also* Affaire Hérouxville; religious differences
reconciliation, 210–12, 215–19, 221–33; cunning of, 215, 223–25, 228–29, 231; dominant discourses of, 211–12, 221–22, 225, 230; logic of, 215
Reder, Deanna, 272n15
redress claims, movements, politics, 209–12, 214–20, 229, 232–33, 294n1, 295n6; "heritage redress," 219–21; Japanese Canadians and, 12, 161. *See also* apology; Japanese Canadian Redress Agreement
refugee claimants, 108
Rehberg Sedo, DeNel, 69, 76, 78, 80, 81, 82, 279–80n1
religious difference(s), 114, 131, 135, 139, 142–44, 148, 251
Renan, Ernest, 114–15, 118, 119, 125, 283n2
representations: crisis of, 43–44; of difference and diversity, 73, 90; of homelessness, 279n5; of immigrants, 136; of knowledge, 33–34; of people of colour, 136; realist, 55; textual and media, 68, 73, 130; of urban spaces, 54, 61; of veiled Muslim women, 131, 146–47
residential schools, 106, 155, 217–18, 220–21, 223–24, 243, 265, 296nn10–11, 296n14–16; apology for, 220–21, 223–24, 228, 230, 296n13. *See also* Indian Residential Schools Settlement Agreement
révolution tranquille. See Quiet Revolution
Ricci, Nino, 72; *Lives of the Saints*, 72
Richardson, Boyce, 300n12, 301n14
rights: civil, 88–89; political, 88–89, 100; social, 87, 88–89
Robinson, David, 177, 179, 181, 185, 292n20
Roman Catholic Church, 132, 147
Royal Canadian Mounted Police (RCMP), 238

Royal Commission on Aboriginal Peoples, 224
Royal Commission on Bilingualism and Biculturalism, 184
Rule, Jane, 61; *The Young in One Another's Arms*, 61
Rüsen, Jörn, 9, 271n14
Ryga, George, 180
Rymhs, Deena, 296n18

Sahlins, Marshall, 255, 300n11
Said, Edward, 236–37, 244, 245
Saito, Eiji, 199–200
Sartre, Jean-Paul, 299n6, 300n9
Saul, John Ralston, 90, 237, 298n1
scale theory, 39–40, 46, 50–51, 60, 62; post-, 95. *See also* spatiality
Scherf, Kathleen, 179
Schlink, Bernhard, 203
Scott, F.R., 182
Scott, Gail, 11
Second World War, 88, 92, 125–26, 183, 195, 225, 226
settler states, colonies, nations, 91, 94–98, 101, 104, 106–8, 215; colonial roots of, 21; nationalism and, 95. *See also* post-settler states; white-settler states
Shaw, Nancy, 59
Sheffield, Gary, 121
Shields, Carol, 189; *The Stone Diaries*, 189
Shinchosha, 191, 193, 194, 201, 203, 205
Shinsui-sha, 200–201
Shklovsky, Viktor, 7
Shreve, Anita, 203
Siegler, Christy, 290n7
Siegler, Karl, 177, 178, 180, 185, 290n7, 291n17
Siemerling, Winfried, 3

Sikh citizens and communities, 225
Silvera, Makeda, 273n18
Simmons, Deborah, 243
Simon, Sherry, 175, 290n2
Smith, Julian, 127
Smith, Malinda, 93
Smith, Neil, 40, 46, 50, 58
Smith, Zadie, 203
social sciences, 75, 76, 78–80; positivist model of, 81
Social Sciences and Humanities Research Council of Canada (SSHRC), 33, 273n20
Le Soleil, 135, 137, 142
Sollors, Werner, 32, 277n49
South Asian Canadians, 92, 103, 218, 219, 225, 288n5
sovereign, sovereignty, 36, 50, 95, 97, 118, 120, 147, 148
Soyinka, Wole, 4
space and spatiality, 39, 46–47, 49, 56
Spariosu, Mihai, 269n1
Speeches from the Throne, 98–108, 282n5; treatment of immigrants in, 100–103; treatment of indigenous peoples in, 103–7
Spivak, Gayatri Chakravorty, 274n25
Stanley, George, 59
state theory, 43
Steele, James Arthur, 270n5
Stewart, Jane, 217
Stone, Marjorie, 85
Strahl, Chuck, 230
Strang, Catriona, 59
Stratford, Philip, 183
Sugai, Rieko, 193, 194, 203, 205
Sugars, Cynthia, 283n1
sui generis rights, 232–33, 245–47
Swift, Graham, 203
Swyngedouw, Eric, 39

Symons, T.H.B., 270n5
Szeman, Imre, 20–21, 38, 47–48, 63

Tallman, Warren, 20–21, 22, 26, 275n36
Talonbooks, 176–86, 290n7, 291n10, 291n14, 291n17, 292n24; fonds, 175–78, 290n6, 292n24
Taussig, Michael, 253
Taylor, Charles, 129, 130, 140, 277n53
Taylor, Timothy, 42, 53; *Stanley Park*, 53–56, 61, 63, 279n5
temporality, 12, 16, 26, 42, 52, 61, 156, 158, 166, 168, 169, 222, 239, 252, 289n7
Tessera, 11, 175, 281n11
throne speeches. *See* Speeches from the Throne
Tickell, Adam, 40–41, 43
Tilly, Charles, 284n3, 284n7
Todorov, Tzvetan, 269n1
Toury, Gideon, 189, 198, 293n11
Toyozaki, Yumi, 206
TransCanada Project, 2–3, 6, 13, 30, 33, 66, 85, 269n2, 273n21
transdisciplinarity, 35–36
translation(s), 36, 59, 173–76, 178, 182–85, 189–93, 196–97, 206. *See also* cultural translation
transnationalism, 51, 59
treaties and treaty rights, 103–5, 236–39, 246, 256, 260, 298n4
Tremblay, Larry, 179
Tremblay, Lise, 179
Tremblay, Michel, 178, 179, 183, 184, 291nn10–11, 291n15; *Les Belles-Soeurs*, 178, 291n11, 291n17
Trouillot, Michel-Rolph, 226
Trudeau, Pierre Elliott, 159, 235, 242

Truth and Reconciliation Commission in Canada, TRC, 221, 223–24, 296n13, 298n25
Turner, Bryan, 89

Ukrainian Canadians, 216, 218, 219
Ukrainian Canadian Civil Liberties Association, 295n6
Ukrainian Canadian Congress, 295n6
Ukrainian Canadian Foundation, 219
United Nations, 57, 225, 230–31, 238, 240. *See* Declaration on the Rights of Indigenous Peoples; Working Group on Indigenous Peoples; World Conference Against Racism
United States (USA), 43, 51, 54, 57, 60, 65, 69–70, 71, 170, 212, 226, 238, 259, 263, 286n7, 295n5; history and culture of, 199, 200. *See also* American literary studies
urban spaces, 41, 47, 61, 133; gentrification of, 53–55
Urquhart, Jane, 73, 128; *The Stone Carvers*, 73, 128

Valpy, Michael, 121, 123, 127
Van Burek, John, 178
Vance, Jonathan, 125
Vancouver Sun, 295n8
van Dijk, Teun, 135, 140
Van Meer, Allan, 178, 184
Véhicule Press, 185
Verduyn, Christl, 269n2
Viau, Robert, 20–21
Vimy Ridge, 111, 116–28; monument, 122–28, 284n9
violence, 51, 109, 111, 113–16, 118, 126; against women, 146, 171; foundation of, 123; founding or originary, 115, 118–20, 122, 128;

imperial and colonial, 237, 284n8; symbolic power of, 284n8
"visible minorities," 96, 107, 282n3
von Flotow, Luise, 290n2
vox populi, 139–40

Wah, Fred, 7–8, 161–63, 169–70, 171
Wakeham, Pauline, 1
Waldram, James, 300n13
Warland, Betsy, 11
Warley, Linda, 20–21
wars. *See* First World War; Second World War
wealth: hierarchies of, 251; reconfiguration and distribution of, 254–57, 260
Weber, Max, 284n3, 284n7
Weech, Terry, 35
Weis, Linda, 43
West, Cornel, 153
West Coast Line, 152 153, 161, 171
white civility, 210–16, 227–28, 231. *See also* Coleman, Daniel
white Enlightenment, 235
whiteness, 95, 168, 210
white settler states and societies, 36, 93–95; diasporic underpinnings of, 282n2

Williams, David, 283nn1–2
Williams, Kevin, 290n7
Williams, Raymond, 11, 271n13
Williams, Vicki, 290n7
Women and Words conference, 10, 25, 273n18
Women's Press, 182, 295n3
Wong, Paul, 153, 272n17, 288n4
Wong, Rita, 59
Wood, Ellen Meiksin, 43
Working Group on Indigenous Peoples, 235
World Conference Against Racism, 226, 230–31
Writing Thru Race conference, 10, 61, 160, 272n17, 273n18, 295n3

Yaffe, Barbara, 295n8
Yamada, Taichi, 204
Yamanouchi, Hisaaki, 293n9
Yee, May, 153–55, 158, 164–65, 168
Yee, Paul, 288n2
Yeğenoğlu, Meyda, 146
Young, Robert, 250–51

Zine, Jasmin, 132–33, 135, 147–48
Zolf, Rachel, 59

Books in the TransCanada Series
Published by Wilfrid Laurier University Press

Smaro Kamboureli and Roy Miki, editors
Trans.Can.Lit: Resituating the Study of Canadian Literature / 2007 / xviii + 234 pp. / ISBN 978-0-88920-513-0

Smaro Kamboureli
Scandalous Bodies: Diasporic Literature in English Canada / 2009 / xviii + 270 pp. / ISBN 978-1-55458-064-4

Kit Dobson
Transnational Canadas: Anglo-Canadian Literature and Globalization / 2009 / xviii + 240 pp. / ISBN 978-1-55458-063-7

Christine Kim, Sophie McCall, and Melina Baum Singer, editors
Cultural Grammars of Nation, Diaspora, and Indigeneity in Canada / 2012 / viii + 276 pp. / ISBN 978-1-55458-336-2

Smaro Kamboureli and Robert Zacharias, editors
Shifting the Ground of Canadian Literary Studies / 2012 / xviii + 350 pp. / ISBN 978-1-55458-365-2

Kit Dobson and Smaro Kamboureli
Producing Canadian Literature: Authors Speak on the Literary Marketplace / forthcoming 2013 / 268 pp. / ISBN 978-1-55458-355-3

Eva C. Karpinski, Jennifer Henderson, Ian Sowton, and Ray Ellenwood, editors
Trans/acting Culture, Writing, and Memory / forthcoming 2013 / 315 pp. / ISBN 978-1-55458-839-8